OPEN MIND,
DISCRIMINATING MIND

ALSO BY CHARLES T. TART

Altered States of Consciousness: A Book of Readings
On Being Stoned: A Psychological Study of Marijuana Intoxication
Transpersonal Psychologies
States of Consciousness
The Application of Learning Theory to ESP Performance
Symposium on Consciousness (with P. Lee, R. Ornstein, D. Galin, and A. Deikman)
Learning to Use Extrasensory Perception
Psi: Scientific Studies of the Psychic Realm
Mind at Large: Institute of Electrical and Electronic Engineers Symposia on the Nature of Extrasensory Perception (with Harold Puthoff and Russell Targ)
Waking Up: Overcoming the Obstacles to Human Potential

OPEN MIND, DISCRIMINATING MIND

Reflections on Human Possibilities

CHARLES T. TART

1817

Harper & Row, Publishers, San Francisco

New York, Grand Rapids, Philadelphia, St. Louis
London, Singapore, Sydney, Tokyo, Toronto

OPEN MIND, DISCRIMINATING MIND: *Reflections on Human Possibilities*. Copyright © 1989 by Charles T. Tart. All rights reserved. Printed in the United States of America. No part of this book may be used or reproduced in any manner whatsoever without written permission except in the case of brief quotations embodied in critical articles and reviews. For information address Harper & Row, Publishers, Inc., 10 East 53rd Street, New York, NY 10022.

FIRST EDITION

Library of Congress Cataloging-in-Publication Data

Tart, Charles T., 1937-
  Open mind, discriminating mind: reflections on human
possibilities / Charles T. Tart.—1st ed.
    p.   cm.
  Bibliography: p.
  Includes index.
  ISBN 0-06-250855-5
  1. Transpersonal psychology.   2. Self-actualization (Psychology)
I. Title.
BF204.7.T37   1989
150-19—dc19   88-46008
                                                                CIP

89 90 91 92 93 KRUEG 10 9 8 7 6 5 4 3 2 1

My research and this book would not have been possible without the generous aid of many people, including my students; my wife, Judy; and Henry Rolfs of the Institute of Noetic Sciences. I particularly want to acknowledge the love and support of my mother, Alma Tart, and the generous and selfless contributions of my loyal assistant, Irene Segrest.

Contents

Introduction   ix

Prologue: The King's Son   xix

PART 1: Dreams   1

1. Lucid Dreams: Entering the Inner World   3

2. Beyond the Dream: Lucid Dreams and Out-of-the-Body Experiences   18

3. The Sun and the Shadow   28

4. Beginning Dream Yoga   35

PART 2: Psychic Phenomena   43

5. Time: The Mystery Nobody Notices   45

6. Subtle Energies, Healing Energies   53

7. Subtle Energies: Life as the PK Target   61

8. ALB: The Misuse of ESP?   67

9. Firewalk   75

10. How to Use a Psychic Reading   84

11. Who's Afraid of Psychic Powers? Me?   101

PART 3: Psychological Growth   115

12. Real Effort   117

13. Identification   121

14. The Game of Games   129

15. Aikido and the Concept of Ki   139

16. Living in Illusion   156

17. Self-Observation   165

PART 4: Spiritual Growth   175

18. Selecting a Spiritual Path   177

19. Prayer   182

20. Altered States of Consciousness and the Search for   190
      Enlightenment

21. Going Home   208

22. What We Believe In   214

23. Cultivating Compassion   224

PART 5: Meditation   243

24. Stray Thoughts on Meditation   245

25. Observations of a Meditation Practice   265

26. Meditation and Psychology: A Dialogue   279

PART 6: Death   317

27. Peace or Destruction?   319

28. A Dream of the Other Side   323

29. Altered States and the Survival of Death   333

Epilogue: The Tale of the Sands   361

Acknowledgments   363

Notes   365

Index   379

Introduction

In 1987 my friend Jo Ann Norris, a founder and director of the Rim Institute, Phoenix's main growth center, called me to tell me about an experience she knew I would appreciate:

One day Jo Ann's four-year-old grandson Tabor lost a toy in her house. Jo Ann and Tabor looked all over for it. Finally they saw it on the living room rug.

As Jo Ann said, "There it is," and started toward it, Tabor suddenly shouted, "Stop, Grandma! It might be an illusion!"

Taken aback, Jo Ann stopped. Then she asked Tabor how you can tell whether something is an illusion or real. "You pick it up and shake it," replied Tabor. "If it's still there after you shake it, it's real, not an illusion."

"Where did you learn about real things and illusions?" asked Jo Ann.

"In school."

"In school?" asked Jo Ann, looking puzzled. Tabor was only four, he didn't go to school.

"Not regular school," Tabor explained, "the school in my head."

Grown-ups are so slow to get things sometimes.

This is an excellent allegory of the human situation. Many of the things we desire and reach for in life are illusions. We need to learn how to "pick up and shake" our ideas and attitudes, our concepts and desires, so that we can distinguish the real from the unreal. We can develop this inner wisdom by going to the school "in our heads."

Closed Mind/Open Mind

When we think we already know everything important we stop learning. When we stop learning we begin dying. I call this "the closed mind." How can you identify a closed mind? The closed mind:

- is insecure; the danger of new knowledge upsetting its balance outweighs the joy of exercising curiosity
- reinforces and guards the borders of the everyday world
- takes either no risks or foolish ones
- has forgotten the joy of using its powers, of testing its limits
- flees from doubt in rigidity or fanatic belief, or poisons itself with useless doubts
- tries to control the universe too much from fear of mystery, and so loses the marvel of existence
- gives too much respect and power to authority and is emotionally and inappropriately dependent on or rebellious to authority
- wants approval from others rather than genuine feedback
- gives too much power to the approval or disapproval of others
- pursues pleasure at the expense of truth and avoids pain at the expense of truth
- has too much distrust of emotions as sources of information
- fails to respect and maintain its body as a source of information and joy

To learn how to discriminate truth from illusion—indeed to experience the joy of life—we have to dare and refresh an open mind. The open mind:

- is curious
- wonders what's beyond the everyday world
- enjoys using its powers
- enjoys testing its limits
- respects authority but doesn't take it too seriously or hesitate to test it when it seems wrong
- appreciates the feedback it gets from sharing its understanding and experience with others, and takes that feedback as more information that may or may not help its understanding
- recognizes its emotions as valid sources of information about reality and itself, as well as possible sources of confusion
- recognizes its body as a further source of information and joy, and respects and maintains it well
- recognizes its limits as current limits rather than absolutes
- is willing to take calculated risks
- cherishes and grows from its doubts
- always takes its beliefs as working tools, not absolutes
- appreciates living in a marvelous and mysterious universe

Growing Beyond Our Present Limits

To be human is an incredible opportunity. We each have a creative mind embodied in a fantastically engineered body, and we live in an exciting, mysterious, alive world.

Although we live in a reality with laws of its own, our minds have enormous powers to alter our perception of and reaction to that reality and thus to strongly control the way we live in it. We have the potential to live either in "heaven" or in "hell"—now, not later. Heaven is a meaningful life with a touch of the eternal present that enlivens all. Hell is pointless, stupid suffering. Yes, there are real problems in the world, but the great tragedy of human life is that so many people waste so much of their lives in useless suffering generated by their own minds.

Modern psychological research has now detailed the long and arduous "developmental" process we have all gone through in "growing up." In too many ways it squeezes out the light of life, inhibits our life energy, and destroys the openness and the simple joy of being alive. The result, as the philosopher and mystic G. I. Gurdjieff observed, is that some of the "normal" people we see on the street are in fact the walking dead, joyless automatons.[1]

Fortunately this deadening process is only partially effective for most of us: That's why I wrote this book and why you are interested in reading it. A vital spark remains in us and we want it to grow. When we enlarge our ideas of what we can be we create an opportunity to grow beyond our present limits. Remember the four-minute mile? That was considered "impossible" until one person ran it. Suddenly lots of people discovered they could run it too—and faster.

The Waking Trance

This book is a collection of related essays from *The Open Mind*, a periodical I published for four years. Publishing the periodical was part of my own life experiment in staying open and learning new skills, just as publishing this book is.[2] Both the periodical and this book were written for people who want to keep questioning and expanding their concepts about who they are and what their possibilities are. The information is intended as a partial antidote to the restrictive and negative views we are constantly given, which are reinforced in us in the course of contemporary life.

We are social animals. We want to be "normal," to fit in with and be accepted by the people around us. Consequently we put ourselves into a kind of "waking trance" in which we automatically give and receive suggestions and orders to ourselves and others, and then we believe them in order to "fit in." Many of these beliefs are depressing when made clearly conscious: "Real happiness is a new car." "God is a stupid idea, long ago disproven by science." "Get all the pleasure you can now. Death is the end; you never know when it will get you." "Existence has no meaning, it's all the mindless manifestation of physical laws and blind chance." If you were conscious of suggestions like these would you want to let them into the deeper parts of your mind, to let them be the primary focus of your approach to life? Just to be "normal"?

Exploring Human Possibilities

Although possessing the skills to be "normal" and handle the ordinary tasks of life skillfully is a necessary foundation for real growth, I have never accepted the ordinary as the ultimate, and I have been fortunate to find friends and colleagues who reinforced my vision with their own explorations of human possibilities.

My interest about human possibilities began as a child, partly because I found the world so interesting, partly because of disturbing experiences. Why did people hide their feelings and lie to each other? Why was I sometimes punished when I expressed the way I felt? What was love? Why were people, including me, sometimes cruel? And especially because of wonder: I can still recall awakening each morning with the intellectual and emotional attitude, "Wow! Another day! I wonder what fantastic things will happen today?"

Ordinary socialization processes made me more and more "normal," however. By my early twenties I was overintellectualized and emotionally constricted, a life-style that is, unfortunately, well suited for a university professor. I had learned to awaken in the mornings with the intellectual and superego-driven attitude of "What do I have to accomplish today and what is the most efficient schedule for doing it?" I was too busy, too filled with delusions of the importance of my ego activity, to look around in wonder.

Yet the feelings of wonder and curiosity, and the belief that there must be a better way than just "normal" for people to live, were always in the background. My scientific career has always reflected these feelings. I focused on such cutting-edge (and usually highly controversial) areas as parapsychology, altered states of consciousness, hypnosis, meditation, dreams, mind-body relationships, humanistic psychology, and transpersonal psychology.

In sciences like physics or chemistry the personality and nature of the physicist or chemist has almost no bearing on the discoveries made. The force conveyed by a moving object hitting something is a product of its mass and the rate at which you slow it down (deceleration), and it doesn't matter whether the physicist solving that particular equation is a Nazi or a saint, a neurotic or a leader, a miser or a charitable person. Many psychologists have long wished that psychology were like that: an "objective" science independent of the human qualities of researchers. Some of my earliest research showed me that, for better or worse, this is seldom true: The researcher is usually an important part of his or her psychological research.[3] Pretending you aren't just makes you more susceptible to fooling yourself, whether your "research" is a formal project in a laboratory or an attempt to understand your current life situation.

So while I have tried to understand and report on our possibilities as objectively as possible, I have been deeply and personally involved in many explorations. Take one human being, shake thoroughly with repeated doses of encounter groups to loosen up feelings and remove dogmatism, thoroughly massage and structurally integrate the physical body with Rolfing to lessen physical blocks, occasionally remove both the "top" and the "bottom" of the mind by participating in psychedelic experiments, confront basic personality fixations with a variety of psychological growth and therapy tools, stretch limits and toughen the mind with scientific objectivity and Gurdjieffian self-observation techniques, warmly nurture softer parts, mellow with basic Theravadan Buddhist mindfulness and Tibetan Buddhist compassion meditations, keep the body stretched and continually educated with Aikido practice, remember that the growth "cooking" process is never finished, season the whole process with a mixture of love, resistance, fear, stubbornness, courage, and blessings, and you get . . . well, you get a lot of the openness and curiosity of childhood back, combined with adult skills, and much more.

This book is my way of sharing some excitement, some possibilities, and some solutions to the human problems we all face in trying to open our minds and hearts. My goal in each chapter is to stimulate you to question your assumptions about yourself and to offer possibilities for psychological and spiritual growth.

We will touch on many exciting ways to shake up our beliefs about our limits. Part 1 is about recent exciting developments in dreaming, including some ways to increase the quality of consciousness to make dreams a time when we can explore our inner world. Psychic phenomena also have the power to shake up our limited worldviews. Part 2 discusses some psychic possibilities from a variety of points of view.

Expanding the open parts of the mind is a matter of psychological growth; we must open not just our intellect but our emotions, our body, our spirit, our personal self, and our social self. Part 3 looks at many facets of personal growth—our concepts of who we are, our identities, the specific ways we can indeed live with closed minds in a world of illusion.

In our materialistic culture it is easy to restrict our idea of growth to personal growth, the ego's growth. Such growth is vitally important but many of us have never been too comfortable with this as an ultimate limit. In Part 4, then, we will explore some ideas about spiritual growth.

Ideas about psychological and spiritual growth are inspiring and are necessary starting places, but what can we do in a practical way? The practice of meditation is central to most spiritual growth practices, so it is the subject of Part 5, which begins with a guest chapter by an American meditation teacher and dear friend of mine, Shinzen Young. Shinzen is one of the first of a small but growing number of Americans I consider treasures for our spiritually starving culture. His personal understanding of Eastern meditation is very deep, and so he is extremely good at explaining what meditation is all about to us Westerners. And, lest meditation sound like some perfect mental action accomplished by perfect people living in exotic realms, this section includes an account of the difficulties and satisfactions I experienced while attempting to meditate, as well as Shinzen's pointers on actual practice.

Finally we come to death, the fate which we can all look forward to, but would usually rather forget about. The Buddha, like many astute observers, remarked that one of the greatest wonders of the world is that we can live surrounded by instances of death all the time and yet almost never believe that death has anything to do with us personally! In Part 6 we will first look at death on the large scale: Can we save our world from destruction? Then I will share my struggles with recent personal experiences of death, and my psychological understanding of what life after death might be like.

This book does not fit into our usual categories. It is a scientific book in that I have tried to clearly share my best scientific understanding of our nature and possibilities. But I do not use jargon or presume the reader has a background of formal scientific training. People also tell me that my writing is far clearer than is usually associated with scientific writing, an accurate but unfortunate comment on the usual quality of scientific writing. It is also a personal book: I do not hide myself behind the fashionable and customary mask of "scientific objectivity." I see psychology as the study of the human mind and spirit. That means I have used my mind and my spirit as the tools of study, so why pretend I didn't?

Discriminating Mind

This book looks at waking and dreams, living in clarity and living in illusion, firewalking, delusions about the psychic, mystical experiences, psychic healing, dream yoga, defenses against reality, bodily intelligence, prayer, altered states of consciousness, and many other "strange" and yet familiar experiences. When you disagree and react strongly I encourage you to open your mind to understanding *why* you disagree. You may still disagree with me but you will have learned more about yourself. When you agree completely I encourage you to open and examine your mind even more strongly: The beliefs we do not examine can be far more dangerous to us than the ones we reject. Yes, I am an "authority." Yes, I write clearly. And I always try to tell the truth to the best of my ability. But part of personal growth is realizing that we can fool ourselves whether we know it or not; I might lead you astray sometimes, even when I think I am clearly telling the truth.

This brings us to the second part of this book's main title, Discriminating Mind. To have an open mind does not mean that you have holes in your head! Our minds can come up with all sorts of wonderful ideas, but just because they feel wonderful and seem obviously true does not mean that they are.

Here's an example. During the time of research on psychedelic drugs, before government and social hysteria essentially stopped all research, two psychiatrists decided to investigate LSD. Neither of them had ever taken any: Should they do so, to get a personal feeling for the reactions they wanted to investigate in others?

Psychedelics were already controversial at the time. One major school insisted that much of the experience produced by the drugs was important but ineffable: If you hadn't experienced it personally you couldn't really understand it. Thus to do research on others when you had not experienced LSD yourself meant that your research would probably be shallow and irrelevant to what was important. The other school insisted that psychedelics drove you crazy and permanently damaged you, leaving, as it were, holes in your brain. Research by a scientist who had personally taken LSD would be very suspect, as he or she was probably incompetent.

Damned if you did, damned if you didn't. What were the psychiatrists to do?

They decided to compromise. One of them would take LSD to get the inside view, the other would not. Then they would design and analyze their research as a team in hopes of getting the best of both points of view and compensating for the worst. They flipped a coin to decide who would take the drug. (When I tell this story in lectures someone usually asks who got to take the LSD, the winner or the loser of the toss? As a little intellectual teaser I will leave the answer unwritten.)

One of the researchers took LSD and had a stimulating and positive experience. At one part of it he was alone in a small room near the laboratory and he happened to glance at a sign on the wall. To his ecstatic astonishment the words of this sign expressed all the Truth of the Universe! Everything that you needed to know!

The sign read, "Please flush after using."

I have had the psychedelic experience myself and learned a great deal from it.[4] I can understand how you can see a lot in that sign. Yet I think we will all agree that there are a few more truths it would be useful to know!

Knowledge or experience of the psychic, meditation, lucid and ordinary dreams, altered states, mystical experiences, psychedelics: All of these can open our minds to new understandings, take us beyond our ordinary limits. They can also temporarily create the most convincing, "obviously" true, excitingly true, ecstatically true delusions. That is when we must practice developing our discrimination. Otherwise the too-open mind can be worse off than a closed but reasonably sane mind.

Sogyal Rinpoche, a Tibetan teacher, some of whose work on developing compassion is described in chapter 23, tells the story of one of his Western students who was losing weight rapidly and getting frail and ill. When he asked the student what was wrong the student replied that Sogyal Rinpoche had appeared to him in a dream and told him that food was impure, so he should not eat it. The student's mind was "open" to the idea that Rinpoche, as a spiritual teacher, would guide him in his dreams, so he stopped eating in order to purify himself. But this kind of openness is just plain stupid.

Rinpoche told the student to sit in front of him. The teacher put some food in front of the student and said, "See me? I'm right here in front of you, and I'm telling you to use your common sense and eat!"

I have shared many exciting ideas and techniques in this book, but I have tried to be discriminating. I seldom mention things that don't have at least some psychological and scientific support (even if they are controversial), and when I am speculating rather than reporting more solid material I try to make that clear. Even so, use your sense. Test ideas that appeal to you and always be open to retesting them. Develop discriminating mind as well as open mind.

I am pleased you are sharing some parts of my adventure in cultivating the open mind.

Prologue

This book is about open-mindedness and human possibilities. I can think of no better way to begin than with this Sufi teaching story.

THE KING'S SON

Once in a country where all men were like kings, there lived a family, who were in every way content, and whose surroundings were such that the human tongue cannot describe them in terms of anything which is known to man today. This country of Sharq seemed satisfactory to the young prince Dhat until one day his parents told him, "Dearest son of ours, it is the necessary custom of our land for each royal prince, when he comes of a certain age, to go forth on a trial. This is in order to fit himself for kingship and so that both in repute and in fact he should have achieved—by watchfulness and effort— a degree of manliness not to be attained in any other way. Thus it has been ordained from the beginning, and thus it will be until the end."

Prince Dhat therefore prepared himself for his journey, and his family provided him with such sustenance as they could: a special food which would nourish him during an exile, but which was of small compass though of illimitable quantity.

They also gave him certain other resources, which it is not possible to mention, to guard him, if they were properly used.

He had to travel to a certain country, called Misr, and he had to go in disguise. He was therefore given guides for the journey, and clothes befitting his new condition: clothes which scarcely resembled one royal-born. His task was to bring back from Misr a certain Jewel, which was guarded by a fearsome monster.

When his guides departed Dhat was alone, but before long he came across someone else who was on a similar mission, and together they were able to keep alive the memory of their sublime origins. But, because of the air and the food of the country, a kind of sleep soon descended upon the pair, and Dhat forgot his mission.

For years he lived in Misr, earning his keep and following a humble vocation, seemingly unaware of what he should be doing.

By a means which was familiar to them but unknown to other people, the inhabitants of Sharq came to know of the dire situation of Dhat, and they worked together in such a way as they could, to help to release him and to enable him to persevere with his mission. A message was sent by a strange means to the princeling, saying: "Awake! For you are the son of a king, sent on a special undertaking, and to us you must return."

This message awoke the prince, who found his way to the monster, and by the use of special sounds, caused it to fall into a sleep; and he seized the priceless gem which it had been guarding.

Now Dhat followed the sounds of the message which had woken him, changed his garb for that of his own land, and retraced his steps, guided by the Sound, to the country of Sharq.

In a surprisingly short time, Dhat again beheld his ancient robes, and the country of his fathers, and reached his home. This time, however, through his experiences, he was able to see that it was somewhere of greater splendor than ever before, a safety to him; and he realized that it was the place commemorated vaguely by the people of Misr as Salamat: which they took to be the word for Submission, but which he now realized meant—peace.[1]

Part 1

DREAMS

CHAPTER 1

Lucid Dreams: Entering the Inner World

Compared to our waking life our dream life is a passive sort of existence. Things usually just happen to us—whether we will them to or not. Modern sleep research has shown that we each spend about 20 percent of our sleep time in the dream state. This means that if you sleep for eight hours you will spend over an hour and a half dreaming. Why not take an active approach to dreaming and have a richer nighttime life? Adding that time to a sixteen-hour conscious day is like adding 10 percent more time to your conscious life. That's not a bad gain.

Some people already do this regularly in lucid dreams. In this special type of dream they experience a pronounced shift in the way their consciousness functions: They know *while dreaming* that they are dreaming, they feel much more in control of their mental functioning, and they are able to exercise much more control over subsequent dream events. You may be surprised to learn that almost everyone has had at least one lucid dream.

The quality of consciousness in a lucid dream is very much like the quality of waking consciousness. If your mind were functioning in pretty much the same manner as it is right now, but you knew that you were actually dreaming and would wake up in bed in a few minutes, you would be having a lucid dream. You can know that you're dreaming and be very rational about it, even though you are standing right there in a dream world that may seem as real—or more real—than the ordinary waking world. In ordinary dreams you may feel dull, passive, and unaware of sensory detail. During a lucid dream, however, your consciousness can become quite clear and can even choose to direct events, even though you are still in the dream world.

The term "lucid dream" was coined by a Dutch physician, Frederick van Eeden, writing about his own experiences in the *Proceedings of the Society for Psychical Research* in 1913. Here is an account of one of van Eeden's lucid dreams:

On September 9, 1904, I dreamt that I stood at a table before a window. On the table were different objects. I was perfectly well aware that I was dreaming and I considered what sorts of experiments I could make. I began by trying to break glass, by beating it with a stone. I put a small tablet of glass on two stones and struck it with another stone. Yet it would not break. Then I took a fine claret glass from the table and struck it with my fist, with all my might, at the same time reflecting how dangerous it would be to do this in waking life: yet the glass remained whole. But lo! when I looked at it again after some time, it was broken.

It broke all right, but a little too late, like an actor who misses his cue. This gave me a very curious impression of being in a fake world, cleverly imitated, but with small failures. I took the broken glass and threw it out of the window, in order to observe whether I could hear the tinkling. I heard the noise all right and I even saw two dogs run away from it quite naturally. I thought what a good imitation this comedy world was. Then I saw a decanter of claret and tasted it, and noted with perfect clearness of mind: "Well, we can also have voluntary impressions of taste in this dream world; this has quite the taste of wine."[1]

The impressive qualities of lucid dreaming are the knowledge that one is dreaming, the feeling of clarity of perception and thought, the ability to call upon relevant knowledge to deal with the dream world, and the greatly enhanced ability to voluntarily control the subsequent dream action. Instead of dreams just happening to you, you begin to actively direct parts of your dream existence.

Some Possibilities for a Richer Dream Life

Our culture conditions us to believe that our dreams are not important, that they just happen to us, and that we have no possibility of active control or creation. We tend to think that there's something suspicious about people who are too involved in their dreams. "Rational" people don't waste time remembering their dreams or thinking about them. It's as if our culture has given us a commandment: Don't think about your dreams! But in so doing we are eliminating 10 percent of our conscious lives. How crazy to throw that away.

What can you do with 10 percent additional conscious time in your life? You can take a useful (but still somewhat passive) approach to your dreams by simply savoring them as part of your life experience. Or you can get analytical about them and try to extract meaning from your dreams. Or you can try to induce lucidity (which doesn't preclude savoring and analyzing your dreams) and enrich your dream life the way you try to enrich your waking life.

Van Eeden's lucid dream illustrates that it is possible to take an experimental attitude toward studying the dream world. Some of the intriguing experiences that have been reported for lucid dreams include

- fascinating and insightful conversations with characters you meet in lucid dreams
- meetings with people you know who have died (or convincing dream simulations of these people)
- extraordinary sexual encounters
- meetings with characters who act as spiritual guides and teachers
- emotionally and aesthetically thrilling experiences like flying
- the use of the lucid dream state as a means for inducing even more exotic altered states of consciousness or, as some express it, using the lucid dream state as a "gateway" to other worlds of experience.

These are heady possibilities for something that requires little more than training your attention and intention, and getting your ordinary amount of sleep each night.

How to Determine Whether You Are Dreaming

Although a number of lucid dreamers have written about the techniques they developed to induce lucid dreams in themselves (major sources are listed at the end of this chapter), we do not know how general these techniques are. A description of a mental technique that works well for one person may not always work for another. In the last decade, however, Paul Tholey (pronounced *toll*-eye), working with the Goethe Universität in Frankfurt, has developed a number of techniques for inducing lucid dreaming that have proven useful for a variety of people.[2] These techniques fall into two broad categories: (1) techniques used during the waking state that are designed to have a later effect during dreaming; and (2) techniques that retain the lucidity of our ordinary waking state while we are falling asleep, so there is continuous lucidity from waking into the dreaming state.

Before we look at Tholey's techniques let's make sure we agree on the general nature of consciousness. When I try to explain what is meant by the concept of a *state* of consciousness I often ask, "Are you dreaming right now?" Some people want to get philosophical about this and debate the nature of reality. But if I rephrase the question and ask, "Are you unsure enough about the distinction between waking and dreaming that you're willing to bet me fifty dollars that you'll wake up in bed within the next half hour without leaving my sight?" the debate evaporates. You know you're not dreaming right now.

How do you know? For most people this isn't difficult. When you hear the question you make an almost instantaneous scan of the overall pattern of your mental functioning. It clearly feels like waking. That holistic pattern-scan test is a major way to define states of consciousness.[3] With it you can tell whether you're dreaming or awake, or in some other altered state such as an emotional state of panic, drunk on alcohol, or under the influence of a psychoactive drug like marijuana.

Another way to determine your state of consciousness is to look for specific characteristics of your experience that you associate with dreaming or waking, and use those as a guide. For example, in my waking state I have very good continuity of memory. I can trace my actions and experiences that have led up to the present moment back a long way in fine and continuous detail. In my usual dreaming state, by contrast, I usually do not know how I got to be where I am.

Different people may have different styles of dreaming, so what works for one person may not work for another. Some people have reported to me, for instance, that they never experience any sensations of touch in their dreams. These people could use the old folk test of pinching themselves: If they feel it they are awake; if they don't they are dreaming.

Some people may have absolute tests of their state of consciousness: If their experience has a particular quality to it they can be certain they are dreaming. If it has some other definite quality they can be certain they are awake. If you are one of those (rare) people who always dream in black and white, for example, you can ask yourself, "Am I seeing color?" If the answer is yes you know you're awake. If the answer is no you're dreaming.

Most tests, however, are relative rather than absolute indicators. If I can easily recall how I came to be sitting in front of my word processor right now, for example, I am probably awake but not certainly so. Some of my dreams have a lot of memory continuity. So I would need to make several tests of the relative kind to answer the question of whether I'm awake or dreaming in a very confident, even if not absolutely certain, manner. These tests lead into Tholey's most general method for inducing lucid dreaming, the Reflection Technique. (Please note that these techniques require you to "make believe" in an intense way. For this reason they could be dangerous to people who already have poor contact with reality. If you intend to try these techniques your mind should be strong and balanced enough that part of you knows you are only imagining.)

The Reflection Technique

Tholey's Reflection Technique is basically a matter of getting in the habit of frequently asking yourself during the day, "Am I awake or dreaming?"

Don't just accept the yes or no answer that comes to mind each time you ask, but further ask yourself, "What specific characteristics of my experience right now lead me to think I'm dreaming or not dreaming? Do the qualities of my experiences in the last few minutes leading up to this moment seem like dream experiences or waking experiences?"

Tholey found that the habit of reflecting on your state of consciousness in this way during the day will eventually transfer itself to your dream state. You will ask yourself these questions while dreaming, and the answer will be that you are dreaming. The act of knowing that you're dreaming is likely to trigger lucidity: a clear shift in the quality of your consciousness so it's like waking, even though you remain in the dream world.

Don't be disappointed if the knowledge that you are dreaming doesn't always trigger lucidity. It's possible to remain in ordinary dream consciousness and have the ordinary dream thought, "This is a dream." Keeping up your examination of why this is or isn't a dream will make the shift to lucidity more and more likely, though.

Tholey stresses that the Reflection Technique must be used frequently. Ask yourself what your state of consciousness is and examine why you think you are awake or dreaming at least five to ten times each day. Tholey also found that it is helpful to use the Reflection Technique close to the time you are going to sleep, and to use it in the kind of waking situations that are frequent dream situations. If you dream a lot about driving, for example, use the Reflection Technique frequently while you are actually driving during the day.

In using the Reflection Technique, habit makes it more likely that you will ask yourself whether you are dreaming during a relatively normal and ordinary set of actions in your dreams. (Presuming your waking life is ordinary and normal, that is when you will usually ask the reflection question while awake, and that will generalize to your dreams.) This, however, makes it somewhat harder to use a generally good test of dreaming, bizarreness of events, as a way to determine that you are dreaming. Thus it is important not only to examine the qualities of the moment's ongoing experience but also to recall what has led up to the present moment. This may bring back memories of bizarre incidents that make you realize you are dreaming.

The Intention Technique

With the Intention Technique you resolve that you will become aware that you are dreaming when you find yourself in a particular dream situation. Suppose, for example, that you frequently dream you are in your car and cannot start the engine. Resolve that from now on when you dream this you will realize that you are dreaming.

How do you make that resolution work in your dream? Practice visualizing the situation—in this case trying to start your car—as if you were dreaming it. After you have visualized it for a while add the new factor: your recognition that you are dreaming. Do this several times a day, week after week, to establish a strong habit that in this situation you will realize you are dreaming.

A variation of the Intention Technique, which you can combine with the above, is to establish an intention that you will actively carry out some specified action in your dreams. The technique Don Juan recommended to Carlos Castaneda—trying to look at his hands during his dreams—is an excellent example of this.[4] Although Tholey doesn't mention it, it is probably a good idea to visualize yourself carrying out your intention in typical dream situations.

The Intention Technique, like the Reflection Technique, involves a shift of interest and desires from one state of consciousness (waking) to another (dreaming). Some may find this easy, some may find it difficult; thus the emphasis on practice, practice, practice, until the desired shift results from strong habit.

The Autosuggestion Technique

Another waking-state technique is based on using autosuggestion to implant the idea of achieving lucidity into the subconscious part of your mind. Autosuggestion techniques, unlike the Intention Technique, do not involve conscious willing. You simply suggest over and over to yourself, in a passive way, that you will become lucid in your dreams. Use a clear and simple verbal formula. For example: "Tonight

I shall know that I am dreaming, and I shall awaken in the dream world."

Mentally repeat the phrase over and over again, say for three or four minutes at a time. Don't vary the wording, and don't grit your teeth or clench your muscles or use other ordinary methods of imposing your "willpower." Just calmly and clearly repeat and repeat. The phrase is simply true, and you're saying it over and over; you don't have to make it true.

Close your eyes and take a few minutes to do this sort of auto-suggestion during your ordinary waking state several times each day. Techniques that increase suggestibility, such as hypnosis, self-hypnosis, or autogenic training, should make this procedure even more effective. I am partial to autogenic training, which is a graded system of self-hypnosis. Most people are successful with it because they don't try to accomplish too much too fast.[5]

The Combined Technique

Tholey and his colleagues have combined the elements of the Reflection, Intention, and Autosuggestion techniques into a series of waking practices. Using this Combined Technique people who have never experienced lucid dreaming before have had a lucid dream within four or five weeks, on the average. There is great individual variation, of course; some people dream lucidly the first night they try the techniques, others take several months.[6]

Here are the elements of the Combined Technique.

1. Practice reflecting. Ask yourself, "Am I dreaming? Why or why not?" at least five to ten times each day.
2. If you answer no to the above then imagine as intensely as possible that you are actually dreaming, that everything you perceive, including yourself, is actually dream stuff. This should further sensitize you to the qualities that distinguish dreaming and strengthen your interest in understanding the nature of your dreams.
3. Remember to consider what has led up to your ongoing experience when you reflect, "Am I dreaming?" A single bit of dream experience may be perfectly ordinary, but are there inexplicable gaps in your experiences leading up to the moment? Were there bizarre experiences just a bit back?
4. Always try to ask yourself the reflection question in waking situations that are also typical dream situations for you. Ask it

whenever you are experiencing strong emotions of any kind. If you have any sorts of recurrent dreams it is especially useful to ask the reflection question during similar waking situations.

5. If frequent dream situations have no waking counterparts, such as teleporting, for example, practice imagining being in the dream situation and then realizing it's a dream.

6. Anything that increases your dream recall in general will be helpful. The simple act of putting a notebook beside your bed with the intention to record your dreams can sometimes dramatically increase dream recall.

7. Create the intention to carry out some simple action, like looking at your hands in your dreams. Keep it up until you succeed. Don't change your intention until you have succeeded at it.

8. As you go to sleep calmly think that you will eventually succeed in becoming lucid in your dreams. Don't will it; just let it be one of your last thoughts as you go to sleep.

Continuous Lucidity: Through the Gate of Sleep

How do we go to sleep?

Ordinarily we pick a quiet, comfortable place where we will be safe and undisturbed. We lie down, relax our muscles, and close our eyes. If we are not lying properly and there is too much pressure on some part of our body, we shift until we are comfortable. "Comfortable" means being able to forget our body.

We also perform a mental act that, unless we are very tired, is essential: We forget ourselves. We can no longer continue to think about all those things that seem so important to our waking self, or review our plans, or sort out our priorities. Our self, that overarching system of priorities, is let go. Whatever comes, comes. Nothing is more or less important than another.

Our self is also a review and control system. It inspects each item of mental content. Sometimes it accepts an item as it is, often it rejects something or changes it to fit with our system of values and priorities. You can't exercise that kind of active control if you want to go to sleep.

For most of us this dropping of priorities means that our ordinary waking self effectively disappears at some point in the process. Consciousness goes from being organized by the self to a period where the self fades and imagery and thought come in seemingly random ways. This period is called the *hypnagogic* state. We forget most of the imagery and thought of the hypnagogic state. It's as if our minds don't bother to record it in memory. This is followed by so-called *stage 2 sleep* (measured by brain-wave criteria), which is a blank in memory the vast majority of the time. After that you find yourself in *stage 1 sleep* (the ordinary dream state that is characterized by rapid eye movements—REMs—and is also called REM sleep) and in your dream.[7]

Some people are naturally able (or have developed the ability) to maintain the continuity of their consciousness as they pass through the hypnagogic "gate of sleep." Tholey and his colleagues at the Goethe Universität have studied several techniques for maintaining lucid awareness as you pass through this gate of sleep. These techniques allow more precise timing of lucid dreaming, that is, of getting a lucid dream the particular night you want one.

The Image Technique

In this method you focus awareness exclusively on the visual images that occur as you move into and through the hypnagogic state. It requires a lot of practice to follow the images while retaining awareness that you are "awake," lucid, and watching the imagery.

Tholey notes that the nature of the imagery varies considerably from person to person. A typical sequence begins with flashes of light and rapidly changing geometrical forms. These can become images of objects and faces, and finally complete scenes. (This geometrical imagery, incidentally, may represent something about the way our nervous systems are constructed. The originators of geometry probably got a lot of their inspiration from these forms; they may be a basis for the idea of archetypal forms, primal forms that exist in a mental space beyond the physical world.)

Now you need to stop being a lucid but passive observer outside the dream scene and move into it. Tholey and his colleagues found it is not desirable to actively try to enter the dream scene as this may wake you up. It is better to let yourself be passively carried into it. Unfortunately sometimes you will lose lucidity as you are carried into the dream scene. If you have previously set up an intention to carry out some particular action when you are dreaming, recalling this intention and carrying it out may create your lucidity.

Techniques to Overcome Immobility

If you focus on your body sensations while falling asleep you may find that your body seems immobile. I suspect that the immobility is the experience of an actual neurological change, namely the active paralysis of our muscles. Paralysis during sleep normally occurs whenever we start dreaming. If you dream of running, for example, impulses go to the muscles of your legs to make you run, just as in waking. If we actually could run while asleep the nighttime world would be a dangerous place. So an active paralysis system keeps our muscles from responding. Ordinarily this paralysis system does not turn on until we start dreaming, and turns off the instant we stop dreaming, so we don't notice it. Occasionally we wake up from a dream before the paralysis mechanism has turned off. This can be a frightening experience and can lead to much struggling, which increases the fear; but it is not harmful.[8]

Overcoming this immobility in either of two ways leads to what Tholey terms the One Body and Dual Body techniques for retaining lucidity as you go into the dream world.

The Dual Body Technique

To overcome immobility in the Dual Body Technique you visualize a second, nonphysical body detaching itself from your physical body and moving away. Your consciousness goes with the second body and you can now move into a dream scene with lucidity. The movement of the second body out of the physical can be one of floating out, falling through, twisting, and so on. You vividly imagine that this is happening so that the imagination (which is far more potent in the dream state) makes it real.[9]

The One Body Technique

Tholey considers the One Body Technique to be simpler than the Dual Body Technique. When you experience your physical body as immobile vividly imagine that you (still embodied in your physical body) are someplace else than in your bed. This can put you in a dream scene with a mobile body again. As long as you think of yourself in bed the obvious immobility of your body is a problem. A variation is to visualize your physical body dissolving into an "airy" form, and then solidifying it into a movable, more solid form.

It is not necessary to experience the state of immobility. Experienced lucid dreamers can apply the above techniques just before the stage of immobility is reached.

The Image-Body Technique

In the Image-Body Technique you concentrate equally on your own body and on the visual imagery you experience as you fall asleep. Passively hold the thought (suggest to yourself) that your body is moving about in the imaged scenes as you experience them, as well as holding the awareness that you are dreaming. You can then glide or otherwise move into dream scenes with lucidity.

The Ego-Point Technique

Why bother having a body in a dream? Yes, we are in the habit of experiencing ourselves as embodied in both waking and dreaming, but do we need to continue this in dreaming? Tholey reports that we don't.

In the Ego-Point Technique you imagine, as you retain consciousness while falling asleep, that you are only a point of consciousness, a point of perception and thought. Passively hold the thought that the physical body will soon fade from perception: You may find yourself a point of consciousness, floating in your bedroom.

The Image-Ego-Point Technique

If you combine the above technique with focusing on the imagery that occurs as you fall asleep you can travel into a developed dream scene. Tholey does not indicate whether active willing to travel is detrimental here, as it was in the Image Technique, so you should experiment as to what is most effective for you.

Tholey reports an unusual application of this technique: You can move your ego point of consciousness into the body of some dream figure and take it over. Now you have a body in the dream world. I think this would be a most unusual experience, and a good one for the philosophically minded to puzzle over.

All of these techniques are generalizations from Tholey's extensive work. You may have to vary them somewhat to make them effective. Some techniques may work better than others for you. Try what appeals to you and see what happens. Keep good notes so you can refine your techniques.

Altering the Content of Lucid Dreams

The techniques we have discussed so far are for inducing lucid dreams. If you are successful with any of Tholey's techniques you will probably be content for a time simply to experience whatever happens in this new phase of your existence. But suppose you don't like what happens naturally, or you wish to deepen or extend some particular aspect of lucid dreaming? We will now consider techniques for altering the content of lucid dreams at will.

Presleep Control

Just as you can use autosuggestion during waking hours to bring about lucid dreaming, Tholey has found that you can use similar techniques to affect the content of lucid dreams once you have learned how to induce them. For example, patients in psychotherapy who had learned how to dream lucidly would wish to learn more about the nature of their conflicts in lucid dreams. This sometimes made the content of their lucid dreams very revealing, either in a symbolic way or, more dramatically, when a dream figure in a lucid dream explained the dreamer's conflicts to them.[10]

The great attraction of lucid dreaming, however, is the possibility of immediate control of their content while you are lucidly dreaming. Apparently such control is not absolute—lucid dream wishing is not the same as ordinary daydream wishing, where you can usually imagine whatever you want as you want it. The dream world seems at times to operate by its own laws, rather than being totally your subjective creation. Nonetheless Tholey has developed a number of useful techniques.

Control by Wishing

If you want your lucid dream to be different you can wish it to be the way you want it. Successful wishes have changed the dream scenery, changed the dreamer's location in dream space and time, altered the actions of other dream characters, and changed the dreamer's own person within the dream.

Direct wishing does not always work, however. Sometimes nothing happens, sometimes something related to the wish happens later, sometimes wishes are fulfilled in quite unexpected ways. Tholey notes that wishes that call for "miraculous" (by waking standards) changes in dreams are the most unlikely to succeed. If you want to talk with someone who isn't present in your dream scene, for instance, it's much more likely to work if you call out to that person to please come there than if you try to conjure the image up out of thin air. Traveling to a location where the person is likely to be is also more successful. If you want to modify your lucid state toward an altered state such as might be induced by drugs, it's more likely to happen if you lucidly dream of taking the drug in appropriate form than if you try to create the state directly.[11]

Control of Inner States

Tholey notes that the environment of a lucid dream—the scenery and, even more, the character and behavior of other dream characters—is strongly affected by your emotional state in the dream. If you meet a threatening figure, for example, and allow yourself to become very afraid, the figure may grow in size, act more aggressively, and attack you. If, on the other hand, you control your fear and don't give energy to it, the figure may physically decrease in size, change its appearance to a less threatening one, and behave less aggressively. There is some parallel to life here, but the correlation between your inner mood and the "outer" reality of the lucid dream is stronger than in ordinary life. The degree of emotional control you have developed in waking life will be reflected in the degree to which you can use this in lucid dreaming.

I don't believe this means you should always exercise strict emotional control, in life or in lucid dreams, to always make things pleasant. When we are seeking psychological knowledge of ourselves we may have to allow or even amplify unpleasant emotions in order to gain insight. It shouldn't be necessary to point this out, but our culture often conditions us to go overboard on emotional control.

Control by Looking

The way you focus your gaze in lucid dreams can have major effects on the dream.

If you fix your gaze on some stationary point in the dream, for example, the entire dream world will begin to fade and dissolve after four to twelve seconds. If you keep your gaze fixed as this happens you will dissolve the dream world completely and wake up. If you glance rapidly about when the fading and dissolving begins you can usually restabilize the dream world. You can also apply the other techniques for controlling the dream world as the fading and dissolving start and sometimes restabilize a changed dream world this way. Tholey hypothesizes that fixing the gaze saturates and thus destabilizes some area of the brain responsible for dreaming, but I believe this is just a first attempt at an understanding of this phenomenon.

Deliberate control of your gaze can also be used as a way to deal with hostile dream figures. Looking hostile figures in the eye tends to rob them of their threatening nature. Unfortunately, if you fix your gaze too long on the hostile figure, this may dissolve the whole dream and produce awakening. This solves the problem of dealing with the hostility, but you have lost the lucid dream, so it's a little too much. Another problem is that some hostile figures don't like to be looked in the eye and will try to avoid your gaze.

Talking to Dream Characters

You can deal with hostile figures in dreams by techniques of counteraggression: stare them in the eye, fight with them, retreat by wishing yourself elsewhere, and so on; but Tholey finds that a more positive approach can be just as useful or even more effective. For example, ask a threatening figure, "Who are you?" This can change the appearance of the dream figure or start a conversation. Your inner readiness for self-knowledge is probably an important factor here. The mythical Senoi have a similar attitude: Fight when you absolutely must, but try to make friends with all dream characters.[12]

Tholey and his colleagues consider conversations with dream characters to be very useful in inducing insights about oneself. Soliciting help from dream characters often helps to produce further lucidity and can alter the nature of the dream experience. In a lucid dream, for instance, you might ask a friendly person to appear in your next ordinary dream and remind you that it's a dream so you can attain lucidity. One of Tholey's subjects was taught to fly by a friendly "ghost" in a lucid dream, another used a dream hypnotist to induce an ecstatic experience. Dream figures have been used to transport the dreamer to different locations.

I am struck by the parallels with shamanistic techniques here. The shaman—often in some sort of altered state—meets other characters, human or animal, and solicits their assistance; many of them then become regular "spirit helpers." The shaman treats these figures as "real" rather than as "just dream characters," but I suspect lucid dream figures appreciate being treated as real while you're with them. That would be common courtesy, after all.[13]

What Can You Do with Your Dreams?

We have looked at a wide variety of techniques for inducing lucidity in dreams, carrying lucidity through the "gate of sleep" into dreaming, and both controlling and learning from experiences in lucid dreams. The methods have been reported to be successful with a wide variety of people. They may be successful with you.

What can you do with the extra conscious time you gain in the altered state of consciousness of lucid dreaming?

The answer to that question depends on your attitude toward life in general. What can you do with your life? Does your life just happen to you? Do you react passively to events, or do you plan your life and initiate actions to lead you to your goals? Of course there are many events that we can't possibly control, so we have no choice but to react after they happen. Conversely, it would be pathological to try to control all aspects of life: Spontaneity is an essential aspect of a satisfying life. Yet we do want to exercise control over our life to some degree, especially if it's unsatisfactory in various ways. So why not take the same attitude toward our dream life?

Suggested Reading

Gackenbach, Jayne, and Stephen LaBerge, eds. 1988. *Conscious Mind, Sleeping Brain.* New York: Plenum Press. This book is excellent for the latest summaries of knowledge about lucid dreaming. Tholey's more recent work is discussed in this book and complements the basic information presented in this chapter.

Green, C. 1968. *Lucid Dreams.* Oxford: Institute of Psychophysical Research.

Harner, Michael. 1980. *The Way of the Shaman.* San Francisco: Harper & Row.

Hervey de Saint-Denys, Marquis de. 1982. In M. Schatzman, ed. *Dreams and How to Guide Them.* London: Duckworth. An English translation, recently published, of a classic work on lucid dreaming.

Lucidity Association. *The Lucidity Letter.* This semiannual journal is must reading if you want to keep up with the latest in lucid dreaming. For more information write to 8216 Rowland Road, Edmonton, Alberta, Canada.

Mitchell, E., and J. White, eds. 1974. *Psychic Exploration: A Challenge for Science.* New York: Putnam.

Monroe, Robert. 1971. *Journeys Out of the Body.* New York: Doubleday.

Tart, Charles T. [1975] 1983. *States of Consciousness.* El Cerrito, Calif.: Psychological Processes.

_____. 1977. *Psi: Scientific Studies of the Psychic Realm.* New York: Dutton.

Tholey, Paul. 1983. Techniques for inducing and manipulating lucid dreams. *Perceptual and Motor Skills* 57:79–90.

CHAPTER 2

Beyond the Dream: Lucid Dreams and Out-of-the-Body Experiences

When we think of the "world" we usually think of the physical world in which we live our daily lives. Yet there are mental worlds of experience, worlds of dreams and inner imaginings, worlds accessible in altered states of consciousness. Conventional wisdom gives full reality only to the physical world; but we have to be careful as to how far we will let a convenient convention become an absolute that limits our minds. In dreams and in some altered-states experiences we are "out" of this world as far as our immediate reality is concerned. Must we always dismiss such experiences as "subjective" and "unreal" when we return to ordinary reality?

In this chapter we will continue to explore dreaming and lucid dreaming, and then we'll take a close look at out-of-body experiences (OBEs) and their meaning for us. Two exciting and important books—Stephen LaBerge's *Lucid Dreaming: The Power of Being Awake and Aware in Your Dreams* and Robert Monroe's *Far Journeys* break new ground in understanding experiences that are out of the ordinary world. I strongly recommend both of these books.[1]

A Lucid Dream

LaBerge's *Lucid Dreaming* introduces the subject with the following dramatic example:

As I wandered through a high-vaulted corridor deep within a mighty citadel, I paused to admire the magnificent architecture. Somehow the contemplation of these majestic surroundings stimulated the realization that I was *dreaming!* In the light of my lucid consciousness, the already impressive splendor of the castle appeared even more of a marvel, and with great excitement I began to explore the imaginary reality of my "castle in the air." Walking down the hall, I could feel the cold hardness of the stones beneath my feet and hear the echo of my steps. Every element of this enchanting spectacle seemed real—in spite of the fact that I remained perfectly aware it was all a dream!

Fantastic as it may sound, I was in full possession of my waking faculties while dreaming and soundly asleep: I could think as clearly as ever, freely remember memory details of my waking life, and act deliberately upon conscious reflection. Yet none of this diminished the vividness of my dream. Paradox or no, I was awake in my dream!

Finding myself before two diverging passageways in the castle, I exercised my free will, choosing to take the right-hand one, and shortly came upon a stairway. Curious about where it might lead, I descended the flight of steps and found myself near the top of an enormous subterranean vault. From where I stood at the foot of the stairs, the floor of the cavern sloped steeply down, fading in the distance into darkness. Several hundred yards below I could see what appeared to be a fountain surrounded by marble statuary. The idea of bathing in these symbolically renewing waters captured my fancy, and I proceeded at once down the hillside. Not on foot, however, for whenever I want to get somewhere in my dreams, I fly. As soon as I landed beside the pool, I was at once startled by the discovery that what from above had seemed merely an inanimate statue now appeared unmistakably and ominously alive. Towering above the fountain stood a huge and intimidating genie, the Guardian of the Spring, as I somehow immediately knew. All my instincts cried out "Flee!" But I remembered that this terrifying sight was only a dream. Emboldened by the thought, I cast aside fear and flew not away, but straight up to the apparition. As is the way of dreams, no sooner was I within reach than we had somehow become of *equal* size and I was able to look him in the eyes, face to face. Realizing that my fear had created his terrible appearance, I resolved to embrace what I had been eager to reject, and with open arms and heart I took both his hands in mine. As the dream slowly faded, the genie's power seemed to flow into me, and I awoke filled with vibrant energy. I felt like I was ready for anything.[2]

Modern Studies of Lucid Dreaming

LaBerge's pioneering work establishes that lucid dreaming usually occurs in a stage 1 rapid eye movement (REM) state, the same physiological state in which ordinary dreaming occurs. This rules out the old idea that it is really impossible to be lucid in a dream, that people who think they have lucid dreams are just vividly imagining things during brief awakenings in the night. His work also shows that lucid dreaming includes a clear recall and understanding of waking-state experimental objectives and a capacity for volitional control of dream action in the laboratory in accordance with these objectives.

To illustrate: A subject capable of having lucid dreams agrees that during such dreams she will signal to the experimenter (who is monitoring her brain waves, eye movements, and other physiological measures) that she is now lucid in her dream. This is not an easy task, given the general paralysis of almost all muscles in stage 1 sleep. How can it be done?

The dreamer's rapid eye movements are being measured, as are electromyogram (tiny electrical signals that control muscular movement) potentials on both wrists. On becoming lucid the dreamer sends a prearranged signal: She rolls her (dream) eyes vertically three times. This is a good signal because pure vertical rapid eye movements are rare in stage 1 REM sleep and are not likely to occur by chance.

Unlikely is not impossible, however, so to be completely sure that the signal really signifies lucidity and is not just a chance set of vertical eye movements, the dreamer then sends her initials in Morse code by selectively tensing the (dream) muscles of her (dream) hands. If the right hand is to signify dots and the left dashes, for example, LaBerge (a proficient lucid dreamer himself) would send his initials, S.L., by tensing his right hand three times (S = *dot-dot-dot* in Morse), pausing a couple of seconds, and then tensing his right hand once, his left hand once, and his right hand twice (L = *dot-dash-dot-dot* in Morse). Electrodes on the dreamer's (physical) wrists pick up the electrical signals produced and record them on the polygraph. These kinds of signals of lucidity have now been sent many times in the laboratory. Keith Hearne, a British psychologist working totally independently of LaBerge, conducted similar successful experiments a little earlier than LaBerge.[3]

Controlled lucidity is a major breakthrough for the scientific study of dreams. Understanding the nature of dreams has always been a slow process because of their uncontrollable, spontaneous nature. They seldom manifest the particular thing you would like to observe more closely when you are ready to study it. LaBerge describes many experiments about the nature of dreams that are much more feasible with a dreamer who is an active coexperimenter.

For example, to discover the rate at which dream time flows we can have a lucid dreamer signal lucidity, then count off an agreed-upon number of seconds in the dream, then signal again. When we compare the polygraph marks signaling a dream-time interval with clock time we discover that dream time flows at much the same rate as ordinary time, at least for short intervals.

To find out whether our breathing in dreams parallels the breathing of the physical body we have the dreamer signal lucidity, take a prearranged number of deep breaths, and signal again. When we compare this to the actual physical record of breathing we find that deliberately breathing in the dream does affect physical breathing. LaBerge described the results of this and several other fascinating experiments, including studies of dream sexuality and right- and left-brain hemisphere functioning and dream consciousness. Many more are possible, yet this research is still in its infancy.

Growth Aspects of Lucid Dreaming

The most obvious possibility of lucid dreaming that strikes us is gratification of our desires: I can experience anything I want! Sex, power, magic, adventure, you name it. This is natural. Yet, as LaBerge recognizes,

. . . after too many wish fulfilling dreams, where the action is motivated by the ego-associated drives, passions, desires, expectations, and goals with which we are so familiar, a point of satiation may be reached. Lucid dreamers . . . grow weary of dreaming the same dream, and equally of being the same self, night after night. It is at this point that the need for self-transcendence may arise. Such lucid dreamers no longer know what they want, only that it is not what they used to want. So they give up deciding what to do, and resign from deliberate dream control.[4]

The lucid dream quoted at the beginning of this article is not just interesting and gratifying: It is a growth experience. The dreamer recognizes the intimate relation of his dream reality to his self; and instead of fleeing from the Guardian of the Spring he looked him in the eye and embraced him, restoring the wholeness in his mind.

In chapter 1 we mentioned the possibility of personal and spiritual growth in lucid dreams. This is a very individualized subject but it has very real potential. Consider the following lucid dream of LaBerge's:

While ascending a mountain path, I began to find it more and more difficult to climb. My legs took on the familiar leaden feeling they sometimes have in dreams, and a dull heaviness spread through my rapidly weakening body. My feelings of weariness deepened relentlessly until I could only continue by crawling—but finally even this was too much for me and I was overcome with the feeling of certainty that I was about to die of exhaustion. The realization of imminent death focused my attention with remarkable clarity upon what I wanted to express with the one act of my life I had left: perfect acceptance. Thus, gladly embracing death, I let go completely of my last breath, when to my amazement and delight, a rainbow flowed out of my heart and I awoke from the dream.

Years after this experience, the profound impact of this dream of death and transcendence continues to influence my beliefs concerning what may happen to us when we die.[5]

We Westerners are a long way from a fully developed discipline of spiritual growth through lucid dreaming—Tibetan Buddhism has such a discipline—but LaBerge gives us some interesting starting points. His book also includes techniques he developed for inducing lucid dreaming, which can supplement the techniques we discussed earlier. In chapter 3 we will look further at growth aspects of lucid dreaming.

Labeling Experience

Everything starts with personal experience. We then *label* our experiences and evaluate them in culturally given categories, habits of thought that are largely automatic and unconscious. For example, what we label a "dream" might be labeled a "journey to another world" by a Native American traditional culture.

Labeling is dangerous. Any label is but an approximation of the full reality of that to which it refers and should never be used to do more than point our attention toward the thing labeled. Yet our minds love labels and use them automatically. The semanticist Alfred Korzybski once said, "The map is not the territory." As a psychologist I am frequently forced to add the qualifier, "Most of the time most of the people *prefer* the map to the territory!" Objectively we can say that we have experiences during the night; but as soon as we automatically call them "dreams" we run the danger that this label will distort our perception of what they actually are.

In ordinary and lucid dreams we are temporarily "out" of this physical world and "in" new worlds of experience; then we automatically devalue these worlds of experience by labeling them "subjective" on our return—"It was just a dream." But suppose we had a nighttime experience in which our consciousness seemed not only quite lucid, as in a lucid dream, but was an experience we were convinced was quite real? Suppose it seemed perfectly clear that we were actually in another world of experience that had an independent existence, like the physical world, rather than existing only in our minds? This would be an OBE: an out-of-the-body experience.

The Out-of-the-Body Experience

In *Far Journeys* Robert Monroe does not begin by talking about his nighttime experiences as dreams, lucid or nonlucid, but about out-of-the-body experiences (OBEs),

a condition where you find yourself outside of your physical body, fully conscious and able to perceive and act as if you were functioning physically—with several exceptions. You can move through space (and time?) slowly or apparently somewhere beyond the speed of light. You can observe, participate in events, make willful decisions based upon what you perceive and do. You can move through physical matter such as walls, steel plates, concrete, earth, oceans, air, even atomic radiation without effort or effect.

You can go into an adjoining room without bothering to open the door. You can visit a friend three thousand miles away. You can explore the moon, the solar system, and the galaxy if these interest you. Or—you can enter other reality systems only dimly perceived and theorized by our time/space consciousness.[6]

Bob Monroe's OBEs began quite unexpectedly in 1958. He was a radio producer and businessman, a solid, sane citizen living in New York's respectable Westchester County. His interests and background definitely did not include the "occult" or the "psychic."

For a few months he had been experiencing some strange "vibration" sensations that worried him. It seemed as if his body were being shaken for a minute or so by some sort of electrical field that was surging through him. His physician found nothing wrong with him. A psychologist friend frankly told him psychology didn't know a thing about it, but it didn't mean he was crazy, and that he ought to take time to explore it. Monroe wasn't at all sure about exploring it, and he had a busy and satisfying life to lead. In retrospect he was quite lucky to have encountered such an open-minded psychologist.

Here is how he describes his first OBE:

It was late at night, and I was lying in bed before sleep. My wife had fallen asleep beside me. There was a surge that seemed to be in my head, and quickly the condition spread through my body. It all seemed the same. As I lay there trying to decide how to analyze the thing in another way, I just happened to think how nice it would be to take a glider up and fly the next afternoon (my hobby at that time). Without considering any consequences—not knowing there would be any—I thought of the pleasure it would bring.

After a moment, I became aware of something pressing against my shoulder. Half-curious, I reached back and up to feel what it was. My hand encountered a smooth wall. I moved my hand along the wall the length of my arm and it continued smooth and unbroken.

My senses fully alert, I tried to see in the dim light. It *was* a wall, and I was lying against it with my shoulder. I immediately reasoned that I had gone to sleep and fallen out of bed. (I had never done so before, but all sorts of strange things were happening, and falling out of bed was quite possible.)

Then I looked again. Something was wrong. This wall had no windows, no furniture against it, no doors. It was not a wall in my bedroom. Yet somehow it was familiar. Identification came instantly. It wasn't a wall, it was the ceiling. I was floating against the ceiling, bouncing gently with any movement I made. I rolled in the air, startled, and looked down. There, in the dim light below me, was the bed. There were two figures lying in the bed. To the right was my wife. Beside her was someone else. Both seemed asleep.

This was a strange dream, I thought. I was curious. Whom would I dream to be in bed with my wife? I looked more closely, and the shock was intense. *I* was the someone on the bed!

My reaction was almost instantaneous. Here I was, there was my body. I was dying, this was death, and I wasn't ready to die. Somehow the vibrations were killing me. Desperately, like a diver, I swooped down to my body and dove in. I then felt the bed and the covers, and when I opened my eyes, I was looking at the room from the perspective of my bed.[7]

Journeys Out of the Body is the story of Monroe's early attempts to make sense out of his OBEs. He had to do this almost entirely on his own; our culture was very ignorant and rejecting of such experiences in the 1950s and early 1960s. His OBEs became the center of meaning in his life and inspired his first book, which has become one of the classics in the field. Since it was first published in 1971 innumerable people have found comfort and help in the knowledge that they weren't alone and they weren't crazy just because they had had OBEs. *Far Journeys* is the story of what has happened to Bob Monroe since 1971, and the story of his search for methods that would help other people have OBEs.[8] It is a fascinating story of the kind of experiences that are prominent in humankind's spiritual heritage.

Are OBEs Real?

How do we know these are the stories of real journeys? They are fascinating, lucid dreams, to be sure, since Monroe describes clear consciousness as part of the OBE. But how do we know they're not just fantasies?

Here we come back to the problem of labeling. I am having an experience right now of sitting in my chair in front of my word processor, typing. How do I know it isn't a dream? That it is real?

My immediate reaction to the question is that it is obviously real.

That is, the overall *feel* of my consciousness is that of my usual waking state, and I have been taught to believe and been rewarded for believing that what I experience in my waking state is absolutely real. I'm a Westerner and a scientist, after all!

I could, of course, have a dream tonight that I am sitting at my word processor typing. After I return to my usual waking state I will say that there is a lack of clarity, of lucidity, about my dream state, compared to my waking state, so that *in retrospect* I can dismiss my dream of typing as unreal. It seems quite real at the time in the dream, of course. Perhaps dreams are set in another reality, an independently existing world whose reality is simply different from ordinary physical reality? Not by Western standards. Dreams show too much variation, too much inconsistency, and it is tempting to conclude that anything so inconsistent must be subjective. We have such a longing for stability.

Lucid dreams bring a whole new dimension to the labeling of dreams as unreal. Your consciousness is no longer cloudy, as in a typical dream, and you seem to possess most or all of your mental abilities to reason, recall, and act, just as you do in your waking state. *And* you label a dream right then and there in the dream world. You still perceive your ongoing experience as real; but you believe, because you've labeled it a dream, that some unknown part of your mind is arbitrarily creating this dream world, and that it only *seems* real. The sandwich in your mouth tastes delicious, but somehow you must really be just imagining it. You make your ongoing experience fit into your theories about the nature of the world.

Further support for this belief comes from the fact that you can sometimes deliberately control the content of your lucid dream by simply willing it to be different. You wish to talk to your dead brother and a moment later he walks into the dream and says hello. We can't do this in our waking world: That would be "magic." Since we have been conditioned not to believe in magic, yet magic is now working, we are therefore dreaming.

Lucid dreamers may be inclined to believe that people who claim to have OBEs are merely misinterpreting their (lucid) dreams. People who have OBEs are inclined to think that those who talk about their lucid dreams may be too readily dismissing what may be actual OBE journeys to other realities. I suspect both may be right sometimes.

LaBerge reports some experiences that are similar to some of Monroe's. LaBerge is open to the possibility of OBEs but he has never experienced one he believes was more than a dream imitating an OBE; thus he labels all of his sleep experiences lucid dreams.

Monroe, in personal conversations, has told me that his OBEs are easily distinguished from lucid dreams because he *cannot* work "magic" in them. He finds himself in places that have their own reality, and he cannot change them by mere acts of will. Many of the other worlds he visits in OBEs show the stability of ordinary reality. Just as the walls of my study keep their same dimensions and spatial relationships to each other each time I walk in, barring lawful changes such as rebuilding, the out-of-this-world places Monroe visits in OBEs maintain their principal characteristics from visit to visit.

Local Validation

Some OBEs are "local," that is, you are out of your body but still located in what seems to be the ordinary physical world. This can present an opportunity to apply a very stringent test of whether you were really there (in at least a perceptual sense of being "located" somewhere), or just dreaming. Can you describe specific, improbable details of the location you believe you visited? Can you be sure there was no normal way you could have known about these details? Finally, can you now verify that these details are correct?

Feeling you were in a large, empty room somewhere won't do; the world is full of large, empty rooms. Certainly you could have just dreamed such a thing, and mislabeled a lucid dream as an OBE. But what if it's a room in a neighbor's house that you've never been in before, and you saw a stuffed badger sitting on top of a pink 55-gallon drum, and this is verified? What then? This is hardly the sort of thing most people have in their house.

The question of whether his OBEs were real in this sense or just unusual dreams was a very pressing one for Monroe for the first few years of his experiences. He gives the question much attention in *Journeys Out of the Body*. Many of his local OBEs couldn't be checked: If you find yourself on a dark street in a strange city for a few seconds, looking at nondescript buildings, how can you check it? Fortunately there were enough instances where he could check and did confirm that his OBE perceptions matched physical reality, and he did finally accept his OBEs as having a reality of their own. I deliberately use the phrase "a reality of their own" because there are enough alterations in OBE perception from the perception of our physical eyes to suggest that a simple model of the OBE traveler just being there in the same way that one is present at a physical location is too simple.

Your Nocturnal Life Will Be . . . ?

So we live in a world in which about twenty percent of our sleep time results in experiences that, as intense and apparently "real" as they can sometimes be, are usually forgotten, with much of the forgetting resulting from the mindset we inherit from our culture. If remembered, they are usually automatically dismissed as nothing but "dreams." Some people don't buy this culture-set, though, and at least consider their dreams important experiences, something to think about in retrospect and learn from. Some go further and "wake up" within the dreamworld and enjoy and grow from lucid dreaming. Some consider these experiences as "real" journeys in another kind of reality, and also explore them for pleasure and growth. If they are smart, they are discreet about whom they mention them to in order to avoid social difficulties (like maybe being institutionalized!) with those of conventional view.

There will be a lot of nights left in your life. What will *you* do?

Suggested Reading

Hearne, Keith. 1978. Lucid dreams: An electrophysiological and psychological study. Ph.D. thesis, University of Liverpool.

LaBerge, Stephen. 1985. *Lucid Dreaming: The Power of Being Awake and Aware in Your Dreams.* Los Angeles: Tarcher.

Monroe, Robert S. 1971. *Journeys Out of the Body.* New York: Doubleday.

_____. 1985. *Far Journeys.* New York: Doubleday.

CHAPTER 3

The Sun and the Shadow

Many publishers send me galley proofs of books they are about to release in the hope that I will read them and say something about the book that they can use in promotion. Many of these books look like they will be of great interest to me; unfortunately I seldom have time to read the galleys.

Recently I received the proofs of Kenneth Kelzer's *The Sun and the Shadow,* and thought once again, "This looks really fascinating, but I don't know when I can find time to read it in the next two months."[1] I decided I should at least read a page or two at breakfast before sending a letter of regret to the publisher. After two pages I was hooked: I took the galleys to work with me and read them at every opportunity. This book will clearly be one of the classics of lucid dream literature.

Kenneth Kelzer is a psychotherapist. In 1980 he decided to induce and explore lucid dreams as part of a personal and spiritual growth program. His book is an account of the dreams that followed and his struggle to integrate their insights into his everyday life. The lessons he learned will be helpful to all of us, even if we don't have lucid dreams.

The purpose of this chapter is to persuade you to read this book. The selected passages that follow will give you the flavor of the book. Even out of context they are useful to growth.

Why Do We Have Lucid Dreams?

One of the purposes of lucid dreaming, I am now convinced, is to give people the experience, however fleeting or temporary, of spiritual and psychological mastery. These tastes of mastery and moments of transformation spur us on to continue the inward journey.

Shouldn't lucid dreams be analyzed like other dreams for hidden messages? As a psychotherapist Kelzer was expert in such analyses and knew their value, yet:

I had no desire to analyze this lucid dream or do therapeutic work with it in any way. It had a sense of completion that is common to many lucid dreams, almost as if the dream were a work of art in itself. This sense of completeness and wholeness is one of the features that clearly distinguishes many lucid dreams from ordinary dreams. Most schools of psychotherapy generally follow or build upon Freud's basic idea that the dream expresses the content of the unconscious mind and usually presents the dreamer with some kind of problem to be solved. Many lucid dreams, however, are simply nonproblematic; they seem to emerge from a different category or realm of the mind. As such, they serve many important purposes other than assisting the dreamer toward the confrontation of personality problems, although such confrontations can certainly be one of their functions. . . . Speaking as a psychotherapist, I do not see any inherent contradictions between the works of Freud, Jung, Perls, and other psychotherapists and the ramifications of lucid dreaming. I do believe, however, that one of the biggest challenges that psychotherapists may have in approaching the lucid dream will be to step aside from their traditional problem-oriented point of view in order to appreciate that the lucid dream is more likely to serve the dreamer on another level. A lucid dream is more likely to be instructional about the nature of consciousness per se than to reveal the dreamer's particular disturbances of consciousness. It is more likely to depict something about the general evolution of consciousness than reveal something about the individual dreamer's particular "arrestment of development." As its first function, the lucid dream is more likely to reveal the dreamer's inner joy and creativity, while addressing his or her emotional problems as a secondary function. In short, the lucid dream is more likely to be the bearer of good news than the bearer of bad news.

Simply to appreciate and enjoy the lucid dream and to bask in its light, its vivid images and colors may well be the primary creative response that we can make to most lucid dreams. Not that lucid dreams do not offer us messages or insight. They often do, though these messages are often of a much higher or much more subtle nature than the meanings of ordinary dreams. The lucid dream is a subtle teacher. As my experiment progressed I began to grasp this concept in many ways.

Fear

As a psychotherapist Kelzer is very sensitive to underlying psychological dynamics in both lucid dreaming and ordinary life. Commenting on a lucid dream in which he met a primitive man riding on a huge creature like an African wildebeest, he notes that:

Eventually, after some reflection, I realized that this lucid dream taught me a lot about fear. Fear is perhaps the most primitive human emotion of all, and we all have a great deal of it inside ourselves. We all need to learn how to confront the objects and sources of our fear in order to thrive and prosper in this world. I realized, too, that the dream was bearing a personal message, telling me that I still have a lot of powerful fears inside myself, which at times threaten to overwhelm my conscious mind. I did not associate the wildebeest to any particular fear, but more to fear in general. The dream reminded me of Franklin D. Roosevelt's statement, "The only thing we have to fear is fear itself." Now I am wondering if this lucid dream was suggesting that I might surrender one step further and give up the fear of fear. To be unafraid of fear itself implies a willingness to face all of my fears, whatever they are, regardless of what plateaus I may already have reached in my personal growth.

I personally find this quite interesting, because at one point in my own growth I too realized that my fear of being afraid was indeed bigger than my fear of anything in particular.

Here is Kelzer's comment on one of his early and powerful lucid dreams:

There is a kind of magic in many lucid dreams. This one had the potential to become a nightmare, but in the moment that I became lucid I experienced total inner transformation. All my fear vanished in an instant, and inside of myself I felt full of courage. Complete clarity of vision, in this dream, yielded instant transformation. This became one of the important principles that I learned from this particular lucid dream. To see fully is to have courage. To see fully is to have no fear. But, as is so evident when we examine our world, we human beings seldom see anything fully in our normal state of consciousness. More often than not, as the apostle Paul wrote: "We see now through a glass, darkly, but then we shall see face to face."

The Shadow Side

Kelzer has to struggle with the shadow side of his nature in his quest, a side that seemed to strengthen as his sun side, his spiritual side, grew. In such struggles it is all too easy to identify with the good and totally reject the bad, a strategy that is quite costly in terms of psychological growth.

Spiritual work, when it is true and genuine, expands awareness and does not *displace* awareness. It leads us to see and appreciate the whole of our humanity, and does not lead us to reflect upon our higher natures only. We need to dwell upon our higher nature in order to grow in a positive direction, but we must not do it by rejecting our dark and primitive side. A whole person, then, is someone who has walked with God *and* wrestled with the devil.

Kelzer, a well-socialized male, brought very masculine attitudes of control to his study of his lucid dreams; but the dreams had something to teach him about this.

My own self-analysis was that for the present my approach to lucid dreaming still contained too much of my *willing* it to happen and not yet enough of my *allowing* it to happen. The "masculine" attitudes of willpower, order, goal setting, intentionality and control are very strong in my personality and always have been since childhood. Correspondingly, the "feminine" attitudes of trust, patience, relaxation about goals and allowing it all to happen have been my less-developed traits. These feminine mental qualities, I realized, would need to be increased within myself if the fullest psychic cross-fertilization was to take place.

Following an especially powerful lucid dream, which he titled "The Arrival of the Serpent Power," Kelzer noted that:

The "Arrival of the Serpent Power" and the life context out of which it came has often led me to reflect upon one of Carl Jung's statements: "I would much rather be a whole person than a good person." His message was a criticism of the commonly misunderstood and truncated version of moral goodness that is so often held up for emulation in civilized society. Goodness has often been equated with qualities such as niceness, patience, kindness and tolerance, with the expectation that these qualities should be displayed at all times and in all circumstances. Such "goodness" unfortunately often makes people into victims because it may unconsciously invite more aggressive individuals to abuse, attack or exploit. In this setting, I was relearning once again that a whole person is someone who feels his own anger and aggression on those appropriate occasions when someone else is exploiting him and can speak out or take effective action to prevent the attack from proceeding any further. In essence, it is not always appropriate nor spiritual to turn the other cheek. For me, Jung's basic idea is so vital because it implies that there is a dark side to love which actually turns out to be a positive human force in the long run. It throws out absolute behavioral guidelines for people to follow and encourages us to commit to the wholeness of the psyche as our overall guiding principle.

In any spiritual path there is the danger that we will identify with a specialness: "Me!" as superior to the common hordes. Kelzer notes that:

Ego inflation was the major two-edged sword that came out of my experiment with lucid dreaming. It was capable of cutting both ways: positively or negatively, creatively or destructively—To inflate or not to inflate, that is not the question. How to respond to one's inflation, if it occurs, is the question. For as Rilke wrote to the young poet, we must give birth to our images, and we must give birth no matter what happens as a by-product in our psychological development. To be human is to love, create and give birth in the real world and to wrestle courageously, if need be, with any negative by-products that may emerge from one's choice to be fully alive.

The Sun Side

We all experience occasional (perhaps too occasional) "peak experiences," moments of joy and clarity when we transcend our ordinary false personality and experience the higher aspects of our self. Some of Kelzer's lucid dreams were peak experiences. But they are rare and fade, so what good are they?

These peak experiences, however, even if they are fleeting and fragile, are no small contribution to the spiritual evolution of the person who receives them. Without them life could easily become drab and dull. In reflecting on my experiment, I have come to see that the ultimate purpose of the peak experience is to provide us with a taste of ecstasy now, because a taste is better than nothing at all and because a taste is all that most of us can bear *now*. In addition, we need to understand that if we were to receive the full impact of ecstasy without adequate preparation, most of us would probably die, because we are simply not yet strong enough internally to bear the fullness of the Light.

For those of us with no or few experiences of lucid dreaming, it is easy to think about them as a curiosity, a funny variation on ordinary dreaming, but yet:

It seems mandatory to me now to rethink and expand upon our present paradigm for dream studies in which we customarily distinguish ordinary dreams from pre-lucid dreams and lucid dreams. I firmly believe that these three categories of distinction are incomplete and insufficient, since in this dream I experienced a lucidity that was so vastly different and beyond the range of anything I had previously encountered. At this point I prefer to apply the concept of the spectrum of consciousness to the lucid dream and assert that within the lucid state a person may have access to a spectrum or range of psychic energy that is so vast, so broad and so unique as to defy classification and to transcend what we ordinarily speak of as "consciousness" from the perspective of the waking state.

I am particularly impressed with Kelzer's clear intent to deal with the whole of reality, not just the parts of it that we label "good." Pursuing the good is fine but very tricky. We easily distort our perception in the pursuit of security and pleasure and thus sow the seeds of useless suffering.

I think you can see why I find this book excellent and fascinating, and a useful illustration of the actual practice of growth through lucid dream work.

Suggested Reading

de Saint-Denys, H. 1982. In M. Schatzman, ed. *Dreams and How to Guide Them.* London: Duckworth.

Delaney, G. M. V. 1988. *Living Your Dreams: Using Sleep to Solve Problems and Enrich Your Life.* San Francisco: Harper & Row.

Domhoff, W. 1985. *The Mystique of Dreams: A Search for Utopia Through Senoi Dream Theory.* Berkeley and Los Angeles: University of California Press.

Evans-Wentz, W. 1935. *Tibetan Yoga and Secret Doctrines.* London: Oxford University Press.

_____. 1964. *The Yoga of the Dream State.* New York: Julian Press.

Faraday, A. 1972. *Dream Power.* New York: Coward, McCann & Geoghegan.

_____. 1976. *The Dream Game.* New York: Harper & Row.

Gackenbach, Jayne, and Stephen LaBerge, eds. 1988. *Conscious Mind, Sleeping Brain.* New York: Plenum Press. This book is excellent for the latest summaries of knowledge about lucid dreaming. Tholey's more recent work is discussed in this book and complements the basic information presented in this chapter.

_____, and Jayne Bosveld. 1990. *Control Your Dreams: How Lucid Dreaming Can Help You Uncover Your Hidden Desires, Confront Your Hidden Fears, and Explore the Frontiers of Human Consciousness.* New York: Harper & Row.

Garfield, P. 1974. *Creative Dreaming.* New York: Ballantine.

_____. 1979. *Pathway to Ecstasy: The Way of the Dream Mandala.* New York: Holt, Rinehart & Winston.

Green, C. 1968. *Lucid Dreams.* Oxford: Institute of Psychophysical Research.

Harner, Michael. 1980. *The Way of the Shaman.* San Francisco: Harper & Row.

Kelzer, K. 1987. *The Sun and the Shadow: My Experiment with Lucid Dreaming.* Virginia Beach, Va.: ARE Press.

LaBerge, S. 1985. *Lucid Dreaming.* Los Angeles: Tarcher.

Lucidity Association. *The Lucidity Letter.* This semiannual journal is must reading if you want to keep up with the latest in lucid dreaming. For more information write to 8216 Rowland Road, Edmonton, Alberta, Canada.

Mitchell, E., and J. White, eds. 1974. *Psychic Exploration: A Challenge for Science.* New York: Putnam.

Monroe, Robert. 1971. *Journeys Out of the Body.* New York: Doubleday.

Stewart, K. 1971. Dream theory in Malaysia. In C. Tart, ed. *Altered States of Consciousness.* New York: Doubleday. 161–70.

Tart, Charles T. [1965] 1969. Toward the experimental control of dreaming: A review of the literature. Reprint. In C. Tart, ed. *Altered States of Consciousness.* New York: John Wiley & Sons. 133–44.

_____. 1979. From spontaneous event to lucidity: A review of attempts to consciously control nocturnal dreaming. In B. Wolman, M. Ullman, and W. Webb, eds. *Handbook of Dreams: Research, Theories, and Applications.* New York: Van Nostrand Reinhold. 226–68.

———. 1983. Lucid dreaming. *Dictionary of Psychology.* Oxford: Basil Blackwell.

———. [1975] 1983. *States of Consciousness.* El Cerrito, Calif.: Psychological Processes.

———. 1984. Terminology in lucid dream research. *Lucidity Letter* 3(1): 4–6.

———. 1985. What do we mean by "lucidity"? *Lucidity Letter* 4(2): 12–17.

Tholey, P. 1983. Techniques for inducing and manipulating lucid dreams. *Perceptual and Motor Skills* 57:79–90.

van Eeden, F. 1971. A study of dreams. In C. Tart, ed. *Altered States of Consciousness.* New York: Doubleday. 147–60.

CHAPTER 4

Beginning Dream Yoga

Western dream research is relatively new, but other traditions have taken dreams seriously for hundreds or thousands of years. For several weeks I explored one of these traditions by way of a simplified version of a Tibetan *dream yoga* meditation technique. Such dream yoga techniques are intended ultimately to induce lucidity in dreams to enable you to use the dream as a vehicle for meditation and liberation. I will describe the technique in detail at the end of this chapter.

My practice was far from proper but I had some interesting experiences. I simply visualized a red, "energetic" spot in the middle of my throat, near my Adam's apple, as I was falling asleep. This is a long way from the precise sort of visualizations Tibetan practices usually call for. I was not exactly sure just where the special *chakra* or energy center in my throat was supposed to be located; nor did I have a precise and steady image of a perfect red lotus. My mind wandered a lot during this meditation and I only remembered to try it every third night or so.

Nevertheless I experienced some changes in my dreams. The main change was that my recall of dreaming went up considerably. Another outcome was much more unusual, as we shall see.

For most of my life I have had excellent dream recall. One year, when I systematically recorded my dreams in the morning, it was easy for me to fill a typed, single-spaced page (sometimes three or four of them) with dream descriptions. The quality of my dreams has almost always been very positive and enjoyable since I was a child—especially after I learned to eliminate occasional nightmares with a self-discovered version of a method Stewart later attributed to the Senoi of Malaya.[1] My dreams are usually fascinating adventures: I go places, do interesting things, triumph over difficulties, and generally have a great time. If you saw the movie *Raiders of the Lost Ark* the statement that I am Indiana Jones in my dreams will convey the flavor nicely.

For the last eight years or so, however, I have been too busy with outer life. On awakening I had been turning my attention to my plans for the day, or practicing a special "priming exercise" to stimulate self-remembering practice during the day, so my dream recall had become quite sparse.[2] Only a few fragments would be with me on awakening, and they would disappear almost immediately. The quality of my dreams remained unchanged—still positive and adventurous.

An Unusual Dream

During my simplified dream yoga practice I began to awaken with long dream sequences in memory, some of which were consistently unusual. Two of the sequences from the dream that inspired this chapter were as follows:

I was standing beside a brick wall on which birds occasionally landed. They then clung to the vertical side of the wall. I believed I was hungry (although I don't recall any actual sensation of hunger in the dream).

Someone said that if I caught one of the birds the heat of my hands would be sufficient to cook it. A bird the size of a large sparrow landed on the wall near me, about three feet above the ground, and looked at me for a moment. I thought it a little odd that birds would land so close to people. It was just behind an ornamental brick that projected a few inches out from the wall. I waited until it settled. Then I inconspicuously sidled a little closer and suddenly batted my hand around the brick and hit the bird hard enough to stun it and knock it to the ground.

I picked it up and held it between my hands. The "heat" from my hands must have been very powerful: To my amazement the bird began to swell up and in a couple of seconds was the size of a football! I threw the bird away from me, fearing it might pop from overheating. This scene than faded into the next. . . .

In the next scene I and a vague number of others were with my friend Arthur Hastings (the well-known transpersonal psychologist) as we walked around a construction site. They were adding buildings to a university or a convention center or some place like that. One of the recently completed buildings was visible a thousand yards or so away. It was a high-rise, rectangular office building about twenty-five stories high. It was green on the outside, covered with the same sort of material that the foundations of the uncompleted buildings were cast from.

In fact only flat foundation slabs of these other buildings were visible and they tended to blend indistinctly into the ground. Both the earth and these slabs were all made of this greenish, sparkling stuff, so it looked as if we were on rolling sand dunes all made of a greenish material with white sparkles in it, like frozen green ice.

Arthur got ahead of me and I started to hurry to follow him. He went down some hills and I had to slide down the greenish stuff after him. It was like sliding down ice banks, although it wasn't cold or steep enough to be dangerous, just interesting.

The bird scene was strange, even for my dreams. The scene where I followed Arthur was not particularly unusual in terms of content, but it was unusual in that I rarely dream about identifiable people whom I know. It wasn't until two events happened the following morning that I suspected these dream scenes were more interesting than I thought, and might be hinting at intriguing possibilities in dream yoga.

The Disturbances

After I woke from this dream I went into the kitchen to make some coffee for myself and my wife, Judy. I was surprised to find a heavy tray, some fruit, and some packages of bread sticks scattered on the kitchen floor. These had come from a shelf about three feet above the floor. Who or what had knocked them down? Judy and I are not sleepwalkers, so my suspicions immediately focused on our cat, Dawn.

The previous evening we had noticed that several peaches in the fruit bowl had had small bites eaten out of them, and one small peach had been half consumed. We discussed the possibility that Dawn had done it. Like many cats, a few hours after she has been fed she can convince herself (and try to convince us) that she is on the verge of death from starvation. She is a picky eater, though, and it was hard to imagine her taking one bite of something as obviously unlike food (by cat standards) as a peach, much less taking several bites from several different peaches or consuming half of one. Nor could we ever recall her jumping up on a kitchen counter or a table.

Perhaps a mouse had gotten into the house? We didn't see any signs of mouse droppings, but it was possible.

When I saw the objects scattered on the kitchen floor in the morning I hypothesized that we did indeed have a mouse in the house, and it had been up on the shelf eating fruit (we saw fresh bites in other peaches) sometime during the night. Dawn must have seen or heard it and jumped up after it, knocking things over in the process.

Arthur's Dream

Later that morning I called my friend Arthur to talk about returning some electronic equipment I had borrowed from him a few weeks before. I had vaguely been intending to call him for several days about this, so he was on my mind.

He mentioned that I had been in a dream of his last night; he only occasionally dreams about me. In his dream he and I had been talking and then he had to return to a hotel where some sort of conference was going on. He could see the hotel, a high-rise building, in the distance. There was some smoke coming from it. He began hurrying back so he could get into it and get his things before fire trucks blocked the entrance. I was following along behind him. His dream faded after this. Naturally I told him about his appearance in my dream.

Since I rarely dream about people I know, and in both my and Arthur's dreams I had been following Arthur toward a high-rise building, I suspected that we had had a small degree of telepathic contact in our dreams. I would not cite this mild coincidence as very evidential for convincing anyone else of the reality of telepathic dreams, but I have had enough of them (as has Arthur) that I am inclined to believe that this one involved some telepathic interaction.

In my study of the telepathic dreams of others I discovered that such dreams may have an unusual event in them that does not convey any telepathic information but acts as a sort of "flag" to call the person's attention to the dream after waking.[3] This is sometimes true in my own telepathic dreams. Could the swelling bird have been such a flag, calling my attention to the telepathic interaction with Arthur?

Perhaps. Or perhaps that and more.

Communicating with Animals

I have always liked animals. In my reading about various kinds of unusual psychic abilities I have always been especially fascinated by the ability to understand the thoughts and experiences of animals. I would love to be able to share an animal's consciousness and experience its world. Might the apparent telepathic interchange with Arthur actually have been the flag rather than the main event, designed to call my attention to a special occurrence?

As soon as my wife heard of the parallel with Arthur's dream she suggested that the earlier scene with the bird in my dream might have been a symbolic telepathic interchange with our cat, Dawn.

Consider the following parallels:

- People don't eat sparrows. Cats do.
- People don't wait for sparrows to settle, sneak up, and then bat them off walls with their hand. Cats do wait and sneak up and bat birds with a paw.
- The sparrow in my dream is about three feet up on the wall, the shelf Dawn probably leaped to is three feet up from the floor.
- A sparrow is very small compared to a person, but a sparrow the size of a football compared to a person is pretty close to the size a sparrow would seem to a cat.

Could my interest in what had been eating the fruit have focused my dreaming consciousness on that shelf and on Dawn? Could a mouse on a shelf three feet from the floor have provoked her to stalk and bat at it, although she must have finally failed to catch it, just as I threw the swollen bird away? Could the dream yoga practice have sensitized my sleep consciousness in some way that let me tune in on this event in a partially symbolic way?

I don't know. But I do know that I'm going to practice this dream yoga technique more seriously. If you would like to try it you can use the simplified technique described above, or the more sophisticated version below.

Lotus Dream Yoga Technique

Tarthang Tulku, one of the leading Tibetan teachers who has chosen to live in the West, wrote the book *Openness Mind* to introduce Tibetan Buddhist meditation practices to Westerners.[4] This very clearly written book advocates the development of lucidity in dreams.

1. Begin at bedtime with relaxation exercises. First you should deeply relax your muscles. Particularly relax your head and eyes, your neck muscles, your back, and finally your whole body. Gently clear your mind of thoughts as much as possible and let any tensions go. Lightly remember some pleasant things to further calm the mind. You should reach a state where your body is relaxed and your mind is not jumping around, where you are feeling calm and peaceful.
2. Now visualize a beautiful lotus flower in your throat, with light pink petals softly curling inward. When you have a clear image of the flower further visualize a flame in its center, a luminous

red-orange flame that is light at the edges and darker in its center. The flame represents awareness, which is inherently luminous. Gently holding the image of this flame as you drift into sleep will maintain a thread of lucidity that can eventually take root in the dream.

3. Continue to hold the visualization of the flame in the lotus while falling asleep. Watch how thoughts arise and disappear. Don't analyze the thoughts, don't think about them, just watch them come and go, keeping the gentle visualization of the flame in the lotus as your central reference point to whatever comes and goes in your mind. If you get distracted and forget all about the visualization, don't get upset about it (this is a further distraction); just gently come back to the visualization as soon as you realize you've slipped away.

At first you may not notice any obvious effect on your dreams. Tarthang Tulku says that as you continue the practice night after night your awareness within the dream state will naturally develop until you start knowing that you are dreaming while it is happening, and you will be able to see the evolution and creation of your dreams.

This deliberate creation of an "anchor point" for consciousness, something deliberately but gently willed for mind to stabilize around, is similar to the self-remembering practice for the waking state discussed in *Waking Up*. The cultivation of lucidity in dreams should assist the cultivation of lucidity in waking life, and vice versa.

Sweet dreams!

Suggested Reading

In addition to the readings suggested for the last two chapters, all of Carlos Castaneda's books about the teachings of his (mythical?) teacher don Juan contain much useful information about working with dreams for spiritual growth. My students and I hope to publish a complete index of his eight books in the future, but meanwhile you must search through the books, a not unpleasant task and the context will add a great deal.

Castaneda, C. 1968. *The Teachings of don Juan: A Yaqui Way of Knowledge.* Berkeley and Los Angeles: University of California Press.
———. 1971. *A Separate Reality: Further Conversations with don Juan.* New York: Simon & Schuster.
———. 1972. *Journey to Ixtlan: The Lessons of don Juan.* New York: Simon & Schuster.

———. 1974. *Tales of Power*. New York: Simon & Schuster.

———. 1977. *The Second Ring of Power*. New York: Simon & Schuster.

———. 1981. *The Eagle's Gift*. New York: Simon & Schuster.

———. 1984. *The Fire from Within*. New York: Simon & Schuster.

———. 1987. *The Power of Silence: Further Lessons from don Juan*. New York: Simon & Schuster.

Part 2

PSYCHIC PHENOMENA

CHAPTER 5

Time: The Mystery Nobody Notices

"Time" is one of the most frequently used words in the English language. We look at our watch and ask, "What time is it?" We meet a friend and remark, "It's been a long time!" We think about our busy lives and complain that we don't have enough time. As often as we use this concept, it seems we should understand it well. We take it for granted, but don't really understand it.

We can be reminded of how little we understand when our experienced time doesn't match clock time: "You only said that a minute ago? It seems like it was an hour ago!" In our culture clock time—"scientific time"—is so predominant, seems so "objective," that we usually give it priority over our own experience. After all, aren't our experiences "subjective" and thus inherently inferior to "objective" knowledge?

Researchers working at the cutting edge of modern physics have begun to wonder about the nature of time, and their ideas may soon challenge our old concepts. For now, however, there is much more direct evidence of how little we know: namely the parapsychological data about *precognition*.

Beliefs about prophecies, visions that foretell the future, forebodings, and premonitions can be found in all cultures. Throughout the ages people have had dreams, visions, hunches, and other experiences that seemed to foretell the future, often with dramatic accuracy. Priests or shamans developed special technical procedures to try to foretell the future on demand. These included trying to induce symbolic, precognitive dreams, and such exotic practices as haruspicy—foretelling the future from examining the entrails of a sacrificial animal—and hepta-

scopy—examining the liver of a sacrificial animal. Sometimes their results were strikingly accurate, sometimes they were totally wrong. Often the impressions of the future were vague and ambiguous, and
interpreting them proved slippery and unsatisfactory. And there has
always been lots of what we might call *psuedo-divination* around. For
example, if I "psychically" predict that a well-known Hollywood star
will get a messy divorce next year as a result of a sex and drug scandal
(a routine sort of prediction of psuedo-psychics), will we really be surprised if this turns out to be true?

Scientific investigators of psychic phenomena have defined precognition very precisely: *Precognition is the successful prediction of the future
state of affairs when there is no way to logically extrapolate that prediction
from current data.* This definition allows us to separate precognition from
other psychologically interesting ways to predict the future, such as a
good ability for rational inference. For example, if I see you release an
object in your hand I can predict it will hit the floor simply by extrapolating from current knowledge: On this planet unsupported objects
fall. But if we are sitting in a restaurant and I predict that a baseball
will come flying out of the kitchen and land on our table, and it does
a minute later, that's precognition.

The Polite but Impossible Request

In the classical laboratory parapsychology test for precognition the
subject is shown a deck of cards. The experimenter says, "In an hour
I'm going to shuffle this deck of cards very, very thoroughly (at least
ten shuffles) without looking at what I'm doing. Would you please
write down *now* what the order of this deck will be when I finish shuffling them in an hour?"

Given what we think we understand about the physical universe
there is no way you can now acquire any ordinary, sensory information
about what the order of the deck will be in an hour. You could thoroughly examine the cards as they are now, but anything you can see
about the current order of the deck is irrelevant because that order will
be destroyed in an unpredictable way by the shuffling process.

The request is straightforward. The goal is clearly defined: Predict
the order of these cards at the specified future time. Given our ordinary
understanding of time, however, the request may be straightforward
but it is also impossible. The past is gone, the future doesn't exist yet,
only the present is real. How can the experimenter ask the subject to
do such an absurd thing?

And yet it works! Absurd or not, the request sometimes produces results. In a recent review of the scientific literature on this and similar types of precognition studies I found thirty-two successful experiments reported. I used a tougher criterion of success than is usually applied, namely that people's scores were clearly higher than they would get just by chance guessing; that is, that they were predicting the future accurately, as they had been asked to do. Statistically, there had to be *at least* 20 to 1 odds against the results being due to chance for me to consider an experiment successful. (Many other studies show more subtle, statistically significant precognition effects, but that wasn't my focus.) So the idea of asking someone to predict the future this way may seem absurd, but sometimes it works. Reality will manifest what it can manifest whether our concepts allow it or not. We can close our minds and live in our concepts or we can open our minds to what is: Sometimes our minds can reach "forward in time" and bring back extrasensorially acquired information about the future.

Precognition is a form of extrasensory perception. The human mind can sometimes transcend not only spatial barriers (as when a target for psychic perception is at a distance or hidden in sealed containers); the mind can sometimes "cross" the "time barrier," go "into" the supposedly not-yet-existent future. I put quotes around these terms to remind us that although we can easily use spatial analogies to talk about time, that doesn't mean we really understand time.

Extrasensory Perception (ESP)

Extrasensory perception (ESP) is a highly controversial topic in orthodox scientific circles. Most establishment scientists, especially older ones, prejudicially reject it out of hand, without even bothering to look at the evidence for it. It seems to be impossible in principle because it doesn't fit with the satisfying and highly effective picture of the physical universe modern science has created. If information about something is going to be perceived by someone, there has to be physical energy or physical matter to convey the information: light waves for sight, sound waves for hearing, paper with a message on it.

Not only have we been unable to reliably associate any physical energy with ESP, ESP doesn't behave the way it should if a physical energy conveys it. Physical energy is detectable with instruments, it declines in strength with increasing distance, and its transmission can be blocked by shielding. Since none of these physical effects have been associated with ESP, the closed mind reasons that ESP can't exist. This presupposes a great faith in one's reasoning abilities.

Precognition seems even more impossible than present-time ESP. Ordinary ESP is about things that exist, at least. The future doesn't exist yet, so how could any kind of "energy," much less matter, "flow" from it to the present to convey information? We won't even think about what such a "flow" might do to our ideas of causality.

Toward Discovery

This apparent lack of relation between ESP and the physical world may change. I recently made a discovery about precognition that relates it to a measurable physical condition. Any discovered relation like this might go a long way toward reducing the psychological resistance of establishment science toward the paranormal.

This discovery came about because of my long-standing interest in understanding the nature of ESP. What does ESP tell us about human nature? About human possibilities? About our transpersonal, spiritual possibilities? How might it be practically applied? Unfortunately, although experimental studies in parapsychology laboratories have demonstrated the existence of ESP, they haven't told us much about its nature. This is because ESP in the laboratory generally shows up weakly and inconsistently, so it's been hard to study its nature. In engineering terms the *signal-to-noise* ratio is very poor.

Here's an analogy: A native genius in an isolated and nontechnological country logically deduces that there must be radio broadcasts and wants to hear what is being said on those broadcasts. After years of experimenting she manages to build a very crude receiver, perhaps like an old crystal set. But her receiver is so insensitive, and there is so much static in the atmosphere from the frequent storms in her country, that all she ever hears is an occasional word or phrase interspersed with hours or days of constant, irritating static. That is what is meant by poor signal-to-noise ratio.

The occasional words might be enough to convince some of our genius's friends that there is such a thing as a radio broadcast. Others will scoff and claim that people only *imagine* they hear an occasional word or phrase; it's just some kind of hallucination induced by listening to all that static hour after hour. This is a long, long way from understanding what the *nature* and *content* of the broadcasts are. That's the situation with our scientific knowledge of ESP today. What might we learn if we could hear and understand all of the "psychic broadcasts" of our universe?

A few years ago I became concerned with the question, "When ESP does clearly manifest in the laboratory, how *strongly* can it manifest?" I was concerned with the upper limits of performance results. Even more specifically: When ESP works, how much information is actually transferred? Drawing on my memory of good results I had read reports on in the past, I reviewed a dozen studies published in the parapsychological journals. I was surprised to discover that all of these very successful studies were of manifestations of present-time ESP, none of precognitive ESP. That is, in these very successful studies people were trying to extrasensorially perceive things that existed *now*, never things that would only come into existence at some future time.

This seemed odd, but perhaps it was only a coincidence. I had only reviewed a dozen out of the hundreds of published parapsychology studies. I decided to thoroughly review all of the successful parapsychology studies. What follows is the essence of the exciting discovery I made.[1]

The Discovery: Precognition Works, but Not Very Well

My initial impression was confirmed. There were lots of both precognitive and present-time ESP studies where *psi* (the term now coming into general use for the various kinds of ESP and psychokinesis) only manifested at low (although statistically significant) levels.[2] *But a substantial number of present-time* ESP studies showed ten times as much information transfer as even the better precognitive ESP studies. In fact several present-time ESP studies had perfect scores: Every target had been correctly perceived, not just some small percentage above chance. Not a single precognitive study came anywhere near perfect scoring.

This is the first solid relationship I know of between ESP and a physical condition. As soon as you go into the future ESP performance falls off drastically. You don't have to go very far into the future: Some of the studies I reviewed involved electronic testing devices where the target to be guessed was randomly created only one- or two-tenths of a second into the future. So present versus future time status makes a difference.

Contrary to what we might expect I saw no indication that the *amount* of time made a difference: The information transfer rate in precognition studies seemed about the same one-tenth of a second into the future as an hour or a day or even a year into the future. I do not

discount the possibility that more extensive research might find relationships between the amount of time and the amount of precognition,
however, as I did not have enough data to map out the space of a year
in seconds.

So we may have a physical correlate of ESP. Having a physical correlate may make it a more acceptable topic of study in orthodox science.
I say *may* for, as we shall see in chapter 11, people have tremendous
psychological (and largely unconscious) resistances to ESP.

The more important aspect of this finding for me personally, as well
as for people in general, is the fresh stimulus it gives to think about
precognition. We *must* question our "common-sense" assumptions and
our apparently "scientific" assumptions about the nature of time. Even
if it doesn't work as well as present-time ESP, precognition does work:
It's real.

What Is the Future?

Does the future already exist in some form? If it already exists in
some form is everything already predetermined? Is it partially predetermined in a sort of probabilistic sense? There might be some form of
existent future, for example, in which you eat breakfast tomorrow
morning; but it's only likely, not certain. Is predetermination testable
for truth or falsity? Is the idea of predetermination a psychologically
useful concept if we are oriented toward growth?

The fact that precognition seems to work much less well than present-time ESP also raises mind-stretching questions. Is precognition a
different kind of ESP than present-time ESP, such that it's just the
nature of it that it doesn't pick up information as well? Are both present-time and precognitive ESP the same human process, but some kind
of "time barrier" exists between the present and the future that greatly
reduces the "intensity" of psychic information that passes "through"
or "across" it? Is the future in some sense less "real," less fully formed,
such that ESP just can't be as sure about it? That possibility fits with
the idea of free will much better.

We should also be alert to a possible psychological explanation for
the difference. Might it be that the very idea of precognition is much
more psychologically unacceptable to people in our culture than the
idea of present-time ESP? If that is so *why* is the idea of precognition
so unacceptable? I am not inclined to put too much weight on this
explanation. Cultural bias is very important, as I emphasize throughout
this book; but in the hundreds of people tested for precognition over

the years you would think there would be an occasional person who hadn't absorbed the cultural prejudice that well, and so might try hard and score very well on precognition.

If I Were Precognitive. . . .

We've come full circle, back to our psychological beliefs and attitudes about time and precognition. Let's put it on a personal level. Suppose you could go to a parapsychology laboratory next week and receive a treatment that made you strongly precognitive. Some advantages are clear: You could call your broker because you have a good idea as to what stocks will go up or down. You could decide not to visit city A next week because you know that an earthquake is coming. This could be appealing.

But do we really want the full burden of precognitive ability? Do you want to know about coming tragedies to loved ones that you may not be able to prevent? Do you want to bear the laughter and rejection of others when you intervene in their lives with the explanation that you're acting on the basis of a "psychic vision"? Do you want to feel the responsibility of intervening? Do you want to have to judge whether you should intervene or not? If a particularly nasty person is going to be run down by a car at the next intersection, do you try to rescue him? Do you want to know when your friends are going to die? When *you* are going to die?

It's easy and socially acceptable to call for more research on the nature of psychic functioning, particularly precognition. That distances it from me, from you. Or we can just remain skeptical, and deny the reality of precognition: If it doesn't exist then I don't have to deal with any of these questions. If you want to stretch your mental horizons, though, and think about the universe in some new ways, do some serious thinking about these questions—and remember to "think" with your heart as well as your head.

Suggested Reading

The subject of precognition is fascinating and there is a large body of literature on it. Below I have listed a few good books on the subject and a few more technical journal articles to start your reading. If you're really fascinated with the laboratory work, most of the experimental reports will be found in the three major journals of parapsychology, the *Journal of the American Society for Psychical Research,* the *Journal of Parapsychology,* and the *Journal of the Society for Psychical Research.*

Dean, E. D. 1974. Precognition and retrocognition. In E. Mitchell and J. White, eds. *Psychic Exploration: A Challenge for Science.* New York: Putnam. 153–78.

Eisenbud, J. 1982. *Paranormal Foreknowledge: Problems and Perplexities.* New York: Human Sciences Press.

Kesner, J., and R. Morris. 1978. A precognition test using guided imagery. In W. Roll, ed. *Research in Parapsychology 1977.* Metuchen, N.J.: Scarecrow Press. 48–51.

MacKenzie, A. 1974. *Riddle of the Future: A Modern Study of Precognition.* New York: Tapplinger.

Priestley, J. B. 1964. *Man and Time.* New York: Doubleday. This classic has especially interesting material on precognitive dreams.

Tart, Charles T. 1979. Improving real-time ESP by suppressing the future: Trans-temporal inhibition. In C. Tart, H. Puthoff, and R. Targ, eds. *Mind at Large: Institute of Electrical and Electronic Engineers Symposia on the Nature of Extrasensory Perception.* New York: Praeger. 137–74.

_____. 1983. Information acquisition rates in forced-choice ESP experiments: Precognition does not work as well as present-time ESP. *Journal of the American Society for Psychical Research* 77:293–310. This is the full technical presentation of the material described in this chapter.

_____. 1983. Laboratory PK: Frequency of manifestation and resemblance to precognition. In W. Roll, J. Beloff, and R. White, eds. *Research in Parapsychology 1982.* Metuchen, N.J.: Scarecrow Press. 101–2.

CHAPTER 6

Subtle Energies, Healing Energies

When we think of the word "energy" we usually think of the qualities that are measured and manipulated by physicists. Electricity, magnetism, heat, and chemical energy are common examples. Carl Jung pointed out many years ago, however, that "energy" is basically a *psychological* experience and concept: We experience being more or less "energetic," and have days of possessing lots of or little "energy." This archetypal psychological concept of energy has extremely useful applications when applied to understanding and controlling the physical world.

Indeed "energy" can be described and quantified in a much more precise way in dealing with its physical manifestations than when dealing with psychological energy. Physical scientists have been so successful with physical energies that their (secondary) ideas have become primary for most of us. We tend to believe that *real* energy is what physicists measure, and "psychological" energy is a subjective, probably unscientific concept.

Nevertheless the experiential, psychological concepts about energy won't go away. For one thing they are too useful in describing our psychological lives. And, whether "official science" scoffs at it or not, we do hear stories about "subtle energies," "psychic forces," and "healing energies"—such as in the laying on of hands for healing—that can't always be dismissed. In this chapter and the next we shall look at what we know about "subtle energies" and their possibilities.

The Laying on of Hands

Healers in virtually all cultures have worked through the laying on of hands. The healer places his or her hands on the afflicted area and tries to "flow energy" into the injury to increase its rate of healing. The healer may also pray or do other things; but the idea that some special quality or energy of the healer's touch promotes healing is central.

With a little effort anyone could document thousands of cures resulting from the laying on of hands. Indeed the laying on of hands is now advocated and taught by some medical professionals.[1] Does that prove there is a special energy emanating from the hands of healers?

There may not be any increase in the rate of healing from the laying on of hands. Most injuries and illnesses get better by themselves in the long run. So, in many of these anecdotes, the patient would have gotten better anyway. And we may not have heard about the failures. Furthermore people seldom have clear ideas of what the normal time course of an illness is, so we don't know if there's any actual speeding up of healing as a result of the laying on of hands.

I haven't specifically searched the medical literature for controlled studies that demonstrate the benefit of this kind of healing. Such studies would be straightforward to carry out: Give some patients the healing treatment and don't give it to others; then have physicians who don't know which patients were treated and which were not make ratings of severity of illness at various time periods. In this way we would see quite readily if we had a higher or a more rapid cure rate.

We could also argue that we don't need such studies because the speeding of healing in some cases is so dramatic. I also believe that studies would show that laying on of hands does have at least some benefit in most cases (and often a lot); like most people I don't get too excited about experimenting to prove things I already accept. Let's assume laying on of hands helps. What are some other possible explanations?

The Value of Touch

All illnesses and injuries take place in a psychophysical system: The physical body's functioning is affected by thoughts and emotions; and thoughts and emotions are affected by what goes on in the physical body. A positive attitude is probably good for healing in general, and having a healer lay on his or her hands probably improves your attitude. A healer gives you a lot of attention. You must be worthwhile to deserve this attention, so it's good for you. Much of the attention is delivered through gentle touch, which communicates positive regard and caring a lot more effectively than mere words usually do.

An example: A few years ago I went in to my clinic for a regular medical checkup. Usually this involves being mechanically tested by technicians in one testing station after another, culminating with a five- or ten-minute physical examination by a physician, who in my experience had always been a man. This time the examiner was a woman, a nurse practitioner. I was amazed: The quality of touch I received from her was so different from all those previous male physicians. Her whole style of touching me during the examination conveyed the feeling that she was paying attention to me as a human being. She even warmed the stethoscope before listening to my chest, as if my comfort was of value.

The fact that she was a woman and a nurse practitioner may have made it more likely, given our cultural roles, that she would be more caring; but there is no reason why a male physician, or any health care professional of either sex, cannot exhibit sensitivity and care in the way they touch patients. Sensitive, caring touch is therapeutic.

The value of touch, then, might account for the effectiveness of much healing by laying on of hands. The warmth of the healer's hands may also be good for healing, as raising the temperature of a body part tends to dilate the blood vessels. These possible alternative explanations do not reduce the value of such healing, but do complicate the question of whether "subtle energies" are also involved in the laying on of hands.

Detecting Subtle Healing Energies

I think it is therapeutically as well as scientifically important to know whether subtle energies are involved here. Perhaps we could build a heated, plastic-covered mechanical hand that would mimic all the effects of a healer's hand. All we would still have to do is fool patients into believing that a real human being is paying attention to them to get the full benefit of laying on of hands without having to invest all the time a healer would ordinarily spend. (In fact some patients do benefit from "talking to" computerized psychotherapy programs. "Attention" from a machine may be better than no real attention from a human being who is only pretending to pay attention to you.)

If, however, humans do emanate a subtle healing energy then we can't simulate a real human healer. We would instead want to know how to train people to put out this subtle energy in the most effective ways, perhaps even learning to train many people to function as healers instead of a select few.[2]

Subtle Healing Energies: The Work of Bernard Grad

Bernard Grad is a biologist with the Alan Memorial Institute of McGill University in Montreal, Canada, where he makes his living doing conventional biological research on cancer. He has contributed more than a hundred studies advancing our understanding of cancer. Clearly he knows his conventional science. He has also been interested in the concept of life energies since he began his graduate training in the 1950s.

In the 1960s Grad met a Hungarian healer named Oscar Estabany, who used the laying-on-of-hands procedure. Intrigued, he decided to investigate whether Estabany was emanating subtle energies. Grad was well aware of the importance of touch in all such healing, and the psychological influence it has on patients, so he decided to begin by diminishing the effects of touch and suggestion. The patients in his first study were mice, who presumably do not have much in the way of expectations about healers.[3]

A large number of mice were selected for the experiment. Grad inflicted approximately equal-sized wounds on the mice by snipping off a piece of skin with a scissors. The size of these wounds (and thus the rate at which the body heals them by growing new skin in from the edges until the lesion is gone) can be precisely measured by tracing the outline of the wound on special paper and then measuring the area of the wound by tracing the transferred outline with a planimeter. The mice were then randomly assigned to experimental (healing) or control (no healing) conditions.

The Mouse in the Bag

For the actual healing treatment an assistant would put one of the mice in the experimental group into a paper bag and close it up, then bring the bag to Estabany in another room. Estabany would hold the bag in his open hands for a few minutes, focusing on healing the mouse by flowing his subtle energy to it through the bag. He didn't regard the bag as a real obstacle. The bag greatly reduced the likelihood that any helpful effects of the healer might be due to the quality of the touch with which he held the mouse, whether he stroked and gentled it, and so on.

To cancel out the effects of putting the mouse in the bag the control mice were put in bags the same number of times and for the same periods as the experimental mice. The assistant then had these bagged mice held by people who were conveniently available but who had no reputation as psychic healers: medical students. (It says something about the impersonal and technological bent of allopathic medicine that people in general see no problem in using medical students as controls for handling effects because we don't expect them to have subtle energy healing powers!)

To avoid biases for or against the idea of subtle healing energy the size of the wounds was measured, on a fixed schedule, by a technician who was blind as to which mice were in the experimental group and which were in the control group.

The Healer Helps

Grad found that the mice that received Estabany's healing treatment showed significantly faster wound healing than those that didn't. This was not just a barely detectible statistical effect: The rate of healing in the treated mice was often double that in the controls.

In a further experiment with these same mice Grad found that the healing treatment had a generally beneficial effect on the vitality of the treated mice—in addition to the specific effect on their wounds. The mice were subjected to near-freezing temperatures overnight, which is very stressful and often fatal. Only 14 percent of the control mice survived the night, but 63 percent of the treated mice did. Did the "extra energy" added by Estabany add itself to their own vitality? Can an animal or a person be given an extra charge of vital energy like this?

In a similar study a sensitive breed of mice were put on an iodine-deficient diet, which interacts with the thyroid gland to produce thyroid cancers. Half the animals received healing treatments from Estabany through the paper bag; the control mice were held in their paper bags by medical students. The measure of healing effect was the weight of the thyroid after the animal was sacrificed at the end of the experiment. If Estabany's healings were effective, the thyroids of the treated mice should weigh significantly less. They did.

These three studies argue strongly for some kind of subtle energy flowing from the healer's hands, an energy that is not stopped by paper. But three more conventional hypotheses might also explain the results.

1. Suppose Estabany has some chemical in his sweat that mice like; or suppose the medical students, probably chronically overworked like most medical students, have stress-related chemicals in their sweat that upset mice. Sweat might pass through paper and so be responsible for the results. (This would be quite interesting in and of itself, of course; it might be useful to identify the positive chemicals and introduce them into sickrooms.)

2. Suppose that Estabany's hands were warmer than those of the medical student controls, and the mice liked the extra warmth.
3. Suppose that Estabany handled the bags more gently and this indeed gentled the mice, who were otherwise stressed by being imprisoned in these paper bags.

The Nonsuggestible Patient

Grad's focus was the question of subtle energies, not chemical ones, so he had to eliminate the problems suggested above. He switched to a new type of "patient" that was not susceptible to suggestion, as in gentling, and a new type of healing procedure that eliminated chemical and thermal contamination. The patients were barley seeds.

Estabany had no direct contact with these "patients." Instead he would come into the laboratory and be given a hermetically sealed jar of the kind of sterile saline solution (0.9 percent) that is used for intravenous feeding in hospitals. Estabany would hold the jar between his hands and give it a healing treatment just as if he were holding his hands on a patient. Because of its hermetic seal there could be no chemical contamination of the saline. It probably would get a little warmer, however; to counteract this the technician put the jar back on a shelf for an hour so it would cool back down to room temperature.

To give the barley seeds a need to be healed they were baked in an oven, which sapped their vitality and killed some of them. They were then randomly divided into experimental and control groups. The experimental seeds were soaked in saline solution that had received the healing treatment from Estabany, the control seeds in otherwise identical saline solution that had not received such a treatment. One effect of this saline soaking was to keep the seeds patients: The salt was not good for them.

The treated and untreated seeds were planted in separate pots. They were regularly watered with ordinary saline solution (to keep up the need for healing) by a technician who did not know which seeds had gotten the healing treatment and which had not. Another technician, who was also blind in this way, took regular measurements of growth.

The Green Thumb Effect

This experiment and subsequent ones Grad has carried out produced a clear effect. For seedlings treated with the "healed" saline solution significantly more seeds sprout, the seedlings grow faster and taller, and the plants weigh more. It can make you wonder whether people who have a "green thumb" do more than just provide better conventional care to their plants.

The Black Thumb Effect

In one experiment Grad put a jar of hermetically sealed saline solution in a paper bag and gave it to a psychotically depressed patient to hold. She was suspicious of and agitated by this request to hold the bag for a few minutes, but she held it. Barley seedlings were then treated with this saline.

Compared to controls treated with ordinary saline significantly fewer of these seedlings sprouted, they didn't grow as tall or as rapidly, and they weighed less. One experiment only; but we do have traditions of people with black thumbs, who can never get plants to grow right in spite of following all the instructions. If "healing energy" can be psychically transmitted, why not "sickening energy"?

What Is the Energy?

Grad's procedure seems to rule out conventional kinds of energies or chemicals and suggests that some form of subtle energy or psychokinetic effect can penetrate glass, "store" itself in water, and then beneficially affect sick organisms.

We have no idea what the ultimate nature of psychokinetic (PK) energy or any other kind of subtle energy is; we only know that it is not a known or readily conceivable form of conventional energies. Grad and some other researchers have a little information about its possible interaction with water, however.

Grad finds that as long as the treated bottles of saline are kept hermetically sealed, they can have healing effects months later. If they are opened to the air, however, their potency rapidly disappears. Also, both Grad and Douglas Dean, a parapsychologist who has worked extensively with healers, have measured some shifts in the infrared transmission spectrum of treated saline.[4] Magnetic fields applied to saline solution can also produce somewhat similar spectral shifts; but to do this these fields must be enormously stronger than the Earth's magnetic field or any conceivable magnetic field we could expect a person to produce. Thus the healing "energy" may produce some kind of shift in the state of water molecules. This shift might be part of the mechanism of accelerated healing, or incidental to it.

"Something Else"

Grad's careful experiments, done in spite of resistance from the orthodox scientific community and with little funding, are truly pioneering and important. I feel he has solidly established that there can be a "subtle energy" involved in healing. Certainly in ordinary laying on of hands there are suggestion effects, positive effects from being paid attention to, and so on; but now that we know there can be a vital "something else," it is important to find out all that we can.

Meanwhile, what about *your* hands? Hold them eight to ten inches apart. Feel whatever the quality of feeling is in your hands. Then feel the quality of the space *between* them. Is there "something" there? Move your hands closer and further apart: Does the feeling change? Try holding your hand near another person's and feeling these things. Try holding your hand over the afflicted area when someone you care for is ill. Yes, there may be some imagination involved, but might there also be something else?

Suggested Reading

Dean, Douglas. 1983. Infrared measurements of heater-treated water. In W. Roll, J. Beloff, and R. White, eds. *Research in Parapsychology 1982*. Metuchen, N.J.: Scarecrow Press. 100–101.

Ehrenwald, J. 1977. Parapsychology and the healing arts. In B. Wolman et al., eds. *Handbook of Parapsychology*. New York: Van Nostrand Reinhold. 541–56.

Grad, Bernard. 1965. Some biological effects of the "laying on of hands": A review of experiments with animals and plants. *Journal of the American Society for Psychical Research* 59:95–127.

————. 1967. The "laying on of hands": Implications for psychotherapy, gentling, and the placebo effect. *Journal of the American Society for Psychical Research* 61:286–305.

Krieger, D. 1979. *The Therapeutic Touch: How to Use Your Hands to Help or Heal*. Englewood Cliffs, N.J.: Prentice-Hall.

Morris, R. 1977. Parapsychology, biology, and anpsi. In B. Wolman et al., eds. *Handbook of Parapsychology*. New York: Van Nostrand Reinhold. 687–715.

CHAPTER 7

Subtle Energies: Life as the PK Target

Psychokinesis (PK) is the general parapsychological term for a direct influence of the mind on matter. A person wishes for a physical result, and even though no known form of physical energy or mechanism intervenes, the result occurs.

The classic testing mechanism for PK was thrown dice. A person called the "agent" tried to influence the fall of dice, often tossed by a machine, and deviations from chance expectancy occurred in the desired direction. Although the psychokinetic effect was often small in absolute terms, it was statistically significant often enough to establish the reality of PK.

Most PK research has used inanimate, mechanical, or electronic systems as targets of the PK energy. If the healing effect in Bernard Grad's experiments (which we discussed in the last chapter) is a form of PK, then it looks as if PK can influence animate, biological target systems as well as inanimate ones. Pioneering research on this idea has been done by William Braud, a psychologist working at the Mind Science Foundation in San Antonio, Texas. He has conducted, with various colleagues, several PK experiments using biological systems as targets.

Controlling Fish

In one of his earliest experiments the biological target system was an electric knife fish (*Gymnotus carapo*). These fish generate a weak electrical field that spreads out through the water and is modified by objects or other creatures in the water. By sensing these modifications the electric knife fish is able to scan its environment when vision is poor, as in muddy water.

By measuring the electric field the fish puts out, its orientation in an aquarium can be automatically recorded. Braud, acting as the PK agent, tried to psychically influence the orientation of an electric knife fish—first one way, then another—in various experimental periods. Over ten sessions he was successful in 52 percent of the trials, rather than the expected 50 percent we would get by chance alone. Although a small effect in absolute terms, this was a statistically significant success rate; that is, it would have occurred so infrequently by chance alone that it is not reasonable to explain it by chance: Something really happened.[1]

In another experiment the British psychic Matthew Manning tried to mentally influence the fish.[2] He showed a significant 53 percent success rate. Two further experiments used a group of unselected volunteer agents.[3] They were not preselected because of known psychic abilities; they were ordinary people who came to the laboratory because they were interested in parapsychology. One experiment only showed a 51 percent overall success rate for the group, which was not statistically significant; but the other group showed an overall 54 percent success rate, which was significant.

We can make a good case, then, that human intention can influence the orientation of these fish. Is it PK in the sense of a direct "energetic" action on the fish, or on the parts of their brains that control orientation? Does it produce something in the water of the aquarium that attracts the fish's attention so it orients in the desired direction? Or is it a telepathic effect, a communication to the fish of the desired direction?

Run, Gerbil, Run!

Gerbils are cute, furry little creatures, similar to hamsters. Cage life, unfortunately, doesn't allow for much physical activity, so they take advantage of the opportunity to run when they are put in a circular activity wheel. Can their activity in the wheel be psychokinetically speeded up or slowed down by the wish of a human agent?

Braud again used himself as agent in a first study. He got a 55 percent success rate instead of the 50 percent expected by chance, but his results were so variable that the success rate wasn't statistically significant. In another experiment Matthew Manning got a much smoother 53 percent success rate, which was significant.[4] Two subsequent experiments with unselected volunteers obtained significant effects—55 percent in the one case, 52 percent in the other.[5]

The activity rate of gerbils, then, can be affected. But is it telepathic communication, or direct PK influence on their brains?

Healing Blood

Human blood is slightly salty (0.9 percent), and the red blood cells are stable under conditions of normal salinity. If a blood sample is diluted with distilled water so it is less salty *hemolysis*, the gradual breakdown of the red blood cells, occurs. A test tube of red blood gradually gets less opaque, and eventually becomes transparent as the cells break down. If you pass a beam of light through the test tube more light will pass through as the fluid gets clearer, so you can conveniently measure the concentration of intact red cells this way. The breakdown rate of cells is stable and well known under standard conditions.

The breakdown of red cells is clearly unhealthy. Could psychic healing promote health by inhibiting this breakdown? Braud tested this directly during Matthew Manning's visit to the Mind Science Foundation.[6] Manning held his hands above the apparatus containing the sealed test tubes and tried to psychically affect them. A strong, statistically significant 7 percent slowdown of the normal breakdown rate resulted. Manning's return to England prevented continuing research, but this healing effect deserves much more study.

Biofeedback

In ordinary biofeedback sensors are attached to a subject in order to measure some physiological activity. This activity could be heart rate, blood pressure, the electrical resistance of the skin (related to overall level of excitement or relaxation), brain waves, skin temperature, and so on. Amplifiers strengthen the weak signals detected from the biofeedback subject's body and use them to run indicating equipment— for example, to move the pen on a chart recorder. When the biofeedback subject can view this output it provides feedback about what that particular physiological system is doing, and he can then try various strategies to increase or decrease the activity. Conventional biofeedback can be called *auto*biofeedback, as the system you control is inside your own body.

For example, we can measure the electrical resistance of the skin by passing an extremely weak (typically 50-millionths of an ampere) electrical current through a pair of electrodes. The most sensitive placements of these electrodes are on the palms of the hands, the forehead, or the soles of the feet. There are many sweat glands in these areas, and presecretory activity of these glands strongly reflects a biofeedback subject's overall activation.

As the biofeedback subject watches the chart recorder he can see his skin resistance going up and down. If something startles him his skin resistance will drop rapidly and take some time to recover. If he relaxes it will go up. If he engages in demanding mental activity, like complex mental arithmetic, it will go down. Now he can deliberately try various kinds of mental activities and see whether and how they change his skin resistance. If he tries to vividly remember a frightening incident, for example, he can probably make the chart recorder's pen move down; if he visualizes relaxing in the sun on a warm beach it will probably move up. In this way he can acquire conscious control of skin resistance. With that control of skin resistance, an external indicator, comes control over level of activation.

Allobiofeedback

Braud's recent research has focused on a new laboratory procedure that he has named *allobiofeedback* in contrast to ordinary or autobiofeedback. In these experiments sensors are attached to the subject to measure a physiological function. Braud has used skin resistance almost exclusively in these experiments.

Unlike autobiofeedback, however, the allobiofeedback subject does not receive any feedback about this measurement. The feedback information is sent to another person, who acts as a PK agent. This agent is shielded from sensory communication with the subject by being in a distant room. The PK agent now tries to mentally influence the subject's physiology, using the feedback as a way of telling how well he is doing. Thus the feedback is *allo*—outside of the subject.

The agent tries to psychokinetically influence the subject's skin resistance during specified trial periods. These results are compared with the results from control periods in which the agent does not watch the feedback display or try to have any influence. A statistically significant difference between the responses in the influence and control periods signifies successful allobiofeedback.

Nine formal experiments in allobiofeedback have now been carried out, using people with known psychic abilities as well as unselected volunteers as agents. Five of the nine experiments have been significant. Differences of up to 10 percent have occurred. It is not a large difference in absolute terms; but it is a quite sizable difference for early experiments when we know so little about psychic functioning.

The subjects in these experiments know what is happening. They are told that someone else will try to influence their physiological responses. They need do nothing special, just sit quietly in their shielded room for less than an hour. I was surprised to learn that almost none of the subjects expressed any negative feelings about being psychically acted on in this way, and many actually liked the idea.

How does the allobiofeedback effect work? Braud mentions four main strategies used by various agents. One is to focus on the polygraph pen, which gives you feedback of what's happening: *Will* the pen to move in the desired direction. Give no thought to the subject. A second strategy is to produce the desired changes in yourself and imagine that they are transmitted to the subject. If you are trying to activate the subject, for example, think of something exciting, such as a dangerous situation you were once in. Do this vividly enough so your body responds with arousal. A third agent strategy is to vividly image the subject in a situation that would produce the desired physiological changes.

The fourth agent strategy is quite different. Many researchers have remarked that psi in general is goal oriented: It seems to get you to a desired outcome even if you don't have much understanding of the necessary steps that would have to occur to produce that goal. So in this strategy the agent doesn't pay much attention at all to the information about the subject's physiological responses provided by the polygraph pen, but instead simply focuses on the idea that the experiment will be successful.

As I reflect on my feelings about Braud's studies, particularly the allobiofeedback experiments, I find myself both encouraged and bothered.

I am bothered because there is something unsettling about the idea of someone else changing physiological processes in *my* body. Like most of us, I think of my body as *mine*, a private place, a place where I call the shots. Actually, our bodies are more like symbiotic communities or well-organized empires, with all sorts of specialized worker populations contributing to the welfare of the whole. The empire analogy is particularly apt, for the empire has a standing and active army, constantly killing barbarian invaders, our immune systems protecting us from bacterial and viral infections. That's all intellectual knowledge though: There is a deep emotional level at which my body is *mine* and I don't like the idea of someone else affecting it. Isn't that what black magic is all about, somebody making you ill by psychic means? Of course that is what psychic healing is about too, so this is a mixed bag.

In addition to the attractiveness of the idea of psychic healing, Braud's findings give some support to the idea the great mystics, those explorers of altered states of consciousness knowledge, have always been telling us, that in reality, we are all one. That is an idea that doesn't make much sense in our ordinary state of consciousness, it's just a philosophical abstraction. But, whether we grasp it or not, is there some literal truth to it? If sometimes one person can affect another's body (and mind, as with ESP) deliberately, what is going on unconsciously all the time? Are the links between us much more important than our well-defended sense of separateness allows us to see? There is much food for thought here.

Suggested Reading

Braud, W. 1978. Allobiofeedback: Immediate feedback for a psychokinetic influence upon another person's physiology. In W. G. Roll, ed. *Research in Parapsychology 1977*. Metuchen, N.J.: Scarecrow Press. 123–34.

————. 1978. Conformance behavior involving living systems. In W. G. Roll, ed. *Research in Parapsychology 1977*. Metuchen, N.J.: Scarecrow Press. 111–15.

Braud, W., G. Davis, and R. Wood. 1979. Experiments with Matthew Manning. *Journal of the Society for Psychical Research* 50:199–223.

Braud, W., and M. Schlitz. 1983. Psychokinetic influence on electrodermal activity. *Journal of Parapsychology* 47:95–119.

CHAPTER 8

ALB: The Misuse of ESP?

Most people who are interested in psychic events take them very seriously. That is appropriate in many ways; but an open mind requires sensitivity to and enjoyment of the inherent humor of our beliefs and lives. This chapter should lighten things up a little.

In this "New Age" we are fascinated by extrasensory perception (ESP), psychic energies, channeling, crystals, auras, holistic healing, and all sorts of other wonderful things that *might* be real and that *might* be used to enhance the quality of life. People like us, however, are knowledgeable and sophisticated. We don't just marvel, we occasionally pause to maturely reflect on the possible *misuse* of these energies. Not that we would ever misuse them ourselves, of course, but we have to recognize that there are some people out there who aren't as mature as we are.

For instance, we always hear the rumor that the Russians are developing telepathic powers in order to put confusing thoughts into the minds of our national leaders, so they will make stupid decisions. I always react as a true patriot to that one, though, and vehemently deny that the Russians' knowledge has advanced that far. Our leaders aren't Communist puppets, they can make their own mistakes!

These discussions of good and evil are usually pretty abstract and theoretical. Now that I've apparently been the personal victim of misused ESP, however, it's not so abstract after all. It's downright disgusting, and good for a big shot of self-righteous moral indignation. Let me tell you my sad story.

My wife, Judy, and I (and any unsuspecting guests we can drag into it) sometimes play a game called Boggle.[1] This fascinating and potentially addicting game is deceptively simple. You have a box with sixteen little compartments in it, a four-square by four-square grid.

There are sixteen dice in the box, each with a letter of the alphabet on each side. You shake the box until the dice settle into the compartments, and then you have two minutes to try to make as many words as possible out of dice that consecutively touch on a side or corner without using the same cube twice in one word.

A legitimate word must be at least three letters long, it must be found in an English-language dictionary (we keep a big unabridged one nearby), and you must know the meaning of the word if there is any question about whether it's really a word. Proper names are not allowed, nor are plurals. You get one point for each three- or four-letter word you find, two for each five-letter word, and so on. If any other player has the same word you don't get any credit for it at all. The winner each time is the one who has the highest score after the common words are taken out.

Suppose you shook the box and got the following arrangement of letters:

        A A K N
        A B D I
        E N L E
        G P N J

This is a very rich throw. Starting at the upper left you can get BAD, BAA, DAB, BAN, NAB, ADE, BADE, AKIN, DIN, LINK, BLINK, LIE, KIN, KID, LED, LID, PEN, BEG, PEND, END, BEND, AND, BAND, PEA, BEAN, BANE, and ANE. The last word, ane, is just the sort of obsolete word I like to find. It's in the dictionary—look it up if you don't believe me. It's an obscure word from the Scottish meaning "one." It's obscure enough that it's unlikely Judy or some other player will spot it, thereby canceling my points.

I frequently am forced to look up words like this, as Judy accuses me of just making words up out of thin air. I think of myself as being creative, as having a feel for the roots of our mother tongue, even if my memory is not too specific; and I'm justified by the dictionary—some of the time. (Just to show you what a competitive player Judy is, she insisted we have a rule that when she challenges a word of mine and I can't find it in the dictionary, or it's in there but I didn't really know the meaning of it, I get penalized a point. I figure that I need all the advantage I can get, since she's better than I am at this game.) I don't really digress here, I am simply filling in the background so you can properly appreciate the misuse of ESP. Now here's the killer.

A week before the incident I read an interesting suspense novel.

One of the characters is a priest, and at one point after a service he takes off his *alb*.

That word leapt right out at me. What a lovely little obscure word to use in Boggle! Hardly an everyday word, except maybe among priests. I doubt that I've ever used it in my life, or that Judy has, so it's really unlikely that she would get it too and cancel my score.

A week later Judy and I decide to play Boggle one evening. As we get ready, I remember: It's my chance to try to use my special new word! Now it's very unlikely that ALB will come up, of course. I've never seen it come up before in the hundreds of games I've played but, what the hell, I can go for it.[2] I announce to Judy (with an intelligent smile on my face, which she probably misperceives as a smirk) that I have a special word in mind I'm going to go for in Boggle tonight. Maybe the gods will be good to me, maybe my unconscious psychokinetic powers (if I have any) will make ALB come up: Who knows? It's a nice chance to kid her at the start of the game. She smiles a lot when I tease her about Boggle.

Naturally I don't tell her what the word is, and I know she hasn't read the novel yet.

Well I imagine you can guess what happens. In about the sixth round we play ALB does come up. Unfortunately *I* don't see it: Judy does. It was the last word she saw before the two-minute timer went off.

If that isn't the misuse of psychic powers I don't know what is. My own loving wife, psychically *stealing* that word out of my mind! Who can you trust?

I think it's about time we established rules and regulations about psychic abilities before it's too late. Once you let them start getting away with things, there's no stopping them. In fact Judy looked at this manuscript and pointed out that I missed KIND, BLED, PLED, PLINK, and DIE in my own example above! I kind of think that I've bled so much after I pled for trying to get my special word that I might as well plink away at my own head with my .22 and die. At least I know that there is at least one more word in the example that she missed.

The Second Incident

But I didn't plink away, of course, for fate had more in store for me.

Judy and I went off for ten days on a wonderful vacation—without the Boggle set. So between vacation and busyness on getting home we hadn't played Boggle for some weeks. Last night we played again.

I managed to win the first set, then she beat me five times in a row that evening—a too typical result. In the middle of this we got a phone call from a well-known psychic, Keith Harary. He and his wife Darlene are close friends of ours, and we talked about getting together for dinner in a couple of weeks. I thought about telling him about the "ALB incident," as I've taken to thinking about it, but didn't get around to it.

Just before our fourth game I told Judy that I wished I could find someone who could simulate Boggle on a computer and have it run a million games or so to find out how often ALB came up. Then I would know if ALB's appearance was indeed quite unlikely, as I suspected, or not that unlikely. If the latter, I couldn't really conclude that there was anything psychic involved in the ALB incident. Before our vacation I had tried to calculate the probability of getting ALB in any one game after the sixteen dice have randomly fallen into their grid, but the math is complex and I gave up. Judy argued that this objective calculation wouldn't mean that much; the probability of seeing any word like ALB depended on your mind set. I replied that this was true, but you still needed to know the objective probability of ALB appearing if you wanted to discuss psi. Between my conversation with Keith and Darlene and this discussion, you might say that ALB was on my mind, but then I forgot about it and went back to playing.

We played our fourth game for the evening. Can you guess what three-letter word came up? Can you guess who saw it and scored when I didn't? Once again, it was the last word she saw just before the timer went off. Once you start on the downward path of using psychic powers to embarrass and humiliate innocent, decent scientists, I guess there's no end to it.

Still, we scientists must try to be objective about these things. So is the appearance of ALB improbable enough to call these events psychic, quite aside from my feelings about these events?

As I said, I tried to work out the probability of ALB coming up theoretically, but the problem is a mess. Different dice have different combinations of letters on them, you have to consider not only whether the right letters—A, L, and B—come up, but the likelihood that they will be adjacent in the needed manner, and so on. Now today's sophisticated scientist (one who is a smart computer programmer or has the money to hire one) would have a computer program simulate randomly selecting one of the sixteen dice; randomly throwing it and noting which face came up; then randomly picking one of the remaining fifteen dice and throwing it, and so on; and finally looking at the positions of any A, L, or B and seeing if they were adjacent in a proper way to make ALB in a single game. The computer would then do this a million times or so (for precision), count the number of ALBs that turned up, and give you a quite exact probability of ALB occurring in any single game. If anyone wants to do it, get a Boggle game (watch out—it's habit forming!) study the layout of the dice, and try it. I'd like to know the results.

Meanwhile, not being that "sophisticated," I resorted to a terribly old-fashioned method: I shook the dice in the Boggle box one hundred times and counted the number of ALBs that came up. This is a pretty good approximation if ALB isn't too rare, not good if it is really rare. As it turned out I got five ALBs in my one hundred tries, so there is approximately a 1 in 20 chance of ALB coming up in any one game. Definitely more frequent than I thought: Judy and I may have never seen it before the first incident, but it must have been around.

In the first incident ALB came up once in six tries when I was looking for it. The (binomial) probability of this happening is 0.27, or roughly 1 in 4. In the second incident ALB came up in the first game following our discussion, which has a probability of 0.05. The conventional rule in science is that the odds against chance have to be at least 20 to 1 (0.05) or greater before it is considered likely that something special did indeed happen, rather than just seeing chance variations. Nobody is going to argue for the psychic nature of an event that happens one in four or five times by chance alone.

So my scientist self concludes that the first ALB, the one that started all this, has probably been much ado about nothing. But the second ALB may have come about through psychic means. Intellectually this is all quite frustrating: The odds are not high enough to be really confident that something psychic happened, but they are not unequivocally low enough to completely dismiss the psychic possibilities. My emotional self, though, knows it was all psychic and that I've been robbed! Both times!

Meditative Perspective

The ALB incident is interesting in itself, but it is even more interesting to me from the perspective of several years of fairly serious meditation.

The kinds of meditation I have been doing, and the years of mindfulness practices preceding that, emphasize an ability to be more aware of and present to the here-and-now reality of the world and myself, while simultaneously not identifying with these events.[3] When done well it leads to a clearer, more intense life, yet with a fluidity and ease that comes from not being overly attached to any particular events or feelings, or being overly attached to a concretized sense of self, of who I must be.

I have written my account of the ALB incident with zest, not in the more usual intellectually cool style associated with scientific writing, because that's the way I experienced it. I was delighted when ALB leaped out at me from the printed page, I was delighted when I thought of getting it that evening and surprising and having a harmless minor triumph over Judy. I was delightfully amazed when she got ALB, and as my feelings of having been psychically robbed arose, I indulged them. I knew that I was actually delighted with the whole set of events, but it was fun to immerse myself in the role of victim of psychic forces.

The same was true in the second incident. As in the first incident my feelings were quite real, I was in them; yet a part of me was aware that I was playing a game and that I could have stopped the game at any time if it were necessary.

So the ALB incident has illustrated a valuable truth to me. All too often in ordinary life we get totally absorbed in and identified with our feelings, ideas, and reactions, in a limited concept of self that defines how we should react, and then we lose the fluidity to change when the situation changes. For example, you may be mildly angry and arguing with a loved one over some minor incident, but something you say touches on a vulnerable point in their psyche and they then hurt badly about something not really related to the present minor incident. If you are stuck in your anger about the present incident you probably won't notice this change and go on arguing, hurting your loved one far more deeply than you would ever want to. This produces reactive anger from your loved one toward you: You are always so damned insensitive and cruel!

This kind of event is what the Buddhists mean by the vicious cycle of *samsara*, illusion (a concept further discussed in chapter 16). If you were more mindful your minor anger may have been no less real, but you would have been present enough to see the change in your loved one, drop this anger, and deal in a loving way with the new event.

I'm deliberately not saying that you should never have been angry in the first place. Maybe saints can be like that, but we're talking about real folks like you and me.

Indeed I worry a lot about the stereotypes we have of saints and "spiritually advanced" people, who sit around all the time with a blissful little smile on their faces and never get upset no matter what happens. You can do that with a steady diet of tranquilizers nowadays. Your feelings are so suppressed that you don't give a damn about anything. But that's not living. At best it's passing time (which we may all need to do sometimes); at the worst it's a living death.

I am a little suspicious about the way some spiritual disciplines are used to produce a similar tranquilizing effect. You can teach yourself to focus all the time on some internal concentration object that is emotionally pleasing, for instance, and so just not notice most external things that might upset you nor have the energy to be upset even if you do notice: All of your energy is involved in your internal concentration object. It's not easy to learn to concentrate that well, but it's possible. The Buddhists have a sophisticated conceptual system about different levels of concentration and the kind of "bliss" (or "blissed-outness") associated with each; but they recognize that while attaining these levels of concentration is a remarkable attainment, by themselves they lead nowhere. They don't give you insight into the nature of your self and reality so you can truly grow.

Mindfulness disciplines, like Gurdjieffian self-remembering or *vipassana* (insight) meditation, do not teach you to detach in some zombie-like way from everything.

I'm a long way from being able to do it all the time, but I see more fully than before that real mindfulness leads to a fuller life, not a reduced one. Perception, emotion, thought, behavior become richer; yet by being mindful in the midst of all these experiences a fluidity is achieved so that you are smarter in dealing with reality.

Could I say that you can have your ALB and eat it too?

Suggested Reading

I have treated the idea of negative uses of psychic abilities lightly here, but I have done some serious scientific writing on it. See also the discussion in chapter 11.

Tart, Charles T. 1979. A survey of expert opinion on potentially negative uses of psi, United States government interest in psi, and the level of research funding of the field. In W. Roll, ed. *Research in Parapsychology 1978*. Metuchen, N.J.: Scarecrow Press. 54–55.

———. 1980. Cultural roots of the communication problem. In W. Roll, ed. *Research in Parapsychology 1979*. Metuchen, N.J.: Scarecrow Press. 39–40.

———. 1983. The controversy about psi: Two psychological theories. *Journal of Parapsychology* 46:313–20.
———. 1984. Acknowledging and dealing with the fear of psi. *Journal of the American Society for Psychical Research* 78:133-43.
———. 1986. Attitudes toward strongly functioning psi: A preliminary study. *Journal of the American Society for Psychical Research* 80:163–73.
———. 1986. Psychics' fear of psychic powers. *Journal of the American Society for Psychical Research* 80:279–92.
———. 1987. Psychological resistance in research on channeling: A discussion of the channeling panel. In D. Weiner and R. Nelson, eds. *Research in Parapsychology 1986*. Metuchen, N.J.: Scarecrow Press. 159–60.
———. 1987. On the mental health of parapsychology and parapsychologists. In D. Weiner and R. Nelson, eds. *Research in Parapsychology 1986*. Metuchen, N.J.: Scarecrow Press. 164–65.

Self-observation and the kind of meditative perspectives that allow a simultaneous vivid enjoyment of but detachment from life experience can be explored in the following books, as well as in chapters 17 and 26.

Goldstein, J. 1987. *The Experience of Insight: A Simple and Direct Guide to Buddhist Meditation*. Boston: Shambhala.
———, and J. Kornfield. 1987. *Seeking the Heart of Wisdom: The Path of Insight Meditation*. Boston: Shambhala.
Hanh, Thich Nhat. 1987. *Being Peace*. Berkeley, Calif.: Parallax Press.
Ouspensky, P. D. 1949. *In Search of the Miraculous*. New York: Harcourt, Brace & World.
Sole-Leris, A. 1986. *Tranquility and Insight: An Introduction to the Oldest Form of Buddhist Meditation*. Boston: Shambhala.
Tulku, T., ed. 1975. *Reflections of Mind: Western Psychology Meets Tibetan Buddhism*. Emeryville, Calif.: Dharma Publishing.

Since we also get too serious about ourselves, I also strongly recommend James Thurber's "Let Your Mind Alone!" for balance: Thurber, J. 1937. *Let Your Mind Alone! and Other More or Less Inspirational Pieces*. New York: Harper & Row.

CHAPTER 9

Firewalk

When I was a child I would get out of bed with a sense of expectation and wonder, curiosity abuzz. I was always wondering. What is this? What is that? Why does this thing work this way? Where did this come from? Why am I thinking what I'm thinking? Why won't that thing work? When I became an adult I lost much of that wonder as my curiosity was channeled into conventionally approved areas.

This childlike attitude and its loss in adulthood are nicely expressed in the first two stanzas of Wordsworth's "Intimations of Immortality":

> There was a time when meadow, grove and stream,
> The earth and every common sight,
> To me did seem
> Apparelled in celestial light,
> The glory and the freshness of a dream.
>
> It is not now as it hath been of yore;
> Turn whereso'er I may,
> By night or day,
> The light which I have seen
> I now can see no more.[1]

One of the most important fruits of the many years of psychological growth work I have participated in has been to reawaken much of my child mind. The little boy in me is again starting to open his eyes in the morning with the open expectation that interesting things will happen. "Interesting" can sometimes include things normally considered negative, but somehow they are different if I really pay attention.

In the last couple of years the adult and the little boy in me have been cooperating more and doing some assessment of my life. As a result both the little boy and the adult are thrilled: I've had a far more interesting life than the little boy who grew up in a very conventional world in New Jersey ever expected. This chapter will share a recent experience that is one of those thrills—and an experience that you could have.

The Firewalk

For the twenty-five years that I have been a psychologist I have been interested in the firewalk. The idea that people all over the world have walked over beds of blazing coals or hot stones is incredible: Surely this is a very high-intensity form of psychokinesis? Certainly something very unusual is going on, and understanding it would be an important step forward in science.

Whenever the subject came up, in casual conversations with friends or in public lectures, I advocated that we investigate firewalking. How could we ignore something that we had good evidence existed, yet seemed so impossible to our Western minds? The result of this advocacy was usually nil.

Reactions to the Idea of the Firewalk

I found that most people simply weren't interested in firewalking: It was a sort of mythical idea, or something "primitive" peoples somewhere did, not something that "civilized" people took seriously. For all practical purposes it didn't happen. Things that don't happen do not challenge our curiosity or belief systems.

Opinions were varied among the small number of people who knew of firewalking and believed it actually occurred. Some thought that it didn't really mean anything because the fires weren't *really* hot, they just *seemed* hot. This has been presented as the idea that the *temperature* of the coals may be hot, but the *heat capacity* and conductivity of the coals is very low, so not enough heat can be conducted into the skin to cause a burn. For example, you can briefly put your hand into an oven that may be at 350 degrees Fahrenheit and not be burned. But if you touch a metal pan in that same oven you will be badly burned. Air has very little heat stored in it and doesn't conduct heat well; metal has a lot and can rapidly conduct that heat to your hand.

If all firewalking were done on soft, powdery ash, a poor heat conductor and storer, this theory would carry a lot of weight. But I have read reports of firewalking on heated stones, which would be more comparable to the metal pan in the oven than to hot air.

Others accepted the idea that the fires were hot but assumed some sort of trick was involved. The favorite mechanism for this trick was a hypothetical paste applied to the feet to protect them. But I do not recall that anyone ever specified what this mysterious paste was supposed to be, and then demonstrated its usefulness by putting some on his feet and showing that he could successfully firewalk. Others had a belief that "primitives" had thick callouses on their feet that protected them from pain.

I remember reading an article in a magazine when I was a teenager in which the author proposed that the firewalk worked because sweat was flashed into tiny globules of steam that protected the feet. When you drop water onto a hot frying pan it forms tiny balls that dance above the surface of the pan for a while. Supposedly the sweat from the firewalker's feet is flashed into such a steam layer by the heat of the fire. If you think of a firewalker as very frightened, "in a cold sweat," this puts that sweat to good use.

What impressed me most about this theory was that its author successfully firewalked. This was much more interesting than the ideas of the armchair theorists, who have never touched a fire.

The most interesting reactions came from a few people I met from countries in which people actually firewalked. "Oh yes," they would say, "they do that each year on the feast of so and so out in the mountain villages, but it's a primitive thing. We moderns aren't interested in it. Let us return to our discussion of sophisticated intellectual topics."

We must answer two questions about the firewalk: Why don't the walkers feel pain during or after the walk? And why don't their feet burn?

Why Don't Firewalkers Feel Pain?

The lack of pain is not hard to explain in terms acceptable to the Western mind. It's some sort of "hypnosis." We know that you can anesthetize the hand of a deeply hypnotized subject by suggestion, and then hold a match under the subject's hand. The flesh will char without the subject reporting any pain. Incredible but true.

I have never done this to a subject myself; the desire to witness it directly was not of enough consequence to me to be worth inflicting such damage on anyone. But I have done experiments where deeply hypnotized subjects received quite painful (but nondamaging) stimuli like strong electrical shocks, where they neither reported pain nor showed any signs of feeling it. So if we must explain the firewalk in conventional Western terms, it's easy to invoke hypnosis as an explanation for the firewalker not feeling pain, during or after the firewalk.

The occasional walkers who do feel pain clearly aren't very talented at hypnosis.

Why Don't Firewalkers Get Burned?

I also remember reading a report when I was young about a fire-walking experiment conducted in 1935 by Harry Price of the University of London Council for Psychical Investigation with the Indian fakirs Kuda Bux and Ahmed Hussain. Several tons of oak logs were burned for hours and then the coals raked into a bed about four feet wide and twelve feet long. This bed of coals was so hot that the experimenters could not stand closer than about three feet without feeling their hair begin to singe! In various experiments, measured surface temperatures ranged from 806 to 1,067 degrees Fahrenheit, with temperatures a few inches into the coals ranging from 1,292 to 2,550 degrees Fahrenheit.

The fakirs prepared themselves for the firewalk by meditating for a while. Their feet were examined and washed. No obvious paste or anything covered their bare soles. They walked the length of the pit at a slightly faster than normal walking pace, showing no sign of pain or discomfort. Immediate examination of their feet as they stepped out of the pit showed no signs of injury. Indeed a measurement of the surface temperature of Hussain's foot indicated it was actually ten degrees Fahrenheit cooler than just before he stepped into the pit.

Price knew of the sweat globule theory for explaining firewalking, but wasn't very impressed by it. He noted that the firewalkers insisted that their feet be dry before walking, and also found that it took several seconds before a wet object actually showed any signs of steaming on the test fires, too long to be of much help for the short time the feet were actually on the coals. He suspected that the main reason for lack of harm was that the firewalkers only took two steps on each side for the walk, so that the feet were in too brief contact with the coals to absorb enough heat to burn. Some Englishmen who gamely volunteered to be control subjects, and who walked somewhat more slowly (and nervously!) did show small burns, as did Ahmed Hussain when Price persuaded him to (reluctantly) walk a pit that was twice as long.[2]

My Firewalk

On a chilly winter night in 1986 the firewalk became real for me as it had never been before.

I had been attending the first Archaeus Congress on Holistic Medicine at the West Pecos River Conference Center, near Santa Fe, New Mexico. A fine and stimulating array of papers concerning the psychological, parapsychological, and spiritual dimensions of health had been presented, and now we reached the program item headed "Transforming Fear into Power," by Eric Best.

Eric Best, an industrial systems analyst, had been giving seminars of this sort for over two years. His prime objective is to show people that they do not have to be limited by their fears, they can overcome them and use the liberated energy to live fuller lives. The primary tool to reveal this to people in a short time period (four hours for us) is firewalking. If you can get yourself into a state where you can walk over a bed of glowing coals without pain or injury, most, if not all, of the things you fear in everyday life will seem trivial. If I can walk over glowing coals who really cares about slighting remarks, lack of appreciation, mundane worries, and the like?

I came to the seminar curious, open-minded, thrilled, and reserved. I would see firewalking firsthand, which would be fascinating. The curious child in me, who had read about firewalking so long ago, was actually going to see it! My adult self felt I might or might not try it myself. I knew Eric insisted that you walked or didn't walk purely on the basis of your internal feelings, not because of social pressure. That was fine: I am accepting enough of myself that I knew I could try it if I felt the inner urging, or not try it if I didn't feel it, and either outcome would be fine. I had no need to prove anything to myself or to anyone else.

We began the seminar by standing in a circle around a huge bonfire. The New Mexico winter night was dark and cold. The stars and deep chill contrasted starkly with the darting flame and smoke of the fire, whipped around unpredictably by strong gusts of wind. We were going to deal with that?

I will not detail the psychological methods Eric used to work us up to the proper, energetic state for firewalking. To get anything out of it you need to experience it, not consider it abstractly. Suffice it to say that I wholeheartedly got into letting all my fears in life come up in me (very unpleasant), and I stayed with them instead of denying them. I found I was still there, still sane, not overwhelmed, and the insights into hidden fears thus found were very valuable. Even if there had been no firewalk I learned a great deal from this process. Knowing the firewalking opportunity was going to come at the end of the evening, of course, made it a lot easier to bring up buried fears!

Walking the Coals

Finally Eric told us that if we thought we *might* firewalk we should take off our socks and roll our pants up six inches or more. I love the implicit suggestion here that we could protect our flesh from burning, but we should not expect to be able to protect the fabric of our pants.

We ran outside. Assistants had taken apart the bonfire. After burning for four hours it was a rich source of glowing coals. With these coals they had prepared a bed about three feet wide and ten feet long. I did not find it at all fearful. Indeed it was attractive, for it was quite cold outside and I liked the fire's heat.

A towel at one end marked the start: You could wipe off any sand or gravel that was on your bare feet. A damp towel at the far end marked the finish. We were specifically instructed to wipe our feet on it as we stepped out of the fire, for pieces of glowing coals sometimes stick to your feet or get stuck between your toes. You don't want any glowing coals sticking to you after you stop concentrating at the end of the walk.

Eric had given us specific steps to follow. They will not be completely meaningful outside of the context of the event, but they consisted of first shouting, "Energy in!" then "Strong focus!" then "Eyes up!" and then (repeatedly, as you walked), "Cool moss!" The group usually (but not always) shouted these along with the walker.

Like a true leader Eric walked first—just a normal walk. It took about four paces to traverse the pit of coals, and he made it look very normal and prosaic.

Now was the time for decision. If you thought you wanted to walk you stood at the end of the fire pit and went through the chant, focusing your energy. If it felt right inside to walk then you walked. If it didn't feel right inside you stepped aside, being true to your inner self, not succumbing to any feelings of obligation or group pressure. A number of people did not walk, and we all respected their decisions.

Person after person walked the coals, without pain, without injury, jumping and shouting with joy at the end. Young women, older women, quiet scientists, physicians, believers, conference center staff, and a physician who was a professed "skeptic." When I decided I wanted to walk my primary difficulty was having to push my way into the line because so many people wanted to walk or repeat their walk!

The Moment of Truth

Finally my turn came. "Energy in!" "Strong Focus!" "Eyes up!" "Cool moss!" And I walked.

Now the point of the psychological ritual is to keep your attention fully focused on the ideas of being full of energy and walking on cool moss. I did this for the first couple of steps and felt no heat or pain. But I'm so curious about what is happening that I hate to miss anything. So I kept most of my attention on the ideas but I had to turn part of it downward to check out the feelings in my feet, to see if the fire felt at all hot.

Sure enough, I could feel *very* hot heat on that step! And yet . . . I walked the fire. Except for that focused look at foot feelings, I felt no other heat or pain. I stepped out, jumped, and shouted for joy! Wow!

Some of the physical scientists in the group were monitoring the fire with thermocouples: Those coals were burning at 1,000 to 1,100 degrees Fahrenheit. Yet I had walked through. I had not completely followed instructions but the only injury I had to show for it was on the one foot to which I had sent my attention: four tiny (1/8-inch to 1/4-inch) round red spots, only one of which was slightly painful if I focused my attention on it. All I did to "treat" that spot was put a Bandaid over it so my shoe wouldn't rub. The spot showed no sensitivity at all twenty-four hours later. Not bad for four steps on 1,000-degree coals.

No mysterious pastes. No fire that only looked hot but wasn't. No "primitive natives"—unless "primitive" can include physicians, psychologists, psychoanalysts, engineers, physicists, and corporate executives.

This experience also showed me the inadequacy of the balls-of-protective-steam-from-sweat theory. When I got back to my room after the firewalk I found that my feet were filthy with soot. All that irregular filth would have absorbed sweat and made it impossible to build up a continuous steam layer, something difficult to do on the irregular surface of the coals anyway. I'm pretty good at monitoring my internal state, and I wasn't afraid or in a cold sweat. While I waited to walk my feet were cold on the sand and gravel. The air temperature was below freezing at that time. So I can also say, "No sweat!" about firewalking.

As a psychologist I note that the main requirement for successful firewalking that we know of currently seems to be that the firewalker have a strong belief in a theory that allows him or her to firewalk. It is not clear to me that it makes any difference whether that theory is about microballs of steam, specific heat, the protection of the goddess Kalibaliwali or Saint Somebody, or cool moss.

The curious little boy in me is very pleased. He did something "miraculous," and he got to eat his cake and have it too—he didn't have to feel the pain or be really injured, and yet he got to take a tiny peek and get a tiny injury just to prove it was really hot. Wow! I wonder what will happen tomorrow?

To Walk or Not to Walk

The child in me is part of my essence, and I am very glad I have been able to nurture it and sometimes be one with its vitality and joy. But childhood essence is only one part of the self, not everything; some adult perspective must be added.

Do you want to firewalk? Should you? There is some real danger involved. You could get burned physically or even psychologically—if you saw it as some sort of test of your worth and you didn't measure up to your standards. Also, some of the firewalk seminars I have heard about strike me as very manipulative, with enormous group pressure to walk. If you succumb to this kind of pressure situation when your inner voice says no, it would be too easy to interpret any burns as a judgment that you are unworthy, or be upset by the feeling of being manipulated even if you are successful. So I don't necessarily recommend firewalking. Nor do I know that it will make a permanent change in anyone's life. Those kind of claims require formal study, and I doubt that any studies have yet been done by disinterested scientists.[3]

I don't think I want to firewalk again, but I'm glad I did it. My scientific curiosity is higher than ever and I want firewalking to be extensively researched. In a way the firewalking is a gimmick, anyhow: The important thing is to face your fears and transform them into power. That is a long-term process as well as a momentary high, but now is the best time to begin.

My restrictive socialization is definitely breaking down. We began this chapter with Wordsworth's poem noting how the light had gone from life. Here are the first two stanzas again:

> There was a time when meadow, grove and stream,
> The earth and every common sight,
> To me did seem
> Apparelled in celestial light,
> The glory and the freshness of a dream.
>
> It is not now as it hath been of yore;
> Turn whereso'er I may,
> By night or day,

The light which I have seen
I now can see no more.

I find I want to rewrite them as follows:

T'will be a time when meadow, friend, sight seen,
This earth and every daily sight
To us will beam,
Apparelled in mind's lucent light,
The emptiness, yet fullness of mind clean.

Life shan't be dulled by words and feelings tight,
Or barriers of old,
Ego's tense hold.
The light which we may share
Shall set our hearts alight!

Suggested Reading

Blake, J. 1985. Attribution of power and the transformation of fear: An empirical study of firewalking. *Psi Research* 4(2): 62–88.

Coe, M. R., Jr. 1958. Fire-walking and related behaviors. *Journal of American Society for Psychical Research* 52:85–97.

Eliade, M. 1964. Shamanism in Southeast Asia and Oceania. *International Journal of Parapsychology* 6:329–61.

Gibson, E. P. 1952. The American Indian and the firewalk. *Journal of American Society for Psychical Research* 46:149–53.

Heinze, R. I. 1985. "Walking on flowers" in Singapore. *Psi Research* 4(2): 46–51.

Iannuzzo, G. 1982. Fire immunity and fire walks: Some historical and anthropological notes. *European Journal of Parapsychology* 4:271–75.

Jamal, M. 1985. The sacred fire. *Psi Research* 4(2): 62–88.

Krechmal, A. 1957. Firewalkers of Greece. *Travel* 108(October): 46–47.

McClenon, J. 1982. Firewalking and psychic surgery: Defining the paranormal by investigating its boundaries. *Journal of Indian Psychology* 4(2).

Price, H. 1939. *Fifty Years of Psychical Research*. London: Longman, Green & Co.

Schwarz, B. E. 1960. Ordeal by serpents, fire and strychnine: A study of some provocative psychosomatic phenomena. *Psychiatric Quarterly* 34:405–29.

Stillings, D. 1985. Observations on firewalking. *Psi Research* 4(2): 51–99.

Vilenskaya, L. 1985. Firewalking and beyond. *Psi Research* 4(2): 51–89.

Walker, J. 1977. The amateur scientist: Drops of water dance on a hot skillet and the experimenter walks on hot coals. *Scientific American* 347(August): 126–31.

CHAPTER 10

How to Use a Psychic Reading

We are an unhappy people: So many of us are unsure of what values and beliefs we can depend on and live by. Our times suffer from widespread "value-deficiency diseases." Traditional religions, the original sources of many of our culture's values, work for some, but for many they seem bankrupt. The preaching is intense about how you *must* believe, but the doctrines don't match experience and seem scientifically nonsensical. Scientific humanism works for a few but is empty for too many: "Facts" may be "facts"; but a world of meaningless physical forces with blind chance leading to "selfish genes" is not a very loving or satisfying view of the world. We are hungry for deep meaning.

Traditional religions have always had occasional competition from paths that say you can have direct experience of spiritual realities and make your own decisions: You don't have to blindly believe or blindly not believe. Today channeling and psychic functioning offer this to many people.

Some people claim to be able to temporarily open their minds to "channel" higher "forces" or "beings" who want to help us and teach us.[1] We certainly would like to believe in channeling because we have made a mess of things here and and more evolved beings who can help are welcome! Shallowness is so common in modern life that beings who claim to be in touch with the eternal verities are just what we need. Other people do not claim to channel higher beings but do claim to have psychic abilities—natural human talents like telepathy, clairvoyance, and precognition that can be practically applied in everyday life and for personal and spiritual growth by someone in whom they are well developed. A person who claims to have developed psi abilities well enough for practical application is generally termed a psychic.

But . . . . Isn't channeling just nonsense? Scientifically impossible? Harmless delusion at best, madness at worst? Fragments of our unconscious minds that are fooling us? Maybe unconscious fragments that are even using ESP sometimes to fool us more thoroughly? Aren't we just demonstrating our weakness and ignorance to hope for help from higher beings? Aren't so-called psychics probably self-deluded people who mistake the ramblings of their imaginings for psychic impressions? Aren't some psychics out-and-out charlatans who use psychological and physical tricks to defraud the gullible?

We are citizens of the twentieth century, a time of science, and we are bound to have these doubts about channeling and psychic functioning. Such doubts are healthy if not taken to excess. Dealing with psychics and channels is an area in which we must develop discriminating mind as well as open mind.

Is Channeling Valid?

I am scientifically convinced—at the 99.9 percent level of confidence—that basic psi abilities (telepathy, clairvoyance, precognition, and PK) do exist. *Sometimes* these phenomena manifest in everyday life, although more ordinary phenomena may be mistaken for psi phenomena; and *sometimes* they manifest under the controlled conditions of the laboratory, where alternative explanations are ruled out with high degrees of confidence. There is also good evidence for a psychic component in healing (see chapters 6 and 7).

I believe the reality of psi phenomena makes an excellent case for understanding the human mind as something that transcends ordinary physical matter.[2] When you combine this with reports of out-of-the-body experiences (OBEs), near-death experiences (NDEs), and phenomena from a variety of altered states of consciousness, I think we have an excellent case for believing that some nonmaterial part of our minds may survive death (see chapter 29) and that there may be intelligent, nonphysical beings in the universe, a matter of great intellectual and spiritual significance to us. (This latter conclusion is not "solid" science, as much research is still to be done; but it's the way I have personally made sense of my world.)

When you go from a general form of this belief to more specific questions—"Is Barbara *really* channeling a super-intelligent being named Higheyeque from Sirius, an entity who will help us improve

our lives, improve the gas mileage of our cars, and save our world?"
or "Will David's psychic readings speed my psychotherapy and let me
make money on the stock market?"—the subject becomes more complex.

I will not go into the intricacies of channeling here.[3] I will, however,
briefly outline our scientific psychological and parapsychological
knowledge about channeling:

- No ostensible channeled entity has *unequivocally* established that
  he/she/it is a nonphysical being or a physical being from some
  other world communicating psychically. But I wouldn't rule it out.
- Channeled entities are strong on philosophical (and pseudophilo-
  sophical) and spiritual (and pseudospiritual) advice, but generally
  have a dismal track record on science and technology. Not one
  has come up with a carburetor design that will improve gas mileage by 10 percent (something that would quite concretely help our
  civilization, for example); and the "scientific knowledge" communicated is usually a rehash of widely known and current scientific ideas or "technobabble," stuff that looks scientific to the
  layperson but is incomprehensible or makes no sense when examined by experts.[4] Some ostensible channeled entities are banal.
  If you are looking for profound spirituality, on the other hand, it
  is difficult to beat the channeled *A Course in Miracles*.[5]
- Knowledge that was probably obtained by use of psychic abilities
  is occasionally manifested by channeled entities, but generally its
  style and magnitude is of the same order as that manifested by
  psychics who only claim that they are using ordinary human abilities.
- Much of what is said by channeled entities is ordinary common
  sense and good advice. Its attribution to an exotic channeled
  source makes it more likely that you will pay attention to this good
  advice than if you got it from your neighbor or your sister. Some
  of what is said is factually wrong or is simply poor advice. Much
  of the glamorous stuff ("I am 35,000 years old and very wise")
  cannot be checked in any way, so you will never have any idea
  whether it is profound knowledge or pure nonsense.
- Some channels are deluded or mentally ill, but the average channel is "normally" healthy: perhaps a little neurotic in some ways,
  but sane enough to live a normal life.
- A few people who claim to channel are charlatans. They use ordinary psychological skills to imitate sincere channels and manip-

ulate their followers to increase their own wealth and power. Some of them may go so far as to use private detectives to dig up useful information on their wealthier followers. Casually dropping the name of a pet dog or deceased relative while "channeling" can shock and impress potential followers so they believe and obey. If you become deeply involved with any channel where there is reason to suspect this you must read Lamar Keene's *The Psychic Mafia,* or some similar book, to realize the disgusting extent to which this kind of deception can go.[6] I have no reason to believe that the frequency of charlatanism is higher in channeling (or practicing as a psychic) than it is in more ordinary areas of life; but it is more shocking because we have higher standards for people who claim to be in the spiritual business than those in ordinary commerce.

Psychics

What about people who do not claim to channel higher intelligences, but only to make reliable use of human psychic abilities?

There are probably thousands of people in the United States alone who call themselves psychics. It would be reassuring if that meant each of them had been thoroughly tested under laboratory conditions and scientifically certified as psychics. Unfortunately that's not the case.

There have only been around two dozen scientists working in parapsychology in the United States for the past few decades, usually with minuscule research budgets—the field is too controversial to receive support from the establishment.[7] Thus the vast majority of psychics have never met a scientific parapsychologist and have not been tested by one.[8] I know many of the psychics who have shown useful ESP results fairly consistently in the laboratory, but they are only a handful. So what would I say about psychics in general, given laboratory knowledge and my general experience of them?

- Almost all psychics are self-proclaimed; they are not laboratory tested in a competent, scientific way. Some of these people are extremely good at psychic functioning and ought to be named as national treasures, others may seldom show genuine psychic functioning.
- Almost all psychics are decent people who honestly believe that what they do involves psi abilities. Their personalities run the full range from some quite mature, spiritual people to garden-variety

neurotics. Most are decent people trying to do a decent job but in an area that society considers odd and to which it gives little support.

- Almost two-thirds of Americans believe they have had at least one psychic experience in their life, and laboratory work shows that occasional ESP ability is widely distributed. Thus it is likely that all these self-proclaimed psychics have at least occasionally and sometimes frequently shown a flash of ESP.[9] Whether this happens regularly enough to support their claim of showing *reliable* ESP—being a psychic—is something we generally don't know.
- A typical psychic reading is mostly good but general advice that could apply to many people; some ideas and statements that are wrong; some guesses; a little drama; and varying amounts of information that was probably obtained psychically. When there is enough psychic information that is really relevant, a psychic reading can be a growthful, even mind-shattering experience that can change your life.
- Even the best psychics who have genuine psi abilities only manifest them part of the time, and they still make mistakes, sometimes big enough mistakes to seriously flaw a psychic reading. Good psychics understand this and admonish you to test their readings for usefulness, not to have blind faith. Be cautious of psychics who claim 100 percent accuracy—or of anybody in life who claims perfection, for that matter.

Petty Charlatans and Cold Readings

Unfortunately a few psychics, like some channels, are charlatans. Some people have been badly hurt in their dealing with psychics and channels, so it is important to look at charlatanism more closely.

Many of the charlatans in this area are what we might call "petty charlatans." The carnival psychic, for example, is interested in lightening your wallet and sending you on your way to make room for the next mark (as the suckers/customers are called), not in changing your way of life or making you a loyal follower. Such people probably, with some justification, think of themselves as entertainers, giving value for fees received, rather than as sinister figures preying on you.

The art of doing such fake psychic readings for a mark who walks in cold off the midway or street is called a *cold reading* and is described in the kind of mentalism books that can be bought from magic supply houses.[10] Here are some highlights:

- You can learn a lot about a mark from observation. Is he or she well dressed? "Reveal" to them that they are successful or that fortune is smiling on them and good things will come their way in the future. Always predict some good things in the future: We all like to hear that! Does the mark talk like an uneducated or educated person? If a physically big, muscular man speaks like he was college educated and is well dressed, for example, come up with a "psychic impression" of "... some kind of injury when you were a young man, was it a leg injury?" The probability is high that a successful big guy who went to college played sports and thus had a leg injury as a young man—but if this guess is right, it will be probably be perceived by the mark as a fantastic psychic hit!
- Watch the mark's eyes and facial expressions while you "go fishing." *Fishing* is casting out a story line in almost any direction and seeing if you get a bite that you can pull in. "I see a thin man in your life who meant a lot to you . . . " If the mark leans forward or his pupils dilate, keep fishing in that direction, otherwise divert into a different line of fishing.[11] Marks usually forget all the fishing you've done if it doesn't pan out and just remember your successes.
- Compliments, phrased in a personal way, are always good. "The spirits tell me you are a very intelligent person, but others don't appreciate your intelligence enough." Who is going to deny the perceptiveness of the spirits? Universal problems, phrased in a personalized way, usually impress. "I have a feeling you were deeply hurt once in a relationship with a loved one . . . you have dealt with it well enough on a conscious level, but inside sometimes it still hurts."
- Casually and conversationally ask questions as the reading goes along to elicit personal information. Feed the answers back, in modified form, as part of the reading later. Marks seldom remember that the reason you "psychically" knew the name of their brother is that they gave it to you in another context earlier.

This last point particularly makes it clear why the clients of such cold readers are cynically referred to as marks or suckers. I deeply believe the psychic and the spiritual are vitally important realities, but there is an enormous amount of human folly, greed, gullibility, and stupidity connected with them. In real estate they say there are three things that determine the value of a commercial property: location, location, and location. The three most important aspects of approaching the psychic and the spiritual are discrimination, discrimination, and discrimination.

Hungry Ghost Charlatans

Discrimination is particularly important when we think about the kind of psychic or spiritual charlatans I will call the *hungry ghost charlatans*. Hungry ghost is a Buddhist term referring to a psychological condition in which a person feels empty inside and consequently tries to fill this hungry vacuum with more and more experience, satisfaction, fulfilled desire, power, and so on. Such a person is always needy, always wanting *more*, even though the more will never satisfy because the basic problem is a wrong relationship with the inner self, not a lack of externals. These people are like ghosts because they identify with these surface desires and lose their real selves, becoming insubstantial in the process.

We have all been like hungry ghosts at times, but in some people the state is chronic and enormous. A hungry ghost who manifests in the role of psychic or channel will not be satisfied with ten dollars for a ten-minute reading and good-bye, send in the next mark.

A hungry ghost charlatan may not be a deliberate, conscious charlatan: She may believe in the phenomena she manifests and fiercely believes she is following a higher calling, but this is (as we will discuss in chapter 16) a way of living in illusion. Your belief is needed to support the hungry ghost charlatan's belief; your doubts are threatening to her. Hungry ghosts need loyal followers, the more the better. They do not see doubt as a sign of an intelligent, inquiring, open mind, but as personal disloyalty. Before you know it you may end up as a loyal cult member with the leader's channeled entities telling you what to eat, what to wear, what to think, who to be friendly with, who is your enemy, and so on—not to mention donating your worldly goods in the process. And if you ever show doubt and leave the cult you are told you will be damned forever.

I don't want this discussion of charlatans to leave the impression you should never be near a psychic or channel, much less talk to one. You would miss some great opportunities. Hungry ghost charlatans are a very small minority of psychics, channels, and spiritual teachers. (Indeed most hungry ghost charlatans are not involved in the psychic and spiritual. They are in more conventional fields like politics or commerce where there is a lot more power and money to be had.) The point is to be open but *discriminatingly* open—and in all areas of life, not just the psychic and spiritual. Now let's go back to the main point of this chapter and look at sensible ways to work with advice from psychics and channels.

Rigorous Testing of Psychic Information Sources

Parapsychologists have worked out tightly controlled methods of testing psychics and channels to see whether they indeed provide information that could only have been obtained by using some kind of ESP. I will just sketch the technical methods involved here, and the interested reader can delve into the technical parapsychological literature for detail.[12] I do not expect an ordinary person to go to this much trouble, and it is *not* a way to test whether the work of a particular psychic or channel is useful for personal and spiritual growth. But it is helpful to see how discriminating we could be about the psychic aspect and inform our actual actions in that light. We will look at a personal growth approach to psychics and channels in Part 3.

To begin rigorous testing you must eliminate *all* ordinary sources of information for the psychic or channel. You, unfortunately, are a source of information, not only in your physical appearance but in your reactions to statements. You might think you can sit there stony-faced and unreacting, but we know from research that it's not only doubtful, it's demanding and boring. The straightforward solution is to eliminate yourself as a source of possible sensory information altogether by having someone else be your proxy. Ideally your first proxy should instruct another person who doesn't even know you to go to a reading as a second proxy and ask the questions you want answers to. The second proxy has an appearance and reacts; but he doesn't know anything in particular about you and can give away nothing systematic by normal means.

Think your questions out carefully. The form of a question can give lots of information about you. "Where can I find my sister Genevieve?" will allow easy inference that she is missing in an unusual way, that ordinary methods of searching have failed, that your overall relationship to her is probably positive, and so on. The psychic or channel might say, for example:

"I sense an unusual family situation in the past, although much of it seemed normal to you while you were growing up. There was love in the family but also conflict, conflict that wasn't completely resolved, some of which still persists today. You have spent much time and effort searching for Genevieve, and it has been trying and frustrating for you. You don't fully understand how deeply you love her, and yet there is also deep conflict. She wants to be found, and yet a part of her doesn't want to be found . . ."

Everything in the above statements is an inference from the form of the question and common psychological knowledge about relationships. If you are emotionally wrought up over finding your sister, however, that kind of statement can hit you deeply and make you feel the reading is right on. Yet there is no new factual information in the above statements at all. Can you evaluate the information that comes back to eliminate such ordinary inferences, and not let it have a halo effect to make other information look better than it actually is?

Parapsychologists have found that everyone is biased in some way when it comes to evaluating psychic readings. You can be biased to see too much, more than is there, or biased to see too little, overlooking genuine psychic information. When a psychic or channel tells me what a wonderful person I am I really appreciate his psychic perceptiveness, but I get bored when he speaks of shortcomings that don't apply to me. The ideal method for evaluating readings in a way that can't be systematically biased was devised by parapsychologist J. Gaither Pratt and statistician William Birge.[13] I helped refine the method as it was applied in remote-viewing experiments conducted at Stanford Research Institute (now known as SRI International) and other parapsychological laboratories.[14]

A remote-viewing experiment goes about like this: You collect a group of psychic readings on hidden targets. The targets could be people, objects hidden in sealed vaults, scenes on hidden slides, remote locations where a "beacon" person is located, and so on. Then you give a "blind" judge transcripts of the readings and a list of the targets, with both sets of data in random order. The judge is blind in that he is not told which readings were supposed to be about which targets. So you have, for example, nine names of remote locations (such as Redwood City Marina, Baylands Nature Preserve, Palo Alto Drive-in Theater, and so on) and nine sets of descriptions ("This place is very spacious, a lot of greenery; This other place, I see a lot of little boats . . . "). The judge must compare the various descriptions with the various target places and decide which reading was intended for which.

If there was no psychic functioning in the readings, the judge will merely be guessing; and statistically we know that the judge will probably only get zero or one correct matches out of the nine. If there was genuine psychic functioning in several of the readings, which gave *specific* and *correct* information that applies to that target and not to targets in general, the judge will be able to score more correct matches. A straightforward statistical test can then tell you if that number of matches would be so unlikely by chance (four or more matches in this case) that it's more reasonable to assume there was psychic functioning.

In applying this procedure with people as "targets," the target people would, of course, have to be unknown to the psychic and have no contact with the psychic during the experiment. The blind judge would have to have an intimate knowledge of all the people, which is difficult to do, so you could have the people who were targets act as judges. You simply give each person *all* of the nine readings with the instructions, "One of these readings was intended to be about you, the other eight are about other people. I can't tell you which is which. Please mark which one best describes you." The same kind of statistical analysis is applied to the result.[15]

This kind of hard-nosed experimental procedure has given many significant results. It has shown ESP operating in a large number of remote-viewing studies and in *ganzfeld* studies. It has only been applied a few times with people (rather than places or objects) as targets, and with mixed results. Jeffrey Smith and I, for example, tried this procedure with the well-known psychic Peter Hurkos some years ago with only chance results, even though we expected a successful outcome.[16]

In an ideal world, if you wanted to consult a psychic, you would hire a psychologist with expertise in parapsychology to run this sort of experiment several times on the prospective psychic. If the results were consistently positive that would give you confidence in the psychic's reliability and then you would just go to the psychic and ask the questions that really interested you and required ESP to get an answer. Extensive experiments could even give a finer picture: "David's information is terrible on the stock market but good on missing persons." Or perhaps, "Higheyeque gives only vague advice that never seems to discriminate one person from another, but his economic predictions over several years have been as good as those of most economists." Even if Higheyeque was good on discriminating people, showing he (or his channel) was using ESP sometimes, that would not tell us if Higheyeque was the entity he claims to be.

This isn't an ideal world, of course, so it's more likely that you'll hear a friend say that Tom T. is a fabulous psychic, tell a few amazing stories, and rouse your curiosity. To be open-minded would be to go and observe Tom T. To be discriminating would be to approximate the hard-nosed procedure as best you can, and remain tentative about your results whatever they are and always open to new information, whether it supports or undermines the particular beliefs you create about Tom T. Too much *attachment* to any beliefs, positive or negative, closes the mind.

How to Work with a Channel or Psychic for Growth

There are two major ways to approach a psychic or channel. One is to test her knowledge: Does she really have access to valid information in a way that transcends normal functioning? That is, does the psychic or channel show evidence of getting information psychically? The other approach is to try to use the *stimulation* provided by the channel or psychic to become a better person. The two attitudes of approach can conflict with each other, so it is best to be clear about which approach you are using at a given time and stick to it.

Suppose, then, that you have some initial confidence in a psychic or channel. You believe that whatever the source of information is, it can be useful to you. How can you use the channel to become a better person, to grow and mature?[17]

Foundations: Self-Appraisal

Begin with an honest and *accurate* recognition of your personal shortcomings. If you are taking the trouble to ask a channel for information with which to form new values and advice on how to improve yourself, you obviously believe you have problems of ignorance about yourself and the world and problems with your usual personality functioning. Otherwise you wouldn't need to ask advice.

Study this situation. Just what is it you feel inadequate about? Be ruthlessly honest with yourself and be *accurate*. If you feel you can never do *anything* right and must have guidance on *everything*, for example, you are almost certainly not being accurate: Even the worst of us do most things right. Perhaps a more accurate statement of your problem is that you do *some* things in a way that seems ineffective or wrong to you, and you also have a bad habit of not giving yourself enough credit. Perhaps you need to explore why you won't give yourself enough credit. (Indeed, if putting yourself down too much is a major issue, an ordinary counselor or psychotherapist is probably more useful to you at this point than an exotic source of stimulation like a psychic, although sometimes the two can be combined fruitfully.)

Don't Try to Bypass Ordinary Developmental Tasks

Another major area to examine before you decide to use a psychic or channel for growth is whether you are trying to ignore and bypass some ordinary growth problems instead of solving them. If you are too shy, for example, or too easily angered, or have a hard time relaxing around people, exotic advice might be useful but it also might be your way to avoid facing the problem. When you avoid ordinary developmental tasks, like learning to get along reasonably well with people, and think you are concentrating on "higher" tasks instead, you are building a house on sand.

Don't Expect Perfection

People expect perfection from psychics and channels and, to some extent, they accept this expectation. This can undermine the situation. A psychic is sometimes expected to be 100 percent accurate and to have access to relevant vital information that is otherwise unknown. If you believe this you will give too much value to what may be casual comments, psychic mistakes, ordinary helpful human suggestions, errors, and misunderstandings, rather than psychically obtained information. You may also create or reinforce fantasies of grandeur in the psychics or channels, which can be dangerous to their mental health.

You wouldn't put such expectations on friends. If you did, the first time they lapsed from perfection you wouldn't have any friendship left. Even when you go to a recognized authority like a physician for advice you reserve the option to seek a second or even a third opinion.

So take what the psychic or channel says as stimulation, not as the final word or authoritative truth. Think about it. Try putting some of the advice into practice to test its results in your life. If you don't like the outcome, or it doesn't make sense, consider that the test didn't prove out the advice or information.

I am tempted to pronounce authoritatively that you should *never* let ostensibly psychic or channeled advice overrule your common sense and basic intelligence. Unfortunately this is one of those pernicious almost-truths that create trouble because it is true most of the time, but there are significant exceptions. It can be the things we don't want to hear for emotional reasons, or can't hear because of automatic habits of thinking, that are the most important for our growth. To explore this let's look at stuck thinking and creative thinking.

Creative Solutions

Why don't we grow? Why are we stuck in some areas of life? *Because we think we already understand our selves and our situation.* Unfortunately we don't really; we are stuck in our habitual concepts and feelings and they don't allow any room for real growth. Sometimes we are stuck just out of habits of thinking, feeling, and perceiving (see chapter 16 on living in illusion); sometimes we have covert emotional investments in not changing. An excellent illustration of this is the Sufi teaching story "Dividing Camels":

There was once a Sufi who wanted to make sure that his disciples would, after his death, find the right teacher of the Way for them.

He therefore, after the obligatory bequests laid down by law, left his disciples seventeen camels, with this order:

"You will divide the camels among the three of you in the following proportions: the oldest shall have half, the middle in age one-third, and the youngest shall have one-ninth."

Here we have an insoluble problem. Seventeen does not divide in halves, thirds, or ninths! We habitually think in terms of arithmetic, and we thus have an impossible situation. We can sympathize with the plight of the disciples as the story continues:

As soon as he was dead and the will was read, the disciples were at first amazed at such an inefficient disposition of their Master's assets. Some said, "Let us own the camels communally," others sought advice and then said, "We have been told to make the nearest possible division," others were told by a judge to sell the camels and divide the money; and yet others held that the will was null and void because its provisions could not be executed.

Luckily the disciples gave a try at being open-minded.

Then they fell to thinking that there might be some hidden wisdom in the Master's bequest, so they made inquiries as to who could solve insoluble problems.

Everyone they tried failed, until they arrived at the door of the son-in-law of the Prophet, Hazrat Ali. He said:

"This is your solution. I will add one camel to the number. Out of the eighteen camels you will give half—nine camels—to the oldest disciple. The second shall have a third of the total, which is six camels. The last disciple may have one-ninth, which is two camels. That makes seventeen. One—my camel—is left over to be returned to me."

That was how the disciples found the teacher for them.[18]

We need to use creative approaches to reframe our understanding of our selves and our world; but just *how* do we do that when we're stuck?

Breaking the Framework

There are probably as many approaches to creativity as there are people and problems. I will share one way of mine here that applies specifically to working with a psychic or channel (or spiritual teacher) for personal growth. We might call it the "be random seriously" approach.

Being stuck means (1) that you have framed your problem in a way that doesn't allow a solution, and (2) that you accept that framework as the logical and sensible way to view things. For example, you are presented with the problem of the division of camels, as above, and you can only see it as a straightforward arithmetic problem. If you can break out of that framework in almost any way and cast the situation in a new light you have a *chance*—not a guarantee but a chance—of seeing a useful solution. Having a chance is better than being stuck. If the first reframing of the situation doesn't work out you can reframe it a second way, and so on, until you get a solution.

Getting psychic input could be helpful for this; but breaking the framework can also be done in an apparently "meaningless," random way. You could consult the venerable Chinese *Book of Changes*, the *I Ching*, for example. This book has hundreds of separate paragraphs of advice. To determine the advice for you, you throw some coins. The numerical value of the outcome of the throw tells you to read some particular paragraphs and take them as the answer to your question.

From an Eastern point of view (habits of thought and perception) you are allowing a holistic, interconnected universe to advise you. From a Western point of view (habits of thought and perception) you are getting advice at random: Most of the universe is disconnected from the rest of it for all practical purposes, the coins are certainly not affected by your life situation, so it is most unlikely that the *I Ching* reading will have much to do with your particular situation. But this is exactly the point at which you must take the answer seriously; you must temporarily believe that the universe has cooperated in some subtle way to give you appropriate, knowledgeable advice. If you don't temporarily give experimental belief to the advice—if you say, "This is silly, it's all random, my problems are too important to waste time being silly"—you will remain stuck in your problem.

Suppose you find yourself stuck in a pattern of overwork and overachievement. You know it's bad for your health and your relationships, but when you try to plan ways to slow down you are troubled by feelings of lack of worth, that you are only valued for what you produce so you have to keep on producing. You don't like those feelings. They are suppressed when you work hard, but then your health and friendships suffer. You think and think and think, but you're stuck. Going on will physically kill you, stopping will psychologically kill you. Seventeen camels don't divide evenly.

In desperation you consult the *I Ching*. To simplify its complex advice, let's say the reading you get basically says, "The wise man looks to the south."

As a typical Western workaholic you might immediately ask if you've had any good job offers from somewhere to the south. You can't recall any and you decide this stuff is all nonsense anyway. You are still stuck in your problem, you don't even want to think about it. Nothing new there, unfortunately. So you must experimentally commit to putting temporary belief energy into this reading. Believe that the universe itself, in its wisdom, has gone to the trouble of responding to you, so you'd better give it a lot of thought.

Now you begin to play with ideas about the reading's view of your problem. What is my understanding of a wise man? What could south mean? How do you go places? What is the connection between work and the south? Do people who live in the south have problems with self-esteem?

Perhaps an insight eventually comes: "People in the south are poor by my community's standards. They work hard, yet when I've traveled in the south I see people sitting on their porches in the evenings socializing and looking relaxed, or working in their gardens looking satisfied. I wonder what gardening might be like? I can call it work—it produces food—yet it can be slow paced. Hmm. Something to try."

So perhaps you try gardening and find it relaxing and you just naturally leave off your work a little earlier to have more time for gardening, and soon you are having relaxed conversations with others who garden, and. . . . You didn't "solve" the problem directly in the way you framed it, but something useful happened that transcends your view of the problem.

I'm not saying that we should all become gardeners, but that playing seriously with a novel perspective on our problems can be growthful. Perhaps, in this example, the universe in some mystical or paranormal sense did influence the fall of your coins to send you to a particular reading, or perhaps it was just a random event; but because you took it seriously you approached your problem in a creative way and found a solution. Does it matter that much what the actual mechanism was? Do we really understand the way the universe works all that well anyway?

Using Psychic Advice for Creative Problem Solving

For personal growth, for stimulation that might lead to creative problem solving, you can treat a psychic or channel just like you treated the *I Ching* in the above example. You don't have to know whether the person has genuine psychic abilities or is really channeling a "real" nonphysical, wise being. Maybe the person is just a good advice giver, a natural counselor. And maybe that psychic has something more. If there is enough minimum plausibility to begin with so that you are willing to play, then you can carry out belief experiments where you choose to take advice and information seriously and see what new perspectives they can give you, test what effects they have on your life. If nothing useful happens then you've wasted some time, but that is common enough in life. If something growthful and good comes out of it, great!

I have applied this kind of belief-experiment approach to my life with good results. At times I have experimentally given others large amounts of authority over me by assuming that a deep and benevolent Source was guiding them and me. Playing the game this way has been particularly necessary when I have had to learn things about myself that I didn't want to know.

Relating to a psychic or channel or spiritual teacher is more complex, of course; it carries all the intricacies of any human relationship and more.[19] If you travel this way, good luck!

Suggested Reading

For readable and technically accurate introductions to the methods for objectively evaluating psychic readings, try the following books.

Targ, R., and H. E. Puthoff. 1977. *Mind Reach: Scientists Look at Psychic Ability.* New York: Delacorte Press/Eleanor Friede.

———, and K. Harary. 1984. *The Mind Race: Understanding and Using Psychic Abilities.* New York: Villard.

Tart, Charles T., H. Puthoff, and R. Targ. 1979. *Mind at Large: Institute of Electrical and Electronic Engineers Symposia on the Nature of Extrasensory Perception.* New York: Praeger.

There are scattered writings on how to use such readings wisely for personal growth, but they are not in the regular scientific and technical literature on parapsychology. Some excellent books of Sufi teaching stories that can both stimulate our interest in growth and puncture a lot of our pretensions are the following.

Shah, I. 1966. *The Exploits of the Incomparable Mulla Nasrudin.* New York: Simon & Schuster.

————. 1968. *Caravan of Dreams.* London: Octagon Press.

————. 1969. *The Book of the Book.* London: Octagon Press.

————. 1970. *Tales of the Dervishes.* New York: Dutton.

————. 1971. *Wisdom of the Idiots.* New York: Dutton.

————. 1972. *The Magic Monastery: Analogical and Action Philosophy of the Middle East and Central Asia.* New York: Dutton.

————. 1973. *The Subtleties of Inimitable Mulla Nasrudin.* New York: Dutton.

————. 1978. *The Hundred Tales of Wisdom.* London: Octagon Press.

————. 1982. *Seeker after Truth: A Handbook of Tales and Teachings.* San Francisco: Harper & Row.

CHAPTER 11

Who's Afraid of Psychic Powers? Me?

Some years ago I was at a reception following a lecture I gave on parapsychology. Those present were leading scientific parapsychologists who had devoted their lives to researching such psi phenomena as telepathy, clairvoyance, precognition, and psychokinesis. Given the career drawbacks of working in a controversial field, these were clearly people with a very strong interest in psi.

I brought up the topic of fear of psychic abilities, mentioning that I had observed occasional fear of psi in myself. I wondered if anyone else had observed this, and how they had dealt with it? Since many of these people had been in the field much longer than I, I expected good information and advice.

As a topic of discussion it fell absolutely flat. No one was interested.

This struck me as odd. Perhaps I was the only one who had ever felt any fear of psi? At the same time, something about the overwhelming lack of interest made me wonder if some people were indeed fearful but didn't want to face it.

To test this I devised what I call a "belief experiment" and tried it on the spot. I have since used variations of this experiment in weekend workshops with quite enlightening results. You will learn a lot if you try it with friends.

A Belief Experiment

I asked everyone if they would give me ten minutes for a belief experiment. All they would need to do was believe, as well as they could, for ten minutes, what I told them, and then observe their reactions to this belief.

They agreed. I told them that I had developed a new drug, "tele-pathine." I had some with me. It changed you such that you could now telepathically receive *all* the thoughts and feelings of everyone within a hundred yards. There was no antidote to the drug, and the effect was permanent: You had no need to take it again.[1] Who wanted the drug?

No hands went up. Instead, in a clear avoidance of the question, an abstract discussion began about possibilities and implications. I asked again, "Who wants the drug?" More abstractions, so I finally shouted, "WHO WANTS THE DRUG?"

No hands went up and there was silence. As people observed their inner mood they realized that when they were faced with the possi-bility that telepathy might work very well indeed, even if only in a belief experiment, reluctance and reservations based on fears arose. My point was made.

Remember that this was in a group of people who were exception-ally interested in psi, willing to sacrifice career success to work in this rejected field. If they have fears what about ordinary people? What about people who vehemently deny that psi exists?[2]

Do you want to know what others *really* think and feel about you? Could you handle the power over others that this secret knowledge gave you? The mental and emotional overload that might result? If others knew would they hate you?

You might not take the drug but others might. How could you keep your secrets? What about your thoughts and feelings that you think are shameful? How could you control the image you present to people if some could see the real thoughts and feelings behind your outer behavior?

A Social Masking Theory of Psi Inhibition

In a 1983 article in the *Journal of Parapsychology* I proposed a *social masking theory* of psi inhibition.[3] Ordinary social interaction is strongly (but not completely) guided by an implicit social contract: "I want to be known, but on *my* terms. If you will accept the image of myself I want to project, I will accept the image of yourself that you want to project, and our relationship will go smoothly."

We do not let ourselves be completely bound by this, of course. Often we wonder what's behind someone's behavior, and may actively try to find out. We are all fairly good at controlling what image we project, though, and psychological observations indicate that we frequently don't use our senses at all well in looking behind others' social facades. We accept them wholesale, *especially* if they fit our expectations.

Psi abilities are thus a potent threat to the social status quo. How can we deal with the threats psi poses?

A Primal Conflict Repression Theory of Psi Inhibition

The social conflicts that strongly functioning psi could bring about are reason enough for fears of psi to exist, but I suspect an even deeper level of conflict. Let's start with socialization.

We are born with an enormous number of potentials that *could* be developed, but many of them won't be. We are not born into a vacuum but into a culture, which in the course of its history only learned about certain parts of the full spectrum of human potentials. Many of our possibilities will be lost to ignorance. Others are suppressed because they are considered distasteful or bad.

Our parents are the prime agents of socialization. Aside from the natural love most parents have for their children, parents have the job of shaping the developing child to become "normal," to give up certain innate potentials and develop only certain others so the child will be like everybody else in fundamentally important respects. The parents have a tough job: Many times they must not show their own true feelings, but must act to train children "properly."

The pressure has been particularly strong on mothers the last few decades. Mothers are taught that their child's health, happiness, and welfare depends on the mother doing the right thing. The pressure is on for mothers to be "supermothers," *always* naturally loving and caring. No woman wants to be considered a bad mother, so this pressure from the culture is usually internalized.

We discussed how the possibility of strong telepathy among adults could be very unsettling. You couldn't control the image you wanted to project. How much more intense might this sort of conflict be if one party were an adult but the other a young child, a relationship in which the distribution of power is very one-sided?

I believe that mothers and children have a strong, innate telepathic link. It conveys emotion more than conceptual information. This link probably has a lot of survival value: Think of the sort of situations where a mother just has a "feeling" that something is wrong with her distant infant and she'd better go check.

How will this telepathic linkage affect the child when the mother

is "acting"? Consider when "supermother" has had a bad day: Everything has gone wrong, and the child has angered her over and over
again. Mother is not full of unadulterated tender love and selfless concern for her child's ultimate welfare, she's angry! At this moment her
child breaks the heirloom vase from her great-grandmother.

A real mother might like to "break" the child at that point, or at
least throw a tantrum herself. But *super*mothers aren't supposed to. A
supermother should gently chide the child and explain why it
shouldn't do things like that. Supermother will try to remind the child
that she loves it, that she's only restraining or punishing it for the sake
of the child's learning the right thing, that any slight emotional upset
supermother shows is based on her concern that her child learn the
right things, not that she's violently angry herself. Whew! It's hard
being a supermother!

What about the telepathic channel in this sort of situation?

The child gets one message on the overt level: "I'm only concerned
for your welfare, I love you." This is the message the child *must* believe:
It is the socially approved message, and the one that reinforces mother's own beliefs about herself and the image she wants to project to
her peers. Yet the child's telepathic sense is picking up the strong,
emotional message, "Mommy is very angry, she hates me, she wants
to make me hurt!"

To explain the primal conflict repression theory I have drawn a
rather extreme picture. Not all mothers accept the pressure to be a
supermother, even those who do let out their real feelings at times,
and there are other and better ways to deal with such feelings than
hiding them. The basic point is that contradictory messages can come
from a mother (or father), and this is hard on the child.

Many of the conflicts and terrors of childhood are much more intense than the conflicts we have as adults. We have much more
strength to handle conflicts, greater perspective to defuse them, more
knowledge and skills to deal with them. But as children conflicting
feelings were so intense! So how does a child deal with the double
message, "Mommy loves me, Mommy hates me!"?

My theory of primal conflict repression is that we deal with these
early, primary, conflicts by actively repressing our psychic abilities. If
you can cut yourself off from the psi information channels, not pay
attention to them, or invalidate them as "fantasy," then you don't hear
one side of the conflicting message and the conflict *seems* to go away.
You only hear the sensory communication you are supposed to hear,
what mother said, the message supermother (and the culture behind

her) wants you to hear. Then you can go along with the image she wants to project to you. When you go along with it this reinforces her own internalized image of being a good mother.

You can't really keep listening to your psi channels and be "normal" anyway. Mommy will get more angry if you tell her, "No, you're lying to me!"; and adults or other children won't like it if you keep responding to their hidden thoughts instead of their projected image.

Triggering Conflict in Adults

Let's assume you are a "normal" adult. Your behavior is in the acceptable range, and most of your thought and feeling processes are "normal." Your culture functions unconsciously inside your head, shaping your thoughts and feelings, as well as controlling your behavior. (Like all "normal" people you probably have some doubts about whether you are really normal. You know you have some thoughts and feelings that are strange and "bad" by social standards, even if you hide them well from others; but you pass as normal.)

Along comes someone talking about psychic powers, reading people's minds, predicting the future, bending spoons, and so on. You may have a conversation with him about it in a perfectly rational way on the surface. But what happens underneath?

There are several possibilities depending on your particular personality structure, your degree of self-knowledge, the intensity and reality of the apparent psi phenomena, and your style of resolving conflicts. Any of the following unconscious reactions could take place to varying degrees and affect your apparently rational, overt response.

Primary Denial

Some part of your unconscious mind may make the connection, "To acknowledge telepathy means to acknowledge that Mommy hated me!" This puts it in rather extreme form, but unconscious thinking tends to be like that, intense and illogical.

The strength and course of this reaction will be affected by the degree to which you have already accepted this fact that sometimes Mommy was indeed really angry at you: She was a real human being and you did drive her crazy at times. On the other hand you may have thoroughly repressed this sort of knowledge and invested your self in an image of a mother who was well-nigh perfect. Then, rather than face the repressed memories, your unconscious may influence your conscious mind to deny the reality of telepathy and other psi abilities.

If there is no telepathy there is no need to examine potentially unpleasant memories.

Secondary Denial

The idea of psi activates concern about those unacceptable parts of
yourself that you don't want others to know about. There is both a
realistic and a neurotic level of concern here.

Realistically we all have secrets that would cause us harm if revealed, although we may or may not be ashamed of them ourselves.
On the other hand many of the things we are ashamed of may actually
be things everybody shares, even if they don't admit to them, or things
that are actually minor embarrassments but which are blown up way
out of proportion in our own minds. I can recall instances from psychological growth work where a person would finally reveal her "terrible secret flaw" and the reaction of others would be, "Is that all?"

Depending on your degree of self-knowledge and self-acceptance
psi powers can seem merely an inconvenience or a terrible threat.
Strong repression of your emotional reaction may take place (perhaps
in conjunction with primal denial), such that you deny that psi abilities
exist, thus apparently avoiding the conflict.

If someone keeps on talking about psi abilities, though, and your
mind has chosen a repression/denial defense, what happens? This ob-
jectionable person keeps right on stimulating your conflict and may
even get angry at you for being defensive. When we are defensive
about something the last thing we want to hear is someone telling us
we are defensive!

We can leave the situation, allow repression to help us forget about
it (at a high psychological price, of course), and hope not to come in
contact with people who talk about (much less demonstrate) psi. Or
we can counterattack.

Counterattack Defenses

We can label the person who talks of psi a "kook," a misguided
fool who ought to know better, or perhaps a charlatan, swindling the
gullible. Derogatory labeling invalidates what they say.

In another form of counterattack defense we accept the existence of
psi abilities but label them "evil." If something is evil you stay away
from it, discourage its manifestation in yourself and others, and try at
least to stop if not actively punish people who represent evil. It's not
so long ago that we burned people as witches when we thought they
had psychic powers. We don't burn people at the stake today, but

sometimes I wonder how many cases there are where someone who had psychic abilities was labeled "insane" and punished with that stigma and loss of liberty, or drugged or otherwise treated until their psychic abilities were suppressed.

How Do You Feel?

How do *you* feel deep inside about psi abilities?

I recommend trying the belief experiment with a group of friends who are willing to share their true reactions. This will further stimulate your own insights.

Parapsychological research limps along now with inadequate funding and only low-level, unreliable psi functioning for the most part. But science sometimes has lucky breaks. "Telepathine," or its equivalent, could be invented tomorrow. Will you be ready?

Why Are Psychic Powers So Dangerous?

The above discussion of why psychic powers could be frightening or dangerous was published in the November 1983 issue of *The Open Mind*. All human powers are subject to abuse and potentially dangerous to their user as well as those they are used on. What's special about psi? Readers of *The Open Mind*, whom I regard as a knowledgeable and thoughtful group, were asked to comment on the question of "why psychic powers should be any *more* dangerous or subject to abuse than ordinary powers." I received a number of quite fascinating and insightful letters, which form the basis of our further exploration.

Fear of Openness

The fears of openness to psychic communication are indeed very similar, if not mostly identical, to the fears we have about being open in general. Abraham Maslow, the founder of humanistic psychology, described us as constantly oscillating between our *growth needs* and our *security needs*. One set of needs is sometimes predominant for a long time, and we have a period of growth or of regression in our lives. There are many other times when both kinds of needs are strong and we take a step backward for each step forward, trapped in indecision and suffering.

The metaphor of taking "telepathine," the hypothetical drug that gives you full intellectual and emotional telepathic abilities for nearby people, is a particular (and extreme) way of talking about being very open generally to other people. In fact we already have marvelously receptive physical senses that can give us *enormous* amounts of information about our world and the other people in it: *if* we pay attention to these senses, *if* we fully use our intellect, our emotions, and our instincts. Unfortunately it's a big *if*.

Many people who inquired about the experimental Awareness Enhancement Training program that I offered for two years, for example, asked if they would learn how to develop psychic abilities. I had to reply that although we would certainly touch on psychic abilities occasionally, I put no particular emphasis on that aspect of development because it's clear that *people don't use the senses they already have.* What's the point of giving an additional channel of information to people who habitually daydream instead of paying attention to the useful and stimulating information they already receive? Why provide more fuel for fantasy when we don't use the real stimulation, what Gurdjieff called the "food of impressions," to nourish our inner essence? I am not against developing psychic abilities; but unless we make it part of a general program of personal and spiritual development it can be wasteful or dangerous.

The information we find out about our fear of psi, then, will usually tell us about our fears of being fully alive to reality. By observing your state of mind when you don't listen, when you turn your eyes away, when you ignore your body feelings, when you suppress your emotions or pretend that they are something else—these tell us how we live an impoverished life.

Who Am I?

Arthur Hastings, former President of the Institute of Transpersonal Psychology, sent me a letter with three related observations about fear of psi based on threats to our beliefs about personal identity.[4]

1. Psychic perceptions go beyond the boundary of the self; thus they are outside the familiar territory of one's motives, perceptions, and feelings. This venture into the void can be as frightening as stepping off a cliff.
2. The reality of psychic perceptions requires one to redefine the self: There seems to be no boundary between one ego and another. Egos do not like this at all!
3. The existence of psychic abilities violates our Western cultural beliefs—that is a big system to contradict, especially since the beliefs are somewhat interdependent, and many of our ideas, actions, and guidelines depend on not having psi communication.

We give a special "This is *me!*" quality to certain aspects of our experience—this is my house, this is my country—thus empowering them to have first and vital priority on our attention, energies, resources, and emotions compared to merely "factual" information and experience. Our cultural conditioning trains us to identify, designates which things are culturally appropriate to identify with, and rewards us with belonging and other forms of social approval when we identify with the approved objects of identification.

Psychic experiences and powers drastically question our individual and cultural beliefs about where "I" leave off and "others" begin. Since our cultural conditioning has made a lot of feelings of happiness, security, and belonging contingent on being "normal"—experiencing, believing, and behaving like others—Hastings is correct in seeing psychic perceptions as very threatening. I think we must attain a high degree of cultural transcendence and reach a mature acceptance of our real, essential self before we can comfortably deal with the full implications of psychic perceptions or psychic powers.

Can I Handle Psi?

This letter to *The Open Mind* from John Haule, a Jungian analyst, raises important questions about how we would integrate psychic abilities into our personality and deeper self.

From a psychological perspective, the goal of every religion is twofold: expand and integrate. To *expand* is to stretch in every direction the horizons of my sense of "me," of my "ego" as the habitual center of my awareness. Expansion may proceed so far as to include the psychological possibilities called "psi," which are well beyond the horizons of the average ego's awareness (though probably not beyond its capabilities). But religion also calls us to *integrate*. This means that I must in some way realize and further the essential wholeness of my being. My wholeness may be lost if I should pursue one aspect of life to the exclusion of all others. Such might be the case of the armchair philosopher who has plenty of theories about life but whose failed relationships testify to his inability to *live* life successfully. By integration, in contrast, the new discoveries and the expanded horizons are lived in a balanced way. . . .

Recognition and development of "psi" abilities belong to the expansive pole of the religious quest. They are extraordinarily fascinating and can be used in an unbalanced manner to further the aims of an ego that is out of touch with its psyche-as-a-whole. In this way, awareness of our "psi" powers may frustrate the religious goal of integration. But the same may be said of the sorrows and delights of sex. These too may become an obsession which sidetracks the integrative dimension of the religious quest.

Are psi powers *more* dangerous? I believe they can be called "more dangerous" in two senses. First, they are typically developed by individuals who have already achieved some success in integrating their more fleshly instincts. Therefore "psi" powers seem more dangerous in that they can lead astray individuals who are no longer so susceptible to more pedestrian temptations. Secondly, there is a broad popular sentiment that a certain balance is necessary in matters of eating, sex, and so forth. Thus while the fleshly libertine tends to be restrained by public sentiment, the libertine of "psi" is apt to be applauded and revered by the same people who would condemn his "less advanced" but equally unintegrated counterpart. In short, the dangers of "psi" do not reside in its nature but in its social and psychological implications.

Suppose you had a sudden increase in psi powers? You can read people's minds, influence events so you become very "lucky," subtly (or not so subtly) affect people's thoughts, pry out hidden knowledge, feel superhuman. What then? How do you behave? How do you think of yourself?

Our culture offers almost nothing in the way of guidelines except the negative one: "You must be deluding yourself that you can do these things, you're crazy!" or "These things come from the Devil!" These won't make you feel very good about your new gifts and will isolate you from support and sympathy from others. If you are not already well integrated this drastic withdrawal of support, the fear of being "caught," or the opposition that results from others' fear when they discover your strange powers may indeed push you toward insanity.

Haule feels that individuals who are already well developed in terms of ordinary goals and needs are more likely to develop psi powers. I also suspect that the opposite is true: If psychic powers come to a person who has not finished with ordinary social/developmental tasks, the injection of psi into areas that should be handled in ordinary ways may create special problems. Although I think the best development of psychic abilities should occur gradually, in tandem with gradual maturation in all areas of life, many of the psychics I have met were not especially mature people. Psychics include a great many "garden-variety neurotics" and some psychotics. There must be "specialized" (and sometimes clearly unhealthy) ways for psychic powers to manifest through people other than by growth and maturity.

Too Much Energy, Too Little Control

In his letter Robin Robinson, therapist and conjurer, further elaborates the potentially disruptive effects of tapping the areas of the unconscious mind associated with the use of psychic powers:

If I would, one way or the other, induce an altered state that was new to me, when I would come out of it, I would have large quantities of excess energy.

I experienced this as flowing emotion, happy one second, angry the next, sad a third. This would flow so rapidly and so without purpose seemingly that I had no way of knowing what was going on. Gradually I would acquire some deeper understanding that gave me a symbolic "container" for this excess energy and it would then be usable and creative periods would follow. But often I couldn't contain this energy for quite a while and I would suffer considerably. Like most everyone, I have ways of retreating from too much emotion—I get depressed—and I'd do that.

Since then I've learned in limited ways to tap that energy for use with my patients, I've learned ritual methods to contain it, etc. But I think perhaps this is the inherent danger in psychic work. Once you break the threshold into the world of the Unconscious, you encounter a great deal of "uncontained" energy . . . when you come back you bring a lot of it with you. Then you have to find some way to "contain" it.

Robinson's comments are a success story: The worst he suffered was rapidly varying emotions and periods of depression, and he eventually learned to contain and control some of the energy released and use it creatively. In less mature people, however, the emergence of archetypal material from the collective unconscious can frequently lead to breakdown of the personality, delusions of grandeur, and temporary or permanent psychosis. If the archetypal material meshes with that of many people, we can get the mass insanity of a Hitler.

Awareness of Suffering

The importance of balanced development *prior* to the development of psychic abilities is stressed in the Sufi tradition. David Jodrey said in a letter to me:

My understanding of the Sufic view of psychic powers and their dangers is: Knowledge of the techniques of paranormal perception and influence is ultimately self-destructive if it is not accompanied by wisdom, knowing when to use these techniques. Wisdom is acquired by overcoming self-centeredness, desire, fear, and expectations and cultural conditioning. The proper use of psychic powers is part of the total development of the individual, and a lopsided partial development of these powers is harmful.

Thus dangers stem not only from the possible activation of powerful archetypal aspects of the collective unconscious but from our human frailty.

In his book *The Dermis Probe* Idries Shah, a leading figure in adapting Sufi knowledge to modern times, presents a teaching story called "The Light Taker." It is about a dervish who was reputed to be able to see into the hearts of men.

A scholar observed that the dervish had been sold a melon that proved to be tasteless. If he could really see into the hearts of men, why had he been cheated by the seller? The dervish offered to teach the scholar why he had not been using his capacity when he bought the melon, but the scholar wouldn't listen. He began denouncing the dervish far and wide as an impostor.

The scholar's attacks on the dervish came to the attention of the king. He rightly understood that "scholarship" that refuses to take a full look at the data is pseudo-scholarship, so he ordered the scholar to go through the dervish's offered training and demonstration.

The dervish took the scholar to a retreat and instructed him. Then they met the king at a pass in the mountains that was a major route for travelers. The dervish announced that he would place his hand on the scholar's head, thereby temporarily transferring his power to see into the hearts of men.

As one person after another passed by, the scholar became agitated and began babbling, sometimes incoherently. One person who looked like a rogue was actually a saint, the saintly looking traveler was a horrible person on his way to do great harm. The scholar's face became lined, his beard turned white. Finally, unable to bear the burden of seeing into all men's hearts, he wrenched himself away from the dervish's hand.

The scholar now understood that if someone remained fully perceptive to the true condition of men at all times, they would go mad.[5]

I find this story very moving. Although I have worked at making myself more aware of what is happening in the world around me, there are times (such as when I see parents being unfairly cruel to little children) when I find reality is too much, and I deliberately become "normally" insensitive. Indeed most of the time it happens automatically, through my conditioned habits: I am unable to stay aware. If this kind of hurt can come from ordinary sensory perceptions, how much worse would it be if you had an even more direct perception of someone's thoughts when they were suffering or being cruel to others?

"There Is No God but Reality"

We can cut ourselves off from reality and avoid the suffering it would bring for the moment, but we can't keep doing it if we really aim at long-term growth. A saying attributed to the legendary Sarmouni Brotherhood states that:

> There is no God but Reality.
> To seek Him elsewhere
> Is the action of the Fall.

When we tune out reality we may seem to get an immediate gain, but it distorts our understanding and our consequent actions and creates suffering and alienation. We are too frail at times, like children, and must protect ourselves at that time. Then we must keep growing, keep looking, open ourselves to reality to become genuinely useful.

Psychic powers that came too suddenly would indeed be a disaster for most of us. Luckily they usually don't. We may be interested in specifically developing psi powers or they may come about naturally as a part of maturation. Studying ourselves to see how we use and misuse our normal sensory channels of information should be a good preparation for eventual psychic development, as well as valuable in itself.[6]

Suggested Reading

Eisenbud, J. 1982. *Paranormal Foreknowledge: Problems and Perplexities*. New York: Human Sciences Press.

———. 1963. Psi and the nature of things. *International Journal of Parapsychology* 5(3): 245–69.

Hastings, Arthur. 1983. A counseling approach to parapsychological experience. *Journal of Transpersonal Psychology* 15(2): 143–68.

Pierce, J. C. 1974. *Exploring the Crack in the Cosmic Egg*. New York: Julian Press.

Shah, Idries. 1970. *The Dermis Probe*. London: Jonathan Cape.

Tart, Charles T. [1975] 1982. *States of Consciousness*. El Cerrito, Calif.: Psychological Processes.

———. 1983. The controversy about psi: Two psychological theories. *Journal of Parapsychology* 46:313–20.

———. 1984. Acknowledging and dealing with the fear of psi. *Journal of the American Society for Psychical Research* 78:133–43.

———. 1986. Attitudes toward strongly functioning psi. A preliminary survey. *Journal of the American Society for Psychical Research* 80:163–73.

———. 1986. Psychic's fear of psychic powers. *Journal of the American Society for Psychical Research* 80:279–92.

Part 3

PSYCHOLOGICAL GROWTH

CHAPTER 12

Real Effort

G. I. Gurdjieff, one of the pioneers in translating Eastern spiritual insights into forms suitable for Westerners, remarked that people have very unrealistic ideas of what they can accomplish. Either they imagine that they can do stupendous things, which they never put to the test, or they grossly underestimate what they could accomplish with a correct aim and sustained effort. Gurdjieff believed that any "normal" (in the sense of *proper* psychological functioning, not culturally relative normality) person should be able to "make his living with his left foot." At another time he stated that a psychologically balanced person should be able to support twenty people by his efforts.[1]

This seems fantastic to us. When self-pity strikes us we feel that we already work too hard (and aren't appreciated enough for it); it's hard enough to support one's self and one's family. Or we associate that kind of hard work with being compulsively driven or with getting rich. Fanaticism and greed make workaholics of people, but isn't not working the goal of life? How easily we forget that right work is one of the greatest joys.

Forestiere's Garden

In the summer of 1982 I saw an illustration of what Gurdjieff meant by real effort. It made a tremendous impression on me. One man's work, guided by an inner sense of vision, produced something so beautiful, and so sensibly practical, that I now list it as one of the seven wonders of my world. Here is a story of what real effort can accomplish.

Baldasare Forestiere was a native of Sicily, born into a prosperous family of fruit merchants. He emigrated to America in 1901. He loved the land and growing things and wanted to have his own orchard. Adverse financial circumstances at first forced him to work as a laborer, digging tunnels for the New York subway. Finally he saved enough to emigrate to California and used his savings to buy a plot of land in the San Joaquin valley, in what is now Fresno.

Forestiere was swindled. The land he bought turned out to have hardpan, a rocklike clay layer, just a few feet under the surface. Trees would not be able to put down enough of a root system for an orchard.

He could have waited a couple of years and then sold the land, probably at a profit, to some new and ignorant immigrant. But he was too honest to do that, so his dreams of an orchard went into cold storage. He built a small house on the land and worked for other farmers to earn a living. "Cold storage" is a poor metaphor for something happening in Fresno, though, where summer temperatures can hit 115 degrees Fahrenheit, and Forestiere often found he could not work in the blistering afternoons.

The Vision and the Realization

To combat the heat Forestiere dug a cellar for his house. One hot summer afternoon in 1906, as he sat in his cool cellar watching a small shaft of sunlight coming through a window, he wondered if enough sunlight would come into a hole in the ground to grow fruit.

Working only with pick, shovel, and wheelbarrow, Forestiere began digging—and he kept digging, year after year, for forty years. He had no assistants; he did all the work in his spare time after his mornings of working for other farmers. (When he was in his sixties he finally accepted a little help, but only because he had gotten a hernia: He hitched a horse to a scraper to drag out the dirt.)

He had no written plans—but he had a clear sense of where to dig. Sometimes he woke from dreams in the night and marked the place where the dream had told him to dig. Sometimes his tunnels collapsed: He laughed and said our Eternal Father hadn't wanted him to dig there after all. Forestiere dug until his death in 1946 and never felt that he had completed his vision.

Forestiere was not a fanatic. People who knew him described him as a happy, honest, friendly man, the kind of person you wanted for a neighbor. He was not "religious" in a conventional sense, but he had his own sense of the sacred: It is apparent over and over in his creation. The creation of beauty has always struck me as one of the finest manifestations of real spirituality.

The Wonder

The Forestiere Underground Gardens are now operated by Baldasare Forestiere's descendants. They are open to the public for self-guided tours during the summer months and are located just off the Shaw Avenue exit from Highway 99 in Fresno, California. There are acres of underground tunnels, rooms, and gardens. Fruit trees will indeed grow underground: in fact they will flourish. Sunlight enters around the trees and grapevines, producing beautiful plays of light and shadow. Yet there's not much shadow: We think an underground building must be gloomy, but that's not the case at all.

Gently curving tunnels connect one garden court with another, with living quarters, with an underground automobile tunnel eight hundred feet long (yes, he dug it by hand), with a giant underground aquarium (not fully operative now, unfortunately) that had a special glass bottom. On really hot days Forestiere could go to the room under the underground room with the aquarium and look up at the fish swimming above him. It is hard to imagine a psychologically "cooler" situation.

My wife and I visited the gardens on a July day. The temperature outside was moving into the nineties by midmorning, but down in the gardens the temperature was very comfortable. The venturi-shaped sunlight and air openings Forestiere had devised draw the coolest air in from the ground surface and let the warmest air out. When we came back to the broiling surface and looked at the vast mass of Fresno all above ground, I couldn't help but think that Forestiere was the first—and unfortunately the last—sensible builder in Fresno.

What cannot be conveyed with words, not even with photographs, is the harmony and beauty of the gardens. Although he worked without any plans, the harmony and flow of his work is quite remarkable. One of my main purposes in writing this description is to encourage a visit. If you're ever in the Fresno area in the summer call the Gardens (they're in the phone book), and plan to spend a leisurely morning or afternoon wandering through. You will sense messages about harmony, tranquility, and right effort as you sit on the benches carved into the walls, or wander the tunnels. You will come away with an uplifting vision of what one person can accomplish.

This all sounds like a fairy tale, of course. A poor immigrant lad, alone in the New World, but guided by an inner vision and creating an everlasting wonder. Does it have anything to do with your life? Suppose you sat down and made up an energy expenditure list: Where does your time and energy routinely go? How much of it is "necessary" because of what the neighbors would think? How much of it comes out of your heart's desire? How much of your effort is quality effort because it represents your love of what you are doing? Is some change in priorities in order?

Suggested Reading

Ouspensky, P. D. 1949. *In Search of the Miraculous*. New York: Harcourt Brace.
Riordan, Kathleen. 1983. Gurdjieff. In Charles T. Tart, ed. *Transpersonal Psychologies*. El Cerrito, Calif.: Psychological Processes. 281–328.
Speeth, Kathleen Riordan. 1976. *The Gurdjieff Work*. Berkeley, Calif.: AND/OR Press. This is a greatly expanded version of Kathleen Riordan Speeth's chapter in *Transpersonal Psychologies*.
Tart, Charles T. 1986. *Waking Up: Overcoming the Obstacles to Human Potential*. Boston: New Science Library.

CHAPTER 13

Identification

The psychological process of *identification* has enormous effects on our lives, yet is seldom recognized in ordinary circumstances. The following introduction to identification is based on a more detailed treatment that became a chapter in my book on the psychology of G. I. Gurdjieff.[1]

To understand the concept of identification think of the month and day of your birthday. We'll call it M-day. My birthday is April 29. Now read the following two statements aloud, thinking of your birthday where the one statement says M-day:

"People born on April 29 are wimps."

"People born on M-day are wimps."

How do you feel about the two statements?

If you're like most people the first statement about people born on *my* birthday will just be *information*. It's a strong statement, but essentially it's the same sort of information as, "The temperature is currently 39 degrees in Fairbanks, Alaska." Just data. The same statement about people born on *your* birthday (that includes *you*) is emotionally different. "Who says I'm a wimp?"

Some years ago, in analyzing the nature of altered states of consciousness, I designated one of the components or subsystems of consciousness as the "Sense of Identity" subsystem.[2]

The primary function of the Sense of Identity subsystem is to attach a "This is *me*" quality to certain aspects of experience, to certain information in consciousness, and thus to create the sense of an ego. Presumably semipermanent structures exist incorporating criteria for what the "This is *me*" quality should be attached to. . . . Any item of information to which the "This is me" quality is attached acquires considerable extra potency and so may arouse strong emotions and otherwise control attention and energy. If I say to you, "The face of someone you don't know, a Mr. Johnson, is ugly and revolting," this information probably will not be very important to you. But if I say to you, *"Your* face is ugly and revolting," that's a different story! . . . under some circumstances such a statement might preface more aggressive action, against which you want to defend yourself, but often such a remark prefaces no more than additional words of the same sort; yet you may well react to those words as if to actual physical attack. Adding the ego quality to information *radically* alters the way that information is treated by the system of consciousness as a whole.

The process of identification is one of the most important factors affecting human life. Let us consider this process without being too concerned with the particular characteristics of the objects of identification, the things to which the "This is *me*" quality is attached.

Pervasiveness of Identification

The reason we need not be too concerned now with the objects of identification is that the process is so powerful and pervasive that I suspect a person can identify with *anything*. Your name, your body, your possessions, your family, your community, "the cause," country, humanity, the planet, the universe, God, your fingernail, a victim in a newspaper story. . . . The list of things people have identified with is endless.

Once we identify with an object we give it preferential attention and greatly increased psychological power, compared to objects or ideas that are just things or information. This power may be limited to the power given by our attention being readily fixated on the object; but it may well link up, consciously or unconsciously, with basic biological self-preservation emotions, so a threat to the object of identification is a strong threat to "me."

To illustrate this in weekend workshops I sometimes put an opened paper bag in the middle of the floor. There is nothing at all special about the bag. An empty milk carton or Styrofoam coffee cup would do just as well. I then ask the participants to focus their gaze and their attention on the bag, and to try to identify with that bag, to think of it as "me," to love the bag and attend to it the way they attend to themselves.

This is no complex hypnotic induction or exotic meditation procedure. I just speak casually about this for a minute, repeating the instructions a couple of times, asking them to focus on seeing the bag as if it were something they cared about, as if it were their own self. I am asking the workshop participants to exert some voluntary control over their own normally involuntary processes of identification.

Suddenly I step forward and stamp on the bag! Gasps come forth involuntarily. People jump. Their faces show a race of emotions. Sometimes they complain about my cruelty. Many people report they felt physical pain in their body when I smashed the bag. Many are just as shocked as if I had physically hit them. But they get the point. *It is all too easy to give the sense of identity to anything, and thereby give away some of our personal power.*

Common Objects of Identification

Some things are easier to identify with than others. Your sensations ("*I* itch") and your body ("*My* arm") are naturals. Your thoughts and feelings ("*I* thought of it first." "*I* am depressed.") are also easy to identify with—we generally take credit for creating our thoughts, and our feelings clearly happen to us. You identify especially deeply with your name.

Remember the old childhood rhyme?

> Sticks and stones will hurt my bones,
> But names will never hurt me!
> Call me this and call me that,
> And call yourself a dirty rat!

As adults we can see that this rhyme was intended as a morale builder, but it is clearly a lie. Most of us do not get injured by sticks or stones or other physical attacks very often today, but how often are we injured by the names people call us? Or the names we want to be called but aren't?

Remember reading about "primitive" cultures in which people have secret names? These "primitives" are supposedly so foolish that they think they would lay themselves open to magical attack if hostile people knew their secret name. "Magic" is often a matter of saying special words. Superstition, or more psychological sophistication than we have?

We usually identify with a number of socially defined roles, such as parent, educated person, good listener, political activist, pillar of the community, and so on. We also commonly identify with other people: An insult to my husband is an insult to me. Spit on my flag and you spit on me. It is also quite common to identify with people we think of as role models, heroes and heroines.

"Advantages" of Identification?

If we personify our culture, as if it had conscious purposes, then from the point of view of the culture identification can be a very useful process. It is useful when people in *consensus trance* (the culture's "ordinary" or "normal" state of consciousness) have been conditioned to identify with socially approved roles and values. Such identification with approved things is part of the implicit definition of "normalcy" for a given culture: You treat the approved objects of identification as respectfully and preciously as if they were your self. If the culture needs tax money those of us who have identified with being "good Americans" always pay all we owe; and we have the psychological reward of feeling superior to tax cheaters, who by definition are "bad Americans." People who automatically identify with the flag and feel personally insulted when they read about flag burners are going to be people who can be counted on to support the official culture.

The process of identification may also seem useful from a personal point of view. When a Student walks up to me and asks me a question, my Professor identity is immediately induced, with no conscious effort on my part. I act professorial and give the Student an answer or tell her where to research the answer for herself. She is reinforced in her orderly worldview, where Professors knowledgeably answer Students' questions. I am reinforced in my orderly worldview, where I am a smart Professor who is looked up to by sincere Students who want to learn. It all seems so effortless (although it actually takes a lot of energy). Indeed it takes deliberate volitional control of attention, Gurdjieff's practice of "self-remembering," to avoid *automatically* falling into the Professor identity in this situation if I don't want to do it.

Here's another example of the apparent usefulness of identification: Suppose I am in the middle of a long and boring task, but one that must be done. I really want to stop doing it and rest or play, do something exciting. Ideas start coming to my mind of other, more interesting things that I think I ought to do instead. I should really clean off my desk, make some phone calls, and I ought to make some back-up copies of my computer diskettes. These ideas are rationalizations to allow me to give up the boring work. It is a lot of effort to force myself to go on. But wait! I just remembered that I am a reliable and dependable man. I have an *identity* as a reliable and dependable person, an identity I can be proud of. By finishing the task I can be rewarded by feeling proud, for reliable people can be justifiably proud of themselves. Now the anticipation of my reward helps me get on with the job.

Identification, then, seems like a useful process for automatically (and efficiently?) mobilizing attention and energy for useful ends. It is, however, a very costly process, as we shall see.

Right now it would be enlightening if you would try to see what are the many things you identify with. Think about this and make lists. What people? What causes? What thoughts, what feelings? Try to observe in the course of your everyday life when you are identifying, and what you identify with. Add these new observations to your list. Try to see if there is a certain internal "feeling" or "taste" that you can recognize that goes with the process of identification so you can learn to distinguish it when it's happening.

The Psychological Costs of Identification

Identification carries some heavy psychological and practical costs. Let's look at some of these.

Cost 1. You Forget That Life Is Not Static

Identification usually has a "static" quality to it. We identify with things that our minds implicitly believe ought to be *permanent* (bodies, cars, possessions, past events, for example). Logically, consciously, we know better; but we seldom think logically and consciously about things we have identified with. Even mental concepts that we identify with have a solid quality to them: What I said a minute ago has become permanent, my decisions are supposed to be right forever. The understandings I have about the world should be absolute truths.

The difficulty inherent in identifying with anything in the real world, or in our own minds, is that reality keeps changing. Many philosophies and spiritual traditions have pointed out that reality is subject to endless change. Thus when we identify with something (physical object, mental concept, feeling, person, social movement) that thing is going to change, not stay what it was when we identified with it. So we will eventually be disappointed because the real thing (as opposed to our static mental image of it) has changed on us. How often have we heard the cry, for example, "My spouse isn't the wonderful person I married any more!" If we want to avoid this disappointment we will have to force ourselves to give up our identifications with things.

The body that is "me" gets sick, ages, and eventually dies. My car breaks down. My possessions break, wear out, get lost, and may get stolen. I may try to hold to my memory of past events, but memory may fade, other people may question whether those events really happened. The apparently brilliant insight I had last year starts to fade: Was it ever true in the first place? A student in class raises her hand and asks, "On page 157 of your *States of Consciousness* book you said . . . " I'm not sure I think that's a very adequate statement now but I must defend it, mustn't I? By identifying with things we set ourselves up for eventual loss.

Cost 2. You Did Not Choose Your Objects of Identification

Most of the things, concepts, feelings, and roles you identify with were not *your* choices in the first place. As part of the enculturation process—the induction of consensus trance—you were cajoled and conditioned to identify with many roles, ideas, people, causes, values, and so on that may have had no interest for your essential self, or were even opposed to it. People typically discover aspects of this late in life. Too often we hear such statements as, "I drove myself to get through law school and practiced law for thirty years before I realized one day that I was never really interested in law. My parents always expected me to follow in my father's footsteps. Something in me has always hated the stress involved and the boredom, and now I've got an ulcer and high blood pressure. I've wasted most of my life doing something I hate!"

Remember that identification gives special attention and energy to the objects of identification. We don't have unlimited amounts of energy and attention available, though, so if we give it to some things we have to take it away from other things. Identification with things that we were seduced and conditioned to identify with, regardless of our innate essence preferences, is a major aspect of what Gurdjieff called "false personality," the conscious self we have that is false to our essential self.

Cost 3. You Live an Automatic Life

The process of identification is too automated. If your various well-developed identities were like a wardrobe, and you *consciously* chose what costumes, what identities, were the most suitable for various occasions given *all* you know and value, identities would be useful tools. What usually happens, however, is that situation K always and automatically evokes Identity K, whether it is the best thing or not.

If the situation is really more complex than Identity K can handle, or inappropriate for the skills of Identity K (which is "you" for the time being), "you" may blow it. All the rest of your identities, and whatever real you is behind them, are left with the consequences of what Identity K did in that situation. Gurdjieff expressed it as the fact that any one of your many identities can sign a promissory note. All the rest of you is obligated to pay, whether you like it or not.

Cost 4. The Things You Identify with Are Not Really You

The final cost of identification stems from the fact that many—perhaps all—of the things you identify with are cases of misleading and false identification. They are not *really* you, even though you have identified with them. Are you really your name? Your roles? Your body? Your feelings? Your mind? Orthodox Western science would identify you completely with your body, of course, but most spiritual traditions would not.[3]

Who Am I?

What are the consequences of identifying with something that really isn't you? Or that is only "you" in a relative sense?

Here is an informative exercise: Write down a list of the things you identify with. Start with which body sensations are most intimately you; work through your habitual feelings and thoughts; list people and causes you identify with; and finally your most sacred and wide-ranging identifications (soul? God? Universal Energy?). Spend enough time on this list to make it reasonably complete. Afterward start to see what you could eliminate, and how easily you could do it. How much can you get rid of? Which things were your own active choice for giving the importance of identification to, and which things came from the pressure of parents, peers, teachers? "Who" or "what" will be left as you eliminate various items? Is this frightening?

Why?

Could you burn the list?

Suggested Reading

Gurdjieff's ideas about the process of identification and its enormous costs are well presented in the following books.

Ouspensky, P. D. 1949. *In Search of the Miraculous*. New York: Harcourt, Brace & World.

Riordan, K. 1983. Gurdjieff. In C. Tart, ed. *Transpersonal Psychologies*. El Cerrito, Calif.: Psychological Processes. 281–328.

Tart, Charles T. 1986. *Waking Up: Overcoming the Obstacles to Human Potential*. Boston: New Science Library.

The way identification works in maintaining our ordinary state of consciousness, as well as its functioning in altering your state of consciousness is described in my *States of Consciousness* (New York: E. P. Dutton, 1975).

Deep consideration of the ultimately illusory nature of our ordinary identity is found in Buddhist writings, as well as in Gurdjieff, such as the following:

Goldstein, J. 1987. *The Experience of Insight: A Simple and Direct Guide to Buddhist Meditation.* Boston: Shambhala.

————, and J. Kornfield. 1987. *Seeking the Heart of Wisdom: The Path of Insight Meditation.* Boston: Shambhala.

CHAPTER 14

The Game of Games

Many factors determine whether groups and nations are at peace with one another: political, economic, religious, ideological, historical, and so on. To progress toward world peace we need to work on all these fronts. This chapter is about working on a psychological front that strongly affects all these other factors, usually in a hidden way.

This chapter is also a call for talented people to devise a training game (or games) designed to help people learn to transcend their cultural blindness and limitations. As people master this they will be more able to genuinely understand, negotiate, and cooperate with people of other groups and nations from the ground of our basic humanity, instead of from the biases of our conflicting "tribal" loyalties.

The Tribal Worldview

We are social animals. From the core of our being we want to belong, to feel accepted in a larger group. The main group is the culture we are born into. "Cultural" is the appropriate anthropological term, but it is not an emotionally useful term for this discussion: It is too easy to contrast us "cultured" folks with those "savages." I'll use "tribe," with its usual connotations, to remind us how limited and primitive we are under our "tribal" veneer.

Any tribe, including our own, only knows about parts of our total potential as human beings. Any tribe, through ignorance or prejudice, may reject or suppress important parts of our humanity. Each tribe has very specialized, particularized, and somewhat arbitrary ways of looking at the world. These must once have been reasonably viable ways of getting along, or the tribe wouldn't have survived in the real world.

The tragedy with these particularistic, tribal ways of seeing reality

is that tribe members do not consciously recognize them as particularistic and somewhat arbitrary; they are automatically and unconsciously thought of as *right*, as the *normal* way of doing things. This
automatically makes "foreigners" *wrong*.

It is hard for us to recognize how deep and pervasive our tribal
conditioning is. It's easier to spot in another tribe. For example, if you
take a vacation in a foreign country now you can see the natives do
many "strange" things, like saying "Guten Tag!" instead of "Good
morning!" or driving on the left side of the road instead of the right
side. As a competent adult you realize that the rules for doing these
sorts of things are basically arbitrary: We could just as well say "Guten
Tag!" in our tribe, or drive on the left side of the road.

When you first came as an infant to live in your particular tribe,
however, you had no knowledge of the world, no confidence in yourself, no reasoning ability. You absolutely depended on your parents
for comfort and survival, and in learning about your tribe through them
you took their (tribally conditioned) actions as *absolute*. They weren't
the quaint and arbitrary ways the natives acted in the funny tribe you
were visiting, they were *the way* things were done. Our early conditioning laid down extremely persistent psychological patterns in our
minds that affect our thoughts, feelings, and actions today.

We can no longer afford the luxury of blind acceptance of our own
tribe's limited worldview. When it's "them" versus "us," and our tribe
is "obviously right," it's always tempting to take a chance and grab
and strike. Unfortunately our tribe and the other tribes are no longer
limited to clubs and spears; we have weapons that can destroy all human life on earth. We *must* transcend the tribal assumptions that automatically polarize our action in terms of "them" and "us."

Soviet-American Relations

Here's a specific example of the pernicious effects of unconscious,
conditioned tribal limitations. We are not very good in negotiating with
the Soviets, even though many of us on both sides share the goal of
not wanting to destroy the world. We blame the Soviets, they blame
us.

Certainly both sides take real military and political actions that deserve blame and hamper negotiations. But let's add in the fact that we
have a communication problem between two tribes that implicitly and
explicitly perceive the world in different ways.

Robert Bathurst, an adjunct professor at the Naval Postgraduate
School in Monterey, has studied the Soviet-American communication

problem and cast important light on it by bringing in a dimension of tribalism that anthropologist Edward Hall called *context*. Bathurst points out that the Soviets are a *high-context* tribe: Particular issues are not seen in isolation but in their relation to many past issues, other current issues, and many potential future issues. Americans, in contrast, are a *low-context* tribe. Our attitude is, "Let's isolate and fix this particular problem, don't worry about the past, and we'll fix the future problems when they arise."[1]

When we try to talk with the Soviets about a trade problem, for example, they keep relating it to something that happened during World War II. We think the Soviets are being irrelevant, deliberately avoiding and confusing the issue, and acting stupid and hostile: Don't they see we could work out an equitable arrangement about trading some wheat for oil? That war was forty years ago, for God's sake!

The Soviets, from their tribal perspective, find us incredibly naive: We can't or won't see the obvious relations between things. If we won't admit to what is obvious, from their point of view, that probably means we are either stupid or deliberately lying because we have hidden motives behind our actions. It goes on and on. The problem doesn't get solved, which builds more suspicion and hostility for the future.

Transcending Tribalism

We could deal much more effectively and more lovingly with people of other tribes if, in all our dealings, we were constantly aware of all the assumptions, attitudes, biases, and blindnesses that we had unwittingly picked up in the course of being conditioned to be "normal" for our tribe, and then *tested them and put them aside when they weren't adaptive.*

It's easy to make an intellectual commitment to do that, of course, but much of our conditioning lies outside consciousness or is connected to our emotions in ways that make it difficult to get at. Of course, there are some psychological growth techniques that can help you to transcend your tribe and find your basic humanity behind that conditioning. The problem is that these methods are long, arduous, don't always work, and work much better at the individual level than the group level. We have to keep developing these individual approaches—the more transcendent individuals on the planet the better —but we need something that can help us transcend our tribal limits much faster and on a mass scale.

Nobody likes to hear that he or she is a limited and biased person, even if it's important to our mutual survival to know that. And we prefer to have fun rather than work hard. Suppose we had a game that helped people transcend the views of their particular tribe, something that was fun to play, with the learning about transcendence coming as part of the fun? We could call it the Game of Games.

How to Play the Game of Games

The basic idea in the Game of Games is that you and others learn to play as if you were a certain kind of tribe. To play well you must learn that tribe's ways of thinking, feeling, acting, and perceiving. After you have taken roles in a variety of tribes you may start to wonder, "If we can play the life game from many different tribal perspectives, what's so absolute about my native tribe's perspective? What's the fundamental human perspective behind all these tribal worldviews?"

My wife, Judy, and I have given this game a lot of thought. The Game of Games is far from being worked out and operationalized, but here are our basic ideas to date.

Tribal Teams

In the Game of Games you and several others would play as a team, playing with/against/for other teams of several individuals each. Each team would be called a Tribe (or you can try to come up with a better term) and would be randomly assigned a set of attitudes, values, roles, perceptions, and worldviews corresponding to some known human tribe. Thus there might be a Japanese Tribe Team, an Iraqi Tribe Team, a German Tribe Team, an Australian Aborigine Tribe Team, and so on. You can draw on all the cultures of the world as potential team identities. To avoid our preconceptions and existing tribal biases about what identifiable cultures are like ("Everybody knows Xians are pushy!"), the Tribal Team would be given some neutral name (for example, number 12, or Blue Team).

Tribal Team members would get background material to read and refer to about what their Tribal Team is like. For example, you might be told that:

- your tribe values group belonging much more than individualism
- naked aggression and violence are feared and shameful and must be avoided whenever possible
- indirect statements that give you time to feel out others' emotional positions are preferred to direct statements that you like or dislike something or are for or against it, as such direct statements might alienate you from your group

- initial reactions to aggression from others should be deflected if possible with polite, noncombative, indirect responses, but others in your tribe will understand and sympathize if you finally reach a breaking point and explode in a violent response
- there are strong status differences in your tribe that must be respected, even while promoting the appearance that we are one happy family. (These happen to be characteristic of an important contemporary culture, but let's leave it unidentified . . .)

You and your teammates will know what values and views have been assigned to your Tribal Team, but you won't be told what values and views have been assigned to the other Tribal Teams in the Game of Games. Naturally you will try to figure that out when play involves interaction with other Tribal Teams, and this will help the transcendence aim of the game. Or you can make the game more complex by giving your Tribal Team stereotyped information about other Tribal teams that is only partly accurate.

Tribal Problems

To simulate real life each Tribal Team will have several categories of problems to deal with. These problems will be randomly selected at various times by the World Model Referee (discussed below). Problems will fall in categories of Internal Tribal Problems, Intertribal Competition, and World/Humanity Problems.

Internal Tribal Problems

Internal Tribal problems will involve the sorts of domestic problems all tribes must face, such as keeping various internal factions and groups happy, maintaining tribal survival and progress, upholding tribal norms and values, and internal tribal humanitarian activities (helping "our" kind of people). This would include political sorts of problems, like the need or desire of a political group in power to maintain itself in power so it was in a position to cope with external problems; or perhaps a needed revolution when the current tribal power structure isn't working effectively enough.

Intertribal Competition

Intertribal competition problems would involve disputes over natural resources, trade, attempts to impose your tribe's values on another (military action or "missionary" work), possibly limited wars, territorial disputes, and so on. The possibility of large-scale wars and total annihilation of life should be built into the structure of the Game of Games as part of its realism: It's possible for everybody to lose.

World/Humanity Problems

World/Humanity problems would involve creating peace and discovering the basic humanity that makes us brothers and sisters, without homogenizing humanity and losing all the richness and value of cultural diversity the way a world dictatorship would.

Intertribal problems and World/Humanity problems would draw different Tribal Teams into negotiations or confrontations. Now each team member has to try to be faithful (to a reasonable and effective, but not necessarily absolute degree) to the assigned values and views of his or her Tribal Team, as well as trying to understand the values of the other Tribal Teams involved, as well as trying to transcend his or her individual tribal limits and discover World/Humanity values.

Multiple Simultaneous Problems

For realism Tribal Teams would have several categories of problems to cope with simultaneously as the game developed. For example, a team might be involved in:

- trying to maintain Tribal Team political power while
- averting a threat of war with some other aggressive Tribal Team while
- trying to minimize the adverse impact of their actions on the world as a whole.

If Tribe W is threatening war, for example, we could use our non-renewable oil at a faster rate and manufacture more weapons, which might scare off Tribe W so we avoid the negative consequences of war. But in the long run our Tribal Team will have needlessly depleted natural resources and imperiled future health through increased pollution.

What is the best course of action in terms of your Tribal Team's assigned values and characteristics, in terms of fundamental transtribal human values, and so on? Trying to maximize success in the several categories of problems will help develop great skill. An obvious World/Humanitarian solution to an Intertribal Competition problem might exist, for example, but be so alien to your Tribal Team's values that proposing it directly would create a massive domestic crisis that might cost you your power base and so make it impossible for you to take any effective World/Humanitarian steps in the future. How far do you compromise?

Referees

The Tribes need a system of referees to make sure the Game of Games doesn't degenerate into a free-for-all. There are at least two levels of referees in the Game of Games.

The Tribal Referees

A Tribal Referee must scrutinize the proposed actions of each Tribal Team to make sure they are consistent with the values and attitudes assigned to that Tribal Team. If you are in a macho tribe, for example, you can't take steps that would be seen as "weak" without paying a price in terms of domestic power. If you are in a Tribal Team that values group harmony you can't take an action that makes you stand out as an individual without paying a price. This helps the players on each team learn to think like someone of that tribe.

The World Model Referee

A World Model underlies the Game of Games. It provides an ultimate refereeing action for actions at all problem levels—Tribal, Intertribal, and World/Humanity. The World Model Referee would include things like limits on certain natural resources, so the Referee might announce a leap of global prices of some basic commodity as a result of actions by one or more Tribal Teams.

If basic and tribal human values are modeled on a worldwide scale, reactions to actions of one Tribal Team by other Tribal Teams must be considered by the World Model Referee. The Referee's actions must be absolute in certain areas. For example, the food crop has been devastated by the Blue Tribal Team's trade embargo on fertilizers, X people must die of starvation and world food prices must rise by so much. In other areas the World Model Referee will have wide latitude and effects will follow primarily from the reactions of various Tribal Teams. For example, the cost of producing TV shows has gone way up: One Tribal Team might be deeply affected by this, another not at all.

The design of the World Model Referee is important. It must be as faithful as possible to the physical constraints of the real world we live in; contemporary work on global economic models will help here. It must also have basic, transtribal characteristics and inherent values of humanity built into it. The design of the World Model Referee will be a learning experience in tribal transcendence in itself, especially when we insist that it be "realistic," not just airy-fairy "humanitarian." We will probably end up with a variety of World Model Referees in different versions of the Game of Games. Indeed, as the game becomes well-developed, versions where you deliberately change some of the assumptions of the world model can be used to test the way our assumptions influence our realities.

The Computer-based Game of Games

An elegant solution to creating the Referees and World Model Referee would be to embody the Game of Games in a computer program. The World Model Referee is then the world model in the program, each Tribal Referee is a tribal model in the program, and so on. All proposed Tribal Team actions (plays) would then be entered into the program and refereed consistently in terms of the world and the various tribal models.

We already have some computer-based games where you have to role-play a character different from yourself. This character is assigned some simple qualities, such as various amounts of intelligence, strength, magical abilities, and so on; and then you and other players, each with their own character, are thrown into various adventurous situations where you must both survive and advance toward goals, such as finding treasure. These games have become extremely fascinating for some players: They get absorbed in their characters, they identify with them and start thinking and feeling like their character would. Some of these games are designed so that cooperation with other players rather than competition increases your chance of survival and reward. And they are fun, which is important in getting people to play. The technical skill developed in creating these games will be extremely valuable in designing more elaborate versions of the Game of Games.

Unfortunately a totally computerized Game of Games would be available only to people in relatively affluent tribes. We also need simpler versions of the Game of Games that are not computer based. A board game, with one or more players assigned the various Referee roles, would be much cheaper and thus available for international distribution.

The mass media could make versions of the Game of Games available globally, just as they do the news. Plays between various Tribal Teams could be followed internationally just as sports teams are, with all the readers/viewers/spectators learning from the action.

Various versions of the Game of Games could be especially useful to various groups. Anthropologists, for example, might find it an ex-

cellent way to teach anthropology. It could be a training tool for dip-
lomats or for business people who must work in another culture.

Transcendence: The Ultimate Goal

It's fascinating to get involved in the mechanics of a project, but
let's remember our goal. The ultimate aim of the Game of Games is to
teach the players to question the implicit, automatic assumptions and
values of their own native tribe, and so begin to transcend tribalism.
If you get good at playing from the point of view of Tribal Team X it
may occur to you that there are alternative points of view about some
things you and your fellow tribespeople take for granted. When you
also get good at thinking and acting like someone from Tribal Team Y
you can further question the things taken for granted in your native
tribe. By the time you've gotten good at playing on many Tribal Teams
perhaps you've become a good intertribal relater/negotiator in the real
world, a global citizen rather than just a tribal citizen.

To question the values of your tribe does not mean to automatically
reject all these values. It means to see them as relative, as perhaps
fallible and certainly changeable *expressions* of something more important than the quaint customs of a single tribe. Then you can join the
spiritual search for our common humanity behind the many diverse
expressions of it in various tribes.

You Can Help

The Game of Games is not a small project that my wife and I and
our friends can develop. It is a large-scale effort calling for some inspired leaders and cooperation from many, many people. Certain people with special technical skills can clearly contribute: anthropologists,
computer programmers, game designers (board and computer), economists, futurists, psychologists, psychiatrists, political scientists—the
list goes on and on. Game players of all sorts can contribute suggestions, try out preliminary versions, and so on. An organization or organizations is needed to do such things as gather suggestions, accept
financial donations, and coordinate projects. I am sure there are many
helpful ideas we haven't thought of, so I leave you with the question,
"How can I help?"

If this idea catches on it could result in a steadily growing international effort to develop the Game of Games. Such a project is far
beyond my personal resources and skills. I am basically a solitary
scholar, without skills in organizing people and big projects, or the free

time and resources to do it. I am hoping that one or more of you will get excited enough about the possibilities of the Game of Games to say, "This is exciting! My organization (or a consortium of organizations) will take this on!" Don't write or call me, just take what is good in the idea and go!

Suggested Reading

There is so much excellent literature on how our culture affects our perceptions, beliefs, thoughts, feelings, and actions that you can start with almost any current textbook on anthropology. I have detailed the process of enculturation whereby we become conditioned to automatically feel and reflect the values of our culture, emphasizing the psychological, rather than the anthropological, aspects of the process in the following two books:

Tart, Charles T. 1975. *States of Consciousness*. New York: E. P. Dutton.
————. 1986. *Waking Up: Overcoming the Obstacles to Human Potential*. Boston: New Science Library.

CHAPTER 15

Aikido and
the Concept of Ki

In contemporary culture when we think of "energy" we usually think of some known kind of *physical* energy, like moving wind or flowing water, gravity, electricity, chemical reactions, or radioactivity. Carl Jung once pointed out that the idea of energy is actually a psychological one, an archetypal idea of energy arising from the human experience of feeling energetic. As a purely psychological idea it is clearly a real aspect of our experience; but it is difficult to be very specific about it once we finish saying things like, "I'm more energetic today than yesterday."

When the physical sciences began to evolve they were exceptionally successful at being specific about energy. They could describe a mechanical device as producing energy of 35 horsepower, or an electrical current as being 10 amperes of current at 50 volts of pressure, thus manifesting exactly 500 watts of power. With this increasing precision in describing physical energy came enormous progress in applying it to useful ends. This kind of success in science in general has led us to think about energy almost exclusively in physical terms, and sometimes we are even rather apologetic about using a vague and subjective term like "psychological energy."

Nevertheless psychological or psychic energies are useful concepts in understanding the mind, and on occasion they have some aspects of reality in the ordinary physical world. We looked at the experimental application of one kind of psychic energy, *psychokinesis* (PK), to living biological organisms in chapter 7, and we looked at its possible role and application to healing in chapter 6. In this chapter we will look at the practical application of psychological (and perhaps psychic) energies in one of the newest of the Oriental martial arts, Aikido.

What Is Aikido?

Aikido (pronounced "eye-*key*-dough") is a Japanese art of self-defense that evolved in just the last few decades through the efforts and mystical understandings of a remarkable man, Morehei Uyeshiba (sometimes spelled in translation as Ueshiba, pronounced uh-yeah-*she*-buh).

From an early age Uyeshiba was interested in the spiritual life, particularly as it was expressed through traditional Shinto beliefs and in phenomena we would call spiritualistic or psychic in Western terms. Throughout his life he was dedicated to searching for enlightenment and spiritual understanding.

In his youth, however, he saw the thugs of the village landlord beat up his father for having some progressive social ideas, and this impressed on him both the reality of physical power and the need for social justice. Thus he spent his youth and early life in two activities that seem a strange combination by Western standards. He spent enormous amounts of time meditating and studying spiritual matters, and he mastered many traditional martial arts: He became a master at injuring and killing, while becoming more and more spiritual. Consequently he sought the true meaning of *budo* warriorship, the inner essence of the martial arts.

One day, in midlife, Uyeshiba was sitting under a persimmon tree when he had a profound mystical experience:

I felt that the universe suddenly quaked, and that a golden spirit sprang up from the ground, veiled my body, and changed my body into one of gold.

At the same time my mind and body became light. I was able to understand the whispering of the birds, and was clearly aware of the mind of God, the Creator of this universe. At that moment I was enlightened: the source of *budo* is God's love—the spirit of loving protection for all beings. Tears of joy streamed down my cheeks.

Since that time I have grown to feel that the whole earth is my house and the sun, the moon and the stars are all my own things. I had become free from all desire, not only for position, fame and property, but also to be strong. I understood: *Budo* is not felling the opponent by our force; nor is it a tool to lead the world into destruction with arms. True *budo* is to accept the spirit of the universe, keep the peace of the world, correctly produce, protect and cultivate all beings in Nature. I understood: The training of *budo* is to take God's love, which correctly produces, protects and cultivates all things in Nature, and assimilate and utilize it in our own mind and body.[1]

These kinds of mystical insights are wonderful, of course, yet there is real and violent disharmony in the world we live in—person against person, nation against nation. How could one deal with disharmony in a spirit of love and harmony? Out of his mystical experience and his mastery of the martial arts Uyeshiba created a new martial art, Aikido. It is simultaneously an effective method of self-defense and an expression of love and harmony.

The word Aikido is often translated as the way (*Do*) of harmony (*Ai*) with the spirit of the universe (*Ki*). Ki is "spirit" or "energy," the flow of love and life energy, the manifestation of Harmony.

Aikido is different in many ways from other martial arts. For one thing there is no competition: no tournaments, no contests, no pitting of one person against another to make one the winner and the other the loser. Yet you do practice attacking your partner and defending against your partner's attacks. The more skilled you get at Aikido, the more intense these attacks are. Your partner may grab, punch, and strike with his or her hands in many different ways, and eventually attack with a wooden staff or sword. Sometimes several partners attack you simultaneously. But the spirit is of working *with* your *partner*, not of grappling or fighting *against* an *opponent*.

The goal of Aikido practice is to manifest love and harmony in all actions, not just in self-defense, and so help make this world a better place to live. It is also intended to be effective in defending yourself if you are physically attacked. A philosophy of nonaggression may be completely empty, however, if not backed up with the actual skill to defend yourself. Psychologically such a surface philosophy may be a cover for deep tears of being attacked or desires to attack others; the surface attitude may crumble completely under stress, and in defending yourself you become just as aggressive and out of harmony with the ki of the universe as the attacker. Long training in Aikido produces an attitude of peacefulness that is built on a foundation of skill that makes it effective.

Three Levels of Self-Defense

How does a practitioner of Aikido react to a personal attack in this imperfect world? In an idealized scheme we can distinguish three levels of self-defense.

Handling an Attack: Level 1

At the highest level of Aikido skill you would have developed a great sensitivity to subtle cues from others. Among other things Aikido is a kind of mindfulness meditation (Buddhist *vipassana*) in action. Thus you would probably sense that the other person was getting upset and might get physically aggressive, so you would leave the room before the potential attacker's feelings reached an overt level. Not being there when someone gets angry is a marvelously effective kind of self-defense, and you certainly don't need to get angry or aggressive yourself in practicing this.

If you were not skilled enough to sense the imminence of the attack before your attacker felt angry, you would still be skilled enough to know how to stay centered and peaceful under the developing tension that proceeds an attack. Remaining calm, present, and centered is an excellent form of self-defense. Note the importance of being *present* as well as calm and centered here. You may be calm because you are so lost in your own fantasy world that you don't know what's happening around you, but that is quite different from being calm and present.

Sometimes in workshops I have the participants carry out an exercise I adapted from Aikido practice. Partners face one another about three to four feet apart. The person designated the attacker is to repeatedly punch at his partner, to try to feel angry and aggressive, without actually hitting. The receiving partner, taking the role of victim, adopts three different attitudes in the three phases of the exercise. In the first the victim is to cringe back. In the second she is to get angry and pantomime punching back (without actually hitting). In the third she is to stand perfectly still, keep a neutral expression, and calmly look the attacker in the eye.

The reactions of both people are quite different in the three phases of the exercise. When the victim cringes back she usually feels genuine fear, almost instantly. What is even more interesting, the attacker almost always gets much angrier and really wants to hit the victim. "I got really angry at that wimp and wanted to hit her, she deserved it!" is a typical reaction from both men and women. This illustrates that putting out what I call "victim signals" actually *provokes attacks that might otherwise not manifest*. There may be some basic biological reflex involved here.

The attackers report a similar reaction of real anger in the phase where the victim actively strikes back. The attack by the former victim in this kind of defense generates more anger and attack feelings in the attacker. The victims, rather than feeling fear, feel angry and want to be attackers themselves.

In the third phase, where the victim remains physically and psychologically present, calmly looking at the attacker, the most unexpected reaction of all almost always occurs: The attacker's feelings of anger fade away. Attackers report that they feel silly even pantomiming attack, it's so obviously ridiculous. Without victim signals or attack signals to support the initial attack, the attacker just can't stay in the role of attacker with any conviction.

Try these exercises with a friend. The actual experience will teach much more than my words can.

The highest level of defense in Aikido, then, is either to leave before an attacker becomes really angry or to remain both peacefully and alertly present as the potential attacker's aggressive feelings are triggered. You give out neither victim signals nor attack signals. The typical result is that the potential attacker never actually attacks; she calms down and you have a chance to peacefully work through whatever source of dispute exists.

This kind of self-defense is applicable in many areas of life. Its main limitation is that sometimes the potential attacker may be so out of touch with reality that he does not notice your reactions or lack of them, he's running on strong internal drives and distorted perceptions. Then he may continue his attack in spite of lack of reinforcement from victim cues or counterattack cues.

Handling an Attack: Level 2

If you were neither skilled enough in Aikido to leave before the attacker got angry enough to think about attacking, nor skilled enough to stay so calmly and solidly present that his anger quickly died away without manifesting in actual physical attack, you would have to defend yourself against actual attack.

It is still important to stay as calm and present as possible, not allowing either anger or fear to develop, and to remember your commitment to love and harmony. Then you can use physical Aikido self-defense techniques in such a way that the attacker doesn't feel that you are attacking or running, giving out attack or victim signals. Instead he seems to keep getting in his own way, or striking wildly and missing, or tripping himself, and this gives him a little time to calm down. He's expressed his anger, and he hasn't found any victim or attack signals to further enrage him.

Handling an Attack: Level 3

If either of the above levels of self-defense is not adequate, or you don't have enough skill to use them successfully, the Aikido practitioner must drop to the lowest level of self-defense and actually restrain, throw, or hurt the attacker. Again you must do it without becoming an attacker yourself, you must try to stay as calm, centered, and harmonious as possible.

Basic Principles of Aikido

The Aikido skills learned in handling physical attacks can also generalize to situations in everyday life. I was not too aware of this until someone who had attended several lectures I had given on parapsychology told me he admired the calm and effective way I handled hostile questions in these lectures. He admired my "technique." I was puzzled: What technique? On reflection I realized I used basic Aikido techniques to handle these kinds of attacks. To explain this we must first look at basic principles underlying Aikido: getting off the line, blending, and leading.

Get Off the Line of Attack

For an effective attack the attacker must flow a burst of concentrated energy along a line directed at you. If the attack is a punch to the belly the attacker's energy, embodied in his fist, moves along a line from his body to your belly. If it hits you can be badly hurt. So what do you do? You get off the line—you move or turn so the energy of that punch doesn't connect with you. You have to be present to what is happening in order to do this in time, of course.

Blend

The second principle is to blend or harmonize with the attack. You practice Ai. Let's take the above example of being punched. If you had spent months strengthening and hardening your abdominal muscles you could defend yourself by not getting off the line and blending, but instead by absorbing your attacker's punch. You are saying, in effect, "Your punch is nothing, wimp!" This easily becomes a way of meeting attack signals with attack signals, however, and the attacker is likely to get angrier. The same reaction would result from actively blocking the attacker's punch with your arms.

To harmonize with the attack you would not only get off the line, you wouldn't slow the punch down or oppose it in any way. In fact you might put your hand on the punching arm and *add* energy to it in the direction it was already going. You have harmonized and blended with the energy of the attack. By projecting your energy in the same direction the attacker projected his, you see, as it were, your attacker's point of view. (Note that I say "his" energy for grammatical convenience, but as many women as men study Aikido.)

Lead

After you have gotten off the line and harmonized with your attacker's energy you lead that energy further than it originally intended to go, thus taking control of it; and then you can throw or otherwise control your attacker. In this way the attacker provides most of the energy for handling his attack.

To return to our example of a punch to the belly, one Aikido way of handling it is to step a little toward your attacker and turn your body 180 degrees as the punch comes in, so you end up standing right beside the attacker, seeing his point of view. Catching his hand you would extend the energy of the punch in its original direction a little, enough to take the attacker a little off balance so you are not only safe but in harmonious control. If the attacker continues to project energy forward you can slide forward, maintaining your lead of his energy, and throw him forward. If he pulls back (giving a new direction to his energy) you can blend with that back-going energy and take it further enough to throw the attacker backward. You got off the line (entered and turned), you blended (extended your energy along the same line as the attack), you led that attack energy into a throw. And, if you did it right, you stayed calm and peaceful and certainly didn't get angry.

Describing a physical Aikido technique in words is similar to describing a mystical insight in words. It may convey something, but at best that something is a poor, hazy reflection of the reality, and at worst the words call up associations that produce a seriously misleading impression of the reality. I would not advise anyone to actually try the above technique if all you have is my words about it. Watching an Aikido demonstration or class is much better. Learning it yourself is the only way to fully understand it.

Aikido in Everyday Life

As you know from chapter 11 we have a great deal of hidden fear of psychic abilities. One way this fear can unconsciously manifest is through hostility toward psychic and spiritual subjects. I frequently lecture on these topics, and I sometimes become the target of this kind of anger.

I certainly don't like to be attacked for any reason, even if the attack is only verbal. I can become afraid, angry, self-righteous, and lose contact with reality as I get absorbed in these reactions. It's not only unpleasant, there is a further frustration: I have lost sight of my goal, which was to communicate useful knowledge. I might seem to "win" an argument; but if I'm angry and self-righteous I probably have not communicated effectively to my audience, and certainly not to my "opponent."

Before I had studied Aikido my reaction to an attack in a lecture question was to counterattack. I would expose logical flaws in my attacker's thinking or show he was ignorant of the facts and shower him with high-status scientific facts to show him the error of his ways. I wanted to make him see the "truth." I would usually "win" the argument, for I was an expert in the subject matter compared to almost all questioners, and a skilled debater. This also made me popular with most of the audience, who were typically "believers" in psychic and spiritual matters, for I had won a victory over the kind of person who attacked them too. I fought force with greater force.

In retrospect I doubt that I actually communicated much of anything useful to my "opponents," though.

After years of studying Aikido (in addition to extensive growth work of other sorts), I unwittingly began to use the Aikido principles of getting off the line, blending, and leading to deal with hostile questions, in the context of wanting to stay present and genuinely harmonize with my questioner for our mutual benefit. I stress the latter point: I had developed more genuine empathy and respect for the positions of these hostile questioners; I had not simply developed a clever technique for "winning."

Today, when a member of an audience asks a skeptical, hostile question, I try to stay present, centered, and peaceful. To do this I remind myself of the following:

- I am being attacked, but I can stay present.
- I do not have to take this attack personally.
- My questioner is a real person, like me, with genuine concerns of his or her own that prompt this attitude and question.
- I am a competent person, I can understand and handle this attack without having to feel threatened or angry.
- I accept myself as who I am, imperfections and all. I may have made an actual mistake, but that does not mean I am a bad per-

son, or that I need to get involved in neurotic worries about myself. I can stay present and be as truthful and effective as possible.

- At the least I can be gentle and not hurt this person, who may
  already be hurting.
- At best I can say or do something that might be genuinely helpful
  to this person or to others in the audience, and perhaps to myself.

This attitude helps me to "get off the line": I see that the attack
may be aimed at me personally from the attacker's point of view, but
is not really personal from a larger perspective. This and remembering
that my attacker has real concerns of his or her own also helps me
blend with the energy of the attack. Intellectually and emotionally I
will specifically try to understand and see the attacker's point of view.

For example, suppose the questioner asks, "I've read about that
experiment you talked about. Couldn't the subjects in that parapsychology experiment have cheated in such and such a way?" Suppose
further that I hear a voice tone or see body movements that tell me
that this is a hostile question—I must be naive to be taken in by such
crap, and be either a fool or a charlatan to encourage the public in their
superstitions by passing along such garbage.

My reply would be to get off the line and blend. I would not counterattack: "If you had read all the report instead of depending on summaries by biased people you would remember that this point was taken
care of." Instead I would sympathize: There is a genuine concern here,
he doesn't want to be fooled, nobody likes to be fooled or misled, I
don't want to be fooled either. Is there a legitimate doubt about that
experiment? I would say something to express how I sympathized with
and shared his concern for not being fooled. If I saw no factual basis
for his remark about the possible flaw in the experiment I would say
why, but in a way that implicitly or explicitly complimented my questioner for having taken the trouble to read and think about this area.
I have gotten off the line—"I'm like you in your concerns, I'm not your
enemy." I have blended—"My feelings are like your feelings. We're in
this together."

The "lead" and the "throw" come naturally from the blend. If the
questioner has sufficiently expressed his feelings I can try to make
some remark that will literally lead us on from there to think about
the implications of psychic and spiritual phenomena for our view of
ourselves. Leading the energy along to a higher level is sufficient for
the attack to dissipate peacefully.

If his hostility continues I might lead the questioner out some more to clarify what the problem is and continue to deal with it as above. Or I can say something that makes the feeling quality of the question overt rather than hidden in an apparently intellectual concern, and see if the questioner wants to deal directly with the feeling level. Often he does not and is silent: The "throw" has taken place, the attack is over. I will not force anyone to continue on the feeling level if they do not want to.

Sometimes the questioner still does not want to communicate but simply wants to continue to use the occasion to be hostile. Then I have to use the lower style of Aikido self-defense and make a final "throw" with a barrage of facts and logic that undercuts the attack. I go away dissatisfied from this kind of outcome, though, wishing I were more skilled at creating genuine understanding and harmony.

It is easy for me to write about Aikido at length: I enjoy it, and practicing it has been vital in giving me some partial balance as a three-brained (body, emotions, intellect) being instead of being nothing but an overintellectualized scholar. I recommend it for anyone in reasonable health as a way to develop the natural intelligence of the body, as well as to get good exercise, enjoy yourself, and learn effective self-defense.[2]

Now let us return to the question of energy.

What Is Ki?

You may have noticed that in writing about Aikido and its applications I constantly used the word energy: the energy of the attack, the direction of energy, blending with energy. In Aikido we speak of *ki* energy all the time. The attacker projects ki in order to attack, you blend your ki with the attacker's ki in order to defend. What is ki?

Ki as an Attitude Toward Reality

The word ki is actually used in several ways in Aikido, and in Eastern thought generally. In its broadest sense, for example, ki is really a subtle philosophical or metaphysical concept, an overall attitude toward and understanding of the universe as the harmonious flow of a "something" that is beyond verbal definition. From this perspective translating it as "spirit" or "energy" is pretty crude, for ki cannot be reduced to precise verbal definition.

Words, by their nature, can only be partial representations of a reality that is much bigger, especially when we go beyond the world of simple physical objects. The word ki only points at something beyond itself. Zen teachings, for example, emphasize that the finger pointing at the moon is not the moon. In this broadest sense, then, ki only points at something subtle yet fundamental about the universe, a something that can only be grasped through meditative and life experiences. I find ki as a philosophical idea very useful to me personally, but difficult to write about.

Ki as a Tool

In a more limited but more specific usage, ki is a mental image— a functionally useful way of imaging or imagining things.

A common way to teach a newcomer about ki in Aikido is to demonstrate the "unbendable arm." Two partners stand facing each other. The learner puts her wrist on the other's shoulder, palm up, arm turned so the natural bend of the elbow is straight down. The partner who will test the learner's strength puts his hands on top of the learner's elbow (the inside of the elbow) and *gradually* tries harder and harder to bend the learner's arm, keeping it up until it either bends or he cannot bend it.

This is done under two conditions. In the first the learner is told to actively resist having her arm bent, clenching her fist, using ordinary muscular strength. In the second, the unbendable arm condition, she is told to flow ki along her arm and out through her fingertips, keeping her hand open and fingers relaxed and outspread. Her arm is relaxed, too.

How should she flow ki? A common (although not the only) way is to tell her to imagine something like water in her arm, to picture it flowing through her arm and out her fingertips as if her arm were a fire hose and great volumes of water were flowing through it and squirting out the end off into the far distance.

People find that their arm can usually be bent when they use ordinary muscle power to resist, especially if a strong partner is gradually increasing his pull. And it is tiring work to resist the pull. When people do the visualization well, though, their arm usually cannot be bent, even by strong partners, and it feels effortless. If their arm is bent they usually find they had stopped visualizing ki flow and switched to ordinary muscular resistance. The unbendable arm is particularly impressive when an athletic, two-hundred-pound man cannot bend the elbow of a one-hundred-pound woman.

If you want to try this exercise with a friend please follow the instructions given above exactly, or you may hurt yourself or your partner. *Be sure* the elbow bends naturally down before putting any pressure on it. Don't go *against* the elbow joint. Apply pressure *gradually*, not as a sudden jerk. Try a couple of slow-motion dry runs with minimal pressure first to be sure you are not going against the elbow joint. Best of all get an experienced Aikido student to show you how to do this safely.

Isn't Ki Just Imagination?

Insofar as ki is just an image it is imaginary, subjective. If ki is imaginary and subjective doesn't that mean it isn't real? That it's useless? Yes and no.

If ki is nothing more than an imagined picture, a deliberate but arbitrary visualization, the forms in which we image it should be almost unlimited, since we can imagine almost anything. While doing the unbendable arm you could picture ki as flowing molasses rather than water, or perhaps as boxes of dynamite moving on a conveyer belt, or as your arm turning into concrete, and so on. You could even try to visualize the various muscles of your arm in an anatomically correct way, with certain ones relaxed and others tense. The fact is, though, that visualizing ki as something fluid that is flowing freely, while subjective, has objective effects: Your arm becomes strong and unbendable with little or no effort on your part. Images, the subjective, can be a very effective way to guide your body.

For example, several years ago a friend took me bowling. I'd never bowled before and was quite awkward. He started giving me tips: Hold the feet like so, grip like this, turn your body like so, twist like this, and on and on. "Stop!" I finally cried, "I can't keep up with all these rules and techniques, I'm getting confused!"

I told him I'd have to try bowling using what I'd learned from Aikido. I would visualize a ki path flowing down the middle of the alley to guide the ball to the center pin. The ki energy would hold the ball in the right channel. I then made a series of strikes and near-strikes, winning the game and disgusting my friend, who was a good bowler. This went to my head, of course. I started thinking about how good I was instead of focusing on visualizing the ki path, and my game went downhill fast.

So ki is subjective and imaginary in some ways, but it can be an effective use of imagination, especially if your visualization is strong and appropriate. By analogy, the electrical flow comprising the program in a computer is subtle and subjective compared to the solid reality of the hardware. Without a correctly written program to guide it, however, the hardware doesn't do anything useful.

So we have an effective and practical use of ki as guiding imagery for controlling your own body movements.

Is Shared Subjectivity Reality?

Let's think about the meaning of "subjective" some more. It usually implies that the subjective contents of someone's mind are unique and individual, imaginary, unreal. But what happens when several people share similar subjective ideas and experiences: When does shared subjectivity become "reality"?

Aikido is not just an art of controlling your own movements through your visualization of ki. If it were you might be very strong and powerful in your physical movements, but probably not very harmonious: Clashes would be common as your strength ran into your attacker's strength. Instead we try to lead the attacker's ki. What is it we lead?

At the least in Aikido we lead the attacker's attention. If your attacker grabs for your shoulder, for example, you draw your shoulder back at just the right speed. If you draw it back too slowly the attacker gets a good grip while maintaining his balance; too quickly and the attacker, seeing that he can't get his grip, breaks off his attack and retreats; just right and the movement catches the attacker's attention at a basic, almost unconscious level. It looks to the attacker as if he is just about to get his grip with just a little more of a reach: He reaches farther than he intended to and you take his balance in a smooth, harmonious movement. You lead his body by leading his attention.

Instead of thinking about this as leading attention, which is a rather abstract thing to think about (what does attention look like?), you can just as usefully think about it, visualize it, as leading the attacker's ki. Ki is much more tangible than attention for me, for example, as I feel and image it as a definite tactile sensation, a wave of something flowing. The attacker puts out a flow of ki in the act of grabbing, you create a flow of (receptive) ki by stepping back. Proper timing is a matter of harmoniously blending the ki flows together so they join.

Now we have an interesting situation. The attacker may not be deliberately visualizing any kind of ki flow, but it is useful for you as the defender to react to the attacker's actions as if these actions involved ki flow, and so join your ki flow to the attacker's to lead it. If we take the idea of ki as "real" it's easy to come to the conclusion that no one can launch an effective attack unless he flows ki out, consciously or not. Visualizing both your and the attacker's actions as ki flow makes your technique smooth, harmonious, and effective. The "subjective" is now becoming rather "objective."

I mentioned above that the visualization of ki should be strong and appropriate. I don't think visualizing ki as boxes of dynamite moving down a conveyer belt, for example, or as your arm turning to concrete, would work anywhere near as effectively as images of air or water or energy flowing. Partly this is because an image like water flowing is an inherently fluid image, and we strive for fluidity in Aikido. Partly it's due to the principle that the closer a subjective image mirrors an objective reality, the more effective it is likely to be in mobilizing your energies. Does this mean that there is a third meaning of ki, that besides being a metaphysical concept and being a "technology" of imagery, there is a way in which ki is objectively real?

Psychokinesis and Ki

We have looked at ki as a philosophical idea and as a psychological reality, a useful kind of imaging that mobilizes the body effectively. But we also have some good scientific evidence for the objective reality of something like ki, so let us look at some of the more interesting bits—and I stress the word "bits"—of scientific knowledge about it. Our Western, scientific knowledge is still in an early, fragmented stage, far from a comprehensive understanding of concepts that resemble ki, and far from regular, practical application of it. But what we do know is fascinating.

Something like ki has been intermittently studied in the West in that tiny branch of science known as parapsychology. Parapsychology researches possible aspects of human nature that seem to go beyond what our current picture of the physical universe deems possible, phenomena like telepathy and clairvoyance. *Psychokinesis (PK)* is the term for "mind over matter," the apparent ability to directly influence physical matter just by will, without using any known physical forces to get the result. If I ask you to give me a cup of coffee and you reach out and hand it to me, that's ordinary. We understand the forces involved. If you just wish, and the cup floats through the air by itself to me, that's PK.

That's also remarkable, rare, frightening, and controversial. "Macro-PK" is the technical term for ordinary size objects being affected by PK. It seemed to be more common in Victorian times in the context of Spiritualist seances, but much (not all) of it was probably fraudulent, done with thin wires, confederates dressed in black, and other tricks in darkened rooms.

Modern parapsychological research on PK under controlled laboratory conditions flowered in the late 1930s in Professor J. B. Rhine's laboratory at Duke University. Rhine and his co-workers used machines to throw dice, while a subject standing off to one side tried to will them to come up in specified ways by PK. We know that by chance alone each face will come up one-sixth of the time, so in the long run we'll get an equal number of ones, twos, threes, fours, fives, and sixes. (As dice wear they can become biased, but that problem is canceled out when you use all faces as targets an equal number of times.) If the target faces come up with a significantly different ratio from the one-sixth proportion expected, something is affecting them.

In dozens of experiments over the years, enough of the dice outcomes showed statistically significant deviations from chance to establish the reality of PK. Sometimes, by willing or wishing, a person could affect the outcome of a mechanical process without using any known forces.

In general these were rather small-scale effects. The dice did not obviously pause in the air and turn over, and the deviations from chance were generally only a few percent at most. While these results were statistically significant, the PK generally seen in the parapsychology lab is a small and unreliable force. If you want that cup of coffee it's a lot smarter at this stage of the game to reach for it, instead of willing it to float over to you. But if you have to affect some process that has some delicate control elements in it, and you can't get at it by normal means, PK is a definite possibility.

Dice tests are now old-fashioned and almost never used. They've been replaced by PK tests on electronic random-number generators. Typically you sit in front of a box that's full of silicon chips and integrated circuits. A red light and a green light on the box blink intermittently. If you time them you find that they blink an equal amount of time. The chance of either light being selected at any particular moment is 50-50. Now the subject gets instructions like, "Make the red light come on more for the next minute."

In a way this experiment is preposterous. What exactly are you supposed to do? In the dice experiment you could at least imagine yourself mentally "pushing" on the dice at the right moment, but what do you "push on" in an integrated circuit chip? In spite of this conceptual impasse the experiment works on many occasions. Instead of 50 percent hits on the target light, some subjects can get 51 percent or 52 percent or a little better, and keep up this deviation long enough so that we know statistically that it's not luck. Their intention is somehow influencing the electronic circuitry. That's PK.

As with PK effects on dice, it doesn't seem to be a big enough force to be useful for willing your coffee cup to float over to you. We're talking about the results of untrained people in an artificial situation, however, so it's hard to limit the possibilities if it were developed properly. It would be like judging the ultimate possibilities of Aikido by watching some beginners during their first week on the mat.

PK, as we get it in the laboratory now, is a big enough effect to be useful (or annoying) if you're trying to affect delicate things like computers and electronic controllers. The Koestler Professor of Parapsychology at Edinburgh University, Robert Morris, is actually studying certain people who have a strange reputation in their companies: The company computer frequently crashes when they're around, even if they don't touch it. These people often get fired or at least ordered not to come anywhere near the computer building. He's also interested in people who can't wear watches because they keep breaking, an effect that seems to work on digital watches as well as old-fashioned mechanical watches.[3]

Does ki involve PK, in addition to the effects the visualization of ki has in producing smooth, strong bodily responses? Is ki, as a philosophical principle about the nature of the universe, an accurate reflection of a fact that PK is a fundamental force of nature? Conceptually they are similar: subtle energies of an unknown kind, directed by will, that can affect material bodies. Practically, though, it's almost impossible to tell in most situations.

In the laboratory study of PK you can isolate the PK effect: Barriers and other procedures make sure the experimental agent can't use ordinary, muscular means to affect the PK target. If anything significant happens you can infer that PK caused it. On the training mat things are far more complicated. The Aikido practitioner is using her muscles, as well as the muscles and movement of the attacker by directing his attention. Those muscular and psychological forces are almost always adequate (given a preference for a "conventional" explanation) to explain why a technique works.

Also, the magnitudes of laboratory demonstrated PK forces are much too small, and their control too unreliable to date, to be useful on the mat. As a scientist I couldn't convincingly argue that occasionally there's some PK being used on the mat in addition to the muscular action.

And yet . . . I have seen films of Morehei Uyeshiba, the founder of Aikido, in which he does some things that make me wonder if PK is involved. There is one, for example, in which Uyeshiba is holding a five-foot-long wooden staff (called a *jo*) out in front of him. Several young black belts are simultaneously pushing together *sideways* on the jo. They have several times Uyeshiba's strength, and a considerable advantage in leverage, but they can't move him. Several seconds later he suddenly makes a movement and the attackers are falling all over the floor. We can't adequately test for PK from old films, though, so we'll never know for sure.

Uyeshiba has been dead for more than two decades, but will some other Aikido practitioners develop his level of skill? I suspect that the mental attitude that results from constantly using visualizations of ki flow in Aikido techniques might have an indirect effect of teaching you better PK control. Several psychologists have wanted to do PK testing on advanced martial arts practitioners, but it's one of those good ideas that has never been implemented for lack of research money.

We know a lot about the world in Western science, but I think that someday a full understanding of "subtle energies" like ki is going to greatly enlarge our view of what energy is, and our view of our own spiritual nature.

Suggested Reading

Heckler, R. S., ed. 1985. *Aikido and the New Warrior.* Berkeley, Calif.: North Atlantic Books.

Lowry, D. 1985. *Autumn Lightning: The Education of an American Samurai.* Boston: Shambhala.

Ming-Dao, Deng 1983. *The Wandering Taoist.* San Francisco: Harper & Row.

Stevens, J., and S. Rinjiro. 1984. *Aikido: The Way of Harmony.* Boston: Shambhala.

Tohei, K. 1966. *Aikido in Daily Life.* Tokyo: Rikugei.

———. 1962. *What Is Aikido?* Tokyo: Rikugei.

Ueshiba, K. 1969. *Aikido.* Tokyo: Hozansha.

———. 1984. *The Spirit of Aikido.* Tokyo: Kodansha International; distributed in the United States by Harper & Row.

Westbrook, A., and O. Ratti. 1970. *Aikido and the Dynamic Sphere.* Rutland, Vt.: Charles E. Tuttle.

Yamada, Y. with S. Pimsler. 1981. *The New Aikido Complete: The Arts of Power and Movement.* Seacaucus, N.J.: Lyle Stuart.

CHAPTER 16

Living in Illusion

People frequently try to understand the mind by drawing analogies between it and the most sophisticated technologies of their time. Thus we have had hydraulic models of the mind, where emotional intensity is like pressure in a pipe; and chemical models, where the intensity of feelings is a function of the "chemical potentials" of the elements going into it. In our own time we are fond of saying that the mind is a complicated computer.

All of these analogies are just that: analogies, not real descriptions of the mind. Models are frequently confused with reality, but as long as we avoid this confusion we can learn a lot about the way our minds work. This chapter will lay a foundation for understanding a concept found in the transpersonal psychologies: We live in an *illusory* world.

The Computer-brain Analogy

Let us assume that the most important aspects of brain functioning are analogous to the functioning of a computer. Indeed we shall treat brains and computers as *identical* to sharpen the discussion, even though I am sure that some aspects of mind cannot be reduced to brain functioning. The neurons in the brain are thus like the electronic switches in a computer; interconnected groups of neurons are like the circuits in a computer. The brain is the "hardware" of the mind; thoughts and feelings are the "software," the particular programs and sets of instructions that control how the physical structure of the brain works. Now we ask two interesting questions: (1) What *is* consciousness? and (2) What is consciousness conscious *of?*

At ordinary levels of discussion the answer to "What is consciousness?" is straightforward: It is the pattern of electrical-chemical impulses operating in a particular set of circuits, the computer-brain. The specific functioning of the computer-brain at any instant is a matter of where electrical-chemical impulses are—what circuits they are activating—at that instant. Computation, "thinking," consists of the movement of electrical-chemical impulses into different patterns in the computer-brain's circuits. Any state of the computer-brain, any "sensation" or "thought" in it, can be specified and understood *exactly* by the distribution of electrical-chemical impulses in the computer-brain's circuits. For the computer-brain consciousness *is* its electrical-chemical state.

As to what the computer-brain is conscious *of*, the answer is again straightforward: It is conscious of electrical-chemical impulses. It does not directly see or otherwise sense real objects in the external world. Rather, when such objects enter the field of vision of our eyes, they cause a pattern of electrical-chemical impulses to be produced and sent to the computer-brain, and it is this pattern of which the computer is conscious. The computer has no *direct* perception of anything in the real world, but only of electrical-chemical patterns that are associated with and caused by events and objects in the real world.

The Construction-Simulation Process

Suppose you are looking at a fire. You experience it as red in color, you feel the heat from it on your skin. If the fire is threatening you or your possessions you perceive it as dangerous. In another situation and mood you might perceive it as beautiful.

These seem like direct perceptions of external reality, but our modern understanding of brain functioning tells us that it is not really direct. It is mediated by many intermediate processes, each one of which can alter the nature of what we perceive. The fire is not "red" or "hot" or "dangerous" or "beautiful" in any absolute sense: For us it is only a certain pattern of electrical-chemical impulses stimulating our eyes and our skin.

Consider the experience of the fire being perceived as red. We believe we understand the physical world well enough to be certain that the fire is emitting electromagnetic radiation. Some of this radiation is in a vibratory range that can stimulate the human eye, so radiation in this range is called light. Light of a particular frequency does not have any attributes of color in and of itself; it is just vibrating at that particular rate.

The radiation strikes special structures on your retina, the cones, which are responsible for color vision. The energy of the light stimulates electrochemical changes in the cones, such that the particular vibratory frequency of the light hitting the cones sends out a particular pattern of electrical-chemical impulses, nerve impulses, that travel up special nerves from the eye to the brain. The brain modifies these nerve impulses in complex ways that we don't fully understand and the final pattern of electrochemical impulses in the brain results in our perception-experience of the fire as red. *It is the structure and activity of the brain and eyes that construct the experience of red; red is not a property of the outside world.*

You have probably seen those oddly colored computer-processed photographs taken by special earth-sensing satellites. Water may appear as shades of red, vegetation as shades of blue, bare earth as shades of green. Such photographs are usually labeled "false color" photographs. But there is nothing "false" in an absolute sense about these colors. Computer processing of photographs involves just the same kind of relatively *arbitrary* simulation of the outside world that your brain carries out. Your brain could just as well, and just as usefully, construct the sight of fire as the experience of green or blue instead of the experience of red. The construction-simulation process enables us to survive in the world when there is a regular, dependable correspondence between some feature of the outside world and your constructed perception of it. If ordinary fires were always green that would be fine.

The colors in a computer-processed photo, then, are not "false" colors; they are simply not simulated or constructed in accordance with the usual human visual system standards. The redness you directly experience when looking at a fire is an arbitrary construction of your brain. Similarly "hotness" could be constructed by the computer-brain so that it would be experienced with the sensations we now think of as coldness. As long as the relation of the experience of coldness to objects and processes associated with higher temperatures in the outside world held constant, so you knew things that felt cold would burn you, it would be just as useful to our survival as the present experience of hotness being associated with high-temperature objects.

Similarly the "dangerousness" or the "beauty" of the fire you see are somewhat arbitrary constructions of your brain, not direct properties of the outside world. Indeed these two qualities involve even more complex construction activity on the part of the brain than redness or hotness, for emotional evaluation of the outside world has now been added to the construction-simulation of the object itself. We can see a fire as a fire and then separately decide it's dangerous or beautiful; but often we instantly see a dangerous fire or a beautiful fire.

What we are directly aware of, then, are the constructions-simulations of our brains, not outside reality itself. We—our consciousness—"live in" a *world simulator*; we do not live directly in physical reality.

Simulation

Living in a simulator does not mean living in some kind of vague, imaginary state. Let's look at how simulators are now commonly used in flight training.

Learning to fly a plane is a difficult and dangerous process. In the old days, after the initial classroom instruction, you simply got in a real plane and took off. An instructor may have guided you at first, and tried to compensate for any mistakes you made, but eventually you had to fly by yourself. You might have encountered emergencies that never came up in training, like sudden clear air turbulence. A mistake could be fatal to you and your passengers.

Today it's possible to train in a flight simulator. From the outside it is a big box mounted in a framework, and it looks nothing like an airplane. Inside, however, it looks exactly like the cockpit of the plane you are learning to fly. The view through the windscreen is of an airport runway. When you start the engines you hear them rev up, and you see their speed indicated on the instruments. As you begin to taxi you feel the forward acceleration of the plane, and you see through the windscreen that you are moving down the runway.

The tower gives you clearance to take off. You feel the acceleration as you gun the engines for takeoff; and the runway falls away beneath you as you feel the nose of the plane come up. Soon you have forgotten the intellectual, abstract knowledge that you are in a simulator. It's too real. You are busy practicing your piloting skills.

Suddenly a flock of birds comes at you—just as the plane has started to lift. One flies into an engine, you hear the sound of an explosion. Your instruments show a fire in that engine and a loss of power and altitude. The plane starts to slip sideways. You must apply what you've learned instantly to save yourself. Oops! Too late! You feel the shock of impact as a wing tips and hits. You have just failed a test. But you're still alive to practice again.

Simulators like this are expensive, but it's much safer to train pilots in simulators than in real planes. What's more, the simulator is "real"

while you are flying it: Your computer-brain is fed enough realistic cues
so you perceive yourself as being in a real plane cockpit.

In everyday life we also live in a simulator: The computer-brain is
taking input from physical reality and constructing a simulation of our
world that we naively believe *is* reality. Usually we believe the simulator does a good job, that is, it creates a simulation that mirrors the
external world with great fidelity. A great deal of the time it is indeed
a good simulation: The car you see on the street is probably actually
driving down the street in the physical world.

Living in a world simulator, then, means that what we think are
direct perceptions of the physical world are somewhat arbitrary *constructions* of our computer-like brains, not the things themselves. Our
apparently direct experience of the world is actually indirect.

If this were all that living in a world simulator meant it would not
be a great problem. Perceptions could be taken for granted in everyday
life: Whatever the real physical nature of fire, whether it makes me
itch, shiver, or feel cold or tense or relaxed or elated, I nevertheless
have learned that fire can burn and so I will treat it carefully. If I am
curious about the nature of the outside world in and of itself, I can
employ scientific instruments and procedures to learn about properties
that are not adequately represented in my (arbitrarily constructed) sensory perceptions. Unfortunately living in the world simulator has much
more important meanings.

Emotional and Psychological Construction of Perception

If perception involves a complex, active construction of a simulation
of reality, why aren't we aware of the construction process? Or of the
effort involved in constructing it? When I turn my head right now I
instantly see a bookcase. I experience no moment of ambiguous shapes
and colors, I expend no effort to compare these with past knowledge
and decide that a bookcase is the best construct I can make of these
particular shapes and colors. My experience is that I instantly see a
bookcase.

The difficulty in realizing that perception is an active construction
is that its work readily becomes automated, and then we don't sense
the effort. Nor does it take any appreciable psychological time. Early
in our lives, as infants, we had to work at constructing perceptions,
but that was long ago and is now forgotten.

We occasionally have experiences of ambiguous perceptions as adults: What is that shape in the dark? Could it be a bush? A crouching person? An animal? Ah, it's a parked motorcycle, viewed end on. Now that you see it as a motorcycle it is difficult to see it again as a bush or animal or crouching person. Such experiences should alert us to the constructed nature of perception, but they are so rare compared to the instant recognition of things in our automated perception that they have little impact.

The Right-side-up, Upside-down World

A striking example of the construction and automation of perception comes from a classical psychological experiment initiated by George Stratton in 1897 and described in most basic psychology texts. A pair of special goggles is put on a subject. Prisms in these goggles invert the visual field both vertically and horizontally so that what was up is now down. The floor is above the subject, the ceiling below. What was on the subject's left is now on his right, and vice versa.

To describe the subject's reaction as confusion is to put it mildly. Moving about is especially difficult, and some subjects feel nauseated. Their lifetime store of visual and motor simulations of the world and their relation to it are now wrong in major ways.

The inverting goggles are worn for days or weeks. Initially the subject must make perception and movement conscious acts instead of letting them run on automatic. His automatized reactions do not work. If he sees an object that he wants and it is obviously to his left, he must move in the direction his body thinks is right, for example.

After a few days an amazing thing happens. The world no longer looks upside down. The subject can reach directly for things without any calculations of where right and left really are. An entirely new set of perceptual simulations has been constructed and automated. He feels as if he perceives reality directly, just as it is: the same feeling he had before donning the inverting goggles.

When the goggles are finally removed the world is suddenly upside down and reversed! Conscious compensation for left and right is again required. After some visual experience, however, the old, "normal" pattern is reestablished. Because the old simulation pattern is so thoroughly learned its reestablishment takes much less time than it took to establish new simulation patterns when the goggles were first put on. The old simulation pattern is just as arbitrary as the new one, of course.

Perceptual Defense

The reality of unconscious processes, mental or emotional, that affect us and yet lie outside conscious awareness is widely accepted in modern psychology.[1] A specific form of unconscious processes, known as perceptual defense, has not been generally accepted, however, in spite of good experimental evidence for it. The haggling over the reality of perceptual defense has been so intense that I have suspected the idea is being actively resisted. It is too clear a reminder of how mechanical we are.

Perceptual defenses are a form of defense mechanism that works to keep us unaware of events in the outside world that would arouse unpleasant or unacceptable emotions. The effect was first noticed experimentally in some studies of perceptual thresholds. If a word is flashed very briefly on a screen what is the minimal time exposure—the perceptual threshold—for correct conscious recognition of it?

If the flash is extremely brief, say a hundredth of a second or less, you will see only a flash of light and will not even perceive the overall patterning of the letters, much less recognize them. If the flash is long, say one-quarter of a second or more, you will readily perceive the word. If you start with flashes too short for recognition and slowly increase the duration of the flashes until correct recognition occurs, the length of flash required is the threshold value.

Such factors as the length and familiarity of a word will affect the threshold of recognition. Long, unfamiliar words will have higher thresholds than short, familiar ones. Researchers also noticed that emotionally charged words, especially those that might create personal conflict in their subjects, had higher thresholds than words of similar length and familiarity that had no threatening emotional connotations. For college student subjects of three generations ago (who would usually not have had a secure sexual identity in those more sexually repressed times) the word *fuck*, for example, would generally have a higher threshold than a word like *flex*.

Psychologists concluded that there are three stages in perception. First is an initial perception-recognition outside of consciousness. This is followed by discrimination of the potential emotional threat of the stimulus. If the stimulus is classified as threatening an influence is exerted on the mind to raise its threshold for the third step of the process, conscious perception of the stimulus.

In terms of our world-simulator model perceptual defense is an understandable phenomenon. A particular stimulus pattern, already modified to some extent by the physical structure of the senses, reaches the computer-brain. Learned computational processes automatically go to work to construct a simulation of this aspect of reality. As part of creating an appropriate construct-perception-simulation, the computer-brain draws on memory data about this kind of particular stimulus.

In the case of perceptual defense the memory data include information that this is also emotionally threatening. This calls up more memory data about how these kinds of emotional threats should be handled. If the defense style is to try to avoid noticing such threats then the simulation of this stimulus is constructed in such a way as to be less noticeable to consciousness. Or the simulation is altered—we could say "distorted" in terms of resemblance to the initiating stimulus—so that the final simulation, what consciousness will perceive, represents something else. This "something else" resembles the original stimulus but is not identical to it. So *fuck* may become just a flash of light with indistinguishable features, or the simulation-perception may become *flux* or *duck* or *tuck*. As long as the stimulus is not too intense, not well above threshold, the automated simulation process can carry out this sort of altered, distorted construction.

For what threatening aspects of reality does your world-simulation process create high perceptual thresholds? How would you discover them?

The Waking Dream

All this discussion of simulation may create a feeling that there is something unreal about a simulation. Yes, there is in one sense. In terms of what is perceived, though, *the simulation in your mind is reality.* The person you clearly see crouching in the shadows is a perfectly real perception, is your reality at the time you perceive it—even if you later realize that it was a misperception, a poor simulation of a bush in the dark. The "flight simulator" you are training in becomes reality for a time. In this model the reality we live in is the simulation.

We can now see an important aspect of Gurdjieff's statement that people are not awake. In an ordinary nighttime dream we see a whole world of things that are not present in physical reality, but we mistake the dream for reality while it is happening. By contrast (we think) in our waking state we perceive reality. But what we perceive is a simulation of reality. If the simulation is seriously distorted, yet we mistake it for reality, we can be accurately described as being in a kind of waking dream, not really awake. In chapter 22 we shall examine some of the major rules programmed into Westerners that control how we simulate reality.

Suggested Reading

Any basic psychology textbook will have numerous examples of the constructed nature of perception in ordinary people, as well as of the obviously pathological distortions of perception in neurotics and psychotics. You will seldom find this basic knowledge elaborated into the realization that we live in a simulation of reality however. For a more elaborate discussion of this, see Tart, Charles T. 1986. *Waking Up: Overcoming the Obstacles to Human Potential.* Boston: New Science Libary.

The Dixon book referred to earlier in the chapter will provide an excellent summary of work on subliminal perception and perceptual defense: Dixon, N. F. 1971. *Subliminal Perception: The Nature of a Controversy.* London: McGraw-Hill.

Skilled Buddhist meditators bring an especially insightful view of the construction of perception as they have learned to actually observe the process, not just its indirect manifestations.

Goldstein, J. 1987. *The Experience of Insight: A Simple and Direct Guide to Buddhist Meditation.* Boston: Shambhala.
————, and J. Kornfield. 1987. *Seeking the Heart of Wisdom: The Path of Insight Meditation.* Boston: Shambhala.
Sole-Leris, A. 1986. *Tranquility and Insight: An Introduction to the Oldest Form of Buddhist Meditation.* Boston: Shambhala.

Claxton's chapter in the following book is especially useful for integrating the Buddhist experiential knowledge with modern psychology: West, M. A., ed. 1987. *The Psychology of Meditation.* Oxford: Clarendon Press.

CHAPTER 17

Self-Observation

At the end of February 1987 I flew to India, to attend the first International Conference on Energy Medicine. We had two days before the conference to explore the city of Madras and surrounding areas. This was my first real trip to a Third World country, so (in terms G. I. Gurdjieff would have used) my "diet of impressions" was far richer and considerably different than my normal fare. The resulting psychological "indigestion," the prolonged plane travel, and the twelve-hour shift in circadian rhythms confused my usual psychological defenses and allowed new material to come to consciousness. This was the perfect ground for self-observation

Self-observation practices set the stage for deep change.[1] Our ordinary state of consensus consciousness functions poorly: We live in a psychological state characterized by distorted perceptions and by both individual and shared illusions (see chapter 16). The idea that illusions can dominate significant parts of our consciousness is intellectually interesting but of little practical value unless we have direct experience of it. To develop an open mind you must observe what is really in your mind, whether you like it or not. Systematic self-observation is an essential, if sometimes rocky, path to growth.

In this chapter we will look at the process of self-observation through a concrete example: the self-observation notes I took on my trip to India. They illustrate the process of and the defenses against self-observation and are of some interest in their inherent content. They are not flattering to me; but sincere self-observation must always be a matter of putting the desire for truth about what is actually going on ahead of the desire to be happy or maintain one's self-image. The following excerpts are from my notes.

Pain

The primary problem I have to deal with in India is the enormous degree of human misery so clearly visible whenever I leave the sanctuary of the hotel. Our conference hotel, the Connamara, is one of the finest hotels in India. Here wealth buffers us from contact with the realities that exist for the vast majority of the population.

My basic problem is how to maintain any degree of psychological openness when even partial openness entails the perception of so much suffering! When I perceive this suffering I have feelings of pain, of compassion, of frustration, and I alternate between depression and anger. The perception of suffering in others leads, at the deepest level, to unhappiness and suffering within me. At some deep level I believe (or at least I suspect and hope I believe) that we are all one. Thus when I see others suffer, I suffer.

I believe that the perception of constant pain would be intolerable for me, or for anyone who wasn't a saint. Indeed I observe that even brief perceptions of this kind of pain are (I believe) intolerable for me, so I must have defense mechanisms to tune it out. The pain is especially bad because of the enormous *frustration* that goes with it: There seems to be nothing that I or anyone can do to make any significant improvement!

Nobody likes pain, whether it is physical or emotional pain. Intellectually I can accept the function of pain as a warning that something needs correction. But it is another story altogether when there is nothing I can *do* about the pain.

When Automatic Defenses Don't Work

If I were to stay here for a long time I know I would adapt. I would at least be as kind as possible to everyone under the circumstances. But little acts of kindness are just a drop in the bucket in this India of such suffering, their futility in solving the real problems is so obvious. Therefore my automatic defense mechanisms try to make me oblivious to what goes on around me. After all, there is suffering in my own everyday world that I have learned to be oblivious to.

Yet the enormity of the suffering is so great that my automatic defenses cannot easily handle it. My emotional responses threaten to overwhelm me. So I observe that I frequently have a reaction of getting *angry* at the poor people around me! It makes me really mad that people around me are poor and suffering!

Logically the idea of becoming angry at people who are suffering seems absurdly inappropriate. Yet it is "sensible" in terms of the way psychological defenses work. Depression is more negative than anger. Anger has components of power, of being alive, of potency. By becoming angry you can avoid the more negative feeling of depression, get "high" by comparison, even though the anger itself is a pathological reaction to this particular situation.

Thought Driven By Defenses

My intellectual mind becomes driven by these feelings of depression and anger, and launches into thoughts that are totally isolated from emotional reality. I think, for example, that an enormous plague that would cut the impoverished population by a factor of ten or so might be a blessing. In reaction part of me is absolutely horrified that my mind can even think such things, much less take them seriously! Another part of me congratulates me on my "realism," my "superiority," in being able to see what is practically needed even if it is horrible. I suppose this kind of disassociated intellectual thinking is the sort of thing that creates real monsters in life, even while it seems "necessary" and "reasonable" in some sense.

Gurdjieff taught that we are three-brained beings, that is, we have intellectual, emotional, and body/instinctive evaluation processes that are of equal importance. In a genuinely (not just culturally) normal person each of these processes would be educated to function at its full potential, using the kind of "logic" appropriate to itself. A center of consciousness transcending each of these three processes would then consider the evaluation of each and reach a balanced decision. Sometimes this would favor the logic of one brain over the others but it would always take account of all three, thus giving us a fuller and less distorted view of reality.

In what passes for "normal," consensus consciousness, a person usually has only one brain well developed; the other two are undeveloped and often neurotic. This results not only in unbalanced perception and understanding, but often further pathology in that one brain inefficiently and distortedly takes over the natural work of another. Intellectual consideration might be applied to a basically emotional problem, for example, but intellect can never fully comprehend the subtleties of an emotional problem.

I have always been unbalanced toward my intellectual brain in spite of much personal growth work toward developing my emotional and body/instinctive sides. Here I at least recognized that my dominant intellectual functioning was presenting me with a distorted view of what was going on, and it was doing so in order to defend me against emotional feelings I believed were intolerable. This kind of recognition of distortion can be used to inhibit inappropriate action, even if it can't be immediately changed to more appropriate three-brained function-ing.

The Children

One of the most striking examples of this kind of psychological defensiveness occurred when our tour bus visited a temple site yesterday. In the bus I felt relieved: I was *"in* the world of India but not *of* it." I was passing through India but was not touched as directly by it as when I had been walking about in Madras. The sensation of moving *through* something is a marvelous isolator!

We got off the bus at some Hindu temples that had been carved out of the living rock at the ocean's edge. This was a very rich, beautiful diet of sensory impressions, but it became more and more difficult to maintain these desirable (by my ego's standards) impressions. We were surrounded by beggars, both children and adults, and by more and more children attempting to sell us things: postcards, statues, incense, food, anything and everything.

These children are beautiful! They are bright-eyed, smiling, vital, very at-tractive. At the same time they are constantly forcing themselves on you, and it becomes more and more difficult not to succumb to them. I wanted to resist them, as there is such a feeling of manipulation from them. There is a feeling that if you buy something from one of them you will never be free of them. I speak not only here of *my* feelings, but of those widely shared by many of my fellow American conferees who were on this bus trip.

At first I found myself politely saying,"No, thank you." As I had to say this more and more often I became more curt, feeling that I was under attack when it was obvious I did not wish to interact. I went to the temple to look at the temples and sculptures, not to fend off a crowd of pushy salesmen! Eventually the "Thank you" disappeared from my speech and was replaced by a sterner and harsher, "No!" Within fifteen minutes after our arrival I found myself regarding these children as *vermin*. I felt under attack by them. My mind produced fantasies of pushing them away, a fantasy greatly strengthened as I felt *contaminated* when one of them brushed against me. Yet I would have to touch the children to push them away, a most unpleasant prospect.

I was horrified by my fantasies and emotions but powerless to stop them. Even though we had half an hour available, at the end of fifteen minutes I got back on the bus, as did several people in our party. Even on the bus they pursued us, trying to beg or sell us things through the open windows. We were glad when the bus began moving again and we escaped!

A Psychological Function of the Caste System

From a psychological point of view I understand an important reason why a caste system could develop and sustain itself in India. You would have an approved, ritualized, efficient, and psychologically automatic system to isolate yourself from a large proportion of the impoverished masses that were always around. Of course, in my fantasy I am a high-caste person myself!

I can see the "usefulness" of a caste system as a psychological defense mechanism on one level, while seeing the horror of it on another level. . . .

When I can, even if just for minutes, think of needy children as vermin, I know more of the depths to which we can sink than I ever wanted to know. I have always thought of myself as a firm believer in democracy, yet I found attractiveness in a caste system. Many, many times in the course of my psychological growth work in the past I have had to recognize negative aspects of my own mind. Each time I have done this I hoped that I was somehow finished, that I had plumbed the bottom. I suspect it is a dangerous delusion to ever think you are finished. While I hope I never act on these negative impulses, I cannot deny their existence.

I note with interest the way my notes talk about the depths to which "we" can sink, even though I am speaking about *my* mind. This sort of automatic, intellectual depersonalization somehow seems to spread the responsibility, make it less mine. It doesn't in reality, of course.

The Illusion of Separation

Lately I have been quite interested in a teaching that is common in the world's great spiritual traditions: the teaching that there is one basic illusion from which we all suffer, and that this is the root of all other illusions. This is the illusion of *separation,* the belief that we are each an isolated, individual entity, an entity with clear boundaries that demarcate our limited and finite selves from the rest of the universe. *A Course in Miracles* talks about this as a forgetting that we are all sons of God.[2] Buddhism, which generally does not speculate on origins, has a tradition of an initial moment of forgetfulness from which all our troubles arose. Our Judeo-Christian tradition has the story of the Fall from grace in the Garden of Eden.

If it is true that we have forgotten or repressed our true Self, a Self unified with the rest of the universe and others, psychological problems can certainly follow. When you identify with a limited, separate self it becomes natural to be needy. The process of identification gives special importance to that fraction of our totality identified with as self, best expressed psychologically as "*I!*" How will "*I!*" get enough of this or enough of that? How can "*I!*" protect what "*I!*" have? "*I!*" am naturally in competition with other people for finite resources.

Compared to the conditions under which most of humankind lived for most of human history, it is clear that in the West most of us, even many of the "poor," live like kings. It is easy while in the West to imagine that, with the proper political and economic distribution system, there would be enough for all to live well. But how is one to imagine this utopian idea while perceiving the reality of India? There is clearly *not* enough for all.

Intellectually I have known this for a long time. Seeing this actual hopeless poverty, feeling from this direct perception, makes it so much more real. The great spiritual systems teach us to try to transcend the illusion of separation. But if I try to transcend it, even to the limited extent of realizing that these poor masses around me are thinking, feeling, hoping people, just like *me*, then I (my ordinary self) believe I take a chance of tuning in to their misery, their frustration, and their despair. Thus my motivation to transcend the illusion of separation is cut off.

As a lifelong victim of the illusion of separation I have tried to adapt to it by being as self-sufficient as possible. Seeing the misery of others is a reminder of my vulnerability, so I don't want to see.

Busyness as a Defense

Not wanting to see others' misery, not wanting to be aware of my own vulnerability, results in psychological defenses of various sorts. One of these is simply keeping busy. By being involved in my own goals, my own concerns, my *personal* worries, by keeping my mind busy with my future plans and daydreams about the future, I have less attention and energy available to notice the present and the others in it who might disturb me. Thus I walk faster and try to look purposeful as, from the corner of my eye, I see a beggar or a salesperson approaching.

To make this busyness defense even more effective I *identify* with and get lost in my fantasies about goals and being in a hurry to get somewhere. This further distracts me from the present reality and reinforces my behavior: If I really believe I have a goal it's perfectly sensible to hurry toward it. The sensory feedback from my body that I'm hurrying further reinforces my illusion that I must be going somewhere!

In the culture that I am used to this "I am in a purposeful hurry" behavior is sufficient to deter most people from approaching. This defense can work so automatically we don't notice it. What bothers me here in India is that the poor Indians' needs are so great that they won't respond to my behavioral cues about busyness. I can't rest secure in my illusions, for they force me to notice them. Then I fall back to another level of defense, separating them even further from myself by becoming angry. They are intruding on me and my purposes, the children become "vermin." It is a horrible process.

As I edit the above note I also observe that a part of me is *still* angry at Indians for pushing on me this way. This anger encourages me to think that it's not their needs so much as their general obnoxious, pushy character! That idea is to be watched carefully: My cultural conditioning is showing!

Jung and India

One night in India Dennis Stillings (who was there representing the Archaeus Foundation) told me an interesting story about the great psychologist Carl Jung. Jung visited India and he did not like it. After his initial exposure to India he got back on his ship and when it stopped in other Indian ports, he didn't bother to go ashore.

Jung was a man who had a tremendous intellectual interest in and understanding of the depths of the mind. He had a great interest in India, a culture that has contributed so much to our understanding of the mind; yet it sounds as if Jung couldn't take it. I get a perverse kind of pleasure to think that Jung had a reaction similar to mine. I think this pleasure is another defense against openness to the suffering around me.

Indeed the writing of this chapter, the intellectualization and "psychologizing" of my reactions, could become another kind of psychological defense against my feelings, a way to distance myself from them. Were it not for the fact that I think this chapter can be psychologically helpful to others, I would not write it.

The (Apparent) Safety of the Familiar

This kind of psychological distancing defense has come out in other ways. This morning, for example, I found myself fantasizing that someone here would start talking about a word-processing program like Wordstar, but not fully understand it. Then they could seek my advice and I could show them some useful technical tricks. This fantasy came from the defensive desire to anchor my mind in the familiar—better yet, a part of the familiar world I have some mastery over—as a way of escaping from unpleasant realities.

The safety of the familiar is an illusion, of course. Reality is what it is, whether it's familiar or not. Trying to stay in the present— whether it's pleasant or unpleasant, familiar or strange, what you want or not what you want—is an essential part of adaptive growth.

Identifying with the Archetypal Tourist

Our conversation at dinner Thursday night was another form of escape. Several of us who had been on the tour to the temple together were trying to cope with our negative feelings toward India. Even though intellectually I didn't want it to happen, I got emotionally and then intellectually caught up in conversations deriding the lack of progress here. I became an archetypal Tourist, huddling together with other Tourists talking about the Homeland and how much better it was than here. Another way of dulling sensitivity. "We are the special people, the real people, not like those around us who we fear to be open to." I understand more of what Gurdjieff meant by ordinary consciousness being a state of dreamy sleep.

The Spiritual as a Defense Mechanism

My main interest in coming to India was seeing a country that had developed such rich spiritual traditions. I still have great (if not greater) respect for these traditions, but I am now much more aware of how an interest in spirituality can be used as a defense mechanism against confronting the reality of suffering. It is tempting, for example, to think that the poor people I see are not *really* impoverished because they have such a rich, inner spiritual life. There might be some truth in this, but I am quite suspicious of the idea because of its obvious psychological defensive function.

I am similarly suspicious now about ideas of reincarnation and karma. It might be true that we live many lives, that we are reborn after we die. If it is true the idea of karma—that we shall reap as we sow—makes sense. It certainly makes psychological sense in this life. If I push people around for my ends it will be no surprise if they push me around when they get the chance. So the principle would probably apply across lives: The kind of psychological character that pushes people around and so causes predictable reactions would get its possessor into similar kinds of trouble in future lives, until he worked through the personality problems that cause the maladaptive behavior in the first place.

Yet ideas of reincarnation and karma can also be used as a psychological defense to cut myself off from others' suffering. "Yes, they are suffering, but it's their karma, they were wicked in a previous life, so naturally they are suffering. Indeed, it would be wrong for me to interfere with their suffering, then they couldn't work out their karma. Let me go about my business now." This is rationalization: I'm special, I don't have to see or feel, let me alone in my illusion of separation.

And there is always the defense of time. A week has gone by since I wrote the above, and I find myself forgetting the experience, watching time dull the emotional impact, watching my normal busy routine soothe the sting . . .

Self-observation is always showing me new things about the craziness of my ordinary life. I don't want to create the impression that self-observation is all negative, however. Much, much beauty that would otherwise be missed comes to light through self-observation and self-remembering. You must be dedicated to self-observation, to knowing the truth regardless of what you would *prefer* to know or feel: This is the key to psychological and spiritual growth.

Suggested Reading

For general information on the construction of perception and on psychological defense mechanisms, any good general psychology textbook will do, such as:

Bourne, L., and B. Ekstrand. 1976. *Psychology: Its Principles and Meanings.* New York: Holt, Rinehart & Winston.
Hilgard, E. R., R. L. Atkinson, and R. C. Atkinson. 1979. *Introduction to Psychology.* New York: Harcourt Brace Jovanovich, 7th edition.
Kretch, D., R. S. Crutchfield, and N. Livson. 1974. *Elements of Psychology.* New York: Knopf, 3d edition.
Morris, C. G. 1988. *Psychology: An Introduction.* Englewood Cliffs, N.J.: Prentice-Hall, 6th edition.

More depth can be found in any good abnormal psychology text, such as:
Bootzin, R. R., and J. R. Acocella. 1988. *Abnormal Psychology: Current Perspectives.* New York: Random House.

The specific relationship of defense mechanisms in normal people to the process of living in illusion is discussed in my *Waking Up: Overcoming the Obstacles to Human Potential* (Boston: New Science Library, 1986).

Part 4

SPIRITUAL GROWTH

CHAPTER 18

Selecting a Spiritual Path

When we become concerned with searching for psychological and spiritual truths beyond the ordinary it is natural to assume there are paths to knowledge or teachers and exemplars of such knowledge that may have the answers to many of our questions. We presume we can get useful assistance from those who have taken the path before us.

As we begin searching we find that there are multitudes of teachers and paths around, yet many of them seem to contradict one another. Who has the truth? Do they all have all the truth we need to know? Do some paths have some of the truth, but lack important parts of it? Do some teachers have dangerous errors mixed in with what they know of truth? What is the minimally acceptable ratio of truth to error that makes a path or teacher worth following? Which path is *best*?

The Search for a Spiritual Consumer Reports

In ordinary life we can often get fairly reliable answers to similar, ordinary questions. If I need the services of an electrician, for example, I can hire any electrician who is state licensed and be reasonably sure that he or she possesses a certain minimal level of competence, probably enough to handle my job. If I want to learn computer programming, I can take a course at a state college and be reasonably certain that whoever the college hires to teach the course knows what they're talking about. I may not get the best, but I'll get basic competence. If I want to buy a new washer I can read *Consumer Reports* magazine and get an objective appraisal of the faults and virtues of various models, balance these against my needs, and make an intelligent decision as to which model to purchase.

If only it were like this in the "spiritual marketplace." Where is the licensing board that guarantees a basic level of competence for spiritual teachers? If only we had a *Spiritual Consumer Reports* that, after objective testing, might make statements like:

For seekers of extroverted temperament and personality traits A, B, Q, and T, Zen meditation produces rapid progress toward enlightenment. It is definitely Not Acceptable if you have traits C or R, however. Seekers with trait C should investigate the new Gestalt Sufism. Unfortunately no satisfactory spiritual path has yet been discovered for those with trait R, who are better off in this lifetime in artistic vocations.

Selecting the best from among the many is a real problem, even if you're only reading about spiritual matters. It is even more important when you are ready for serious practice. Traditions and teachers make conflicting claims; many paths implicitly or explicitly consider others inferior; and there is no objective authority to turn to for guidance. What can an intelligent person do?

Trust Your Feelings

Selecting a spiritual path is not just a matter of verbal, *intellectual* intelligence, it is also a matter of our feelings and our instincts. In our culture our intellectual intelligence has been highly developed, but our instincts and our feelings have been grossly neglected and often suppressed and distorted in their functioning. This distorted functioning of our instincts and feelings in turn can distort our intellectual functioning, so that much "rationality" is actually rationalization.

Part of our approach to choosing spiritual paths, then, should be based on a continual effort to understand and mature our emotional and instinctual nature. For example, one of the reasons I was attracted to several spiritual paths in my past was that I had an immature need to feel superior to other people, in order to mask feelings of inferiority in myself. That was *my* problem, not the problem of those various paths; yet there are teachers and systems around that have probably lost touch with their original spiritual impetus and now cater to those sorts of immature emotions. Continual increase in our self-knowledge is essential.

Recognize Your Limitations

Intelligence requires us to recognize our current limitations and practice humility. I would like to believe that I can assess the real quality of various spiritual paths and teachers, but I know that's too grandiose to be true. I, and you, can certainly recognize, at one extreme, some of the charlatans, and we can sometimes recognize (intellectually and/or emotionally and/or instinctually) higher ideas and actions. We can do our best to choose—but sometimes we will be wrong. If we learn from our mistakes we have little objective cause for regret.

I am a scientist and a pragmatist as well as someone interested in spiritual growth. When I encounter a spiritual system or teacher, I try to "listen" and evaluate with my mind, my heart, and my instincts, drawing on what I think I know, and remembering that I've made mistakes before and will probably make more in the future. If I decide I can learn from a system or teacher, or do something useful for myself or others by getting involved, I get involved.

Why Not "Go to the Source"?

In an early issue of *The Open Mind* I mentioned that I was working on a book that would integrate the psychological and spiritual ideas of G. I. Gurdjieff (one of the pioneers in adapting Eastern spiritual ideas to Western culture) with modern psychology.[1] This prompted the following letter:

Why continue to focus on Gurdjieff when it is clear that most of his system derives from Sufism? Why not, instead, go to the source?
    D. J., Buffalo, NY

G. I. Gurdjieff was one of the first moderns who made a systematic attempt to translate knowledge and wisdom he acquired from Eastern and Near Eastern teachers into a form that would be suitable for Westerners of his time. He realized that what may be an efficient formulation of psychological and spiritual knowledge for one culture may not work properly in another, so he experimented with forms of teaching that would effectively transmit his knowledge.

I am familiar with a variety of claims about what path is superior. These include the Sufi claim (via the excellent writings of Idries Shah) that Gurdjieff's ideas were useful but are incomplete and now outmoded; the feeling among some followers of Gurdjieff that Shah's Sufi stories are useful but limited; and Oscar Ichazo's claim that his Arica training comes from the secret school that is behind both Gurdjieff and Sufism and supersedes both of them.[2] I have immense respect for the teachings of Gurdjieff, Shah, and Ichazo: All of these systems have been of great value to me and to friends of mine. Since I don't know the address of the "spiritual licensing bureau," however, I can't check on who really has legitimate credentials and who doesn't. Nor have I been able to locate the issue of "Spiritual Consumer Reports" that gives the "objective" evaluation of these systems, or rates one or more as a Best Buy. As a limited being I can only conclude that all (and many other systems) have something to give *to at least some people,* and I hope that the right people will get involved with the right path for them.[3]

I think one of the things a more enlightened science could do for spiritual paths would be to develop something like a "Spiritual Consumer Reports." That is a huge project for several generations of researchers, but it would be possible to assess the characteristics of many people, let them become involved with various spiritual paths, and then see what kinds of outcomes occurred for what kinds of people. It is only a part of the answer, but it would help.

The Spiritual Emergence Network

Sometimes, inevitably, spiritual seekers end up on the wrong path, or on a path that suddenly leads them into new experiences they are unable to handle, or for which they have no reference. This can be frightening, and potentially damaging to the person. The Spiritual Emergence Network (SEN) was formed to help with such problems. The following information is excerpted from an *Open Mind* article written by my wife, Judy Tart:

Many travelers on the spiritual path have found the going rough, or have suddenly found themselves at a level of awareness or energy transformation they were not prepared to handle. Perhaps others around them have also had difficulty in dealing with the enormous new levels of knowledge, insight, and energy their friends are experiencing. Even worse, many people who do not consider themselves seekers or spiritual wake up one morning to find their world suddenly changed—they begin hearing voices, seeing visions, knowing the thoughts and secret feelings of others around them.

We know what usually happens to anyone in our society who not only has these experiences but is foolish enough to talk about them to others: a seventy-two-hour hold in the nearest "spiritual correction" center and some massive doses of Thorazine to bring them back to "normal." I recently reread Bert Kaplan's *The Inner World of Mental Illness,* and was struck by the almost universal themes of spiritual awakening that run through diverse firsthand accounts of people's experience with madness, along with the equally striking lack of recognition of the same by the so-called authorities. It is also frightening to realize that today, with our antipsychotic medications, people aren't even allowed to experience their mystical states in the privacy of their own minds. SEN fills an urgent need for help with spiritual and psychic experiences without automatically invalidating them.

In order to avoid this situation, and to help those who are trying to figure out if they're becoming enlightened or going crazy, Stan and Christina Grof and Rita Rohan established the Spiritual Emergence Network.

Anyone experiencing altered states of awareness, energy, or insights, and who needs some nurturing, reassurance, and help while going through this transformation can call SEN. The network will try to put them in touch with someone nearby who has had similar experiences, or with a therapist who is sensitive to and aware of spiritual dimensions of reality, whom they can contact for assistance. A large part of SEN's energy is spent in networking people and providing information to facilitate a more general emergence of spiritual potentials. For many people a little reassurance that they are not alone, that there are some words that describe their experiences, and books that they can read, is enough to help them on their spiritual journey.[4]

Suggested Reading

An excellent book on choosing a spiritual path has recently appeared that will be very helpful here:

Anthony, D., B. Ecker, and K. Wilber. 1987. *Spiritual Choices: The Problem of Recognizing Authentic Paths to Inner Transformation.* New York: Paragon House.

A sensitive account of the experiences of the mentally ill is Kaplan's classic book:

Kaplan, B., ed. 1964. *The Inner World of Mental Illness.* New York: Harper & Row.

The psychologies inherent in many spiritual paths, including important discussions of what is considered psychopathological from a spiritual point of view, are discussed in:

Tart, Charles T., ed. 1975. *Transpersonal Psychologies.* New York: Harper & Row.

Excellent discussions of general growth problems on the spiritual path can be found in:

Vaughan, F. 1985. *The Inward Arc: Healing and Wholeness in Psychotherapy and Spirituality.* Boston: Shambhala.

A classic work on counseling people who are disturbed by apparent psychic or spiritual experiences is:

Hastings, A. 1983. A counseling approach to parapsychological experience. *Journal of Transpersonal Psychology* 15:143–68.

CHAPTER 19

Prayer

Once a year at the University of California I teach a course in humanistic and transpersonal psychology for advanced psychology majors.[1] We first look at traditional humanistic concerns for meaning, authenticity, love, and relationships, and then we explore transpersonal concerns. We survey the conflict between science and religion and ways of resolving it, discuss the implications of psi phenomena in establishing a reality base for the transpersonal, and then look at specific transpersonal psychologies embodied in such spiritual traditions as Yoga, Buddhism, and Sufism. These non-Western spiritual traditions are rich sources of stimulation for the students, who frequently begin to think seriously about aspects of life they had never considered before.

In the very last part of the course we discuss the Christian mystical tradition. I have learned to save this until last, as it is by far the most difficult topic for students to handle. In some years it seems as if the students cannot get *any* useful ideas from the Christian tradition: For the students it is too close to home and too thoroughly associated with fanatical excesses, stupidity, incomprehensibility, and often painful personal experiences. Buddhism or Sufism are exotic ideas from a faraway place that can be looked at openly; but Christianity is too often the bigot next door who practices cruelty in the name of Jesus.

Prayer is not a fashionable topic in contemporary intellectual circles, partly because of this association with people's rejected Christian backgrounds. Meditation (preferably of an interesting and exotic Oriental variety) may be in, but prayer? That is left for the uneducated, who need superstitious practices to comfort them.

The terms prayer and meditation often cause confusion. An atheist can meditate, even if he or she cannot pray. Meditation properly refers to internal psychological practices intended to change the quality or state of consciousness of your mind. Its efficacy comes exclusively from the meditator. Prayer, on the other hand, is effective insofar as there is a "supernatural" or nonordinary order of Being or beings who might respond to it. Some practices—which may be commonly called meditation, prayer, or something else entirely—have both the qualities of meditation and prayer as we are using the terms.

The most typical kind of prayer is more accurately termed *petitionary* prayer, a petition to "someone" more powerful than yourself, someone who has the power to grant a request if they are so inclined. In our culture "someone" usually means God, Jesus, a saint, or an angel.

Scientism (science distorted by human needs so it has the worst characteristics of dogmatic religions), in its most charitable mood, sees prayer as nothing more than a subjective effort of possible psychological or psychiatric interest. Perhaps prayer occasionally does something psychologically useful for the person who prays. In its more typical mood scientism sees prayer as a degraded example of superstition and nonsense that we would be much better off without.

I doubt that scientism's attitude toward prayer is based on what we would describe as extensive and high-quality scientific research on the effects of prayer. I know of almost no quality scientific research at all on prayer. A genuinely *scientific* (as opposed to *scientistic*) attitude toward prayer would be to admit that factually we know almost nothing about it. It doesn't fit in theoretically with the main body of scientific knowledge, but in genuine science facts take precedence over theories.

Personal Attitudes Toward Prayer

Attitudes toward prayer probably derive mostly from personal experience. We may pray to be granted something that we want very much. Sometimes we get it, sometimes we don't. If we think that prayer should be infallible—especially fervent prayer stemming from strong desires—we are terribly disappointed if we don't get what we want, and we may then reject prayer. Failed prayer can be a deep emotional hurt that colors our attitudes the rest of our lives. Answered prayer can similarly affect us in a positive way. Such experiences of apparent answers or lack of answers to prayer are especially formative in childhood, when emotional intensity is so high.

Efficacy of Petitionary Prayer

G. I. Gurdjieff's ideas about prayer are quite interesting. He looked at the efficacy of petitionary prayer in terms of the intensity and consistency of a person's desires, rather than just as a formal action conventionally defined as prayer. Although he did not spell out the psychic mechanisms of connection, he believed that our thoughts and feelings have effects on higher levels of reality. Thus a consistently held desire for something acts as an unwitting "prayer," a petition or direction of intention to higher levels of reality, whether that desire was expressed as a formal petitionary prayer or not. The man who thinks about getting money all the time is in effect praying for money with unwitting prayer, whether he thinks of himself as a religious person or not, whether he gets down on his knees and formally asks God for money or not. The woman who constantly imagines tragedies befalling her is effectively praying for them. Our habitual attitudes affect our life in many ordinary, psychologically understandable ways; but unwitting prayer is another way in which we create our life, sometimes with tragic (even if wished for unconsciously) consequences. As Gurdjieff frequently expressed it, your being attracts your life.

Effective petitionary prayer in Gurdjieff's view, then, is intense and consistent desire and thought. Most petitionary prayer, however—formal or unwitting—has almost no effect. There are several reasons for this, given Gurdjieff's view of ordinary consciousness.

First, because ordinary people are plagued by shifting identities with disparate and often conflicting desires, the unwitting prayers of various identities contradict and largely cancel one another. Gurdjieff argued that we all have many different identity states, and some of them are at odds with one another. Random alternations of "I desire X," and "I'm not interested in X, give me Y," and "I hate X," and so on, do not give any consistent message to higher levels of the universe.

Another obstacle to effective prayer is our inability to be *consciously* intense. Ordinary emotions, triggered by external events and reacting predictably and mechanically with our personality patterns, may temporarily produce strong desires, strong formal or unwitting prayers; but external events change and the instigating desires disappear. A person in a life-threatening situation may genuinely and intensely pray, "Dear God, save my loved one's life and I will never sin again!" The loved one recovers (which may or may not have any relation to this prayer), the stress disappears, and the promise never to sin again fades away.

This lack of control over emotions is also related to the uncontrolled alterations in what Gurdjieff termed our "false personalities," or subselves, what I have called identity states.[2] Most "false personalities" have specific emotional cores, so when a situation evokes different emotions it can cause a change from one "false personality" to another. The new on-stage subself isn't interested in the same things the previous one was. The thing that makes these subselves "false" personalities is that we unwittingly identify with them at the time they are active and thus mistake them for our whole personality, our whole self.

Effective petitionary prayer would be possible for a person who was genuinely conscious; who, at will and for extended periods, deliberately summoned up his or her intellectual and emotional intensity to consciously pray; and who prayed "from" his or her more integrated and constructive subpersonalities or from his or her essence.[3]

Is Prayer Magic?

Some might object that this emphasis on controlling the quality of consciousness and emotion to achieve more effective prayer smacks of magic or some sort of power play: If I am *deliberately* intense, if I create an emotion, then can I force God (or something at some higher level) to give me what I want? Am I at least getting better odds by my actions? In one sense yes, in another no.

Gurdjieff made a somewhat paradoxical statement on this subject: "Work as if everything depends on work. Pray as if everything depends on prayer." What did he mean?

Gurdjieff felt strongly that we must work on understanding and transforming ourselves with no expectation of receiving any sort of outside help, natural or supernatural. Only *I* can transform myself, only *my* efforts count. The strength I have is the strength that comes from making efforts. I cannot grow stronger muscles by just wishing for them, nor can someone else magically make my muscles stronger. I have to push and pull and strain, pushing myself to and a little beyond my limits over and over again: then I get stronger muscles. Why should psychological growth be any different? From this view it seems clear that wishing and praying are fantasies that divert us from what we actually need to do, so we are better off to just get on with the work.

Yet Gurdjieff also said to pray as if everything depended on prayer, to beseech help from a higher level, recognizing that our work efforts will come to nothing unless we are helped from above. After all, the ordinary self that makes efforts is something of an illusion from the mystical point of view, so it is the higher self that really works. In his practical teaching he emphasized work effort, not prayer, probably because he found that his students had so many distorted and incorrect ideas about ideas like prayer that there was no point in teaching much about it until they had done enough psychological work on themselves to clean out the aspects of false personality that would otherwise sabotage most efforts at genuine prayer.

State-specific Views on Prayer

The paradox between the injunctions to work as if everything depended on effort and to pray as if everything depended on prayer can only be partially resolved in our ordinary state of consciousness. I have found that a fuller resolution requires considerations derived from altered states of consciousness.

When I proposed the idea of *state-specific* sciences some years ago I noted that our ordinary state of consciousness is limited and arbitrary in many ways.[4] In our ordinary state we do not have access to the full range of human perceptions, logics, emotions, and possibilities of action, but only to a specialized selection of them. (The point is further elaborated in the discussion of enlightenment in chapter 20.) This selection is generally highly useful for everyday problems of survival and fulfillment in our particular culture (we call a person neurotic or stupid or crazy if it is not), but quite inadequate for other human issues that go beyond the everyday.

From the point of view of my ordinary consciousness, for example, it is perfectly clear that everything depends on my own efforts. Realistically I also recognize that the effects of my efforts are modified by the desires of others, the limits imposed by physical laws, and chance. I can pray for a million dollars to materialize in the middle of the floor so I can finance my next research project. I'm sure it's a worthy project, but nothing happens. I'd be better off reading books on how to raise funds through normal channels. If higher levels intervene they do so rarely, and often in ways that are contradictory to what I (my ordinary-consciousness I) think that I want. Ordinary consciousness makes it clear that we are separate, finite, quite undivine beings who had better depend on our own efforts.

As I write this in my ordinary state of consciousness, however, I dimly remember insights and understandings I have had in some altered states. At times it has been perfectly clear to me that we are not separate, isolated beings; that we are a part of a divine plan; that our prayers come from our deeper selves, which are also a part of that plan; and that they are answered in the ways that are best for our evolution. From the altered-states perspective I know how limited my ordinary perspective is, and how foolish I am, in my ordinary state, to identify completely with my ordinary perspective as if it were all of the truth.

Unfortunately these are "dim" memories. If I completely identify with my ordinary-states perspective, I can easily talk myself out of them: They were strange ideas in a state of temporary "craziness," and are best ignored. Yet I know that the next time I consider these ideas while in an altered state they will not be "dim," they will be as clear and obviously truthful as the ideas I have now in my ordinary state. So I have learned to try to remember that they are part of my overall understanding and should not be simply ignored, even if they may not see to be too applicable to everyday life.

This does not mean, incidentally, that altered-states knowledge is always true, just that it is part of our overall knowledge base as fully functioning human beings. Altered-states knowledge, like ordinary knowledge, needs to be constantly tested, refined, and developed.

The paradox about work being all and prayer being all, then, is a paradox only from the limitations of a single state of consciousness. When I use my intelligence in either my ordinary state or in an altered state to remember that there are other points of view, and that all these points of view may be fragmentary rather than any one being "truer" than any other, the paradox disappears.

Conscious Prayer

Gurdjieff dismissed most prayer as useless fantasy, but he described a process of *conscious prayer* that was effective.[5] Conscious prayer is a process of *recapitulation*, in which you consciously remind yourself of your knowledge and intentions. The effectiveness of such recapitulation is a function of the degree of consciousness we bring to it.

Suppose you decide, "I want to be serious." Merely praying this over and over mechanically, while daydreaming about other things you'd rather be doing, is a waste of time. To be effective, when you say "I" you must understand what you know about "I." For Gurdjieff this would mean:

- realizing that you had many "I's" rather than a single unified "I"
- realizing that many of the identity states (see chapter 13) we accept as "I" when they are active have mutually contradictory desires and perspectives

• feeling your desire to create a single, unified "I"

When you say "want," you have to recall, for example:

• how these many "I's" in you have many wants
• how these wants come and go with your moods
• what you know about creating a want that carries more weight than these mechanical wants

When you say "to be," what does "being" mean? Is it only mechanical being, in the sense of simply existing, or is it the being of a person who can *do*, a "being" that has will?

How exactly do you define "serious"? How much of that definition is your own and how much is your superego's, forced on you in the innocence of childhood?

Gurdjieff believed that conscious prayer can be very effective, so you had better be very clear about exactly what it is you want.

In many ways Gurdjieff's description of conscious prayer fits the definition of meditation given at the beginning of this chapter better than the definition of petitionary prayer. Indeed Gurdjieff states that the focused, conscious attention and recapitulation in consciously praying something like, "God have mercy upon me!" may well have the effects that God is being asked to provide. This throws us back to the paradox: Work as if everything depends on effort. Pray as if everything depends on prayer. From one point of view the effort of conscious prayer automatically, lawfully, produces beneficial results, including possible connections to higher levels of our selves. From another point of view our efforts may be pleasing to higher aspects of being and attract help and blessings. Probably both and neither views are true, depending on your state of consciousness and being.

Shall We Pray?

Prayer is not fashionable in today's modern growth circles; indeed it is ridiculous given the biases of scientism. The cultural rejection of prayer makes it difficult for many of us to seriously try it. My own psychological, parapsychological, and altered-states studies, as well as personal experience, have convinced me that prayer is a valuable avenue for our growth, and I intend to spend more time in prayer. The "scientific psychologist" part of me winces as I write the above statement: Your colleagues will ridicule you for saying such a thing! But this is what I have learned in examining personal psychological growth, and that is what I will say. I do not know exactly what we should pray for, but I think we would do well to pray for further understanding of ourselves, and wisdom in what to pray for.

Suggested Reading

Nicoll, Maurice. 1970. Note on prayer and the teaching about prayer in the work. *Psychological Commentaries on the Teaching of G. I. Gurdjieff and P. D. Ouspensky*. London: Stuart & Watkins. 155–59.

Ouspensky, P. D. 1949. *In Search of the Miraculous*. New York: Harcourt, Brace & World.

Tart, Charles T. 1972. States of consciousness and state-specific sciences. *Science* 176:1203–10.

_____. 1983. *Transpersonal Psychologies*. El Cerrito, Calif.: Psychological Processes.

CHAPTER 20

Altered States of Consciousness and the Search for Enlightenment

In the East the idea of "enlightenment" is familiar and forms an essential part of traditions such as Hinduism Buddhism. For Westerners, however, the concept of enlightenment is often clouded in confusion and misconception.[1] Perhaps our grounding in the "reality" of consensus consciousness has contributed to this. My work has led me to believe that altered states of consciousness are essential to full enlightenment.

This chapter will address three main ideas: What are altered states of consciousness? What do we mean by enlightenment? What are some ways in which various altered states can be used for growth toward enlightenment?

What Are Altered States of Consciousness?

I would like to be able to discuss enlightenment and altered states from an exclusively scientific perspective, citing evidence from dozens of experiments, and drawing on knowledge tested through the critical review of hundreds of colleagues. Unfortunately, if I restricted myself to this kind of scientific knowledge, I would have almost nothing to say about enlightenment.

Western scientific knowledge about altered states is uneven. For some states, such as hypnosis, we have made a good beginning at detailed scientific knowledge. For others, such as those that can arise from meditative practices, we know hardly anything at all. I have been studying altered states long enough to believe I understand some things about them that have not yet been scientifically investigated, and I will draw on this personal knowledge in this chapter.

My personal interest in altered states began when I was a child. For as far back as I can remember my dream life was real and vivid. My parents, being "normal," taught me that dreams were not "real," and that I needn't pay attention to them, but my direct experience contradicted the usual Western point of view. How could people dismiss such real aspects of life? Why did I forget my dreams so readily? How could I improve the quality of my dream life? One question that especially intrigued me: I could fly in dreams by a certain act of will: Why couldn't I make that same act work in waking life so I could fly here?

States of Consciousness

Let us start by sharpening our use of the term "state of consciousness."[2] For example, if I asked, "Are you experiencing a nighttime dream right now, just dreaming that you are here listening to me, but soon you'll wake up at home in bed?" I would not expect you to say yes. Occasionally people raise their hands when I've asked this in lectures, but such people want to play word games or be philosophical, even though I've said I'm using these words with their ordinary meaning. If I ask these people whether they are willing to bet me fifty dollars that they will wake up in bed from this dream in five minutes, there are no takers!

We make common-sense distinctions about states. There is a pattern to our mental functioning that we can examine, and after examining, classify. If we examine the pattern of our mental functioning at this moment, it doesn't feel like the pattern we usually call "dreaming," it feels like the pattern we call "waking" or "ordinary consciousness." The difference is clear; and, for the vast majority of us, dreaming is discretely different from waking.

To be more precise: In my systems approach to understanding states I defined a discrete state of consciousness (or d-SoC) *for a given individual* (individual differences are important here) as "a unique *configuration* or *system* of psychological structures or subsystems." The "parts" or aspects of the mind we can distinguish for analytical purposes are arranged in a certain kind of pattern or system. There is always some variation in the exact way our mind functions at any moment, even though the pattern remains recognizably the same.

"The structures operative within a discrete state of consciousness make up a *system* where the operation of the parts, the psychological structures . . . stabilize each other's functioning by feedback control, so that the system, the d-SoC, maintains its overall pattern of functioning in spite of changes in the environment."[3] I can suddenly clap my hands, you are startled: There was a change in the environment and your momentary internal mental functioning, but you don't suddenly go into some state of "trance," attain enlightenment, pass out, and so on. Your state of consciousness maintains its integrity in a changing world.

A state is an *altered* state if it is significantly and discretely different from some baseline to which we want to compare it. Since we usually take ordinary waking consciousness as our standard of comparison, a state like nocturnal dreaming is an altered state. Other well-known examples of altered states are the hypnotic state; states induced by psychoactive drugs such as alcohol; states centered around strong emotions, such as rage, panic, depression, and elation; and states that can be induced by meditative practices.

The Power of Altered States: Hypnosis

My childhood interest in dreams was one factor in my choice to become a psychologist, and many of my early research projects involved dreaming. The altered state that most impressed me early in my research career, however, was hypnosis, and it illustrates the enormous power of altered states to change "reality."

To induce hypnosis I would sit down with a volunteer who wanted to be hypnotized. We were both "normal" people. With our eyes we saw the same room around us that others saw, with our ears we heard the ordinary and "real" sounds in the room, smelled what smells were there, and felt the solidity of the real objects in the room. Then I began to talk to the subject. We gave the style of talking the special name of a "hypnotic induction procedure," but basically it was just talking. The subject had not been given any powerful drugs, was not in a special environment, had nothing external done to her brain . . . and yet, with a talented subject, in twenty minutes I could change her universe.

With a few words the subject could not lift her arm. With a few more she heard voices talking when no one was there. A few more words and she could open her eyes and see something that no one else could see; or, with the right suggestion, an object in plain sight in the room could be made invisible to her.

Another suggestion and the subject would have a dream, sometimes as vivid or more vivid than her nighttime dreams. Another suggestion and the subject would forget the present and be five years old, feeling and acting as she did when she was five. Another suggestion, and when she woke up she would not remember what had happened while she was hypnotized.

Hypnosis can abolish a sense as basic as pain. In spite of the number of times I have seen it a test procedure we called "anosmia to ammonia" still amazes me. I would tell a subject that he could no longer smell anything. Then I would hold a bottle of household ammonia an inch under his nose and ask him to take a good sniff. The smell of ammonia is not only a strong *smell*, it is an extremely painful sensation, as if your nostrils were set on fire. (If you are inclined to refresh your memory I advise starting with *very small* sniff!) A talented hypnotic subject would take a deep sniff, while I winced. No reaction. No tears would form in his eyes, he wouldn't jerk his head away, or show signs that anything was wrong. "Did you smell anything?" I would ask. "No."

So-called ordinary reality can disappear as a result of a few minutes of talking. Yet in *Waking Up* I have shown that the induction procedure for creating "ordinary consciousness" (or consensus trance, as I prefer to call it) is even stronger than that for hypnosis.[4] Given this, can we really take the "common-sense" wisdom of ordinary consciousness for granted?

What Is Enlightenment?

A part of my mind is highly amused when I plan to write about the nature of enlightenment. What presumption! Isn't enlightenment something possessed only by superhuman beings, and understood only by them? What in the world can a Western psychologist have to say about it? Well, we have to start somewhere.

Many of the most important aspects of enlightenment are nonverbal. Words cannot capture the essence of this knowledge. Enlightenment also involves knowledge that we cannot adequately comprehend in our ordinary state of consciousness; yet here we are, using words in our ordinary state of consciousness. Nevertheless, words in our ordinary state can be *useful* in thinking about enlightenment, especially if we are careful not to confuse the words with the realities. Let's consider some aspects of what enlightenment is.

Enlightenment as a Continuum

I find it helpful to think about enlightenment as a continuum rather than an all-or-none state. Seeing it as a totally-incomprehensible-to-us absolute end point, with no intermediate steps, makes it difficult to talk about and difficult to do anything about. Compared to the rest of us, for example, a pilot is enlightened about flying airplanes, but she didn't get that way in a single, magical act. She studied for a long time, moving along a continuum from being completely unenlightened about flying to knowing more and more about it. When we think about enlightenment on a continuum, we can see it as a *process*, not just a final state, and as a process in which we can take part.

Enlightenment is a kind of intelligence. This intelligence is emotional and intuitive as well as intellectual; it has the "logics" of several states of consciousness available, rather than only the logic of consensus consciousness.

Basic Assumptions

We will take the following assumptions as given for the purposes of this chapter, even though each could be explored at length in some other context.

1. *Awareness is.* Our basic ability to have experiences, to know that we are, to be aware of things, has never been satisfactorily explained in terms of anything else. Current Western science likes to assume that awareness will be explained as an aspect of brain functioning, reduced to "nothing but" some action of the brain; but this is an item of current faith and fashion, not good science. Although I do not believe we will ever be able to "explain" awareness in terms of something else, we can be aware: That is an axiom.

2. *A primary function of consciousness is the simulation of the environment.* Consciousness, as opposed to basic awareness, is that enormously elaborated, educated, habituated, and conditioned system we normally experience as mind. Consciousness is the creation of an internal representation of the outside world and of oneself, such that we have a good-quality "map" of the world and our place in it.[5] Remember the flight-simulator analogy we discussed in chapter 16? Modern science has created a useful model of mental functioning in which we "live inside" a simulator. "Consciousness" is seen as being inside the brain. Consciousness in itself has no *direct* access to the world around us (ignoring for now the reality of extrasensory perception, as conventional scientists do), but only to processes inside the brain. These brain processes take the information that our senses pro-

vide us about the world and create a simulation of that world, just as the machinery of the flight simulator creates a simulation of being in an airplane. This brain simulation is our major tool for coping with ordinary reality, and so it is important that the simulation be accurate. The degree to which the simulation is accurate is an aspect of enlightenment. The degree to which the simulation is a poor representation of external reality, and the degree to which we mistakenly identify the simulation—experienced reality—with actual reality, are important aspects of lack of enlightenment.

3. *We have a basic nature.* To be "human" is to have characteristics, potentials, limits. It is important, however, not to confuse what our ultimate nature is or might be with what we currently think it is, or with what our culture has told us it is.

4. *We have an acquired nature.* Our basic nature has been subjected to an enormous amount of shaping, bending, conditioning, indoctrination, development, repression, and so on in the course of our personal enculturation. Our perception, our thinking, our feelings, our assumptions and intuitions, and our behaviors have all been strongly molded. This has given us many useful skills and many insane sources of useless suffering. It is a great mistake to confuse our acquired nature, the product of our cultural and personal histories, with our basic nature. Most people do make this confusion and thus cut themselves off from many basic human possibilities.

The Tool Analogy

We can now consider the question of what enlightenment is by means of an analogy.

A carpenter is a person who has to solve a variety of problems in the physical world by using tools to build things. A good carpenter has many tools available (including the necessary ones) and knows how to use them. He has hammers, saws, rulers, squares, nails, pencils, and so on. He uses the saws to cut, not to hammer; the hammer to drive nails, not to chop through boards; and so on. A poor carpenter would be one who doesn't have the necessary tools to do the job, or who can't improvise adequately from the tools at hand. A poor carpenter would also be one who has the necessary tools but doesn't know how to use them properly, or, for whatever reason, *won't* use them properly.

These two dimensions of adequacy in carpentry—having the right tools and knowing how to use them properly—are analogous to two dimensions of enlightenment. The tools are like the skills (including access to various altered states) that you have. The ability to use each tool intelligently and properly, according to its inherent characteristics and the needs of the job, is analogous to the degree of enlightenment you show within a particular state of consciousness.

Thus there are two independent dimensions of enlightenment for any person. What states are available to you, with their particular characteristics, talents, and costs? We will call that the *available-states dimension* of enlightenment. Within any of these states how intelligently do you understand and use the characteristics of that state? We will call that kind of intelligence the *within-states dimension* of enlightenment.

A person may be relatively enlightened on one of these dimensions and not on another. Like a carpenter with only a few tools a person might be "stuck" in consensus consciousness, for example, with no access to altered states; yet she may be very mature, intelligent, and enlightened in the way she uses the mental qualities she has. (Since "ordinary consciousness" has unavoidable connotations of "normality," I use the term *consensus consciousness* to remind us how much our everyday consciousness has been shaped by the consensus of belief in our particular culture.)[6]

She is relatively enlightened within that one state, but deficient in access to other states. Another person might be like a sloppy carpenter who has access to many tools but uses them poorly. I have certainly known people who could enter many exotic altered states, but whose unintelligent and neurotic behavior in several states showed they certainly weren't very enlightened.

Qualities of Within-state Enlightenment

Let's look more closely at the qualities we would expect of within-state enlightenment.

1. *The ability to focus one's awareness as desired*, within the limits of the natural capacity of that state. Such limits should be found by effort, not by preestablished beliefs that might artificially limit the capacity. Thus one could focus on any aspect of the state and bring it to awareness. Since initial awareness is usually the prerequisite for using a capacity, this sets the stage for use.

2. *The ability to focus awareness as required by your survival and growth needs.* You might desire, for instance, to focus on a pleasing aspect of a situation you are in, say the taste of a good meal you are eating. But if there is a potentially dangerous aspect of the situation you had better perceive *it,* even if it is unpleasant and you would rather be aware of pleasant things. The lurking figure outside the window may frighten you and spoil your meal, but you are more able to do something constructive in this situation if you know about the figure than if you keep it out of your conscious awareness. Giving priority to basic needs over less important desires is a quality of within-state enlightenment.

3. *Undistorted perception/simulation of the world, within the inherent limits of the state.* In any state, for example, the nature of the human eye sets some ultimate limits on what can be visually perceived; but the constructed nature of visual perception after the initial stimulation of the eye can vary greatly in its accuracy. Perceiving people as threatening when they are friendly, for example, can lead to treating them in a hostile manner and evoking a consequent hostile reaction, all of which is unenlightened and leads to useless suffering.

4. *Recognition of the state of consciousness you are currently in, and knowledge of its advantages and disadvantages, leading to optimal use of the state.* I am not sure that there is any one state of consciousness that offers totally unlimited and undistorted perception of the world around us. Every state that I know of seems to offer perceptual, cognitive, and emotional advantages and disadvantages.

5. *Recognition that your current state of consciousness may not be very useful for handling your current life-situation.* This quality of enlightenment also applies to the available-states dimension.

Qualities of Available-states Enlightenment

What are some of the qualities of the available-states dimension of enlightenment?

1. *The recognition that you are in a state that may not be useful, or at least not optimal, for dealing with a current situation.* You might be called on, for example, to help settle an argument between lovers, but be in a state of rage from an earlier, unrelated encounter with someone else. A state of rage might be highly useful for saving your life in certain kinds of situations where you are at-

tacked, but its characteristics do not include the calm sensitivity about hurt feelings between lovers that are required to help them remember their basic love after their argument.

2. *Knowing what state is optimal for the situation you are currently in and knowing how to end your current, inappropriate state and induce the optimal one.* If you recognize your current state and understand it enough to know it is not a good one in which to deal with your current situation, you could try to postpone action until you happen to be in a more appropriate state.

3. *Knowledge and action in any particular state must be tempered by the memory of knowledge gained in other states of consciousness.* For example, I may be in a state of rage. As I get the advantage of my opponent it is perfectly "natural" and "reasonable," given my state, to want to destroy him utterly and to enjoy destroying him. That is the inherent "logic" of a state of rage. There may be relatively unenlightened inhibition of my urge to destroy: It may be checked by the emotional conditioning of my superego, or by my fear of the consequences of my action. More enlightened control may occur if, in my state of rage, I recall other states in which I recognize our kinship and have compassion for my opponent. Then I may terminate my state of rage and enter a more appropriate state, assuming that compassion is a higher value for me than winning every fight. If I cannot voluntarily end the state of rage at will, I can at least keep myself from acting wholeheartedly on the basis of my current rage.

Suppose you are in some state where you are full of compassion, but you are dealing with someone who is enraged. The enraged state may be available to you: You could use the other's rage as an induction technique to enrage yourself if you thought that would be the optimal state to deal with your opponent. Or you could draw on your personal memory of what it is like to be enraged to more fully understand the enraged person you are dealing with, and then act compassionately in a more effective way because of this available-states enlightenment.

This ability to recognize what state you are in and draw on relevant knowledge from other states, as well as having the ability to enter those other states if you desire, implies some aspect of consciousness, of our basic awareness, that transcends any particular state we are in at the time. The nature of that quality is of profound interest, and I suspect some of the higher types of Buddhist meditation practices deal with it.

4. *Access to multiple states of consciousness allows sharper discrimination between our basic and our acquired natures.* The bulk of the conditioning and shaping of our acquired nature, our enculturation, took place in consensus consciousness or in some emotional state that is ordinarily accessed from consensus consciousness. Sometimes simply being in an altered state gives an "outside" perspective on the conditioned, restrictive quality of consensus consciousness or of some emotional states, due to the nature of the "logic" inherent in the altered state, or may at least form a basis for focused work on the problems in the other states.

5. *A realistic assessment of your capacities, including the fact that at present some may only be potentials requiring development.* A quality experienced in a particular state may need considerable work to become robust and usable in that state, or for you to learn to transfer that quality into some other state, such as consensus consciousness. An experience of great compassion experienced in a meditative state, for example, may carry over into consensus consciousness, making you feel like an enlightened being—until someone insults you and the feeling of compassion is immediately replaced by anger. This kind of discrimination between developed reality and potential is particularly important when there is excessive attachment to an altered-states experience, such that you want to believe that you have made it permanent.

Enlightenment and Suffering

Much of our suffering is useless suffering: We unwittingly create it through unenlightened, unintelligent use of our human capacities. We misperceive the world or our own self, act in a way that is contrary to the realities of our situation, and then reap the unpleasant consequences. Within-state enlightenment leads to more realistic perception of the world and our selves, and consequently the more effective action that results can eliminate much useless suffering.

Much of our suffering occurs in various altered states, particularly emotional states, as well as in consensus consciousness. Emotions are powerful conditioners. By understanding the nature of altered states we can relieve suffering in those states: The remedy to suffering in some particular state is often specific to that state, and our attempts to apply a remedy suitable to some other state lead to frustration and more suffering. For example, my fear may trigger an altered state and consequent maladaptive behavior. I spend many hours with a psychotherapist trying to get at the root of this fear. Unfortunately the hours with the therapist are in consensus consciousness, but the heart of the fear is in experiences only fully accessible in the altered state, so the therapy proves only partially effective.

How Can We Use Altered States to Seek Enlightenment?

I believe there are many, highly specific uses of various altered states in seeking enlightenment, but this belief goes well beyond well-established Western scientific knowledge. The primary use of altered states, though, is to gain a perspective on consensus consciousness that reveals many of its arbitrary, crippling, unenlightened characteristics. Such a perspective can both motivate us to try to change our consensus consciousness in a more enlightened way, and sometimes give us specific insights into the kind of changes we need to make. Consensus consciousness holds an immense power over us, and this opportunity to gain a more enlightened perspective on consensus consciousness is a very great gift indeed.[7]

Let us now look at some specific altered states with the question in mind, "How could a person seeking more enlightenment use each of these states to grow?" All of these altered states involve risks and can also be used for other purposes than seeking enlightenment, including ways that increase the suffering of the user and the people with whom the user interacts. Here, however, we will focus on intelligent, growthful uses of these states.

Dreaming

To begin to use dreams for growth we must overcome the cultural conditioning that dismisses and trivializes them as not "real." You should not confuse them with waking life, but you should strive to discover what their own unique reality is.

Analysis

A major growth use for dreams, practiced by some people in Western culture, has been to analyze them for clues about hidden aspects of waking life. This is an intelligent use: Dreams can tell us things about ourselves and our attitudes that we did not consciously know before. Science does not know whether this is actually more efficient than studying experiences from waking life for clues to the hidden sides of ourselves, but almost any kind of self-study can contribute to enlightenment. Studying waking, consensus-consciousness experiences can contribute to within-state enlightenment about consensus consciousness. Study of your dream experience can also contribute to within-state enlightenment about consensus consciousness *and* may lead toward within-state enlightenment in the dreaming state, as well as developing some available-states enlightenment.

Analogy

A second major growth use for dreams is analogical. Most dreams illustrate a much less enlightened functioning of consciousness than is possible in consensus consciousness. In dreams we find ourselves in a world of experience, just as we live in a world of experience in waking life. In the dream world we are often passive toward the events of this world when being active could have led to much more satisfying experiences. We often forget who we are, what our real values are. We often do not remember relevant knowledge that would greatly improve our ability to cope with dream situations. How many times, for example, have you had some very frustrating dream where you were stupidly unable to operate some device, like a telephone, that you can use perfectly competently in waking life? In this sense of comparatively wide access to our accumulated knowledge and the ability to take an active role in shaping our world, consensus consciousness is a higher or more enlightened state of consciousness than dream consciousness.

Once we have established the idea of a more enlightened state of consciousness in this way we can apply it to consensus consciousness: Is there a possibility of some new state that is as superior in this way to consensus consciousness as consensus consciousness can be to dream consciousness? Grasping the possibility can lead to beginning the work toward such states as Gurdjieff called real awakening.[8]

Creative Problem Solving

A third growth use for dreams is creative problem solving. Sometimes a dream will spontaneously happen in a way that gives us important insights into some ordinary life problem. It is possible to use dream incubation techniques, in which waking procedures applied before sleep increase the probability that useful, insightful dreams will occur.[9]

Lucid Dreaming

One of the most exciting possibilities for growth in the dream state is its use as a gateway or stepping-stone to other altered states of consciousness. (This is another area in which I suspect Buddhist knowledge will be very helpful.) The state we know something about in current Western knowledge is *lucid dreaming,* which we have discussed in Part 1 of this book. Lucid dreaming is much more enlightened than ordinary dreaming consciousness.

Lucid dreaming is a state in which there is a major shift in the quality of dreaming consciousness, such that (1) you know you are dreaming and (2) new (to usual dreaming) abilities are added to consciousness that make it much closer to the functioning of consensus consciousness than dream consciousness. These abilities include not only the within-state enlightenment quality of knowing your state (knowing that you are in a dream); they also include enhanced abilities to recall relevant ordinary-world knowledge about things, to plan, to exercise will, to question the apparent reality and plot of the dream and take deliberate action instead of being passively swept along by the dream action. You are still located in the dream world, but the pattern of functioning of your consciousness is much more like its waking style than its ordinary dreaming style.

Creative problem solving can thus occur directly within the dream. One of the most creative procedures is to seek (or create) a "wise man" or "wise woman" in your lucid dream and hold a conversation with him or her. One of the least useful applications of lucid dreaming is to simply gratify consensus consciousness wishes and fantasies; it is much better to use this opportunity to study yourself. Not that I'm against pleasure, but I do think it's wasteful to throw away opportunities that could lead to real growth and true happiness.

Just as the comparative enlightenment of consensus consciousness relative to ordinary dreaming can suggest the possibility of "waking up" from consensus consciousness, lucid dreaming can similarly suggest the possibility of "lucid waking." There is a state of lucidity attainable from the waking state, and from this point of view consensus consciousness is indeed a "waking dream."[10]

Emotional States

Emotional states, like dreams, are universal in normal human beings. Emotions per se should be distinguished from emotional states. Within consensus consciousness or various other altered states we can experience mild to moderate intensities of emotions; but the *pattern* of consciousness is not basically altered from what it was before the emotion occurred. You can be a little angry, moderately sad, somewhat excited, all within consensus consciousness. As emotions increase in intensity, however, they induce a discrete altered state organized around that emotion. When we speak of rage, for example, or depression or mania, we speak of states, more than just strong amounts of anger or sadness or excitement. The emotion in such altered states "constellates" other mental processes around it so perception and cognition alter their style to support the dominant emotion.

Our Western attitudes toward emotions and emotional states are not very sane, and this interferes with possible enlightened use of such states. We become attached to positive emotions and emotional states, try to maintain them when they are no longer appropriate, and generate them through fantasy. This then cuts us off from reality and thus sows the seeds of future suffering. We shun negative emotions and states even when they might be appropriate, or become attached to them and covertly generate them for unconscious reasons.

G. I. Gurdjieff stated that we have emotional "brains," that our emotions should perceive and evaluate data and guide us intelligently in reality. Such functioning of our emotions is all too rare, so our emotional "brains" remain at childish, undeveloped, and usually neurotic levels. I suspect there are many enlightening uses of emotions within and across states of consciousness, but we are not developed enough to use them effectively. If psychotherapy were put in a context of enlightenment rather than simply adjusting to a culture that is itself neurotic, we would see rapid progress here. Since the evolving field of transpersonal psychology has that aim, we should see interesting developments.

Sexual States of Consciousness

Sexual ecstasy is an excellent example of an emotional state. A small degree of sexual interest or excitement is possible within consensus consciousness or other altered states without fundamentally affecting the organization and pattern of that state. Beyond a certain point, however, the sexual excitement becomes the central organizing point of consciousness, and most other perceptions and thoughts become sexualized. A gesture that ordinarily evokes no emotions is perceived as obviously seductive, and further contributes to the intensity of the sexual state.

There are degrees of intensity within the sexual state, and there may even be several discrete sexual states for some people. Consciousness during orgasm, for instance, can be a discrete state quite separable in more than a quantitative way from the sexual state of consciousness preceding it.

Sexual states clearly illustrate the power of the processes of attachment and of the ability of a state to constellate perception, thought, and feeling in a highly particularistic, biased way. Take the "obviously" seductive quality of another's gesture we mentioned above: Perhaps it is a correct perception of a sexual signal that you might overlook if you were not in a sexual state of consciousness; but can you simultaneously remember that there are alternative, nonsexual perceptions of that gesture that will be "obviously" true in other, nonsexual states? Can you learn to enjoy the sexualized quality of that gesture and the way it feeds your own excitement without becoming so attached to that pleasure and maintaining it that you ignore your other across-states knowledge about the possible meaning of that gesture? Perhaps the other person is expressing agitation, not sexual desire, and compassionate understanding would be more appropriate than further sexual behavior? Can you draw knowledge from the available-states dimension of enlightenment and remember that you value compassion as well as sexual pleasure?

It may be difficult to learn aspects of enlightenment within the sexual state because it is exceptionally powerful. On the other hand the sensitization to these processes that can be achieved in a sexual state can let us recognize them in other contexts where they may not be so obvious.[11]

Psychedelic Drug-induced States

In workshops on the nature of consciousness I sometimes give the participants a task: Describe your qualities when you were a young child, four to six years of age, emphasizing the qualities that are different from the way you are now. I then list the qualities people report, divided into positive (people wish they were more like that now) and negative.

The positive qualities from childhood show great similarities from group to group. They include living more in the here-and-now; being more open to new experience; a vitality and happiness in just being alive; more feeling of having a natural place in the universe; happiness in experiencing the simple, basic things of life; and perceiving the world as more sensorially intense and alive. In the course of becoming adults we somehow become closed, stale, and abstracted, cut off from the natural vitality and beauty of the world around us. I use this exercise to generate curiosity about how our consciousness was molded as we grew up.

I then describe my study of the nature of marijuana intoxication in experienced users.[12] The desirable, childlike characteristics of consciousness listed by my workshop group turn out to be some of the major characteristics of marijuana intoxication.

The deliberate use of psychedelic drugs in the pursuit of enlightenment is controversial in the West because the very idea of enlightenment is generally not accepted. When connected with drugs, which are thought to produce many illusions, the concept of enlightenment is further degraded as one more kind of illusion. In the East some spiritual teachers condemn the use of psychedelic drugs as producing inferior counterfeits of enlightenment, while others sometimes use them.[13]

When I tell my workshop participants that the qualities of consciousness they find desirable are common in marijuana intoxication I am not trying to persuade them to use marijuana. The important point is to realize how much of our basic nature has been repressed in developing our acquired nature, and to realize there are ways to regain our full capacities. Marijuana intoxication is one way. Like any altered state it has disadvantages as well as advantages. Some meditative practices, psychotherapy practices, sensory awareness training, and self-remembering techniques, among others, can allow us to regain some of those qualities of consciousness.

Nevertheless psychedelic and psychoactive drugs are common and with us to stay, regardless of attempts to legislate them away. Indeed new ones are being invented all the time. My observations of Westerners who have used psychedelic drugs, such as marijuana or LSD, indicate that for some of them the results are enlightening in the sense that the glimpses of alternative ways of functioning and of more enlightened ways of being that they have motivate them to begin other spiritual practices to make these possibilities *realities* in their everyday lives. Others do not show any obvious signs of personal growth as a result of their psychedelic drug use, and some become more obviously disturbed and unenlightened.

We need research to learn how to minimize the negative effects of psychedelic drugs and optimize their enlightening effects. Western science, once biases against altered states in general are overcome, has the capacity to do such research within the "personal growth" portion of the spectrum of enlightenment.

Lucid Waking

Just as we can have a lucid dream, in which we "wake up" in terms of mental functioning, we can similarly transform consensus consciousness to become more lucid. The technique I am most familiar with is

what Gurdjieff called "self-remembering," practiced as a part of all ordinary life. Self-remembering involves deliberately splitting your attention into two parts. The ordinary part gets involved in the usual way
in what is happening in your world and your reactions to it. The extraordinary part monitors the first part in a *nonjudgmental* way, producing genuine self-consciousness: an awareness of being aware.[14]

Self-remembering can lead to many insights about the automatic,
semiconscious aspects of our mental functioning. As you become able
to prolong the act of self-remembering it develops into a discretely
different state from consensus consciousness. You have a clearer,
fresher perception of the world around you, experience a more natural
and lucid functioning of both cognition and emotion, and are able to
function in a less automatic, more intelligent way. The self-remembering state seems more enlightened than consensus consciousness.

You can also practice the process of self-remembering in a variety
of altered states, with a potential for transforming them in an enlightening way. This process is widely applicable but is, unfortunately,
almost unknown to the Western scientific community.[15]

Asking the Right Questions

In the West we have a large and rather disorganized body of knowledge about altered states of consciousness. One's purposes determine
the kinds of questions one asks about reality, and the kinds of answers
one gets. Our Western questions about altered states have been motivated by a variety of purposes—simple curiosity, the desire to alleviate suffering in others, the pursuit of personal power, and the pursuit
of enlightenment. Our knowledge is relatively deep in some areas,
quite shallow in others.

In Buddhism (as I understand it) the motivation behind the acquisition of knowledge about altered states has been more focused: How
can we alleviate suffering in ourselves and in others? I suspect that has
led to a more coherent body of knowledge, but perhaps one that is
narrower in some ways. I share the desire to alleviate suffering, yet
I'm also just curious. We live in a wonderful, mysterious, intriguing
universe. Altered states are some of those wonders. I hope that these
interchanges between East and West will enrich us all in both satisfying
our curiosity and relieving the suffering of all sentient beings.

Enlightenment. A funny idea, and one I don't really understand.
Yet I certainly understand "endarkenment" far better than I wish I did!
When we honestly reflect back on the many moments of stupidity,

ignorance, malice, inattentions, and craziness in our lives we want there to be something better.

In this chapter and others we have looked at various bits and pieces of that something better, hopefully in a way that gives us some ideas about directions we can try to grow in. Whether it's ordinary state or altered state, psychic phenomena or taking out the garbage, intense relationship or boredom and alienation, though, the key dimension that runs through all is to seek truth above all else and *pay attention!*

Suggested Reading

Ouspensky, P. D. 1949. *In Search of the Miraculous*. New York: Harcourt, Brace & World.

Some more technical ideas of mine on enlightenment can be found in the following:

Tart, Charles T. 1975. Samsara: A psychological view. In T. Tulku, ed. *Reflections of Mind*. Emeryville, Calif.: Dharma Press. 53–68.
———. 1975. *States of Consciousness*. New York: E. P. Dutton.
———, ed. 1975. *Transpersonal Psychologies*. New York: Harper & Row.
———. 1977. Beyond consensus reality: Psychotherapy, altered states of consciousness, and the cultivation of awareness. In O. L. McCabe, ed. *Psychotherapy and Behavior Change: Trends, Innovations and Future Directions*. New York: Grune & Stratton. 173–87.
———. 1977. Drug-induced states of consciousness. In B. Wolman et al., eds. *Handbook of Parapsychology*. New York: Van Nostrand Reinhold. 500–25.
———. 1981. Transpersonal realities or neurophysiological illusions? Toward a dualistic theory of consciousness. In R. Valle and R. von Eckartsberg, eds. *The Metaphors of Consciousness*. New York: Plenum. 199–222.
———. 1989. Parapsychology and our contemporary spiritual crisis. *Fringes of Reason: A Whole Earth Catalog*. New York: Crown.

The Goldstein and the Goldstein and Kornfield books mentioned earlier are also quite relevant in understanding enlightenment, as well as Gurdjieff's ideas:

Goldstein, J. 1987. *The Experience of Insight: A Simple and Direct Guide to Buddhist Meditation*. Boston: Shambhala.
———, and J. Kornfield. 1987. *Seeking the Heart of Wisdom: The Path of Insight Meditation*. Boston: Shambhala.

CHAPTER 21

Going Home

The great spiritual systems all speak of "Home." We feel there is something essential in our being that is of a different and higher nature than the physical world we live in. One of the main goals of the spiritual path is to find the way Home, to recontact our essential nature.

Please read this theme, this chapter, with your heart rather than your head.

The Idea of Home

A Course in Miracles, one of the great channeled works of all time, speaks to this feeling:

This world you seem to live in is not home to you. And somewhere in your mind you know that this is true. A memory of home keeps haunting you, as if there were a place that called you to return, although you do not recognize the voice, nor what it is the voice reminds you of. Yet still you feel an alien here, from somewhere all unknown. Nothing so definite that you could say with certainty you are an exile here. Just a persistent feeling, sometimes not more than a tiny throb, at other times hardly remembered, actively dismissed, but surely to return to mind again.

No one but knows whereof we speak. Yet some try to put by their suffering in games they play to occupy their time, and keep their sadness from them. Others will deny that they are sad, and do not recognize their tears at all. Still others will maintain that what we speak of is illusion, not to be considered more than but a dream. Yet who, in simple honesty, without defensiveness and self-deception, would deny he understands the words we speak?

We speak today for everyone who walks this world, for he is not at home. He goes uncertainly about in endless search, seeking in darkness what he cannot find; not recognizing what it is he seeks. A thousand homes he makes, yet none contents his restless mind. He does not understand he builds in vain.

The home he seeks can not be made by him. There is no substitute for Heaven. All he ever made was hell.

Perhaps you think it is your childhood home that you would find again. The childhood of your body, and its place of shelter, are a memory now so distorted that you merely hold a picture of a past that never happened. Yet there is a Child in you Who seeks His Father's house, and knows that He is alien here. This childhood is eternal, with an innocence that will endure forever. Where this Child shall go is holy ground. It is His holiness that lights up Heaven, and that brings to earth the pure reflection of the light above, wherein are earth and Heaven joined as one.[1]

The Experience of Home

The idea of home is more than just an intuition within us or a statement from a source outside of us. It can be a deep human experience. Both Stephen LaBerge (a pioneer in the study of lucid dreaming, discussed in chapters 1, 2 and 3, and a talented lucid dreamer) and Robert Monroe (whose out-of-the-body experiences (OBEs) are discussed in chapter 2) have had such experiences.

LaBerge describes lucid dreaming as a way of having all sorts of pleasant experiences, but pleasant personal experiences are not enough for our full development. Lucid dreaming can be used in a more growthful way. LaBerge describes a lucid dream experience that reflects the experience of being Home:

Late one summer morning several years ago, I was lying quietly in bed, reviewing the dream I had just awakened from. A vivid image of a road appeared, and by focusing my attention on it, I was able to enter the scene. At this point, I was no longer able to feel my body, from which I concluded I was, in fact, asleep. I found myself driving in my sports car down the dream road, perfectly aware that I was dreaming. I was delighted by the vibrantly beautiful scenery my lucid dream was presenting. After driving a short distance farther, I was confronted with a very attractive, I might say a "dream," of a hitchhiker beside me on the road just ahead. I need hardly say that I felt strongly inclined to stop and pick her up. But I said to myself, "I've had that dream before. How about something new?" So I passed her by, resolving to seek "The Highest" instead. As soon as I opened myself to guidance, my car took off into the air, flying rapidly upward, until it fell behind me like the first stage of a rocket. I continued to fly higher into the clouds, where I passed a cross on a steeple, a star of David, and other religious symbols. As I rose still higher, beyond the clouds, I entered a space that seemed a vast mystical realm: a vast emptiness that was yet full of love; an unbounded space that somehow felt like home. My mood had lifted to corresponding heights, and I began to sing with ecstatic inspiration. The quality of my voice was truly amazing—it spanned the entire range from deepest bass to highest soprano—and I felt as if I were embracing the entire cosmos in the resonance of my voice. As I improvised a melody that seemed more sublime than any I had heard before, the meaning of my song revealed itself and I sang the words, "I praise Thee, O Lord!"

Upon awakening from this remarkable lucid dream, I reflected that it had been one of the most satisfying experiences of my life. It felt as if it were of profound significance. However, I was unable to say in exactly what way it was profound, nor was I able to evaluate its significance. When I tried to understand the words that had somehow contained the full significance of the experience—"I praise Thee, O Lord!"—I realized that, in contrast to my understanding while in the dream, I only now understood the phrase in the sense it would have in our realm. It seemed the esoteric sense that I comprehended while I dreamed was beyond my cloudy understanding while awake. About what the praise did not mean, I can say this: in that transcendent state of unity, there was no "I" and "Thee." It was a place that had no room for "I" and "Thee," but for one only. So which of us, then, was there? My personal "I," my dream-ego sense of individuality, was absent. Thus, what was present was "Thee." But in that realm, "I" was "Thee." So I might just as well have sung "I praise Me . . . " except that there was really no "me" either! In any case, it should be clear why I have called this lucid dream a transpersonal experience.[2]

Monroe similarly describes his OBEs as usually pleasant and adventurous, but sometimes also going well beyond the personal level to the transpersonal. Here is his description of Home:

Three times I have "gone" to a place that I cannot find words to describe accurately. Again, it is this vision, this interpretation, the temporary visitation to this "place" or state of being that brings the message we have heard so often throughout the history of man. I am sure that this may be part of the ultimate heaven as our religions conceive it. It must also be the nirvana, the Samadhi, the supreme experience related to us by the mystics of the ages. It is truly a state of being, very likely interpreted by the individual in many different ways.

To me, it was a place or condition of pure peace, yet exquisite emotion. It was as if you were floating in warm soft clouds where there is no up or down, where nothing exists as a separate piece of matter. The warmth is not merely around you, it is of you and through you. Your perception is dazzled and overwhelmed by the Perfect Environment.

The cloud in which you float is swept by rays of light in shapes and hues that are constantly changing, and each is good as you bathe in them as they pass over you. Ruby-red rays of light, or something beyond what we know as light, because no light ever felt this meaningful. All the colors of the spectrum come and go constantly, never harshly, and each brings a different soothing or restful happiness. It is as if you are within and a part of the clouds surrounding an eternally glowing sunset, and with every changing pattern of living color, you also change. You respond and drink into you the eternity of the blues, yellows, greens, and reds, and the complexities of the intermediates. All are familiar to you. This is where you belong. This is Home.

As you move slowly and effortlessly through the cloud, there is music around you. It is not something of which you become aware. It is there all the time, and you vibrate in harmony with the Music. Again, this is more than the music you knew back there. It is only those harmonies, the delicate and dynamic melodic passages, the multivoiced counterpoint, the poignant over-tones—it is only those that have evoked in you the deep, incoherent emotion back there. The mundane is missing. Choirs of human-sounding voices echo in wordless song. Infinite patterns of strings in all shades of subtle harmony interweave in cyclical yet developing themes, and you resonate with them. There is no source from which the Music comes. It is there, all around you, in you, you are a part of it, and it is you.

It is the purity of a truth of which you have had only a glimpse. This is the feast, and the tiny tidbits you tasted before, back there, had made you hope for the existence of the Whole. The nameless emotion, longing, nostalgia, sense of destiny that you felt back there when you stared at the cloud-layered sunset in Hawaii, when you stood quietly among the tall, waving trees in the silent forest, when a musical selection, passage, or song recalled memories of the past or brought forth a longing for which there was no associated memory, when you longed for the place where you belonged, whether city, town, coun-try, nation, or family—these are now fulfilled. You are Home. You are where you belong. Where you always should have been.

Most important, you are not alone. With you, beside you, interlocked in you are others. They do not have names, nor are you aware of them as shapes, but you know them and you are bonded to them with a great single knowledge. They are exactly like you, they are you, and like you, they are Home. You feel with them, like gentle waves of electricity passing between you, a completeness of love, of which all the facets you have experienced are but segments and incomplete portions. Only here, the emotion is without need of intense display or demonstration. You give and receive as an automatic action, with no delib-erate effort. It is not something you need or that needs you. The "reaching out" is gone. The interchange flows naturally. You are unaware of differences in sex, you yourself as a part of the whole are both male and female, positive and negative, electron and proton. Man-woman love moves to you and from you, parent-child-sibling-idol and idyll and ideal—all interplay in soft waves about you, in you, and through you. You are in perfect balance because you are where you belong. You are Home.

Within all of this, yet not a part of it, you are aware of the source of the entire span of your experience, of you, of the vastness beyond your ability to perceive and/or imagine. Here, you know and easily accept the existence of the Father. The Father, the Creator of all that is or was. You are one of His countless creations. How or why, you do not know. This is not important. You are happy simply because you are in your Right Place, where you truly belong.

Each of the three times I went There, I did not return voluntarily. I came back sadly, reluctantly. Someone helped me return. Each time after I returned, I suffered intense nostalgia and loneliness for days. I felt as an alien might among strangers in a land where things were not "right," where everything and everyone was so different and so "wrong" when compared with where you belonged. Acute loneliness, nostalgia, and something akin to homesickness. So great was it that I have not tried to go There again.[3]

Much of the experiences that people have of Home are what I have termed "state-specific knowledge."[4] They are perfectly clear in the altered state of consciousness in which they occur; but in ordinary consciousness only part of the understanding is clear, vital aspects remain just thin hints. Attenuated as the ordinary-state memory is, it can function as a vital reminder of a greater reality, beckoning us on.

Since his first book Monroe has touched Home again. Once touched, something vital remains. He writes:

On a clear night before going to bed, I might go out and stand on the sun deck and look up. When I do, sometimes the stars disappear and there is nothing but blackness overhead. From beyond the blackness comes an unseen and eternal song that is hauntingly familiar, a reminder, if needed, cutting sharply through the noise of local traffic . . . [5]

I think *A Course in Miracles* is correct: We all have some kind of recollection of Home, however faint. May this be a reminder.

Suggested Reading

Adamson, S., ed. 1985. *Through the Gateway of the Heart: Accounts of Experiences with MDMA and Other Empathogenic Substances*. San Francisco: Four Trees Publications.

Anonymous. 1975. *A Course in Miracles*. Tiburon, Calif.: Foundation for Inner Peace.

Hanh, Thich Nhat. 1987. *Being Peace*. Berkeley, Calif.: Parallax Press.

Goldstein, J., and J. Kornfield. 1987. *Seeking the Heart of Wisdom: The Path of Insight Meditation*. Boston: Shambhala.

Gyatso, T. (The Dalai Lama). 1984. *Kindness, Clarity, and Insight*. Ithaca, N.Y.: Snow Lion Publications (P.O. Box 6483).

LaBerge, S. 1985. *Lucid Dreaming*. Los Angeles: Tarcher.

Masters, R. E. L., and J. Houston. 1966. *The Varieties of Psychedelic Experience*. New York: Holt, Rinehart & Winston.

Metzner, R. 1980. Ten classical metaphors of self-transformation. *Journal of Transpersonal Psychology* 12:47–62.

———. 1986. *Opening to Inner Light: The Transformation of Human Nature and Consciousness.* Los Angeles: Tarcher.

Monroe, R., ed. 1971. *Journeys Out of the Body.* New York: Doubleday.

Monroe, R. S. 1985. *Far Journeys.* New York: Doubleday.

Sole-Leris, A. 1986. *Tranquility and Insight: An Introduction to the Oldest Form of Buddhist Meditation.* Boston: Shambhala.

CHAPTER 22

What We Believe In

Once you begin to understand that our consciousness "lives in" a simulation of reality (as discussed in chapter 16), important questions come to mind. How accurate is my simulation of the actual external world? How can I check its accuracy? What is my simulation-construction of such inner representations as values and meanings? Do I like my habitual simulation? What are its effects on me? How can I come into more direct contact with outer reality? With inner realities?

Modern psychology describes inaccurate simulations of the external world as pathologies of perception and cognition. When your simulation is sufficiently distorted compared to those of "normal" people we describe you as neurotic. A social situation that is simulated by most people as a "fun party," for example, is simulated by you as an anxiety-provoking test of your popularity. If the reality you simulate is grossly different from that of normal people, such as hearing voices, you are called crazy or psychotic. Whether you are really crazy or not is another question.

"Normal" simulation then becomes a matter of what the majority of people in your culture do.

Many spiritual traditions have a deeper concern about the way we simulate the world than whether it is "normal." They believe that even the normal simulation of reality is badly flawed. The similar Hindu and Buddhist concepts of *maya* or *samsara* illustrate this.

The idea of samsara or maya is that we live in a world of unreality, of illusion. It is not the world or even ourselves that is illusory, though, but our *ideas* about reality and ourselves that create illusion. The simulation our consciousness lives in, which we identify with as a direct perception of reality, is very inaccurate. It's good enough in many ordinary ways, of course: We can cross the street without being run down

WHAT WE BELIEVE IN

by cars (generally), behave in an appropriate manner to buy food in a supermarket, and so on. But when it comes to questions about the meaning of our existence and the way we should live our lives and relate to others, the "normal" simulation of reality is often badly distorted. By living in illusion, by acting on the basis of a worldview that is badly distorted, we inevitably make mistakes that then create unfortunate consequences. Clearer perception-simulation of our world and ourselves would allow us to avoid much suffering.

To illustrate poor functioning of the world simulation process on an ordinary level, consider an all too typical example in the human relations area. You may have been conditioned in childhood to fear authority figures and expect them to be critical of you and punish you. Now you're in a situation of being asked directions by a well-dressed stranger. You know the place he wants to get to, although it is complicated to get there. That is all that is happening in reality: All this man wants from you is directions.

Your world simulation process, operating automatically outside your consciousness, not only presents you with an "obviously real" image of a well-dressed man, but of an *authoritative* man. A part of you cringes; your directions come out much more complex than they need to be; you probably can't do it right anyway. The expectation of messing up makes it worse. He frowns as you give him these complex directions. He's concentrating on understanding them, but you automatically perceive the frown as obvious disapproval of *you*.

The result is a confused stranger who may not find the place he wants after all without asking someone else and a reinforced feeling of inability to perform well and rejection by authorities. A malfunctioning world simulation process can create difficulties for many more people than just its owner!

The mystical traditions might illustrate malfunctioning of the world simulation process with this kind of example. You read about a nasty murder, the search for the killer, and her eventual apprehension and punishment. You feel righteously angry at this murderess and satisfied that she will be deprived of freedom forever. It is *obvious*, that is, the world simulation process vividly constructs your perceptions this way, that *you* are righteous and *she* is a sinful beast. Reprehensible as her crime was on an ordinary level, though, the mystical experience teaches people that at some profound level we are all one. The murderer will suffer, but so will some deep part of you, even more than necessary from the objective aspects of what happened because you refuse to accept the savage parts of your own mind that might kill in similar circumstances and your real kinship with all life. Insofar as the mystics are right, our faulty world simulation process is further fragmenting us from our real wholeness.

How can we overcome the limitations of our world simulator and get in better touch with reality? Two major ways are open to us. One way involves attention-training processes that promote a volitional type of more direct access to perceptual input, before the automated world-simulation process can work it over and distort it so much. (A good example of this would be insight meditation, discussed in part 5.) The second way, complementary, involves getting insights into the particular contents of your world-simulation process, and bringing to consciousness the *specifics* of how you construct your experienced world. Such insights remove energy from these automated simulation processes so you can choose to allow them to operate or not. We will concentrate on an important aspect of the second way in this chapter.

Reinforcement of the Rules

Implicit Reinforcement

Many of the criteria for constructing our world are indoctrinated in us in our early years and become automated, but these criteria generally work more effectively if they are occasionally reinforced. Much "normal" social interaction does this. For example, when I meet you and say, "Hi! How are you?" on one level I am greeting you and asking about your health. On another level I am reminding you of cultural rules about being normal: Normal people greet each other in a ritualized manner when they meet.

Your "Hi there! I'm fine, how are you?" is, in turn, not just a suitable response to the overt content of my greeting. You have been reminded about the cultural rules for greeting and you respond in a way that acknowledges these rules and shows that you understand them and belong to the class of normal people. These reminders about and reinforcements of normal behavior further reinforce our internal simulations of the world and ourselves in normal ways: The more your habitual construction of the world and yourself fits the external rules, the more "natural" and easy your behavior, your fitting in. This kind of automatized behavior seems easy but it is eventually quite costly.[1]

An enormous amount of reminding and reinforcing of cultural rules for simulating reality goes on in everyday behavior. The reinforcing of the rules is all the more effective for our unconsciousness of what we are doing.

Explicit Reinforcement

Sometimes we are quite explicit about reinforcing the cultural rules as to how we construct-simulate our world. Consider the Apostle's Creed, recited in only slightly varying forms by millions of Christians every Sunday:

I believe in God the Father Almighty, Maker of Heaven and Earth;

And in Jesus Christ his only Son, our Lord: Who was conceived by the Holy Ghost, Born of the Virgin Mary; Suffered under Pontius Pilate, was crucified, dead, and buried;

He descended into Hell; The third day He rose again from the dead; He ascended into heaven, and sitteth on the right hand of God the Father Almighty; From there he shall come to judge the quick and the dead.

I believe in the Holy Ghost; The Holy Catholic Church; the Communion of Saints; The forgiveness of sins; The Resurrection of the body; and the Life Everlasting. Amen.

Here we have an explicit statement of some of the central criteria for simulating a formally Christian world; other criteria, not explicitly stated but associated with these, are brought to mind by reciting the creed.

The recitation of the Apostle's Creed is a social ritual. You do it in church, witnessed by fellow believers. Our natural social instinct, the desire to belong, is harnessed to reinforce the Creed.

Contemporary secular Western culture has beliefs about our nature, the world's nature, and the purpose of life. These beliefs control the way our brains simulate our reality. We generally do not express them so explicitly as the Apostle's Creed expresses core Christian beliefs. Lack of explicitness is a mixed blessing. On the one hand our beliefs may not get as much reinforcement as the beliefs of an explicit creed. On the other, by not being *explicitly* made conscious, they are subject to less potential examination and so can affect us more unconsciously.

The Scientistic Creation Myth

What does modern science seem to say about the nature of reality? Consider this simplified sketch of what is supposedly scientific fact about ourselves and our world.

In the beginning, a long time ago, all the matter in the universe got together in a single massive point. There was no external "reason" for it to be there, mechanical gravitational attraction just got it all together. As a result of the unimaginable pressures, temperatures, and nuclear reactions that developed in this ultra-dense matter, the Big Bang occurred, an explosion of matter and energy outward. *This explosion created the physical world we know today.*

In its outward rush physical forces resulted in some matter clumping together and creating stars and planets. On Earth the ceaseless, mindless interaction of matter with matter went on for billions of years, driven by its own material properties, fueled by energy from the sun and the Earth's own internal heat. Elements reacted with each other to form simple chemicals, and simple chemicals reacted with each other to form more complex chemical compounds.

In this immense span of time some complex chemical compounds were randomly created. These compounds absorbed other chemicals and energy from their environment and turned them into themselves, so they preserved and enlarged themselves for a time against the changes in their environments.

At least one of these complex compounds accidentally developed an even more interesting property: It reproduced copies of itself that preserved its two inherent properties. That is, the new copies also absorbed other chemical compounds and energies from their environments to preserve and enlarge themselves, and they in turn produced copies of themselves with these properties. *We call this the emergence of life.*

As billions of years went by the chemical compounds we call living continued to interact with their environment. There was no choice, of course, for the laws of physics required such interaction. Living organisms either died out when conditions were unfavorable or got more complex. *We call the process of being mechanically pushed by physical laws into more complex forms evolution.*

One of these complex organic forms became us. Because our ancestors had developed an elaborate network of specialized chemical compounds, the nervous system and brain, in the course of adapting to the environment, we developed intelligence. Intelligence is, among other things, the ability to simulate the external environment inside the nervous system, to estimate "What would happen if . . .?" without actually doing something externally. *Partial awareness of this simulation process is what we call consciousness.*

The question "What would happen if I poked at this sleeping bear with a stick?" could be answered by internal images drawn from memories of what happened when other, smaller animals were annoyed, so you went away from the sleeping bear without actually poking it!

The nervous system and brain, those specialized chemical bodies, went on to develop elaborate simulations, sometimes so elaborate that they simulate things that don't exist. That is, we get imaginary, subjective ideas about things, such as an invisible black sky dragon temporarily eating the moon as an explanation of lunar eclipses. We also get ideas, even what seem to be actual experiences, of supernatural beings like God.

As long as basic physical survival needs are attended to (which is likely if the simulation of the physical world is good) the physically intact unit—the person—survives and can continue the subjective luxury of ideas about imaginary things like altruism, social systems, enlightenment, salvation, and so on.

Social groups that form around some of these ideas then further reinforce the ideas in their members, even if they have no basis in physical reality. If these subjective simulations get strong enough to disrupt the basic simulation of the real physical world, trouble results, which can lead to the destruction of the organism.

When the organism dies the physical-electrical-chemical integrity of the brain and nervous system is broken and so consciousness, a subjective reflection of brain functioning, disappears. *We call this death.*

This is the creation myth of contemporary *scientism*, science ossifying and acting as a belief system instead of as a continual challenge to further thought. These ideas have a fair amount of utility in making sense of our experience of the physical world. They also function as a creation myth and as a set of values by telling us the way things are.

Unfortunately this set of ideas is not explicitly presented as a myth or as a set of values, but simply as the closest thing we have to actual truth and often as the truth. By thinking of them as *factual* we overlook the way in which they function as a myth about why we are here and what we are here for. After all, you wouldn't want to have values that contradicted "reality." Living in our contemporary world constantly exposes us to this myth, and we are socially reinforced for accepting it. Wouldn't you prefer to hear, "She has a sound, scientific mind," rather than, "She falls for every flaky idea that comes along"?

The Western Creed: A Belief Experiment

To illustrate the effects of the way we simulate our world and ourselves along the lines of scientism, let us consider the following training exercise, which I developed several years ago.

The Western Creed exercise is a form of *belief experiment*. First I ask people if they are willing to participate in a belief experiment. This means that for ten or twenty minutes they are to give the material I will soon present as much unconditional belief and energy as possible, while a detached part of their mind observes their reactions.

I have taken the apparent scientific "facts" about the nature of reality narrated above and put them and some of their implications into the Western Creed, a form that parallels the Apostle's Creed. I use it in workshops, where there is time for me to discuss individual's reactions with them. Here you will get it on your own, but I suggest that you try it with a group of friends. The belief experiment may not be pleasant, but almost everyone who does it feels wiser as a result.

In workshops I pass out copies of the Western Creed and then have people stand up, at attention, in neat rows, with their right hands over their hearts. This deliberately invokes a situation every American has been in: pledging allegiance to the flag. I do this to use and illustrate the importance of shared social activity in influencing our beliefs.

Then we read the Western Creed aloud in unison. Following that I ask people to sit down quietly and reflect on their experience, particularly the emotional reactions aroused by the creed; abstract intellectual analysis at this point will distract from what you can learn. After a few minutes we share reactions.

You might want to try a modified version of the above procedure. Get permission from yourself to temporarily believe the Western Creed (preferably before reading it), then stand with your hand on your heart and recite it aloud. Sit down and reflect on your experience.

Remember, after a few minutes you can stop believing it. Of course you might find that you believe parts of it anyway . . .

Please examine your own *emotional* reactions after reading the Creed. It may be helpful to take notes. Once you are clear about your emotional reactions you can intellectually analyze your thoughts and feelings about whatever the Creed has brought up in you.

Please remember that this Western Creed does not reflect my actual beliefs, or my best scientific opinion about the nature of reality. It is a parody of genuine religious creeds, created in order to illustrate the degree to which a distorted form of science, "scientism," has affected our Western beliefs and values.

THE WESTERN CREED

I BELIEVE in the material universe as the only and ultimate reality, a universe controlled by fixed physical laws and blind chance.

I AFFIRM that the universe has no creator, no objective purpose, and no objective meaning or destiny.

I MAINTAIN that all ideas about God or gods, enlightened beings, prophets and saviors, or other nonphysical beings or forces are superstitions and delusions. Life and consciousness are totally identical to physical processes and arose from chance interactions of blind physical forces. Like the rest of life, my life and my consciousness have no objective purpose, meaning, or destiny.

I BELIEVE that all judgments, values, and moralities, whether my own or others, are subjective, arising solely from biological determinants, personal history, and chance.

Free will is an illusion. Therefore the most rational values I can personally live by must be based on the knowledge that for me what pleases me is Good, what pains me is Bad. Those who please me or help me avoid pain are my friends; those who pain me or keep me from my pleasure are my enemies.

Rationality requires that friends and enemies be used in ways that maximize my pleasure and minimize my pain.

I AFFIRM that churches have no real use other than social support; that there are no objective sins to commit or be forgiven for; that there is no retribution for sin or reward for virtue other than that which I can arrange, directly or through others. Virtue for me is getting what I want without being caught and punished by others.

I MAINTAIN that the death of the body is the death of the mind. There is no afterlife and all hope of such is nonsense.

Please pause for a few minutes before reading on, and check your emotional reactions.

When you are ready to think about it more, ask yourself some questions. What parts seem like obviously true descriptions of reality? How do you *personally* know they are true? Have you tested them for yourself, as scientists are supposed to do, or just accepted them on authority? Do you have any fears of looking at some of these ideas too deeply? If so, why? Who would you be displeasing? How many of these beliefs did you consciously *choose*?

I have deliberately chosen not to make any intellectual resolution of the issues raised. You need to resolve them in your personal life, and we Westerners need to resolve them as a culture.

A Transpersonal Creed

The Western Creed is a grim experience for most people. I would like to balance that grimness by presenting another creed, a transpersonal creed that affirms basic spiritual values.

I can't really balance things this way, of course. Partly it's because the transpersonal creed below is too much for your head, not your heart. By making small, easy leaps from conventional science and by trying to be nondenominational, I have to hedge too much: The creed makes sense but it's not inspiring. The forces of Western society exert a lot more influence on us than a single exercise can. But if either the Western Creed or this transpersonal creed gets you thinking or feeling about what really matters to you, it will have value.

This creed should be used experimentally, like the Western Creed.

A TRANSPERSONAL CREED

I BELIEVE that the universe is spiritual as well as material, and that what happens to us is controlled by a combination of both physical and spiritual laws.

I AFFIRM that human beings are part of an integrated Order of life; that we have considerable potential to evolve toward higher levels of this Order; and that seeking to evolve toward this Order is one of the highest values of human life.

I MAINTAIN that there are higher spiritual beings and enlightened humans. Life and consciousness seek to evolve toward these higher, nonphysical manifestations, even though currently rooted in the physical. Like the rest of life, my life and my consciousness share this purpose and destiny.

I BELIEVE that while some judgments, values, and moralities are subjective and personal, some are based on a valid intuition of higher possibilities. Satisfactory personal values and morality must be based on a continual dedication to understanding and living my and others' higher possibilities. Those who help me understand and develop these higher possibilities are my friends and teachers; those who hinder me should be helped as much as possible. Insofar as all Life may be one Being, in a real and transpersonal sense, we should seek to maximize our love of and minimize our harm to all Life.

I AFFIRM that churches or other transpersonally oriented activities may sometimes be useful for aiding my and others' spiritual evolution; that there are actions that are objectively wrong, which we should avoid committing once we understand their nature; that there is a real and objective sense in which harming others harms myself and life; that the universe is lawful on mental and transpersonal levels as well as physical levels, so all acts have consequences that must eventually be faced. Virtue for me is loving and helping myself and others, so I and Life may evolve.

I MAINTAIN that the death of the body may not be the death of the mind. While hope of an afterlife can be a rationalization for lack of evolutionary effort in this life, the probable reality of transpersonal levels of existence not dependent on a physical body may mean that individual life is much greater than physical life.

My best wishes for greater wisdom, even at the risk of some temporary sadness.

Suggested Reading

Modern psychology knows a great deal about the processes that construct and maintain the world simulation process, but is usually caught in cultural delusions itself and so does not see the culturally relative and frequently maladaptive aspects of our world simulation processes. The following suggested books are primarily basic psychology texts, to be examined in the perspective of this chapter:

Bootzin, R. R., and J. R. Acocella. 1988. *Abnormal Psychology: Current Perspectives*. New York: Random House.

Bourne, L., and B. Ekstrand. 1976. *Psychology: Its Principles and Meanings.* New York: Holt, Rinehart & Winston.

Green, M. 1989. *Theories of Human Development: A Comparative Approach.* Englewood Cliffs, N.J.: Prentice-Hall.

Hilgard, E., R. L. Atkinson, and R. C. Atkinson. 1979. *Introduction to Psychology.* New York: Harcourt Brace Jovanovich.

Kretch, D., R. S. Crutchfield, and N. Livson. 1974. *Elements of Psychology.* New York: Knopf, 3d edition.

From a more humanistic and spiritual perspective, I would recommend the following:

Feinstein, D., and S. Krippner. 1988. *Personal Mythology: The Psychology of Your Evolving Self.* Los Angeles: Tarcher.

Tageson, C. W. 1982. *Humanistic Psychology: A Synthesis.* Homewood, Ill.: Dorsey.

CHAPTER 23

Cultivating Compassion

I have attempted to practice a kind of mindfulness, what Gurdjieff called self-remembering, for some years. Its value has been to help me become more fully and realistically aware of the world around me and of the workings of my own mind. The major shortcoming of this practice for me, however, is that it does not deal directly with the heart.

I understand intellectually and practically that, in the long run, clearing away obstacles to natural functioning through self-observation and self-remembering will allow a natural development of love and compassion, and I have seen some growth in myself in this way. Since I regard myself as too intellectual and too lacking in love and compassion to begin with, however, I am impatient and have always wanted to encourage the growth of these aspects of myself more actively. In this chapter we will look at compassion, the obstacles to developing it, and some practices to assist its development.

Clearing the Ground

Most Gurdjieff work does not encourage active development of love and compassion until after years of practice of more basic work. If the development of love and compassion were encouraged at the beginning, before you had much understanding of your own mind and feelings, it would probably result in the growth of more illusions and create further support for false personality.

An analogy to support this policy of not actively encouraging the growth of love in beginners is that of a man who asks what to do to grow beautiful flowers. He has heard of "powerful fertilizers" that really help flowers to grow, and wants some. You look in his backyard and see it is overgrown with weeds. In that case there is no point yet in discussing fertilizers and varieties of flower seeds: A lot of work must first be done to get rid of weeds. Indeed to tell such a person about fertilizers before he has gotten rid of the weeds would be worse than doing nothing. The idea of "fertilizers," of spiritual practices, is exciting, not just to our essence but to many parts of our false personality. The application of fertilizer at this stage would just make the weeds worse.

This reasoning makes perfect sense to me, both intellectually and from personal experience. There have been too many occasions in my life where actions I thought of as using and developing love and kindness turned out to be fertilization of the weeds of my unconscious, of the automatized parts of my false personality. Mindfulness, self-understanding, self-remembering are clearly necessary. Balanced development of all three major aspects of our being—body/intuition mind, intellectual mind, emotional mind—is also necessary. The kind of self-observation and self-remembering advocated by Gurdjieff, as well as some kinds of body work, facilitate development of body/intuition and intellectual mind directly. Because insight removes energy from the automated operation of false personality, it also sets the stage for the growth of the heart. Yet I have always felt a lack of more direct development exercises for the heart, for love, in the basic Gurdjieff work to which I have been exposed.

In 1984 I had the good fortune to attend two lectures by the venerable Sogyal Rinpoche, a leading teacher of Tibetan Buddhism in the West.[1] The emphasis in Rinpoche's lectures was on mindfulness, not just as a special meditative practice but, more important, mindfulness in everyday life. The parallels with Gurdjieff's focus on self-observation and self-remembering were striking; but I was even more interested in his specific emphasis on the active development of compassion within the overall context of the cultivation of mindfulness. I do not fully understand the ideas he presented in terms of their comprehensive development in the Tibetan Buddhist tradition, but I want to share my personal understanding of them here, combined with some of my psychological knowledge of compassion, in the hope that they may be of value to others.

Note that these ideas and practices are embedded in the practice of a general cultivation of mindfulness. I suspect the concepts and methods described below would not have the same effect if used outside a personal commitment to constantly expand your mindfulness of yourself and the world. They might not be as effective, and sometimes they might amount to putting fertilizer on the weeds. Please treat them with caution.

Aspects of Compassion

What is compassion? Standard dictionaries trace its origin to the Latin roots *com*, meaning "with," and *pati*, "to bear or suffer," and they define the word as meaning a sympathetic consciousness of others' suffering and a desire to help them. (It is a sad commentary on our times that a major encyclopedic dictionary of psychology I turned to for more clarification doesn't even list compassion, a lack reflected in most introductory psychology textbooks.)

We can't really define compassion in any exact sense, of course. It is primarily a quality of emotional intelligence, and words relate primarily to intellectual intelligence. But we can talk about some of its qualities.

Breadth of Self-knowledge

Compassion requires the development of breadth of self-knowledge: If you don't experience, recognize, and understand a wide range of human experiences in yourself, you will have difficulty recognizing and understanding them in others. If you never acknowledge anger in yourself, for example, you can't adequately understand what it is and how it functions in someone else, or sympathize with the way that it can constellate other contents of the mind so they are perceived as reasons to justify the initial anger and fuel further anger.

Empathy

A second requirement for the development of compassion is empathy. Empathy is a recognition of a feeling/thinking state in another, and an ability to at least partially experience that same state in yourself. Thus empathy ties in with self-knowledge. To recognize that someone is "depressed," for example, could be done in a cold, intellectual way. You could learn that certain facial expressions, body postures, and styles of speaking usually mean that a person is "depressed." But the emotional knowledge of what it is like to feel depressed, from your own experience, leads to the experience of empathy. This does not necessarily mean that you must feel as depressed as the depressed person with whom you are empathizing; but your personal emotional knowledge must be readily available to consciousness.

Modern psychology has thought of empathy as a late developmental function, but recent research is suggesting it begins to develop within the first few years of life and is part of our essential nature. It may also be partly related to bodily/instinctive intelligence, such that mimicking others' postures and expressions helps us feel what they feel.

Desire to Help Others

A third requirement for compassion is the desire to help suffering beings find relief from their suffering. My own feeling is that this desire is natural, a part of our essence that is naturally aroused by the empathic perception of others' suffering. It is the defenses we have erected around ourselves that keep us from being aware of this natural desire to help others.

Effective Compassion and Intelligence

A fourth requirement for *effective* compassion stems from the fact that compassion should work in concert with intelligence. Compassion is not just an exaggerated empathy, where you feel another's negative emotions very strongly. If that was all there was to it compassion would be a crippling emotion, adding others' sufferings to your own and probably catching you up in some of the maladaptive behaviors in which suffering people often engage, and which prolong their sufferings or make them worse.

Intelligent, effective compassion thus involves

- the open self-knowledge and maturity that gives you intimate, experiential knowledge of a wide range of human suffering (and abilities)
- empathy that allows you to correctly perceive the nature of another's suffering
- a basic caring for others, a motivation and commitment to help alleviate their suffering
- the application of intelligence (mental, emotional, instinctive, spiritual) to eliminate the *cause* of another's suffering, rather than just lessening the symptoms. This aspect is important for efficacy of results.

To illustrate: Suppose you see a woman drowning near the shore. Assuming you are a good enough swimmer to rescue her, compassion would lead you to jump in and tow her to shore. But suppose that you weren't sure that your swimming abilities were good enough for this particular situation? To jump right in anyway would be noble, but stupid, and would probably lead to two drowning tragedies instead of one. The addition of intelligence to compassion would lead you to look around before jumping in. Perhaps there's a life preserver or other buoyant object that could be thrown to the person in the water? Or towed out by you to protect both of you? Is another person who is a better swimmer close enough to ask for help?

Let's suppose you jump in and rescue the woman. She is very grateful, and you feel wonderful about your noble and compassionate act. A week later you again see her shouting for help in the water, and again rescue her. You find out that this person often gets rescued from drowning, either because she won't bother to learn to swim well or she keeps taking foolish chances. Will it be compassionate to keep rescuing her, so she won't come to terms with the consequences of her foolishness?

In this instance the immediate cause of the woman's suffering is being in the water and in danger of drowning. But the root cause of her suffering is not learning (or refusing to learn) about the dangerous consequences of taking chances on the water even though she is a poor swimmer. By continuing to rescue her you compassionately save her; but, on another level, you are keeping her from facing the root cause of her suffering. If she does not face the root cause, chances are that someday she will take a chance when no one is around who can save her, and she will drown.

Would it be more compassionate to tell her that the next time you will *not* attempt to rescue her, so she had better learn either to swim better or not take chances? Or perhaps you should decide to rescue her the next time but take your time about it, so she will go under a few times and have a fearful and painful experience that might force her to become more intelligent by facing and changing the deep cause of her suffering? Is it worth taking the risk that she will actually drown right away?

Such questions do not have easy answers. This illustration is somewhat contrived to make it clear, but people do similar, if more complex things in life all the time. I am using this kind of example to illustrate that intelligent and effective compassion must deal with the problem that we must sometimes let people suffer if it will make them deal with the causes of their suffering and so lead to the permanent cure of suffering.

Obstacles to Compassion

To be compassionate is both natural and satisfying, yet it is all too rare a part of human behavior. Why? Let's look at some of the obstacles to compassion.

Childhood Rejections of Our Love: The Vulnerability of Openness

We have all had experiences of loving someone and trying to give to him or her, but finding our love and generosity rejected. Such experiences embitter us greatly, especially when we are children. Consequently we are all emotionally scarred (and scared) when it comes to acting openly from love and generosity. Indeed, to avoid the pain of rejection of this tender, vital, loving part of ourselves, we create active defenses to live behind.

When you give from your essence you are open and vulnerable. You are being your deep self. When that giving is rejected you feel rejected on a very deep level. Suppose as a child you loved your mother so much that you suddenly gave her your most prized possession to show her how much you cared. Your prized possession happened to be the dead frog you had been hiding in the yard for a week. To you the frog is beautiful and you are wide open, functioning from pure love. To your mother the partly decayed frog is filthy and disgusting, and she yells at you: "Take that filthy thing out of the house this minute and throw it in the garbage, then go wash your hands! You're a disgusting child! When will you learn how to behave?"

An experience like this can be devastating. From your current adult perspective you can understand why your mother acted like that and forgive it; but you weren't an adult when it happened, and you understood and learned quite different things as a child. You learned that acting spontaneously from love gets you into trouble. That you must be mistaken as to what you think love is, or you wouldn't get such a reaction from someone who must, you believe, love you. That you can't depend on your own judgment in important matters. That you are a disgusting child. That you are dumb, since you are much too slow in learning how to behave. That being spontaneously loving leads to great rejection, pain, and confusion. That spontaneity in general is dangerous.

Many of our childhood experiences are this dramatic. Even more of them are less dramatic, but make up in frequency what they lack in individual intensity. Is it any wonder that you wall off your essential self? That you lose touch with your essence and replace it with "safe" behaviors, habits, learned feelings? The "safety" of your defense is an illusion, of course, for any position that isolates you from knowing what is really happening in your world leads to actions that are flawed. And your life now has a constant undercurrent of anxiety from a new worry: Suppose the defenses break down?

Attempts at Invulnerability

You try to become invulnerable so you won't hurt so much. Unfortunately you usually do too good a job of it, walling off your natural love and compassion so well that your life becomes dry and stale. Our many defense mechanisms, Gurdjieff's "buffers," come into play and our natural vitality is stolen and automatically channeled into the habitual perception, thoughts, feelings, and body movements of false personality. In adult life you may then want to be compassionate and loving, try to be that way, but you feel nothing. Worse yet you are led astray down the subjective paths set up by false personality, experiencing the pathologically distorted versions of "love" you were conditioned to accept in childhood, so true compassion and love are absent. To note that this leads to sterile lives with far too much useless, stupid suffering is to put it mildly.

Avoiding the Pain of Incompetence

There is another important reason for staying defended and closed down. As children and as adults we have had experiences where we were compassionate, we felt another's suffering and tried to help, *and it didn't work.* We lacked skillful means so our efforts to help were to no avail—all we did was suffer without accomplishing anything.

How easy to build up a feeling of "Don't notice, don't feel, then you won't get hurt." This is the all-to-prevalent modern philosophy of not getting involved.

Reducing "I!" as a Way Toward Compassion

In chapter 13 we discussed the psychological process of identification, the way in which unconsciously and habitually adding the feeling of "I!" or "This is *me!*" to some contents of the mind gives those contents greatly increased psychological and emotional power. I can consider information about selfishness, for example, much more effectively and objectively when I am thinking about some stranger's selfishness rather than my own selfishness.

We have a huge amount of stored information in our minds. Some of this information has the "I!" tone attached to it: For example, "This is *my* valuable understanding of the sacred," rather than, "This is one understanding among many about the sacred." Our defense mechanisms were initially developed to defend our vital, essential selves, but over the years they begin to automatically defend almost anything that has this "I!" quality attached to it. What was once an essential maneuver by a relatively powerless child to protect its essence has become an automated style of (largely unconscious) emotional and mental functioning that unnecessarily constricts our being.[2]

As an adult, then, you want to be open and compassionate but you don't know how. Our fears and our ingrained habits of mental and emotional functioning cut us off from the parts of our essential selves that generate love and compassion. While you can try to deal with obvious, conscious fears about openness, the ingrained habits and unconscious fears are more difficult. They require various combinations of mindfulness, vulnerability, psychotherapy-like growth, and reduction of the process of identification.

Mindfulness

Becoming mindful—observing and remembering your self, being increasingly sensitive to the exact nature of your reactions to the world—allows increased insight into the functioning of false personality, as well as greater sensitivity to your genuine, essential feelings. Such mindfulness gradually dissolves some obstacles to compassion: Many of our automated constrictions and defenses fade away when exposed to the light of greater consciousness. It may also highlight other aspects of your self that need more specific work.

Vulnerability

Vulnerability seems most undesirable, and yet is absolutely necessary to fully recover your essential self. When you were a little child you were tremendously vulnerable in real ways. Your physical survival, as well as your psychological well-being, depended on your parents. Your lack of experience of the world gave an *absolute* quality to what your parents said and did, which enormously increased their power to love you and their power to (consciously or unconsciously) hurt you. With your own resources so small and your parents' power so huge, was it any wonder that the times they hurt you were so incredibly bad? Was it any wonder that sometimes you thought you would die from the pain of psychological wounds? Friends and strangers, often acting from far less love or even anger, hurt us very badly at times too. It is not surprising at all that you created such powerful defenses: You felt you were fighting for your life and, in many ways, you were.

The psychological habit of fighting for your life is still with you in unconscious and habitual ways. It is as if you received blows from giants and so encased yourself in thick armor for protection. You are still wearing that thick armor, but you have grown into a giant yourself and it's very cramped inside.

Suppose you are walking in the woods with a loved one today and you see a dead frog. Biology fascinates you (and you were fortunate enough to not have the particular childhood experience used as an example above) so you pick it up and show it to your beloved, a spontaneous gesture of sharing one of the wonderful things of the world. You may get another version of, "Take that filthy thing away from me this minute and throw it away and clean your hands! You're disgusting, like a little child! When will you grow up?" The automatic defense mechanisms of false personality begin to operate, the armor closes a little tighter around what's left of your essential self, and you may yell back and start a fight, and feel hurt or angry. But in reality:

- You're not a little child, you're an adult.
- You're a competent adult who can take care of yourself, and need not feel more than mildly hurt by this attack.
- Compared to your current, adult resources this is a very minor attack, you can directly experience the rejection. If you are vulnerable you don't need to deny what you feel. It doesn't feel good but you can handle it. Indeed you can handle far more intense attacks than this. You don't need armor.
- By using empathy, intelligence, and compassion you can understand how your loved one feels, make a good guess why he or she feels this way (social conditioning or traumatic personal experience), and—without denying the reality of her feelings—realize that he or she can't help it. There is no need to feel deeply attacked, as it is not really an attack on you *personally*, any more than rain falling on you is a personal attack by nature.

Intelligent compassion would allow you to empathize with your loved one, take the frog away to stop the immediate upset, and then skillfully apologize and, perhaps, help your beloved understand why he or she is so bothered by dead frogs, so that the root cause of this particular suffering might be eliminated.

Allowing yourself to be vulnerable, then, removes the need for much of your automatic defensiveness and so allows much greater openness to and compassion for other people.

Therapeutically Aided Growth

Sometimes mindfulness and vulnerability are not enough. Some kinds of attacks, even if they really are quite minor in reality, cause such intense hurt that you can't keep your attention in reality or feel compassionate. You must retreat or attack, your defenses take over despite your intentions. Sometimes help and understanding from a friend can get us over these blocks, but sometimes not. This is where Western-style psychotherapy techniques can be helpful.

A therapist is a trained person who is "outside" your delusions and problems and so has a more objective perspective on them. A therapist who is empathic and intelligent can help you to see things you can't otherwise see and feel things you can't otherwise feel. In return for the immediate pain of facing the unfaceable, you get at its root cause and eliminate the years of suffering you would otherwise have.

Reducing the Sense of "I!"

Because our defenses spring into operation when "I!" am attacked, reducing the intensity and frequency of the identification process creates a more relaxed style of mental and emotional functioning that allows our natural compassion, love, and intelligence to function more effectively. Self-remembering and many kinds of meditation can help reduce our sense of "I!"

Self-remembering reduces the intensity of the identification process. Under ordinary circumstances you only have so much attention to give. If you exercise little voluntary control over that attention then it largely goes where the circumstances of the moment—predictably and automatically reacted to by false personality—take it. We are "stimulus driven," to borrow a term from conventional psychology; *re*active rather than genuinely active.

When you self-remember you voluntarily direct your attention so that you simultaneously pay more active attention to what is happening outside you and inside you, as well as keep some reference object (such as specific body sensations) in mind. The simple act of voluntarily putting attention where you want it means that there is now less attention/ energy available to power your false personality and your identification processes and defense mechanisms. Quite aside from specific changes in the functioning of your mind, this reduces the automatic defensiveness that comes from too much "I!" and allows greater empathy and compassion toward others. The traditional Buddhist practice of keeping part of the mind always watching your breath, applied regularly in daily life, similarly reduces the sense of "I!" by diverting energy from the identification process.

Meditation practices, done deliberately—at times specially designated as "meditation" time rather than during ordinary life—can also lead to a temporary lessening of the identification process. If you spend fifteen minutes just observing your breathing while sitting still, for example, you have fifteen minutes in which your mind has been filled with the simple, emotionally neutral experience of breathing, rather than the typical mental/emotional activities that reinforce false personality and its multitudinous identifications. In his lectures Sogyal Rinpoche emphasized that one of the best times to try to practice compassion is right after meditation. Indeed, for the beginner (practically all of us), this may be one of the few times when compassion can be successfully practiced.

The Cultivation of Compassion

We have looked at some common obstacles to openness and compassion at some length, for understanding the obstacles to doing something automatically suggests ways of circumventing or dismantling those obstacles. Learning to meditate in some fashion that reduces our sense of "I!" is a way to indirectly set the stage for more compassion to manifest naturally. Learning to be mindful in everyday life, trusting yourself enough to be more vulnerable, and using the type of help developed for psychotherapy to work on specific obstacles to free mental and emotional functioning, similarly set the stage for more frequent and natural functioning of compassion. What more can you do?

It would be wonderful if you could just decide, "I will be compassionate and open from now on!"—but it isn't that easy. That is why Sogyal Rinpoche used the phrase "courting compassion." You will have more luck if you try to gradually work your way up to being compassionate than if you try to get there all at once.

Remembering Love: A Preliminary Practice

One of the practices Sogyal Rinpoche suggests invokes a feeling of compassion by building on earlier experiences when you were loved by someone else. Here is an outline of the practice. It is best done when your identification process is not working so intensely. A good time to do it is right after a meditation practice that has succeeded (meditation doesn't always work, as we shall see in Part 5) in producing a calm state of mind.

1. Think about someone who loved you a lot. It's tricky to use parents for this purpose, as many of us have unresolved psychological tensions about our parents; but a grandparent is often excellent. Think about the ways this person loved you and was kind to you.
2. Realize that you must be a worthwhile person to have been loved by another. Focus on that, rather than any doubts you have about yourself.
3. Experience the feeling of being loved, of how that person felt in loving you.
4. Now feel loving yourself and call up images of other people and give your love and compassion to them.
5. At first use images of other people who have been good to you.
6. As you get successful at this extend the giving of love to images of people who have treated you neutrally.
7. As you get more practiced extend your love to images of people who have treated you badly.
8. When you get good at the above extend the love to images of people with whom your relationship was mixed and complicated, such as your parents.
9. Now extend your love to all beings.

When you first do this practice you may not get beyond step 2, or you might go on easily to step 5. Don't try to jump directly to the most advanced steps if you're having difficulty with earlier steps. You might set yourself up for failure, and thus reinforce all that early defensiveness that closed you up in the first place. You needn't be perfect at each step, but experience some success at it before you go on to the next one.

The Dalai Lama recommends a similar practice for actively developing compassion.[3] His Holiness's version starts with recognizing the incredible kindness your mother performed in giving birth to you and raising you, and then trying to see all beings as mothers, so you will feel kindness and closeness toward them. I understand the principle involved here, but my psychological knowledge of the two-sided nature of the mother-child relationship leads me to prefer Sogyal Rinpoche's suggestion to base this exercise on a person who was more one-sidedly positive toward you than your mother, lest you have many negative, unconscious associations implicit in your model of a loving person.

Tong Len

Tong Len is a Tibetan practice Sogyal Rinpoche describes for developing greater openness and compassion. It can be used as a way to review unpleasant or problematical events of the day to open your mind to compassionate options for future events. Doing it right after a meditation period, when your sense of "I!" is less, is a good time.

1. Recall the specific problem or unpleasant situation that this Tong Len practice is to focus on.
2. Reflect on the various aspects of the problem situation, its atmosphere, as well as its specifics. Accept the problem; don't deny its reality. See the multiple sides of the situation, the positive as well as the negative aspects. Don't deny any of its reality.
3. As you reflect on these positive and negative aspects of the situation and people involved, as you "breathe them in," also keep track of the equanimity, happiness, and compassion you experienced to some degree in your meditation and give these positive feelings to the problem situation and people: "Breathe out" your happiness as an *unconditional* gift to them. You are not denying the negative, you are simply loving it anyway.
4. Reflect on yourself with regard to this situation. We are all wondrously complex, many-sided beings, so reflect on how different parts of you are responding to the situation. Don't deny anything you see about yourself, even if it's fearful or shameful. Accept all these different aspects of yourself, the "good" sides and the "bad" sides, *and* give your happiness as an unconditional gift to them.
5. Don't force changes. But if aspects of your self change as a result of putting the positive and negative together, give your love to the negative sides: Accept the change.

I believe the Tong Len practice or similar practices can significantly restructure your mind. Instead of having a steadily growing store of totally negative memories of situations in which you were not compassionate—which will, of course, increase your convictions that life is unpleasant and that you are not and can't be a compassionate person—you have processed memories to allow for compassion. The negativity is not denied—that would be pathological—but it is put in a context where compassionate alternatives are seen.

Ultimately, of course, the intent is to sensitize yourself to compassionate alternatives so that they become available in real time, when the next unpleasant situation is starting to happen, not when it's over.

Developing Compassion for Yourself

It is often difficult to develop simple tolerance for many other people, much less compassion: They can be so difficult! It is a real accomplishment to bear the difficult manifestations of others without always having to try to correct them, or being unnecessarily caught up in them. We can learn great and realistic tolerance, though, and even develop our capacity for compassion.

The more difficult accomplishment, however, is to accept yourself and develop compassion for yourself.

I have given students difficult and trying assignments for self-development that involve observation of their negative sides. They can be very unpleasant, and I am always impressed by how hard students will work at them. I have also given students the assignment to be nice to themselves, something just as (and at later stages of work much more) important for self-development. These were no big deals, just little things, like looking in a mirror and smiling at themselves for a moment, or thinking nice thoughts about themselves for five minutes a day.

The resistance to being nice to yourself is enormous. Students forget all about doing the exercises. Even after being forcibly and repeatedly reminded they come up with all sorts of "reasons" (really rationalizations) as to why they don't have time to be nice to themselves for five minutes a day. Work on the feelings behind these resistances usually shows they have a deep-seated set of feelings that says they don't deserve to have *anyone* be nice to them. Anyone includes themselves, often especially themselves, because of feelings of lack of self-worth. Some people feel this more strongly than others, but almost everyone has these feelings to some degree.

That we harbor strong dislikes for and rejections of ourselves is not surprising in light of what we have discussed about the enculturation process. We have all experienced rejection that made no sense to us. We have all had our essential feelings invalidated too many times. We have all learned to identify with socially desirable aspects of ourselves and not to identify with those that didn't fit into consensus reality. It was "natural" to develop a general feeling like, "What I basically am is not good enough, is bad. I can only be accepted and loved if I am careful to do the right thing and don't act spontaneously." This general negative feeling acted in conjunction with specific negative feelings toward particular aspects of ourselves that we felt were bad. We are strongly defended against important parts of our essential nature and have a complex system of social gains to compensate.

Gurdjieff observed this same kind of resistance to letting go of the apparent security of false personality and consensus trance when he remarked that his students would gladly do unpleasant tasks requiring heroic efforts, taking on deliberate, conscious suffering in the hope of growth; but when he asked them to give up their own suffering, that was another story!

The practices of self-observation and self-remembering are a general way of giving attention to our essence (as well as false personality). Attention is energy, so deliberately paying attention to your self is a way of nourishing it. After all, you only pay attention to what is valuable, so *you* must be valuable if you give yourself attention.

To have compassion toward yourself is vital. Self-observation, in its various forms, eventually leads to a depth of understanding we seldom dream of. A vital part of that understanding will be of how pure and marvelous you essentially are. There will be resistance to self-understanding on the way, as you see negative parts of yourself, but the process is worth it.

Until you learn to understand and have compassion toward yourself, all your tolerance, love, and compassion toward others rests on a very shaky foundation.

I will not attempt to give detailed advice about emotional development, as I am an overintellectualized person. I will suggest a couple of basic but powerful exercises that are helpful in nourishing your essence, in promoting self-liking.

Do these exercises occasionally, once a week or so. They generally produce quite pleasant experiences, which is fine; but remember the goal is awakening, achievement of genuine self-consciousness. That requires prolonged self-observation and self-remembering. Since much of that means looking at unpleasant aspects of yourself and reality, neither reject pleasure, nor substitute it for genuine knowledge. Remember,

> There is no God but Reality.
> To seek Him elsewhere
> Is the action of the Fall.

The Musical Body

The Musical Body exercise should be done lying down in a warm, reasonably dark, and comfortable place, where you will not be disturbed. This exercise can sometimes create very powerful emotions. You can modify the directions as you go along to keep any emotional reactions within the range where you can learn from them.

1. Pick one of your favorite musical selections that lasts for about fifteen to twenty-five minutes. Don't use vocal music, as you don't want to get involved in verbal meanings. Flowing, peaceful music that is relatively even throughout is best.
2. Start the music and take a minute or two to just relax.
3. Now listen to the music in both of your feet. Put your attention on whatever sensations are in your feet and gently let the music be there too. Don't force: You're not trying for some very specific sensation. Sense whatever is there and sense the music there. Don't worry about intellectual arguments that you really hear with your ears, not your feet. You really don't, anyway: You hear with your *mind*. By wishing to hear in any specific part of your body, you will have the experience of hearing there, and that's what matters. The music helps you focus attention and a pleasant, positive feeling in the part of your body you are listening in. *Enjoy* the music in your feet and the sensations in your feet.
4. After about a minute move your attention up into the calves of your legs, from the ankles to the knees. Pay attention to whatever sensations are there, and hear the music there. *Enjoy* the music in your calves and the sensations in your calves.
5. Again in a minute or so (timing is not crucial) move your attention to your thighs and sense and listen there. At about one-minute intervals continue to go through your body in the following order: genitals; pelvis, with particular attention to an area about two finger-widths below your navel and about three finger-widths in; belly; chest and back (don't focus strongly on your heart yet); shoulders; upper arms; forearms; hands; neck; and face and scalp.
6. Focus on the inside of your head for a minute or so.
7. Listen to the music in your heart. Strong positive feelings will probably result here, especially if your choice of music has been appropriate. Immerse yourself in and enjoy these feelings for the minute.

8. Finally spread the sensing and the listening to the music and any positive feelings associated with your heart throughout your whole body. After a minute or two of this let your attention relax and just drift into a relaxed state for a few minutes until the music ends.

9. When the music ends get up slowly; jumping up from a relaxed state can make you faint. Stay as present to reality as you can. Live!

The above sequence for listening with the body is not the only one that is useful, so feel free to try different sequences. Just include all of the body.[4]

The Morning Liking Exercise

Do the Morning Liking exercise once a week. It takes about half an hour. You should take particular note of any resistances you have to doing this exercise. You can do it with or without music.

1. To begin, think "I like me." Feel it a little. Put a little smile on your face.

2. Now gently move your attention through your body, starting with the feet and working your way upward, as in the Musical Body exercise. Keep that little smile on your face, and emotionally smile at your body parts as you sense them. Don't force too hard or try to overdo it. Just aim for a gentle physical and emotional smile, a gentle liking, not a big deal.

When you don't have half an hour available you can shorten this exercise by first going over your feet to thighs, then your hands to shoulders, skipping the central core of your body. If you encounter strong resistance to the Morning Liking exercise this abbreviated form is also better.

So many of us have such little liking for ourselves that it can actually be a big deal indeed to spend a few minutes deliberately paying attention to and deliberately liking ourselves, but it is within everyone's ability to like themselves at least a little—and eventually quite a lot.

Both the Morning Liking exercise and the Musical Body exercise can be made much more powerful by asking that you *love* yourself, instead of just liking yourself. If this triggers too much resistance just like yourself. When you can practice this as loving yourself, you will be well along the way to developing compassion—for yourself and for others.

Suggested Reading

Goldstein, J. 1987. *The Experience of Insight: A Simple and Direct Guide to Buddhist Meditation.* Boston: Shambhala.

————, and J. Kornfield. 1987. *Seeking the Heart of Wisdom: The Path of Insight Meditation.* Boston: Shambhala.

Gyatso, T. (The Dalai Lama). 1984. *Kindness, Clarity, and Insight.* Ithaca, N.Y.: Snow Lion Publications (P.O. Box 6483).

Tageson, C. W. 1982. *Humanistic Psychology: A Synthesis.* Homewood, Ill.: Dorsey.

Tart, Charles T. [1975] 1983. *States of Consciousness.* El Cerrito, Calif.: Psychological Processes.

————. 1986. *Waking Up: Overcoming the Obstacles to Human Potential.* Boston: New Science Library.

Part 5

MEDITATION

CHAPTER 24

Stray Thoughts on Meditation

One of our greatest problems in life is that we don't know how to really concentrate. As a consequence we lose much of the force of the decisions and insights that we try to use to guide our life. We are too easily diverted from our intended goals. We also miss many important but delicate intuitions because we haven't trained ourselves to listen to the quiet, rapid, more subtle levels of our mind, emotions, and body.

Meditation is a centuries-old tool that can teach us to listen to these quiet messages and move beyond our ordinary lives and selves. The two general forms of meditation are (1) concentrative meditation, where you learn to focus steadily on a selected aspect of experience; and (2) insight meditation, where you learn to observe the rapid flow of experience in its totality without becoming lost in limited aspects of it.

I have practiced various forms of meditation off and on for many years, but never very successfully. I sometimes half-jokingly (and half-sadly) describe myself as an expert on the difficulties of meditation because I've had so much experience of my mind wandering off instead of focusing. I understand the importance of meditation practice; but my confusion and frustration over the proper way to meditate has sapped my motivation.

In January 1986 I met a remarkable man, Shinzen Young. The occasion was the First Archaeus Congress at the Pecos River Conference Center near Santa Fe, New Mexico. This was one of the most exciting conferences I have ever attended. Shinzen Young's lecture on meditation and his subsequent early morning meditation practice sessions were the high point of the conference for me. Years of graduate training in Eastern religions and philosophy have given him the intellectual knowledge to bridge the gap between the Eastern meditative traditions and our modern Western minds. Even more important is the fact that Shinzen, an American, has spent many years in the Orient as a student of various kinds of Buddhist practices; he speaks from direct experience. His goal is to make meditative practice a viable path for Westerners.

Shinzen's lecture and practice sessions changed my attitude and motivation about meditation drastically. He was so clear and lucid in explaining and guiding meditation practice that, to my great surprise, I found myself looking forward to getting up at 5:30 each morning to meditate for an hour before breakfast! This is quite a contrast to my usual habit of waking up, getting a cup of coffee, and going back to bed with it until I feel awake.

I have continued regular meditation since that conference. I would not describe myself as good at it yet, but I am enormously better at it than I used to be, I am continuing to improve, and I am enjoying it.

To share some of Shinzen Young's clarity with you, I have devoted this chapter to reprinting his "Stray Thoughts on Meditation."[1]

Principles of Meditation

The Buddhist world comprises three broad traditions. Much of Southeast Asia (Ceylon, Burma, Thailand, Laos, and Cambodia) preserves an early form of Indian Buddhism, the Theravada. A very late and highly evolved expression of Indian Buddhism, Vajrayana or Tantra, has dominated in Tibet, Mongolia, and Nepal. In East Asia we find Buddhism greatly transformed at the hands of the Chinese. It is this "Sinified" form of Buddhism which enters Korea, Japan, and Vietnam. Zen is a product of East Asia.

Within each of these three spheres numerous schools, traditions, and individual approaches exist for the practice of meditation. Yet, concerning basic principles, there is remarkable agreement among Buddhists as to what is involved in the meditative process.

This distinctive Buddhist orientation toward meditation can be summed up concisely. Meditation consists of two aspects or components. The first, called *samatha* in Sanskrit, is the step-by-step development of mental and physical calmness. The second, *vipassana*, is the step-by-step heightening of awareness, sensitivity, and clarity.[2] These two components complement each other and should be practiced simultaneously. Some techniques develop primarily calming, others primarily clarity, still others both equally. It is of utmost importance, however, that one component not be enhanced at the expense of the other. To do so is no longer meditation. Tranquility at the expense of awareness is dozing; awareness at the expense of calm is "tripping."

Samatha, if taken to an extreme, leads to special trance states; these may be of value but they are not the ultimate goal of Buddhism. The practice of clear observation on the other hand, if developed with sufficient intensity and consistency, leads to a moment of insight into the nature of the identification process. At that moment awareness penetrates into the normally unconscious chain of mental events that gives us rock-solid convictions like "I *am* so-and-so" or "such-and-such *really* matters." This insight brings with it a radical and permanent change in perspective—a refreshing sense of freedom that is not dependent upon circumstances.[3] The attainment of this perspective and the full manifestation of its implications in daily life are the goals of Buddhist meditation.

What follows will amplify upon the above ideas and describe briefly a few specific practices drawn from the three Buddhist cultural spheres of East Asia, Southeast Asia, and Tibet.

Samatha

Samatha is the practice of stilling the mind through letting go. In Buddhist usage it is virtually synonymous with the term *samadhi*. This latter term is usually translated as "one-pointedness" or concentration. Unfortunately the word concentration often carries the connotation of repressing the mind, forcing it not to wander from a certain object. Such a tug of war between the desire of the mind to hold an object and its desire to wander is exhausting and produces unconscious tensions. This is the very antithesis of the samatha state.

The nature of concentration is detachment. Realizing this marks an important step along the path to the attainment of mental power. In real concentration one simply rests the mind on the object at hand and then proceeds to let go of everything else in the universe. The mind then remains on that object until it is appropriate to shift attention. Thus the ability to focus, to totally concentrate on one thing, is essentially equivalent to the ability to let go of everything. But in order to do this it is necessary to relax the body in a special way.

First one learns to keep the body upright and utterly motionless entirely through balance and relaxation, without using muscular effort. The ideal posture for this is the cross-legged lotus, although satisfactory results can be achieved with a variety of postures, even sitting in a chair.[4] The important thing is to align the vertebrae, find a position of equilibrium, and simply let the body hang from the spine by its own weight. This feeling of letting go then extends to the breath and finally to the mind itself.

Since samatha has the dual nature of letting go and one-pointed-ness, two approaches to the mind are possible. One is simply to allow the emotional and conceptual content of the mind to settle of its own weight. A way this may be achieved is through the elegant technique of "analogy" (*anumana*). One feels a part of the body, such as the arm, relaxing, then discovers the mental analog of that feeling, that is, what it feels like to relax thought.

The second approach is to rest the attention on a specific object and gently return it there each time it wanders off. Eventually this wandering habit weakens, then disappears. The object may be physical or visualized, outside the body or within. The so-called "elephant taming pictures" of Tibet portray this process in detail.[5]

It is common in all Buddhist traditions to give beginners some form of meditation that brings the mind to rest on the breathing. In Zen this usually involves counting the breaths or following the breath in and out. In the Theravada approach one typically cultivates awareness of the touch feeling of the breath at the nose tip or lip. Here no attempt whatsoever is made to control the breath. In Vajrayana elaborate channels for the breath are visualized in the body, and cycles of inhalation, retention, and exhalation in fixed ratios are practiced as in Hatha yoga.

Chanting is also common to all traditions. When done with proper posture and intention it can be very tranquilizing. In East Asia chanting the Buddha Amitabha's name is especially popular. The Chinese call this practice *Nien-Fo*, the Japanese *Nembutsu*, the Koreans *Yombul*, and the Vietnamese *Niem-Phat*. Many Tibetans incessantly chant mantras aloud or silently. Even in Theravada countries the chanting of special scriptures called *pirit* represents a major event in the monastic year, often going on unbroken for many days and nights. The mind-stabilizing nature of chant and mantra recitation was also recognized in Christianity, as witnessed by the "prayer of the heart" so popular in Eastern Orthodox spirituality. Chanting has a strong samatha effect, but, as usually practiced, there is little of the vipassana component; thus its power to bring liberating insight is weak.

Physical Effects

As body, breath, and mind settle, a distinctive slowing down of the overall metabolism begins to take effect. One needs to sleep less, eat less, breathe less. In fact spontaneous slowing of breath is probably the most easily observed physical barometer of depth of samadhi. Normal adults at sea level breathe about fifteen times per minute. During seated meditation, at a middle level of samatha, the breathing rate may drop to only two or three breaths a minute. Because samatha practice produces such conspicuous changes in the body's function there has recently been a good deal of physiological research on meditators. A few results of this research will be summarized here.

Meditators' brain waves are usually highly synchronized; typically this takes the form of increase in the alpha rhythm, whose frequency ranges from eight to twelve cycles per second. This enhanced alpha production in meditators continues even when their eyes are open. In nonmeditators opening of the eyes normally stops production of alpha waves. Electromyography reveals deep-muscle relaxation in spite of the upright, unsupported posture. Skin conductivity (GSR) decreases, perhaps indicating less sweating and hence decreased sympathetic activity. This too implies relaxation.

Researchers at Tokyo University made an interesting discovery about brain-wave behavior in Zen practitioners. A group of meditators and a group of nonmeditators were asked to sit quietly with electrodes attached to monitor brain waves. A click sound was repeatedly presented to both groups. At first both groups showed momentary "blocking" of alpha. This was as expected, for such blocking is part of the normal orienting response to a new stimulus. After several clicks the nonmeditator group no longer showed this blocking. This also is normal. They had accommodated to the stimulus; it was no longer new and fresh. But the Zen practitioners continued to momentarily block alpha with every click as if each time they were hearing the click for the first time. This fits nicely with the Zen ideal of "living in the moment." In India a similar click experiment was done with some yogis. They showed no alpha blocking. Apparently, withdrawn in trance, they did not hear the sound.[6]

Samatha is thus a continuum of states of progressive settling of the mind associated with growth in detachment, concentration power, and a distinctive set of physiological changes. At the deep end of this continuum these phenomena become extreme, and states called in Pali *jhanas* (Sanskrit *dhyana*) are entered. In deep jhana the drives to which everyone is normally subject are actually suspended, though not necessarily extinguished. This may last for a few hours or several days. One does not feel driven to move, eat, sleep, or think. Indeed the metabolism so slows that the breath *seems* nonexistent. The mind, which in its uncultivated state is like a torrential cataract, becomes a rippleless, limpid lake. The deepest jhana is a kind of trance, but by no means is every trance a jhana state. The characteristics of the jhanas are distinct and well-defined in the Abhidharma literature. In all, nine levels are distinguished.

Development and Use of Samatha

Samatha is best developed by a daily sitting meditation practice. What are the typical experiences of a person who takes up such a practice? How is it likely to affect his or her day-to-day life?

At first the body strains to remain upright during sitting, the breath is rough, piston-like, and the mind wanders terribly. One may even feel more agitated than usual. Actually one is just becoming aware for the first time of the appalling extent and intensity of the chaos within. This awareness is really the first stage of progress. In the Tibetan tradition it is called "realizing the mind as a waterfall."

As with any other art, however, time and regular practice bring skill at samatha. Body learns to settle into the posture, breath becomes smooth and slow, and irrelevant thoughts no longer scream for attention but whisper and are more easily ignored. By the end of each half-hour or hour meditation period, one experiences a noticeable calm, lightness, and openness. Then the task is to remember this calm state and to remain in it throughout the activities of the day!

At first it may be possible to recapture this settling effect only during the simplest mechanical tasks such as walking, sweeping, or gardening. The emphasis on manual labor in all forms of monasticism, East and West, is meant to provide situations wherein it is relatively easy to preserve inner silence while moving the body. After sufficient experience the awareness of calm can be preserved throughout the day, though its depth may vary depending on circumstances. One can drive a car, make love, even have arguments and write books without leaving the samatha state. One even dreams in it.

Even a person with no meditation experience can appreciate the advantage of a calm and concentrated mind in carrying out physical or mental tasks. With the deepening of samatha most activities of daily life are enhanced as one brings this ever more powerful, ever more stable mind to bear on them. In addition the associated settling of the body produces an abundance of energy. Further, samatha is a state of openness and acceptance, key factors in successful interpersonal relationships. The detachment associated with samatha makes it much easier to stick to one's principles and approach one's moral ideal.

For many samatha practitioners the events of the day are seen as a sequence of opportunities to deepen and apply skill at one-pointedness. Peculiar inversions in values may take place. Normally unpleasant situations turn into gold. Overwork and physical discomfort become "negative-feedback devices." Uncomfortable? Go deeper! Chaotic and fearful situations are accepted as challenges to one's meditative prowess. Wasting time is no longer conceivable. Being unexpectedly kept waiting for an hour somewhere means an hour of "secret use, hidden enjoyment."[7] The Sung dynasty Ch'an master Wu-Men summed it up when he said, "Most people are used twenty-four hours a day; the meditator uses twenty-four hours a day."

The states along this "samatha continuum" from superficial calming to total trance are known outside Buddhism. *Indeed, they are central to the systematic cultivation of mystical experience in all religious traditions.* For example, in the Roman Catholic church, cover terms for such states are *oratio quies* (prayer of quiet) and *recollection.*[8] Sometimes these states are referred to as "nondiscursive prayer" as opposed to usual prayer, which uses words and thoughts. There is copious literature on the subject in both the Eastern and Western churches. Different authors use different terminologies to distinguish benchmarks along the continuum.[9] The deepest trance level of prayer of quiet was sometimes called *infused contemplation* or simply *contemplation.* After the sixteenth century the practice of nondiscursive prayer declined in the Western church for interesting historical reasons. This, however, is beyond the scope of the present discussion.

The classical Raja yoga of Patanjali, another non-Buddhist system, distinguishes three stages along the continuum of settling, which are referred to as the "inner branches" of yoga. The first is *dharana* (holding on), during which the yogi strives to hold the object of concentration, returning to it each time the mind wanders. When the second stage, *dhyana,* is reached, concentration upon the object is unbroken, "like a flowing stream of oil." Finally all mental fluctuations cease, trance is attained, and the yogi feels that mundane limitations have been transcended. Patanjali calls this last stage *samadhi.* Note that, while in Buddhism the word samadhi is usually used as a general term for any state of one-pointedness, here in classical yoga it refers only to the very deepest of such states.[10]

Nor is the experience of samatha found only within the context of religious mysticism; it sometimes crops up in the arts, sports, and other "secular" activities that require intense concentration and relaxation.

It is interesting to see how beliefs and attitudes influence people's perceptions of the samatha process. The musician who sometimes experiences a light transient samadhi while performing will likely asso-

ciate this state only with the art and, being unaware of its broader
potentials, will not strive to deepen and maintain it. In this case the
artist's daily life will never be engulfed and transformed by the experience.

The Value of Trance

Mystics in traditions with dualistic philosophical outlooks tend to
see trance as the pinnacle and ultimate goal of the mystic path. This
makes perfect sense. If you believe in the dichotomy of spirit versus
matter, as did the Neoplatonists and the Sankhya theorists of ancient
India, then your goal will be conceived of in terms of freeing spirit
from the trammels of matter. The absence of drives and extreme withdrawal, which characterize the deep end of the samatha continuum,
will allow you to do this—but, of course, only for limited periods of
time. Eventually one must come out of trance, at which time there may
or may not be a permanent transformation of consciousness. Patanjali's
Raja yoga is, in fact, simply the practice associated with the Sankhya
philosophy, which postulates a radical dichotomy between *purusa*
(spirit) and *prakrti* (matter). Likewise, if you believe in a God who
stands outside creation, then the way to meet God directly is to pull
out of creation for a while. Furthermore, if you are theistically inclined,
you will likely perceive these states of tranquility, particularly the
deeper ones, as special graces conferred by God. In her *Interior Castle*
the sixteenth-century Spanish saint, Teresa of Avila, vividly describes
the various levels of prayer of quiet, culminating in what she calls perfect union, which roughly corresponds to the very deep jhana in Buddhism or samadhi in Patanjali's yoga.

For Buddhists the attainment of samadhi at its various depths is
more a skill than a preternatural grace. Like piano playing or golf, it
is something that can be learned reasonably well by most people with
sufficient motivation and regular practice. Of course it is a special skill
because of its great generality and power. Most other skills are enhanced by this one skill. More important, it is special because of the
changes it brings to one's life.

However, samatha, no matter how deep, is not the ultimate goal of
the Buddhist. The intensity and enrichment that habitual one-pointedness brings to daily life are but pleasant by-products of the meditative process. Even the jhanas, though purifying and refreshing, are
conditioned, impermanent, and ultimately unsatisfying. They may
even become a hindrance to realizing the true Buddhist goal, *Nirvana,*

the undriven life.[11] Samatha is merely a tool that facilitates the attainment of Nirvana.

The word Nirvana literally means extinction. Not the extinction of self, but extinction of the *klesas*, the "afflictions" that prevent happiness. The klesas may be broadly grouped under three headings: *raga*, *dvesa*, and *moha*. Raga (desire) is the drive to repeat pleasant experiences. Dvesa (aversion, hate, or antipathy) is the rejection of unpleasant experience. Moha is confusion and lack of clarity. Moha is responsible for our sense of limited identity and prevents us from noticing the subtle malaise and discomfort that underlie all experience.

Concerning raga and dvesa, there is an important point that is sometimes missed. Raga means hankering for mental and physical pleasure, not the pleasure itself. The serious Buddhist seeks to eliminate this hankering because it is a source of suffering. Pleasure of itself is most definitely not evil and need not be abjured. Likewise dvesa is the reaction of rejecting psychologically and physically painful situations. Fighting with pain causes suffering. Pain, if not frantically rejected, causes little suffering. One who has come to grips with raga and dvesa, then, enjoys the pleasant without feeling frustrated when the pleasant cannot be had. Likewise he or she naturally avoids hurt yet does not feel imposed upon when hurt is unavoidable. Such a person no longer carries around that internal sword of Damocles under which the majority of humanity labors, that is, the constant threat of hell within if we don't get what we want.

So Nirvana is what life feels like to a person for whom:

No matter how assailed, anger need not arise.

No matter what the pleasure, compulsive longing need not arise.

No matter what the circumstances, a feeling of limitation need not arise.

Such a person is in a position to live exuberantly, to experience life fully, and also to fully experience death. The former is called "Nirvana with a remnant," the latter "Nirvana without a remnant."

There are two ways in which samatha serves as a tool for attaining Nirvana. First it confers a sense of letting go, which aids in the gradual renunciation of desire and aversion. Second it gives the mental stability and one-pointedness necessary for effective vipassana practice. Vipassana destroys moha.

Moha means basically not knowing what is going on within oneself. According to Buddhism it is the fundamental klesa, lying at the root of all our problems. The cure lies in extending clarity and awareness down into the normally unconscious processes. This sounds like much of Western psychology. The difference lies in the fact that, in meditation, awareness is cultivated within the samatha state, that distinctive profound settling of mind and body described above. This allows for an exposing of the unconscious that is far more direct, unrelenting, and keener than that usually attained in psychotherapy. Not surprisingly the results are somewhat different. Therapy, when successful, solves specific problems. Meditation, when successful, provides a general solution applicable to any problem, even "biggies" like guilt, loss of loved ones, failure, intractable disease, old age, and death. Psychology tells us something about how a person's problems arise. Meditation reveals something about how the idea of "person" arises and, in doing so, frees one from the necessity to always identify with being a particular person. Within the context of such radical objectivity personal problems can then be dealt with very efficiently.

Liberating Insight

Sustained vipassana leads to a moment of liberating insight when a huge mass of moha falls away like a chunk of concrete, revealing a vista of freedom. In scholastic Buddhism this is called "entering the stream of nobles." The Rinzai school speaks of *kensho* (seeing one's nature) or *satori* ("catching on"). Sometimes in English it is referred to as initial enlightenment or breakthrough. At that moment the wisdom eye opens, but wider for some than for others. In any case it never closes again. This is no "peak experience" that later fades. It is a permanent change in perspective, a revolution in the basis of the mind.

A breakthrough of insight into oneness sometimes occurs spontaneously to people who have never practiced meditation and may not even be particularly "spiritually" inclined. However, without some background in cultivating calm and clarity, it is difficult to hold on to and integrate such an insight and the experience usually fades into a pleasant memory after a few moments, hours, or days. Occasionally such an unsought experience does work a permanent transformation; but, even then, without systematic practice it is difficult to realize its full implications in daily life.[12]

Late in life Saint Teresa de Avila came to an experience of God that was permanent and independent of trance. She called it spiritual marriage and says it was occasioned by an "intellectual vision." From her description it seems similar to the initial breakthrough in Buddhism, though conceived of entirely in Christian terms, of course. Concerning this experience she makes the remarkable statement, "There is a selfforgetfullness which is so complete that it really seems as though the soul no longer existed."[13]

According to Buddhist concepts at this first breakthrough one realizes "no-self." But this expression, no-self, which Buddhists are so fond of, can be very misleading. At first blush the idea seems uninviting if not absurd. It sounds like a negation of individuality, a frightening loss of controlling center, or a kind of deluded regression. *But what is meant by no-self is becoming free from the concept of self (satkayadrsti).* And this is not quite the same thing as losing self nor does it even imply the *absence* of a concept of self.

What is meant by "becoming free from a concept"? *One is free from a particular thought or concept if that thought always arises without the slightest unconscious tension, repression, or break in awareness of the thought as thought.* Then one is experiencing the thought so fully that there is not time for the mind to tense and solidify the thought. And so the thought ceases to be in one's way. In other words a thought, concept, mental image, or memory has no hold over us if we always experience it totally (vipassana) and yet remain relaxed (samatha). This is no easy matter in any case. Initial enlightenment comes when we discover that it is possible to allow our deepest moment-to-moment image of "me and mine" to arise in this full, empty way. From then on the distinction between self and other (or between enlightenment and nonenlightenment) loses its hold. This, of course, is but one of many ways of interpreting the experience.

Later tradition dilates upon the great merit and karmic resources necessary to achieve this. However, it should be strongly emphasized that, with skillful guidance, a person may well come to such an experience within a few years of highly motivated practice.

Most people, even after such a breakthrough, still find themselves becoming confused, doing wrong things, feeling bad, giving in to unwholesome habits, and so on, though they are no longer constrained to identify with these negativities. So they continue to practice, even more assiduously than before, working to eliminate raga and dvesa, rooting out subtle remaining moha, eradicating the stubborn sway of old bad habits.

Along the way, as one moves closer and closer to complete Nirvana, there may come a point where priorities shift from "wisdom" to "compassion," that is, from meditation to action.[14]

If you really feel oneness with everything it is only natural to take responsibility for all your parts. Helpful words and actions begin to flow forth spontaneously.

Although in Mahayana compassion (really love) is conceived of on a par with wisdom, in practice priority is usually initially placed on gaining liberation. It's just more efficient that way. Clearing away some moha first makes it less likely that one's efforts to help others will be misguided. Eliminating raga and dvesa makes it less likely that one's zeal will lead to aggressiveness and the sacrificing of principles for an end. Further, after one is free from the concepts of helper, helped, and helping, there need be no feeling of chagrin or loss of enthusiasm when one's efforts to help fail.

The specific direction that such activities take depends upon the culture, circumstances, abilities, and personality of the individual. They range from wizardry to political activities.

To summarize what has been said so far: Samatha and vipassana are tools for attaining "enlightenment," a nonself-centered perspective. That perspective is a tool that facilitates the achievement of complete Nirvana. According to some Mahayana conceptualizations Nirvana itself is a kind of tool, a tool that allows a person to effortlessly and efficaciously exert a beneficial influence on others. If you are completely free and if your influence is such that it helps a great many people to also become free (as did that of Sakyamuni), you are a Buddha.

The following are a few specific techniques for developing the liberating awareness described above.

Theravada Vipassana Meditation

A common approach used in the Theravada tradition is to flood the consciousness with more and more complete and precise information about matter-of-fact mental and physical events. Typically one first learns to experience this intense "vipassana mode" of observation for a single simple event. Once learned this can be generalized and applied to any aspect of experience. With practice a suppleness is developed that allows one to perceive each event in the stream of daily life in this totally aware way.

Take, for example, the act of walking. Most people do it unconsciously. There's nothing wrong with that, but suppose you would like to enhance awareness of this event "walking." You could start by mentally noting which foot is swinging at any particular time. This gives you a tiny bit more information about the reality of walking than doing it unconsciously. Next, with regard to each foot, try to note the very instant when the foot begins to rise and the instant when it again touches the ground.[15] Left up, left swing, left down, right up, right swing, right. . . . For still more detailed observation it is useful at the beginning to walk much more slowly than normal and perhaps to pause between each component of the walking. Now note the instant the left heel rises, note the sweep of tactile sensation as the sole lifts away from the ground. Note the moment the toes leave the ground, the beginning of the forward swing, the swing itself, the end point of the swing, the beginning of lowering the foot, the lowering, the instant the foot touches ground, again the sweep of tactile sensation, and the instant when the foot has completely returned to the ground. Now pause. Note when the will to move the right foot arises. Now begin to move the right foot, observing each component as before.

Such an exercise builds much samadhi, but this is a by-product. The important thing is increased *clarity* about the process. After more practice it is possible to apply an even finer analysis. Within each component of the motion (lifting, swinging, lowering, and so on) can be distinguished numerous subcomponents, tiny jerks each with distinct beginning and end points and each preceded by a separate will to move.

If this keen observation is sustained alterations in perception begin to occur. The event seems to slow down, a subjective sensation independent of any actual physical slowness. Each component of the event seems to contain vast expanses of time and space within which to perceive information in an unhurried way.[16]

But wait. As your information about the foot gets fuller and fuller, the foot seems to be less and less there! It expands, becomes light and hollow, merges with things, disappears and reappears. Without being seduced or frightened just keep on noting the simple reality of the foot's moment to moment motion.

This "vipassana mode" of awareness can be applied to every type of experience. One can gently move the eye over an object, drinking in information about it so rapidly and fully that the consciousness has no time to solidify and limit the object. Likewise with other senses, touch, taste, smell, hearing, etc. *This is the fundamental paradox of meditation:* see something *fully* and it is transparent, hear *fully* and there is silence. The feeling of solidity and separateness of objects, which most people take for granted, turns out to be merely an unnecessary and toxic by-product of the process of perception. It clogs the flowing stream of life. One can function quite well without it.

Applying this total mode of awareness to emotions, concepts, and mental images is the most difficult but most productive exercise of all. The stream of a person's thoughts and feelings is so unpredictable and gripping . . . not at all like raising and lowering a foot! Yet with the detachment and one-pointedness of samatha one can catch a thought at its very onset and note each minute permutation until the very end in that same slowed down, complete, unsolidified mode of awareness. A person who can unrelentingly apply this mode to his or her deepest images of self will enter a refreshing new world.

Zen Koan Practice

The meditator attempts to establish direct contact with deep processes. One approach is to pose a question that can be readily answered by the deep spontaneous mind but is utterly intractable for the discursive surface. This approach was developed within certain schools of the Ch'an-Zen tradition, that important East Asian expression of Buddhism. Nowadays it is particularly associated with Rinzai-shu, one of the two major schools of Japanese Zen. Such a conundrum is called a *koan* in Japanese; "What is the sound of one hand clapping?" and "Mu" are two famous ones. The koan question is mercilessly pressed to deeper and deeper levels, and, in the process, great samadhi power is developed. When an answer wells up it carries with it a valuable insight. In this way, by answering many such koans, the wisdom faculty is gradually exercised. However, if the question is pressed deeply enough, the insight accompanying its solution will be sufficient to crack moha and bring kensho (initial enlightenment). It is important to remember, however, that there are many kinds of koans for specific purposes and that individual teachers use koans in different ways.

Meditation is sometimes described as a journey . . . a journey from the surface mind to the unobstructed Mind, a journey made by progressively extending calmness and awareness to subtler and subtler levels, eliminating layer after layer of unconsciousness in great sheets. But along this journey one may experience various phenomena that have significance, though are not in themselves the goal. The meditator may experience warm, blissful energy flowing in parts of the body, see dazzling light, hear symphonies of internal sound, seem to float out of the body, and so on. Or one may encounter what appear to be archetypic entities: gods, goddesses, sages, and demons. In most traditions of Buddhism such experiences are denigrated as stray paths and impediments along the "main line" to liberation. Zen teachers usually dismiss them as *makyo* (obstructive hallucination) and recommend simply ignoring them.

The Tantric Tradition

The Tantric tradition takes a different tack. The Tantrics systematically explored and cultivated these byways. But, and this is really the point, they interpreted these experiences in Buddhist terms and skillfully harnessed them toward the realization of the twin ideals of Mahayana, wisdom and compassion. Herein lies the distinctive and powerful contribution of Buddhist Tantra. It successfully incorporates experiences from the subtle "realms of power" in a way that is both philosophically and practically consonant with the goals of Buddhism. This is part of what is meant by "skillful means," of which the Tibetans so often speak.

Tibetan tradition has thus preserved and developed a rich repertoire of contemplative techniques. Here we will discuss just one, that of "visualization," which perhaps could be more accurately described as mental creation.

We have pointed out how Buddhist meditation seeks to understand the process of identification with a particular self. One way to go about this is to, step by step, build another self from scratch! One visualizes body parts, imputes mental states, speech, and personality until one can see this artificial being as vividly as anything in the natural world. This, of course, is no easy task, but it is made possible through the great mental stability that samatha confers. The practitioner then learns to fully identify with the created being for a specific period of time. Here we are talking about something very different from shamanism and possession phenomena. This is a learning process that, when done properly, is perfectly controlled, lucid, and contrived to bring insight into the arbitrary nature of self-identification. But it confers even more, because the alternate self that is created and identified with is an archetype, an ideal image: a Buddha, Bodhisattva, or Guardian. Not only is concentration power and liberating insight developed by this practice, but one begins to take on the virtues and positive attributes of that ideal, quickly eliminating the subtle remaining klesa blocks to Nirvana. In this way visualization is a skillful means for rapid progress toward complete liberation. It is, however, also relevant to the compassion aspect of Buddhism. This is because habitually perceiving oneself as a spiritual archetype has a subtle and pervasive influence on other people, drawing them in and fostering their own spiritual growth.

Liberating insight achieves the *dharmakaya* that, being merely the absence of any sense of obstruction, is formless. Within, there is constant identification with an ideal image. This is called technically *sam-*

bhogakaya. Outwardly the visualizer appears to others as a normal human being, the *nirmanakaya*—normal but somehow special, magic in a way that people can't quite put their finger on.

The Paradox of Meditation

So far we have spoken of meditation in terms of growth, development, rewards, and attainments. In Japan there is a school that approaches meditation in an utterly different way, refusing to speak of any "attainment" such as samadhi, enlightenment, or Nirvana. According to Soto Zen, meditation is most emphatically not a tool, a means to an end. Rather it is an expression of the fact that the means and the end are not separate. Soto Zen advocates something called "just sitting." To appreciate this we must consider for a moment a "fundamental paradox" of the meditation process.

At the end of "Little Gidding," T. S. Eliot speaks of life as a constant process of exploration, in which we "arrive where we started/And know the place for the first time." If meditation is a journey, it is a journey to where one is. The distance separating starting point and goal is zero. The mystic's freedom is none other than noticing that the bonds don't exist to begin with. In ultimate terms, to create in people's minds a solidified concept of enlightenment as a future goal is already to mislead them in some way. Soto Zen refuses to speak in any but ultimate terms. This is the perspective of the so-called "original enlightenment" school of thought that Dogen, the founder of Japanese Soto Zen, had studied as a youth under Tendai masters.

Then, if everything is already perfect, what should we do? Soto Zen says, every day, for a period of time, place the body in meditation posture and just sit. Let go of everything but the reality of sitting. Don't daydream; don't seek Buddhahood. In a sense Soto Zen is the ultimately simple form of vipassana practice in which one is simply totally aware from moment to moment of the fact of the body sitting. But it is much more, because this is done within the context of the Mahayana philosophy of original enlightenment and, moreover, with the deepest faith that such sitting is the perfect expression of that inherent perfection. This last element, faith, characterized the ethos of the Kamakura period during which Dogen lived and during which pietistic sects like Pureland and Nichiren-Shu flourished.

Misconceptions

Finally I would like to deal with misconceptions and misapplications of meditation. To begin with it is common for people to fool themselves into thinking they meditate when in fact they don't. One often hears statements like, "I meditate with kung-fu" or "Life is my meditation." This is possible. It is also extremely rare. By Buddhist criteria only a practice that palpably and relentlessly destroys the grip of desire, aversion, and confusion is worthy of the name meditation.

Glorifying the guru is another aberration. True, one needs guidance and encouragement, but people who are searching for *the* guru often fail to make solid progress. The Buddha Sakyamuni urged self-reliance and downplayed the role of authority in spiritual life.

Some people meditate for one-upmanship and special powers. They think meditation will give them an edge on the other guy. Actually, the purpose of meditation is to learn to embrace failure as effortlessly as success. As for special powers, Buddhism (particularly Tantric Buddhism) says it is legitimate to explore those realms in order to help others. However, in general, it is best to do this after liberation has been glimpsed. Only then do special powers cease to be seductive, frightening, or at all impressive.

Everyone who develops habitual samatha will sometimes misuse it. If one does something wrong, it will be done wrong very one-pointedly! There is even a technical term for this. It's called *miccha* samadhi. Also, it is easy to use the withdrawal of samatha to avoid facing unpleasant realities. In particular, one can silence the internal voice of conscience with it. This is why cultivating *sila* (wholesome character, morality) is a prerequisite to cultivating samadhi. It is also another reason why vipassana awareness should accompany samatha detachment.

"If some is good, more is better" is not necessarily true of sitting meditation. Some people who sit all day and night for years have amazingly little to show for their suffering.

One of the most insidious traps on the meditative path is getting stuck in a good place. By this is meant achieving some good results and becoming complacent, not moving on to the incomparably better results that lie around the corner. In Zen, a person who gets a taste of enlightenment and does not move forward is referred to as "a worm in the mud."

Deep contemplative attainment does not make a person perfect; it confers mind-power, a sense of happiness that is not dependent on circumstances, and a basically loving orientation toward one's environment. It does not, however, automatically guarantee immunity from stupidity, poor judgment, or cultural myopia.

Furthermore, each meditative system has its characteristic weaknesses. Theravada "vipassana" meditation could make one humorless and depersonalized if not balanced with "friendliness meditation." Tantric practice can easily degenerate into manipulativeness, sterile ritual, and obscurantism. Belief in original enlightenment and just sitting could get in the way of rapid growth. In Japan Zen training, particularly Rinzai training, can be brutal and imbue a tendency toward authoritarianism. In fact Zen suffered a temporary eclipse in Japan following World War II precisely because it had been widely used as an underpinning for militarism. The practice of meditation to get tough and the cultivation of detached repose so that one may kill and be killed without fear or compunction represents a tragic perversion.

Finally it is a mistake to identify meditation with a particular lifestyle. Obviously if one's daily life is seamy and chaotic, it will be difficult to attain a settled mind, but it is ludicrous to think that a person must be a vegetarian or enter a monastery to make headway in meditation. Such externals can help. They can also distract. The path to freedom is systematic and open to all. You don't even need to be a Buddhist to profit from Buddhist meditation.

That these aberrations and misdirections exist should not in the least surprise, dismay, or discourage us. Every tool can be misapplied. The fact is that each of the above approaches to meditation, if skillfully and persistently cultivated, produces a well-balanced, fulfilled individual whose very presence benefits his or her fellows. As such they represent significant and powerful contributions to human culture.

To Sum It Up

There are many paths for entering the reality of Nirvana, but in essence they are all contained with two practices: stopping and seeing.

Stopping is the primary gate for overcoming the bonds of compulsiveness. Seeing is the essential requisite for ending confusion.

Stopping is the wholesome resource that nurtures the mind. Seeing is the marvelous art that fosters intuitive understanding.

Stopping is the effective cause of attaining concentrative repose. Seeing is the very basis of enlightened wisdom.

A person who attains both concentration and wisdom has all the requisites for self-help and for helping others. . . . It should be known, then, that these two techniques are like the two wheels of a chariot, the two wings of a bird. If their practice is lopsided, you will fall from the path. Therefore, the sutra says: To one-sidedly cultivate the merits of concentrative repose without practicing understanding is called dullness. To one-sidedly cultivate knowledge without practicing repose is called being crazed. Dullness and craziness, although they are somewhat different, are the same in that they both perpetuate an unwholesome perspective.

Hsiao Chih-Kuan
by Master T'ien-T'ai
sixth-century China

Suggested Reading

Carrington, P. 1977. *Freedom in Meditation.* Garden City, N.Y.: Anchor.

Emmons, M. L. 1978. *The Inner Source: A Guide to Meditative Therapy.* San Luis Obispo, Calif.: Impact Pubs.

Goldstein, J., and J. Kornfield. 1987. *Seeking the Heart of Wisdom: The Path of Insight Meditation.* Boston: Shambhala.

Goldstein, J. 1987. *The Experience of Insight: A Simple and Direct Guide to Buddhist Meditation.* Boston: Shambhala.

Goleman, D. 1988. *The Meditative Mind: The Varieties of Meditative Experience.* Los Angeles: Jeremy P. Tarcher.

Gyatso, T. (The Dalai Lama). 1984. *Kindness, Clarity, and Insight.* Ithaca, N.Y.: Snow Lion Publications (P.O. Box 6483).

Hanh, Thich Nhat. 1987. *Being Peace.* Berkeley, Calif.: Parallax Press.

Hayward, J. 1984. *Perceiving Ordinary Magic: Science and Intuitive Wisdom.* Boulder, Colo.: Shambhala.

Hirai, T. 1978. *Zen and the Mind.* Tokyo: Japan Publications.

Johansson, R. E. A. 1969. *The Psychology of Nirvana.* London: Allen & Unwin.

Kadloubovsky, E., and E. M. Palmer, trans. 1978. *The Art of Prayer, an Orthodox Anthology.* London: Faber and Faber Limited.

Mullin, G. 1985. *Selected Works of the Dalai Lama III: Essence of Refined Gold.* Ithaca, N.Y.: Snow Lion Publications (P.O. Box 6483).

Murphy, M., and S. Donovan. 1988. *The Physical and Psychological Effects of Meditation: A Review of Contemporary Meditation Research with a Comprehensive Bibliography 1931–1988.* Big Sur, Calif.: Esalen Institute.

Naranjo, C., and R. E. Ornstein. 1971. *On the Psychology of Meditation.* New York: Viking.

Owens, C. M. 1979. *Zen and the Lady: Memoirs—Personal and Transpersonal—in a World in Transition.* New York: Baraka Books.

Shaffi, M. 1985. *Freedom from the Self: Sufism, Meditation and Psychotherapy.* New York: Human Sciences Press.

Shapiro, D., and R. Walsh, eds. 1984. *Meditation: Classic and Contemporary Perspectives.* New York: Aldine.

Shapiro, D. H. 1978. *Precision Nirvana.* Englewood Cliffs, N.J.: Prentice-Hall.

Shapiro, D. 1980. *Meditation: Self-Regulation Strategy and Altered State of Consciousness.* New York: Aldine.

Smith, H. 1982. *Beyond the Post-Modern Mind.* New York: Crossroad.

Sole-Leris, A. 1986. *Tranquility and Insight: An Introduction to the Oldest Form of Buddhist Meditation.* Boston: Shambhala.

Tart, Charles T. 1972. A psychologist's experience with transcendental medi-
     tation. *Journal of Transpersonal Psychology* 3:135–40.
Tulku, T., ed. 1975. *Reflections of Mind: Western Psychology Meets Tibetan Bud-
     dhism.* Emeryville, Calif.: Dharma Publishing.
————. 1978. *Openness Mind.* Berkeley, Calif.: Dharma Publishing.
Walker, S., ed. 1987. *Speaking of Silence: Christians and Buddhists on the Contem-
     plative Way.* New York: Paulist Press.
West, M. A., ed. 1987. *The Psychology of Meditation.* Oxford: Clarendon Press.
Willis, J. D. 1972. *The Diamond Light of the Eastern Dawn.* New York: Touchstone
     Books, Simon and Schuster.

CHAPTER 25

Observations of a Meditation Practice

In this chapter I want to share some of my experiences with meditation, both for their inherent interest and as a way of perhaps further motivating you to begin some kind of meditation practice: I've found something good and want to spread the word around. I've also found that it can be useful to hear about experiences from other meditators who are not "expert," and thus not very different from oneself.

I had tried a little of various kinds of meditation years ago, with very poor results. My main practice was concentrative meditation, trying to focus just on the process of breathing, without thinking anything. My mind was too active to be stilled from thinking for more than a few seconds at a time, though, and I was too concerned with whether I was doing it correctly to be able to relax into the process. This was quite frustrating. I also practiced Transcendental Meditation for a year, with positive but mild results, described elsewhere.[1]

Some years ago I became involved in Transcendental Meditation (TM), which proved helpful on some levels but was ultimately unsatisfying. The following fourteen years were exceptionally rich in psychological insight, practice, struggle, and growth. They involved many years of practice of self-observation and self-remembering, along the lines discussed in *Waking Up* and in some other chapters in this book.[2] Recently I have begun a new cycle of meditation practice, which has been both fruitful and frustrating. In this chapter I shall try an unusual experiment: I shall try to describe my own meditation practice by actually beginning to meditate as I sit in front of the word processor, interrupting the process to write descriptions.

This is ironic in a way, as one of the most common difficulties in meditation for me has always been the appearance of fascinating thoughts about how I would describe meditation if I were writing about it. I have always had to dismiss these as interruptions, but now the devil will get his due.

Beginning

I begin meditation with a minute or two devoted to settling my body down to a comfortable, stable position that I can maintain for forty minutes or so without wiggling around. Sitting in my desk chair in front of the word processor is not my usual or optimal position, but it should be solid and comfortable enough for this session.

I start to settle my body and turn my attention more inward. I am very aware of sensations in my head and body. They are tense, "Go for it!" sorts of sensations. There is a tightness around my head, as if the skull and brain were pushing against my skin, as if they were hardened against the world, and a tension in my neck and shoulders, a straining forward.

One of the by-products of my meditation practice is that I pay more conscious attention to my psychophysiological state during my everyday activities. Consequently I recognize this as an all too common over-excitement that comes over me when I want to get something done. This is a frequent body pattern of mine, but since such physical tension is rarely required to actually accomplish anything effectively, I regard it as pathological: By analogy, I'm revving my engine when only a small touch is required on the gas pedal. My level of activation is much too high for the task at hand.

Even though writing about it has kept me from paying full attention to this tension pattern, some attention has gone to it and it has relaxed moderately. I say "it" because I didn't consciously choose to be this tense, nor does it instantly go away if I command it to. I generally find that conscious attention to tension patterns in my body relaxes them fairly quickly, though, even if I don't deliberately try to relax them. With more attention to or full consciousness of a useless tension pattern, I naturally perceive it as useless and relaxation comes pretty automatically. Now I shall stop writing a minute and deliberately pay full attention. . . .

The first effect of fuller attention is a deeper understanding of how useless this tension is. Since useless tension is a dumb thing to have, this is a little upsetting to my self-image as a smart and efficient person. I know from past experience that insights that upset my self-image tend to make me resist looking inward, but I've also learned that such defensiveness gets me nowhere. So I'll just accept the feeling of dumbness and again get on with paying full attention to settle my body down for meditation.

Settling In

As I settle in a little more a specific component of the head tension stands out more clearly. I am still wearing my glasses. Even though I have closed my eyes, my eye muscles are still straining a little for "proper" focus through my glasses. They have become conditioned to the touch of the glasses upon my nose and ears.

I need my glasses to type. Since I don't want to keep taking them on and off I decide I will relax this sensation as much as I can and then ignore it. This involves setting up a sort of "background" intention during meditating. I won't keep thinking about it all the time, but I'll set up the intention to ignore this sensation, let the intention go, and hopefully only have to give the intention a second or so of attention once in a great while to keep it effective.

I have spent a long time describing the settling-in process and still haven't gotten very far. Such settling down processes are common for me in starting a meditation session.

As I again close my eyes and go inward the tension sensations relax and become a more general feeling of aliveness and awakeness, a pattern of sensations that is more generally spread through my body. I take this as a sign of success, for I have learned that this pattern means that the energy that was being automatically expressed as tension is now available to me for more conscious direction: I have acquired "fuel" to "burn" in the way I want.

Opening my eyes and writing interrupts the settling-down process and takes me back into the tension pattern. Rather than be upset about this I consider it a necessary price to pay in order to get a real-time account of the meditation experience. I have decided to bring mindfulness to this cycling in and out of meditation and so make it a part of the meditation process itself. Thus my process is not interrupted as deeply and I am settling down in a cyclical pattern, a little deeper each time, rather than settling down in a more linear pattern of steadily increasing relaxation.

Concentrative Meditation

My plan is to practice concentrative meditation at first, putting my attention as fully as possible on my breathing. I will feel the sensations associated with my belly moving in and out as my breathing goes on automatically. I will regard anything other than these sensations as a distraction.

This definition of what is appropriate experience (feeling the sensations of breathing) and what is not (anything else) is another of those intentions that will work in the background of consciousness to influence the course of the meditation process. I should not "fight" distractions—that just gives them more energy. Instead I should gently drop them from the focus of attention as soon as I become aware that I have drifted off.

I feel my body settling and relaxing. My breathing starts to become more prominent among the mass of body sensations, and I gently give myself the mind-set to gradually focus more and more on the motions of my belly, rather than forcibly concentrate on it all at once. This gentleness feels right: Being forcible in my intentions usually produces unnecessary tension.

The sensation/energy level is high throughout my body. I can feel my pulse beating all through it, my arms are tingling (my intellectual mind jumps in to "explain" that as a result of the activity of typing— my intellectual mind is addicted to explaining everything!), there is a constriction around my waist from my belt, a slight fullness in my stomach from breakfast an hour ago. I don't want to push away any of these nonbreathing sensations. I decide to be aware of them *from the perspective of the part of my belly that moves when I breathe.* Thus I put more attention into my breathing without actively rejecting anything else.

I also decide that since this is still the initial settling-in period it would be OK to loosen my belt, which I do. If I had been more than five minutes into this meditation I would regard loosening my belt as a kind of "cheating," since I believe I should be as still as possible once I've really gotten going. An older student of meditation who I respect once stated that the first five minutes is usually the squirming period, and I accept that.

I hear my wife, Judy, making a phone call just outside my study door. I'm annoyed. She is interrupting my meditation. She should have more consideration! She doesn't know I'm meditating, of course, but she does know I'm writing and that I don't want to be interrupted. These thoughts go on and on. Finally I call out to her, "Be quiet, I'm writing!" A long train of thoughts of annoyance with her, of annoyance with myself for being so petty, about how I ought to be able to be unaffected by such distractions, and so on, follows.

This long-winded thought-diversion event is all too typical of meditation for me when something external distracts me. I've learned that the best thing to do at this point is to drop the whole thing and get back to being focused on meditating.

Now I've focused on my breathing for a dozen breaths or so, with only occasional distractions. (That I can say "only occasional distractions" represents tremendous progress for me.) I am getting into this meditation. I can feel my body settling and relaxing more, with a kind of warm, heavy, comfortable sensation enveloping it. I sense this in the awareness that is peripheral to my primary focus on the sensation of my abdomen moving in breathing.

My mind is focused on my breathing sensations, but it is also getting more relaxed and contented. I'm getting deeper into my breathing. This warm, comfortable feeling in mind and body feels very like the one that occurs when I'm falling asleep. My meditation experience of these last months is that this is an almost certain indication that in a moment I am going to drift off into some hypnagogic fantasy and so totally lose my focus on my breathing for a period that might be moments or minutes in length. Since I don't think falling asleep into hypnagogic fantasies is the purpose of concentrative meditation, I must increase my level of alertness. In this case the desire to open my eyes and record this event is a very convenient way to increase my alertness, although I lose awareness of my breathing and stop meditation for the time it takes to write this.

An aside: Note that if I could learn to hover continuously at this point between clear focus on my breathing and starting to fall asleep, I would like it a lot. The pleasant body sensations, the calmness, the forgetting of troubles are very enjoyable. If my ordinary consciousness was usually a state of agitation and worry, I would regard this kind of meditative experience as a real "high" and use words like "peace," "bliss," and "tranquility" to describe it. Since I usually enjoy my ordinary state of consciousness, however, I find this particular aspect of meditation experience pleasant but not all that worthwhile; I want much more than that, so I don't want to learn to just hover there.

Seductive Thoughts

Meditating again. For several breaths in a row I was calmly and strongly focused on my breathing. Suddenly I find that I am all wrapped up in a fascinating train of thought about how I might connect the two telephone lines running into the house together so that I could have conference calls with three people, whether this would damage the telephone system, how to try it using a resistor to test without allowing damage, where to mount the switch box for connecting the lines, and so on. I have been on this thought line for somewhere between thirty seconds and a minute or so. It has been a combination of thoughts and mild-intensity image—not as intense as hypnagogic imagery, but vivid enough in its own way. I don't know when I lost track of my breathing. That's my biggest problem with concentrative meditation: I seldom know when a thought is taking me away from concentration.

I love my thoughts. Almost every thought seduces me, charms me, casts its spell over me. It's as if I'm doing something boring when a beautiful woman walks in front of me, smiles, and beckons me to come with her. I instantly forget what I was doing. With a feeling of happiness and anticipation I automatically follow my enchantress. Every step of this journey is interesting, every step promises more pleasure with the next step, and on I go. When the part of my mind dedicated to meditating finally reactivates enough so I realize I have gone away on an enchanted journey, *I* suddenly reappear, the enchanted landscape fades. The mindful, present part that I call "I" is so real, so vivid at this moment, compared to the enchanted mind that I usually wonder, "Where have I been?" The real part of me exists now but it was gone, totally gone, disassembled, scattered to the breeze, under a fairy enchantment.

This part of meditation experience remains the biggest puzzle to me. I am so real, so vivid, when I am mindfully present, whether in concentrative meditation or insight meditation. During this existence as a vivid mindful *I*, I cannot conceive of giving it up voluntarily, of disappearing. Yet it happens all the time. Most of my life is spent on an enchanted journey in the Land of Thought and Fantasy, where this most real kind of "I" does not exist.

Back to meditation practice. I spend several minutes trying to recenter my awareness on my breathing. Miscellaneous thoughts come and go. Body sensations appear and disappear. A slight itch on my scalp appears, disappears, reappears, becomes very prominent, and "tempts" me: "I'm distracting you, there might be a real reason for this itch, like a bug or something, why don't you scratch me so I'll go away permanently?" My background intention to ignore distractions and sit still is not enough and I have to remind myself in the foreground of my attention that I am not going to scratch this itch. Past experience reminds me that it will indeed be very satisfying if I scratch this itch, but a dozen new itches will spring up to replace it, each further tempting me to scratch it "one last time so you can settle down!" Forget scratching the itch, go back to my breathing.

Now I have become sleepy. My mind drifts a lot. I seldom follow my breathing for more than a breath or two before drifting off on some train of thought. I want to focus, so I modify my concentration practice to try to compensate for excessive sleepiness: I begin counting each breath. I think "one" through the first inhalation and exhalation sensations, "two" through the next, and so on up through "ten," where I start again at "one." Since my automatic mind is addicted to thinking something, this is sort of an intellectual sop to it: Here, you can keep track of the count.

This is often, although not invariably, helpful. It doesn't help if I'm very sleepy. It is also somewhat tricky. I want the counting to be a *secondary* activity that helps me focus on the breathing sensations, but it is easy for the counting to become primary, with little attention on breathing. I have to monitor the balance of my attention: Is the actual sensation of my abdomen moving still primary? If not, make it primary.

This brings me to a constant problem I have with concentrative meditation. It seems to me that the point seems to be to become *totally* absorbed in the object of concentration—in this case, breathing. Every other sensation, thought, feeling, and so on, other than the concentration object, should cease to exist for the meditator with this degree of total absorption. But in my experience moments when I start to become totally absorbed in my breathing, with everything else fading away, have always turned out to be moments when I either fell asleep or became enchanted by some thought train. When I am totally absorbed a dullness of mind occurs, and there is nothing or no one left to notice that I'm about to lose the concentration I do have.

I have not satisfactorily dealt with this conflict. Sometimes during concentrative meditation I think I should just keep trying to be totally focused and hope that someday a novel state of total absorption in my breathing that isn't falling asleep or being enchanted by a thought will occur. At other times it seems perfectly clear to me that you cannot literally be totally absorbed in the object of concentration. At least 1 percent has to be devoted to detecting the approach of a seductive thought or the sensations announcing that sleep is coming, and then initiating action to preserve the 99 percent concentration on the breath. I am inclined toward the latter view now, given my experience to date, but the idea of total absorption seems to be so clearly stated in the meditation literature that I remain open to the possiblity that my understanding is quite incomplete. For the present I try to stay about 90 percent focused on my breathing and let the other 10 percent of my mind monitor my state and make little adjustments now and then.

Vipassana: Mindfulness Meditation

Usually I meditate for forty minutes. I devote the first twenty to concentration on my breathing, as described above, and the second twenty to *vipassana*, mindfulness meditation. I like to feel that I have gotten somewhere with the concentrative meditation before switching over when my timer sounds. "Gotten somewhere" I now take as a criterion of at least ten breaths in a row where most of my attention was on my breathing and this attention was continuous, that is to say that even if part of my attention wandered elsewhere at least some part of it stayed aware of the abdominal sensations of breathing all the time. (This criterion of ten breaths is a major achievement for me.) If my concentrative meditation hasn't met this criterion I will do it more "forcibly" (even while trying to keep my concentration relaxed) toward the end of the first twenty minutes, or even continue into the mindfulness period until I've achieved it.

So now the particular form of mindfulness meditation I usually practice begins. My goal is to be completely attentive to whatever physical sensations come along. As a sensation arises in my body I will pay attention to it. I won't try to create or reject any particular sensations. I will pay attention to the sensation as it persists or changes. When it goes away by itself I let it go and turn my full attention to whatever replaces it.

I close my eyes. My attention broadens out from my abdomen, where it was focused in concentrative meditation, moving out to encompass my whole body. I notice a tightness in my head that I wasn't aware of a moment before, but which feels like a familiar tension pattern. Some of it is jaw and temple tightness, which partly relaxes as I perceive it more fully.

I recall that I'm not focusing on what's happening in my body in order to relax it or make it feel better; I'm just focusing on whatever is there. If it relaxes and feels better, that's fine. If it doesn't relax, that's also fine. My goal is to sense it completely and follow whatever happens by itself, not control it.

My mind fills with a sensation of "vibration" through my whole body. "Vibration" seems a grandiose sort of word, maybe tingling would be better. My intellectual mind cuts in: "Is this an *important* feeling? A *useful* sensation?" Realizing I'm not here to *think about* my sensations in this meditation, I let the thought go. Fortunately, I feel, it goes readily, without generating more thoughts.

More subtly my intellect slips in the thought, "But you should relax the obvious tensions; after all, you meditate to break through to profound experiences. You've felt muscle tension and tingling a million times already and they get in the way of the *real* experience, so take just a moment to deliberately relax and clear your mind." The thought catches me, and before I can think again about the purpose of my meditation I deliberately relax my body. The idea seems so sensible, after all. Then again, practically all the thoughts that distract me from meditating seem so sensible.

Well, I have relaxed, there's no point getting further distracted in thinking about whether I should have relaxed, so I'll just go back to sensing whatever sensations there are in my body.

"But remember that important, enjoyable phone call you want to remember to make to your friend?" whispers my intellect. Later. Back to sensing.

A sensation of fullness in my stomach fills my mind. As I watch it awareness of breathing through my whole chest and abdomen takes over. Then this fades and the tension in my temples becomes prominent again. But I am doing it: I am following the natural play of sensation.

Expectations

My mind makes an interesting observation. After stopping to write the above paragraph I again close my eyes and automatically go back to the sensations in my head that were there when I stopped. I can't believe I really put the body's processes on "hold," since sensations usually change rapidly by themselves. Obviously my expectation that I should take up where I left off for the sake of this writing has influenced where my attention goes when I start again. Even though the intention wasn't conscious it played its part. How much do such background intentions and expectations guide all of meditation, even when I am supposedly being completely open to whatever happens by itself?

I hear the humming of the fans that cool my word processor, I feel a tingling in my body that seems to be associated with the humming. I frequently notice that the distinction between "outside sensations" and "inside" sensations of events in my body is not always that clear. Sounds and the like usually generate some distinctly localized and specific feelings somewhere in my body. The humming of the fans spreads through my torso, for example, as well as in a narrow, tubular channel running from each ear down into my torso. A heavy, distant rumbling sound, presumably from some distant truck, is associated with a delicate vibration in the central part of my neck. An airplane sound is like a ball of vibration in the bottom part of my neck.

My intellectual mind would like to construct an encyclopedia, a master map of just where every kind of sound vibrates in my body. Not now, though: I'm trying to meditate, not think up conceptual schemes. I don't want to build up expectations that sound X always is felt in body part Y, and so on. I'm here to fully experience the natural flow of things, not try to pin it down in some scheme. My seductive thoughts—so full of interest and implied promise—are my major distractions to being mindful of my body sensations. The kind of mindfulness meditation that calls for watching one's thoughts is almost impossible for me at this stage.

A small burp. I retaste the sandwich I had for lunch. It is enjoyable. "Ugh!" says the intellectual part of my mind, "What would someone think if they read that? How will you maintain any dignity? When are you going to have some interesting and uplifting experience to report, anyway?" I can get into an intellectual argument with myself about this, but it's better to just drop it and get on with meditating.

I regard drifting off into thought as a failure of my meditation: I already know what thinking is like and how I can drift with it. So I shall meditate without writing for a few minutes until a different kind of experience occurs. Although it doesn't sound *intellectually* convincing I must report that it is pleasing, at some level of my mind, to just clearly follow sensation after sensation. I am a very clear part of my consciousness while doing this and that's relaxing and gratifying. You will probably have to experience this yourself to fully understand what I mean.

Pleasure and Pain

Now I have a kind of experience that is just beginning to happen to me. I slip into thinking about a novel I am reading, thinking how I would enjoy sitting on the living room couch with the sun shining on me, savoring the strange imagery of the novel. Although I am fairly (but not completely) lost in the thought, I notice that my body makes preparatory adjustments to get up and go read the novel, and that there is a feeling of enjoyment in my body at the anticipation of reading the novel.

Shinzen Young has told me that deep mindfulness meditation allows a realization that mental pleasures involve a pleasurable sensation in some part of the body, but this is one of the first times I have actually had some direct experience of this. What would happen if I looked even more directly at that pleasurable sensation in the body? What is behind pleasure?

Odd. I wanted to add, "What is behind pain?" as the last sentence of the previous paragraph but I stopped myself, thinking I wasn't experiencing any pain at the moment, so it wasn't representative of my ongoing experience to discuss pain, and it sounded too grandiose anyway. So I closed my eyes to go back to meditating by being mindful of my body sensations, and a second later I felt a sudden sharp pain in the ball of my left foot, like something had jabbed me. It was too fleeting to focus on closely. Perhaps it was a coincidence; or perhaps it resulted from the intentional set produced by thinking about pain, with a little help from some part of my mind then producing pain so I would be justified in reflecting on and writing about it. I hope it will return and last as I shut my eyes again and turn inward. I shouldn't be hoping for anything in particular, of course, if I'm going to do this meditation properly.

Pain is quite interesting, depending on its intensity. In my experience to date a mild pain coming along gives me "energy." If I have been drowsy it wakes me and helps me feel clearer. If I have been drifting off into thoughts a mild pain brings me back to my body. Then I can focus on the mild pain and it often becomes an interesting *sensation* instead of *pain*.

Some pains are more difficult to deal with, especially if they are the kind that seem to carry the inherent message, "This pain may represent a *real* problem, not just a painful sensation, so quick, move this part of your body and you'll feel more comfortable and prevent real damage!" I usually move automatically on these thoughts, and only afterward realize that most of these are not real dangers of any sort. My biological instincts to avoid pain are very strong and usually overcome my conscious decision to sit still and experience what is.

Awareness

I now notice that although I have not been thinking much, I haven't been very clearly present to sensation either. I've moved toward that pleasant but dull near-sleep state I described earlier. I don't want to be here. It is far more satisfying, in my experience, to be alert and relaxed in this meditation. Indeed the snatches of that simultaneously relaxed and alert state that come along are my main reward for doing mindfulness meditation.

Now, as in other meditation times, I reach a fairly quiet state of mind, following sensations for half a minute or so at a time before being distracted by a thought. I get intrigued with trying to follow or focus on my attention itself. What is it that is aware?

At first this makes me more aware of sensations of tension inside my head and in the back of my neck. But this does not satisfy me. Yes, I remember that I'm trying to focus on whatever is but I want something more than this, I want to "get behind" ordinary mind; I expect something unusual to happen but I don't know what that is. Surely "I," my basic awareness, is more than sensations of tension in my head? I reach some kind of barrier here that frustrates going beyond it. Or perhaps the idea that I must go beyond what is to something else creates the very barrier that frustrates me? This is one of the most interesting and frustrating aspects of my mindfulness meditation to date, the place where I am stuck. I go back to just observing whatever sensations there are, but with a feeling that someday I'll get around that "barrier," I'll find out something. So I end this meditation.

Satisfaction

Given the expectation I brought to the practice of meditation when I first started years ago, this observation of my practice should strike me as examples of frustration. Nothing spectacular is happening, nothing obviously "spiritual." No visions, no revelations.

Yet I look forward to my next meditation period. There is a quiet satisfaction inherent in the moments of concentration and mindfulness in both the concentrative and mindfulness meditation practices that is very fulfilling. I usually meditate in the late afternoon, after I finish working, and most days I start anticipating the pleasure of meditation by early afternoon.

I am not very concerned about doing it "right," now, but somehow I suspect that by being less concerned about how I meditate I am indeed doing it better.

Ending Meditation Practice

My timer goes off, my formal meditation period is over. I feel relaxed and calm. I can destroy this feeling quite quickly if I overstimulate my mind with too many concerns of no real importance in the long run (this is called being normal), but I decide I will carry this calm, centered feeling with me into my daily activities.

Intrigued? Try it! I hope you find these notes of a beginner on the meditative way useful on your own way.

Suggested Reading

Carrington, P. 1977. *Freedom in Meditation*. Garden City, N.Y.: Anchor.

Emmons, M. L. 1978. *The Inner Source: A Guide to Meditative Therapy*. San Luis Obispo, Calif.: Impact Pubs.

Goldstein, J. 1987. *The Experience of Insight: A Simple and Direct Guide to Buddhist Meditation*. Boston: Shambhala.

Goldstein, J., and J. Kornfield. 1987. *Seeking the Heart of Wisdom: The Path of Insight Meditation*. Boston: Shambhala.

Goleman, D. 1988. *The Meditative Mind: The Varieties of Meditative Experience*. Los Angeles: Jeremy P. Tarcher.

Gyatso, T. (The Dalai Lama). 1984. *Kindness, Clarity, and Insight*. Ithaca, N.Y.: Snow Lion Publications (P.O. Box 6483).

Hanh, Thich Nhat. 1987. *Being Peace*. Berkeley, Calif.: Parallax Press.

Hayward, J. 1984. *Perceiving Ordinary Magic: Science and Intuitive Wisdom*. Boulder, Colo.: Shambhala.

Hirai, T. 1978. *Zen and the Mind*. Tokyo: Japan Publications.

Johansson, R. E. A. 1969. *The Psychology of Nirvana*. London: Allen & Unwin.

Kadloubovsky, E., and E. M. Palmer, trans. 1978. *The Art of Prayer, an Orthodox Anthology*. London: Faber and Faber Limited.

Mullin, G. 1985. *Selected Works of the Dalai Lama III: Essence of Refined Gold*. Ithaca, N.Y.: Snow Lion Publications (P.O. Box 6483).

Murphy, M., and S. Donovan. 1988. *The Physical and Psychological Effects of Meditation: A Review of Contemporary Meditation Research with a Comprehensive Bibliography 1931–1988*. Big Sur, Calif.: Esalen Institute.

Naranjo, C., and R. E. Ornstein. 1971. *On the Psychology of Meditation*. New York: Viking.

Owens, C. M. 1979. *Zen and the Lady. Memoirs—Personal and Transpersonal—in a World in Transition*. New York: Baraka Books.

Shaffi, M. 1985. *Freedom from the Self: Sufism, Meditation and Psychotherapy*. New York: Human Sciences Press.

Shapiro, D., and R. Walsh, eds. 1984. *Meditation: Classic and Contemporary Perspectives*. New York: Aldine.

Shapiro, D. H. 1978. *Precision Nirvana*. Englewood Cliffs, N.J.: Prentice-Hall.

Shapiro, D. 1980. *Meditation: Self-Regulation Strategy and Altered State of Consciousness*. New York: Aldine.

Smith, H. 1982. *Beyond the Post-Modern Mind*. New York: Crossroad.

Sole-Leris, A. 1986. *Tranquility and Insight: An Introduction to the Oldest Form of Buddhist Meditation*. Boston: Shambhala.

Tart, Charles T. 1972. A psychologist's experience with transcendental meditation. *Journal of Transpersonal Psychology* 3:135–40.

Tulku, T., ed. 1975. *Reflections of Mind: Western Psychology Meets Tibetan Buddhism*. Emeryville, Calif.: Dharma Publishing.

_____. 1978. *Openness Mind.* Berkeley, Calif.: Dharma Publishing.

Walker, S., ed. 1987. *Speaking of Silence: Christians and Buddhists on the Contem-
    plative Way.* New York: Paulist Press.

West, M. A., ed. 1987. *The Psychology of Meditation.* Oxford: Clarendon Press.

Willis, J. D. 1972. *The Diamond Light of the Eastern Dawn.* New York: Touchstone
    Books, Simon and Schuster.

CHAPTER 26

Meditation and Psychology: A Dialogue

Learning meditation by yourself can be tricky: It is easy to misunderstand simple instructions and not know it. My wife, Judy, and I were fortunate enough to have an extended discussion with Shinzen Young (see chapter 24).

This chapter is an edited version of that. The focus was initially around my meditation experiences, but we ranged much wider and it turned into a fascinating illumination of meditation and our spiritual search.

To begin: as I said in my earlier report,

In this report I want to share some of my experiences with practicing, both for their inherent interest and as a way of perhaps further motivating you to begin some kind of meditation practice: I've found something good and want to spread the word around! I've also found that it can be useful to hear about experiences from other meditators who are not "expert," and thus not very different from oneself, so I hope the following will be of value to you who have just started meditating or are thinking of starting.

Peer Teaching

Charles T. Tart: Now, Shinzen, we're going to discuss aspects of my meditation experiences from two perspectives. One perspective is for you to treat me as a beginning student of meditation, somewhat confused about what I'm doing, and probably reporting aspects of meditation in a misleading way: What would you say as a teacher of meditation if you were trying to tell me how to meditate more effectively? The other perspective is to treat my experiences as reports from a colleague who has studied different areas of consciousness than formal meditation. We both have a shared interest in communicating new ideas about the mind, consciousness, and meditation with the scientific world. Some times these perspectives will overlap.

Do you know of anything in the Buddhist tradition or other meditation traditions that goes along with the idea of having a nonexpert like myself try to teach something to people about meditation?

Shinzen Young: There are various traditional concepts about who is qualified to teach meditation. The general idea is that anybody who knows more than you do would be qualified, so you go with whoever you can get. For example, somebody once asked the Buddha who to study with, and he replied, "Study with an Arhat, a fully enlightened being." And what if there's no Arhat available? "Well, study with a Nonreturner." (That's the next lower level.) And what if there's no Nonreturner to study with? "Then study with a Once Returner," and so on, until he finally said, "Well, study with someone that knows a word or two of the Dharma."

That's one way to look at it. On the other hand, in some traditions, particularly the Zen tradition, they don't really want you teaching until you are pretty far along in your practice. The vipassana tradition tends to be a little more liberal in that respect. If you have done a few years of practice, and you have some knowledge, then you can teach.

There is one historical precedent for this sort of peer sharing experience you're asking about, a Zen group in Japan called the Formless Self Society. That group was founded by a Japanese university professor named Professor Hisamatsu, who obtained a high degree of enlightenment doing traditional Japanese Zen. It was in a period when Japan was starting to modernize, and he was an intellectual. He broke away from some of the classical traditions.

One thing that is stressed in Zen is *sanzen*, an interview with the Master. In this Formless Self Society, which is a major group in the Kyoto area, the practitioners go to each other for interviews. You go up to just anybody who happens to be doing the retreat, on a complete peer basis, and give each other mutual interviews. So there is at least one traditional Buddhist setting where this was done.

Peer teaching is something that I am personally in favor of, and something that I've tried to foster in my center. I am creating a network of peer meditators who are willing to call each other and support each other in the practice and share their experience. I give a special training that lasts for six to eight weeks to people who have completed the basic theory of meditation study and have done some meditation. The training sensitizes them on how to help each other, as well as beginners, in the practice.

This is really quite revolutionary in the Buddhist world. People relate to it. It's not just that it's a peer thing and they can talk about the same type of problems; it's also a practical matter: To continue with meditation a person usually needs huge amounts of reinforcement. No one teacher could possibly give all this reinforcement.

I took my inspiration from the Alcoholics Anonymous Twelve Step program. These programs have found that an immense amount of daily input and contact and networking is required to help a person become free from a compulsion around one piece of experience, whether it revolves around a substance, around eating, or whatever. So how much more networking is necessary to help a person break the compulsiveness around experience itself?

Projections on the Teacher

C. T. T.: I'm not *just* a beginner at meditation. I'm a potentially *dangerous* beginner because I'm an influential writer. There are people who believe I am very knowledgeable about the nature of consciousness: That is partially true, which makes my writings potentially dangerous. It's possible for me to lucidly explain certain aspects of meditation and have a lot of influence on certain people—even if I'm actually off on the wrong track. How do you make sure that your peer network doesn't take off into it's own subjective reality? Do you check in with these people once in a while to share your more experienced understanding of meditation?

S. Y.: You framed your report of your meditation experiences (see chapter 25) as a *sharing* of your experience, not in an authoritarian way. This is similar to the way I work. I want my peer support people to be straightforward about their amount of experience: "I've been meditating for this many months and this is what I've experienced, but I don't know any further than this." There's a built-in safety factor as long as you are honest about your level of experience and you are not misrepresenting yourself.

I have the same misgivings as you about people who believe what you say just because you say it and you are the expert. I think that people who meditate twenty years, forty years, sixty years still feel that in some ways they are misleading students. They may properly lead more than they relatively mislead, but they still feel that they are not communicating perfectly. So it's all relative.

C. T. T.: I ran a growth group called Awareness Enhancement Training for about two-and-a-half years, teaching Gurdjieffian-type self-remembering and related psychological practices. Before beginning I was aware of the dangers of being taken too authoritatively, so *rationally* I did the kinds of thing you're suggesting. I frequently made statements like, "Look I've been studying this for a few years, I know some things about these practices, *but* I don't know when I'm actually mistaken about some things. Just take what I say as *hypotheses*, not as the *truth*." But in spite of my efforts there seemed to be irrational, unconscious factors—psychological Freudian transference and the like—that made people overevaluate my words. This is a real and constant problem with psychological and spiritual growth groups.

S. Y.: That is quite true. Projections on the teacher are very hard to become free of. The very fact that you show such humility and sincerity can then be taken by the projector as proof that you really are the Avatar of the age! So, it's a catch-22 that is pretty hard to get out of.

C. T. T.: Sometimes, when my group was on a weekend retreat and the formal training work for the day was over with the rest of the evening free, I would deliberately have a lot of wine before dinner. I did this partly because I needed to relax and partly because I wanted my students to be able to say, "Hey, he's just an ordinary guy, he's a little tipsy." Yet sometimes I'd get the feeling that they were thinking, "Oh, look, he's so advanced. He's drinking some wine so that he can look like an ordinary guy."

S. Y.: People will find a way to project what their unconscious wants to project. No matter what you do it'll be taken as proof: If you acted in a really spiritual way that's proof that you're spiritual; if you acted in a screwed-up way that's proof that you're so spiritual that you can afford to give the appearance of being screwed up!

One phrase from one of my teachers has stuck with me, with respect to one's level of understanding: "Today's enlightenment is tomorrow's mistake." You have to learn not to fixate yourself, especially if you're in a teaching role.

Getting Beyond Our Biases

C. T. T.: OK, turning now to the specifics of the last chapter, my report was done with an unusual kind of meditation practice. Instead of sitting in a classical posture for a long time I continually interrupted myself to type phenomenological reports on my word processor. What do you think the effects of this interruption might have been? Might it have created atypical results?

S. Y.: It seemed to me, judging from the continuity of the writing, that it didn't have much effect at all. It's also been my experience that consciousness does have the power to go on hold and then just go right back to where it was, even though there's been some intervening activity.

C. T. T.: Given what you said, I'm going to ask one of the toughest questions of all. Vipassana meditation is supposedly about observing the flow of consciousness as it naturally is, without disturbing it. The fact that, in a sense, I could "freeze" consciousness, write something about it, and then go back and pick up that experience where I left off suggests that, to an important extent, I'm deliberately *creating* what my experience is going to be, not just observing. This implicit creation of experience is in apparent contradiction to what vipassana is all about.

We talk about developing an objective quality of mind, a "hands-off" quality, so we can discover truth beyond our desires; and yet my expectations are clearly influencing what's going to happen. I've seen this problem of bias arise over and over again in psychological experiments. One of the great discoveries of our time is that so often we think we're objectively observing what's there, but in fact the biases of the experimenter are creating constraints.

Now, when you begin to do meditation, you already have some concepts about what the mind is like, what meditation is likely to do, and so forth. Even if you try to reduce them you are bound to have some biases. To sharpen our discussion, take an extreme position and argue that the idea of insight meditation in a truly open-minded manner is nonsensical. All you're ever going to find are your own biases. Even when you start seeing some of the surface biases there may be deeper biases beyond that. You're simply going to confirm whatever belief system or spiritual system you already believed in before you began insight meditation, because your meditation is going to be subtly biased and simply create particular experiences that appear to confirm your beliefs. What do you think about that argument?

S. Y.: One way to remedy that is to realize that what you're trying to do is *always* going to be relative: then you're ahead of the game if you are watching with relatively less interference. You may not be able to do it exactly perfectly. Your biases may enter; but then what you try to do is watch your biases, relatively.

In other words instead of being 100 percent sucked into your biases because you are trying to be objective during the meditation, you're only 50 percent confirming your biases and you're 50 percent just observing with equanimity. Then, as time goes on, you can grow with that. Now maybe you're only 25 percent confirming your biases and 75 percent seeing things just as they are. I think that one should not have the expectation to be able to do it perfectly to begin with, but just try to be more objective and equanimous than you would otherwise. And that's something! Does that make sense?

C. T. T.: Yes, and that's the mode I work with operationally in my own explorations, in my own mind. I assume I'm biased to begin with, but I try to see what the biases are and to maintain an intention to see the truth.

Sometimes I use some technical methods that will help me catch my biases. I assume that gradually my experiences will become more and more clear observations and less and less just implicitly creating what it is I already want to believe in. Practically, I don't see how one could do anything better.

Judging from many statements in the traditional spiritual literature, however, there's a belief that ultimately it's possible to become fully "enlightened," insofar as one aspect of enlightenment is totally unbiased observation of reality. So we think of someone like the Buddha, for instance, as having gotten through all the distortions of subjectivity and finally seeing things the way they really are. Could it be that he was 98 percent objective? Compared to everybody else that was absolutely incredible. Is it possible that even the Buddha may still have been stuck in a particular aspect of subjectivity that was so widespread in his culture that it wouldn't even have occurred to people to question it?

S. Y.: I think it might be helpful at this point to clarify what we mean by bias. All the great liberated individuals I have known had cultural biases that markedly influenced their perception or behavior. Sometimes I felt these biases might interfere with their activities as teachers.

It is also true, however, that their relationship with their biases was different from the relationship of the average person in that culture to those biases. One sensed much less of a grasping or holding of these biases, or a defensiveness about them. They were influenced by these biases, the biases were there, but they were held much more lightly.

Mindfulness: The First Axiom of Meditative Practice

Instead of using the word bias we might use the word presupposition or axiom. I reduce the basic principles of meditation to a small set of axioms. When I meditate I apply these axioms.

The first axiom is, *clarity of awareness is preferable to murkiness of awareness.*

To illustrate: You might say, "I feel angry." That represents a certain amount of clarity. You know you're angry versus not angry.

But you could be more clear by saying, "I have a sequence of negative thoughts about this situation, and at the same time I have certain sensations that are rising within my body." That represents a greater clarity instead of the one piece of information, "I'm angry."

You could become even clearer still and recount the exact sequence of thoughts and their interrelationships and the locations and the body sensations. This is what I mean by clarity. It's better to be clear than to be murky about one's own processes. That's one of the "biases."

C. T. T.: From a conventional scientific perspective or even a "common-sense" perspective someone might ask, "How do you know that increased articulation is *true* detail of what is there? What is truly clearer perception and what is vivid fantasy about perception?" I might have a muscle tension due to anger and generate many fantasies starting from that tension, as opposed to clearly perceiving how those muscles actually feel. How is the distinction made?

S. Y.: In meditation we just want to be more clear about what seems to be real. So, in a sense, the distinction between fantasy and actuality is not so important.

C. T. T.: You just made thousands of philosophers roll over in their graves!

S. Y.: From my point of view the process of meditation is not the same as the endeavors of philosophy or of science.

The endeavor of meditation is utilitarian: *to know the truth of one's own internal processes.* Even if those processes are "illusory" you strive to have more knowledge about the specifics of the "illusion." Meditation has a "goal": to allow a person to experience the mind-body process without feeling limited by and trapped within that process. It's not to find some kind of cosmic truth outside of whatever truth you need to know in order to be a free person.

C. T. T.: Let's push that a little further. I practice Aikido, a Japanese martial art that has a lot of connections with the meditative tradition (see chapter 15). I try to meditatively mindful as I do Aikido. I find in Aikido that I can make clear distinctions about the clarity of my mind, which has strong consequences in the physical world. I can be training on the mat and start having *thoughts* that take up much of my attention, thoughts about how good (or bad) I am at Aikido, or about something elsewhere. But when I get lost in these thoughts I am rudely brought back to ordinary consciousness because my partner's attack seems very sudden. She is punching at me and suddenly the punch is right there, practically hitting me, and I wonder where that punch came from as I clumsily react.

On the other hand, when I deliberately practice keeping my mind in the present, aware of what's happening *here and now,* it's more than just a subjective experience: My actions are far smoother, I see the punch or grab coming early on and it's easy to deal with it. There's an obvious difference in what I do. I notice it, outside observers notice it. My meditative practice of trying to be in the present has definitely made things work better. Perhaps the *feeling* of clarity you can get from a meditative practice might mean you genuinely are more present.

S. Y.: I think in a relative way that's probably true; but when you are doing the process of meditation—at least as I understand it, using the approach that I like to use—you are simply observing the mind and body as it is experienced in the moment. If they happen to be lost in illusion then your job is merely to trace the course of the illusion, to experience its comings and goings, rather than trying to get rid of it. That's one approach to meditation.

Equanimity: The Second Axiom of Meditative Practice

Let's continue to clarify the concept of bias. One presupposition we've already discussed—which we called the first axiom of meditative practice—is that clarity is more desirable than murkiness.

The second axiom is, *it is desirable not to grasp or block the flow of the mind-body process.*

Our ordinary tendency is to grasp or block, to fixate or freeze the ongoing process of consciousness, and that is what brings us a sense of limitation and suffering. So we sit down and we begin to observe, to develop heightened clarity. And we make a conscious effort to be, moment by moment, as accepting of this process as possible.

Enlightenment: The Third Axiom of Meditative Practice

I've discussed two axioms: one in favor of awareness, and the other in favor of noninterference with the mind-body process.

The third axiom is, *when we meditate in accordance with these two axioms important transformations will take place within us.*

These transformations will culminate with some very dramatic experiences which are permanent, such that we no longer feel trapped in the mind-body process. Therefore we will have an abiding, constant sense of freedom and fulfillment, a sense that is independent of what may be going on in the mind-body processes. So we presuppose that the consistent application of the principles of awareness and noninterference will bring us to what we might call "true happiness."

I think these are fairly innocent biases.

C. T. T.: Those biases are in accordance with what I think is the essence of scientific method: recognition that you don't know much, and some of what you think you know is probably wrong. But you do want to know the *truth* about whatever you're studying, regardless of what you *prefer* to believe. So you always try to improve the observing process.

You then take a further important step. Science recognizes you'll never be content with just observing something: You're going to want to *theorize*, to make *sense* of your observations, to fit them into a framework. So essential science acknowledges that since you're going to do that then be *logical* about it. Specify what logic you are using (e.g., arithmetic or a particular non-Euclidian geometry), try not to make mistakes in its use, and try to make it fit all the data you've observed.

Essential science then goes further and recognizes a problem with logic in general, which I think of as the universal principle of rationalization: *In retrospect you can always take any set of events that are unrelated in reality and "find" an apparent logical connection if you really want to.*

So you must then take this further step: You must test your theories. If you think your theory and logic do indeed "explain" what is really going on, then keep working the logic of the theory, make predictions about things you haven't checked out yet, and then go back into the field of experience and test: Do your predictions actually come true? If they don't it doesn't matter how elegant or rational your theory is; if it says A is going to happen in these circumstances and A doesn't happen, your theory is bad.

In principle science says that data is primary and theory secondary. In practice, however, the motivation for collecting the data, observing things, is to put it into a theory/formulation. Our intellects love theories! Many meditative traditions seem content to mostly let experience speak for itself.

Meditation Postures

C. T. T.: Let's talk about posture. One tradition simply says sit up straight and don't fall over. Other traditions are very strict and elaborate about posture, with beliefs about energy flows and the like. You have to be sitting in exactly the specified traditional position, with your hands just right, and on and on. None of these traditions anticipated that during my meditation session I would be sitting in a chair in front of my word processor!

Has there been, to your knowledge, any actual collection of what we in the West would call empirical or experimental data about the effects of position? To clarify my question, people may have sat in a certain posture because it's been done that way for thousands of years. They accept that posture without question, but perhaps meditation processes work as well as they do or as poorly as they do for a given person with no actual relationship to the traditional posture. But, given the bias issue we discussed earlier, perhaps people are being taught to believe that a certain position is necessary when it may not actually have much effect on the meditation process at all. Is there anything that might correspond to something like experimental work, or experiential experimental work, on what effects position actually has on meditation?

S. Y.: In order to have that kind of research you would have to discount the effects of other things people were doing, their mental activities. You would have to have people doing the same mental practice, but in different positions. I don't know if anyone has tried that kind of research yet.

As you pointed out there's a lot of variation in teachings with respect to the importance of the position. From the perspective of my tradition, vipassana meditation, there are really two aspects that go on in meditation. One is the *settling* of the mind-body process, which generically in Buddhism is called *samadhi*. There's also the *clarification* of the mind-body process, which ultimately leads to this sense of liberation. Those two aspects are both important.

The posture aspect is more related, I would say, to developing the calmness of the mind and body. Calmness of the mind and body is virtually identical with one's ability to focus and concentrate, and concentration plays the role of what we might call a microscope. You then turn that microscope toward aspects of the mind-body process and observe them. So if you sit in a posture that is "perfect," it is true that it is easier to get a settling of the mind-body, which at the same time involves an alertness. That settling, plus the alertness, is the microscope, and then you start to observe.

It is also true that a person can begin a process of observation without having a particularly deep state of microscopic awareness, and it is also true that it is possible to develop an attachment to certain positions and postures. I have heard of teachers who discourage the use of special postures, and make you do your meditation as a day-to-day activity, while you work, play, eat, go to the bathroom, and so on. This might seem a hard way to go, but that is the method of what is sometimes called *sukkha-vipassana,* or dry vipassana. It's just completely dry awareness, it's not watered by any of the bliss of special concentration states. And you can do that in any posture at all.

C. T. T.: Most of my personal experience is in what you call dry vipassana. It's been work I've done in the Gurdjieff tradition, which says develop *self-remembering,* a simultaneous awareness of body and psychological self coupled with simultaneous enhanced awareness of what is going on around you. Certainly there is no special posture involved; you do it in the midst of life. For me to practice traditional meditation, where I'm sitting still in a quiet place, is very different.

Traditional meditation takes place in a setting where you deliberately lower the intensity of events and stimulation. You're not interacting with people, you're not walking around, you're not even responsible for the balance of your body beyond a minimal level because you're sitting still in a reasonably comfortable position. Self-remembering involves trying to develop mindfulness in the midst of comparatively intense activity.

S. Y.: Remember though, some traditional teachings are that way too, like what you call the nontraditional. There are two ways that people can fool themselves. One is to believe, "I have to sit in a certain posture, and have the body absolutely aligned perfectly, in order to meditate." The second way to fool yourself is, "I don't ever need to sit in a posture like that, I meditate in daily life."

The way that you know if you're meditating in action is if you can stop on a dime anytime you want. Close your eyes: Does the "momentum" of your activity really stop? You should be able to go, at any time, into an absolutely stable, motionless state without struggle if you're really "meditating in daily life."

C. T. T.: I've found that these two methods both seem necessary to complement each other. I've learned to produce a certain kind of mindfulness through self-remembering in the midst of intense activity. It's valuable in a variety of ways. But it's like learning to balance on an actively moving surface, like surfing must be. The kind of self-remembering I do does not generally get me in touch with very subtle mind-body processes, although they may be going on in the background and ultimately affect my foreground experience.

When I sit down and practice the traditional sort of vipassana meditation the subtle processes are much more visible—they're not being swamped by the activity and noise of everyday life. At the same time this awareness at a more subtle level feels like a problem in some ways. A level of thought, for instance, that would not interfere in the hurly-burly of life with a certain high degree of mindfulness now seems like the rampaging storm!

S. Y.: You've raised a lot of interesting issues. We can branch out in a number of ways from here. Before we go any further, though, I'd like to clear up a couple of things about posture.

Essentials of a Meditation Posture

A special meditation posture is a posture that allows for *stability with alertness.* Any posture that allows for that is valid. There is nothing magic about twisting yourself into a pretzel: Any posture is useful only insofar as it allows for stability and alertness. The fact that the spine is kept upright affects the posture sensors that are connected to the reticular activating system. An upright posture keeps the activational level of the mind up. If you start to allow the posture to degenerate in different ways you get a direct physiological impact on alertness.

On the other hand you want a good meditation posture that gives you not just wakefulness, but a real sense of "settled-in-ness." The Japanese have been doing physiological research on Zen meditation since before World War II. They did electromyographic studies of the muscles. People could hold these upright Zen positions for hours and their muscles were showing readouts as though they were asleep! They were that relaxed. A profound physiological change is taking place in the musculature to allow this.

So it's not so much that the legs have to be crossed, or anything like that; but the position has to give relaxation *and* alertness at the same time. You can achieve that in a chair if you don't slouch.

Pain and Suffering

C. T. T.: My personal bias toward posture is that I don't like pain. Is it really necessary?

S. Y.: I described these traditional meditation postures as being stable, settled, comfortable. In point of fact, though, to learn them, you may have to go through some discomfort. Many people have physical pain as their first meditation experience. The pain and tension that you have go through in order to learn how to retain one of these postures is part and parcel of the learning experience. Of course there are degrees of pain.

When I first started to meditate I was very gung-ho on perfect posture. I trained myself to sit in the paradigmatic full lotus posture. I started this when I was in Japan. I'll be eternally grateful for the type of training I was given there. It is not the kind of training that I would give my students here, though.

I'm glad that I was trained that way, but I sometimes refer to it as the "Samurai boot camp" approach. I forced myself into the full lotus and it was very, very painful. In fact the first two or three years of meditation was basically an experience of severe physical pain caused by forcing myself into that posture.

I found that when I would do retreats I'd be spending long periods of time in states of great physical discomfort because I was forcing myself in the posture. I spent long periods of time that way; not just an hour or two hours, but day after day after day. It gave enough time for the "law of averages" to catch up. You may wonder what I mean by that!

As you're sitting there holding one of these postures you have discomfort that becomes a baseline of discomfort. You begin to notice that your sense of *suffering* around that baseline of discomfort ebbs and flows. Every once in a while you'll have an experience that the discomfort will not have changed, but something in your relationship to it changes spontaneously.

That's because there are changes in your sense of grasping. *Psychological grasping is your main source of suffering, not the physical sensations in your legs.* It is how much you are tightening *psychologically* around those sensations that is the main source of suffering.

You may be spending most of your time in habitual tightening or resisting of the sensations; but if you sit there in discomfort long enough, every once in a while—just because of the impermanent nature of the mind-body process—your resistance or fighting with it will spontaneously lessen for a moment. At that time you begin to make a correlation: Diminishing "resistance" brings about diminishing suffering. You literally train yourself out of the habit of suffering.

What you learn in this way with respect to pain of physical origin is immediately generalizable to pain of psychological origin. Suffering is a function of two variables, one's discomfort and one's habit of resisting that discomfort.

I learned immensely from that. But nowadays when I teach I find that I don't emphasize posture that much. I emphasize that people practice awareness and equanimity and that they can do that in any posture. There is a danger that posture can become an attachment in and of itself. It's the "I've got to run off and get my meditation cushion in order to meditate" attitude.

Western Efficiency

C. T. T.: Now let me play devil's advocate for Western culture. There is no doubt that your attitude was splendid. You decided to really learn from the situation you had stuck yourself in, and you did an excellent job of it. But one of our big concerns in the West is *efficiency*. I'm fifty years old; I feel that I don't have a lot of time to go down inefficient or dead-end paths.

A likely conclusion from what you've just said, from a Western point of view, is this: If you want to efficiently teach someone meditation you should sit them down in various postures, put a bunch of electromyograph electrodes on them to find out what their muscle-tension level is, and measure their brain waves. Then you can find a posture for that particular individual that is comfortable in terms of low muscle tension, but also has adequate alertness in terms of brain waves. Who cares whether it's traditional or not?

As I mentioned earlier, my personal bias, in addition to the logic of this conclusion, is that I don't like pain, *especially* if I believe it's unnecessary. I doubt that I am alone in having this bias!

I think that there's an important question here for Westerners in general, and for people bringing the Eastern teachings to Western culture. You said earlier that some of your teachers were still stuck in their cultural biases. One of those biases may be, "I learned meditation in this traditional position, which is painful, and I transcended it, so everybody has to." I don't think that you personally have gotten stuck that way, but it could be a general problem.

Judy Tart: It seems to me that what I've heard you saying, Shinzen, is that it is important not to resist psychological pain, and that psychological and physical pain are really kind of the same thing. So, Charley, you can't try to avoid all those things in your life. If you always want something comfortable, then you're not going to get what you're seeking.

C. T. T.: I agree. Compulsive avoidance is dangerous, and it's a personal problem for me, but I'm focusing here on "unnecessary" pain. For instance, Shinzen, you don't have us wear hair shirts when we meditate. Hair shirts, as were used in medieval Christian mysticism, would definitely add to the pain. You don't have us lean sideways ten degrees, which would considerably increase the muscle strain and consequent physical pain.

S. Y.: Pain does two things. If pain is experienced in a "skillful" way the energy will break up the knotty, hard parts of one's being. This is true whether the pain is of physical or psychological origin. If pain is experienced in an unskillful way it does just the opposite, creates more knots, making a person brittle and rigid.

Therefore there is nothing whatsoever to be said in favor of pain in and of itself for meditators. It can just as much create new blockages as it can break up old ones. Everything depends on one's degree of skill in experiencing it. Very little depends on the intensity of the discomfort per se. A small discomfort greeted with a huge amount of skill will break up knots. A small discomfort greeted with great lack of skill will create knots. This is true with respect to big discomforts. The trick is not so much to endure massive doses of pain, but to develop that *skill* that will allow you to get the maximum growth out of whatever happens to come up.

For example, my most profound experiences of the softening of my being through pain are not so much through the intense pains as through the subtle pains. Sometimes I'll do a practice where I'll lay on the floor and be completely motionless. Then somewhere along the line I'll feel that I want to move. I'd like to move some little part of my body. I get subtle pressures here or there. I find that if I can open up to those subtle pressures completely I really get somewhere.

As Judy said, these minor irritations are likely to come up at any time, so if you can greet each with great skill, they are opportunities for growth.

"Skill" with sensation means to be relatively more clearly aware of the sensation and relatively more accepting of the sensation than you would be otherwise. When a person greets a minor pain with great awareness and great acceptance, then it has a much more powerful growth effect than to greet a major pain with grudging endurance. This was nicely summarized by Thomas Merton. Merton was a Christian monk with a great appreciation of the Eastern meditative traditions, which is not an uncommon combination nowadays. I'm paraphrasing, but somewhere I remember him saying something like, "I did not become a monk to suffer more than other people, I became a monk to suffer more effectively."

Relaxing and Settling In

C. T. T.: When I settle down to meditate one of my first experiences is of tension patterns. Sometimes just being aware of them results in their automatic relaxation, sometimes it doesn't. It's variable. If you feel an obviously useless tension, such as noticing that you're clenching your hand for no good reason, should you deliberately relax the tension, or should you just study it as it is?

S. Y.: You've asked a really interesting question. I believe that there are really two ways of learning relaxation, because there are two distinct levels at which a person can relax. I call them *top-to-bottom* relaxation versus *bottom-to-top* relaxation. "Top" refers to the surface conscious mind, "bottom" to the deep unconscious.

Top-to-bottom relaxation is what most people think of when they think of relaxation. It's voluntary relaxation, like a progressive relaxation where you make an effort to relax. When a person sits to meditate I think it is good to do whatever one can to relax the overall body. I usually try to get this overall sense of the body relaxing. I call it a "settled-in" sense. For example, I notice that during sitting sometimes my shoulders will come up, so I'll relax them as an act of conscious intention.

This form of relaxation, although it's valid and useful, is also limited, because there are certain things that you can't relax intentionally, like the kind of intense sensations that come up when you stub your toe. You can't go through a progressive relaxation, and just relax the sensations going on in your stubbed toe. And what about the sensations that go with a stubbed ego? For that type of phenomenon it is desirable to learn about a second kind of relaxation, which I call bottom-to-top.

Bottom-to-top relaxation deals with the source of tension that is deep within the unconscious mind and way out of the range of conscious control. How can you relax tensions that are not within conscious control? By *observing* them with skill. "Skill" means heightened awareness, a sense of accepting the tension as is. Bottom-to-top relaxation is an attitude. You watch the tension very, very carefully. You get very specific in terms of location, shape, flavor, areas of change, and so on. You just keep pouring out awareness and equanimity, awareness and equanimity, on the tension pattern.

That tension pattern is a conduit into the unconscious mind. By flooding the tension area with the "super adult" qualities of "witness awareness" you are helping the unconscious infant/animal levels of the mind to untie their own "knots." The tension pattern will start to break up on its own. *The quickest way to have that happen is to not want it to break up.* The attitude of wanting it to break up adds subtle new knots. For the really deep relaxation a person has to be willing to watch tension in a skillful way, without desiring relaxation.

Observing Thought

C. T. T.: Sometimes as I'm meditating I get both angry and bored with the tension pattern I'm watching. I say to myself, "Yes there is a discomfort in the back muscle right here in this position, and I've clearly experienced this one a hundred times already in this session. It's not exactly the same, but I already know what muscle tension feels like. I'm here to have more of a spiritual experience than to watch this damned muscle tension pattern over and over again!" Can I go beyond this somehow?

S. Y.: You've asked two excellent questions. The first question is, "What do I do when I've been watching a pattern of tension and I'm suddenly bored and irritated with the process of watching?" The second question is, "I thought I was here to have a spiritual experience, not to watch some muscle spasming!" That's quite a question: How does the experience of watching my butt ache relate to the experience of God? It's the essence of a question that often comes up.

Consistency: The Fourth Axiom of Meditative Practice

We'll start with the practical side. This is just my opinion, but remember I said that I liked to reduce the teaching of meditation to certain basic axioms. I mentioned three of them already. Let's review.

- *Axiom 1. Mindfulness:* To be as alert and precise as possible with respect to events in the mind-body process.
- *Axiom 2. Equanimity:* To maintain an even-minded, matter-of-fact attitude while observing.
- *Axiom 3. Enlightenment:* The habitual practice of mindfulness and equanimity will bring about dramatic, positive transformations in a person's life.

There is a fourth axiom I call the *axiom of consistency*, which states that *reactions arise as the result of observing the mind-body process* (fear, bliss, boredom, irritation, and so on). These reactions are themselves part of the mind-body process and should be *consistently* observed with even-minded awareness.

You've talked about observing tension, then getting bored. Observe the bored and annoyed! How to observe it? Well, your boredom and annoyance can only present themselves to you through two "doors." One is the door of thinking, which is ideas, concepts, images, inner dialogue. The second is the door of sensation: feelings that pop up in the body. So when you feel bored you know it because your mind says, "I'm bored." That's a thought. And at the same time you may feel a heaviness in the body, or a little bit of "yuckiness" all over your body.

Now you can watch the patterns of your internal conversation. You say: "I'm bored. I'm really bored." That's a pattern. Note the contour and cadence of your thoughts. You've been observing a pattern of tension, then you get a reaction of boredom and irritation. So observe the reaction. You just *consistently* keep on applying the first two axioms.

C. T. T.: It is extremely difficult for me to observe thoughts and images. I can observe body sensation much better. When thoughts or visual images come along they almost always catch my attention *completely* and I forget all about meditating, about being there for a purpose. I no longer have any mindfulness about the condition of my mind.

As soon as I realize this has happened I let go of the thought or image immediately and direct my attention back to body sensation. So I don't really know how to observe the thoughts about boredom. I only know how to stop thinking or to be drifting in imagery and try to come back to sensation.

S. Y.: Didn't Fritz Perls frequently say something like, "Go out of your mind and come to your senses"? What you are doing is one possible strategy, and it's quite a good one. It's one of the strategies that I would use if I were teaching someone to meditate.

There are, however, ways to teach a person how to observe thought with exactly the same detachment you use to observe body. If a student came to me and wanted to learn to be able to observe the thought component, I would sit down with her for about an hour and give her a guided meditation with an interactive feedback. I usually can get the person to get some sense of what it's like to observe thoughts in a detached way.

C. T. T.: Let's go into this more deeply. There are two conditions that happen to me in mindfulness meditation. In one I'm aware of some sensation or pattern of sensation somewhere in my body and I'm somewhat aware that I'm aware in this way. In the other condition I'm lost in thought or imagery. I'm *literally* disconnected from my body once that happens. It feels to me in retrospect, as if my body has been switched off.

There are rare moments—well, not quite so rare—when I'm in partial contact with sensation and experiencing some thinking or imagery at the same time, but a part of me is still able to keep track of the sensation. I still am somewhat mindful.

At this time I say that I'm "succeeding" in meditation if I'm having at least partial contact with body sensations, and I'm "failing" at meditation as soon as I get lost in thought or imagery. I tend to think of thought as the enemy.

S. Y.: The way that you're meditating now is a good way to meditate. It's a very practical thing to ground oneself in body sensation. Some vipassana teachers emphasize body sensation as the only domain of investigation. Other teachers say that you should watch any aspect of the mind-body process, including thoughts, sounds, images, and things like that. So one could almost say that there do exist two major trends. One is a trend to just stay with the body sensation as your primary object, and the other is a trend that says watch any of the six senses. (Sense number six is the thinking sense.) And you get arguments (not violent arguments, of course, but *mellow* arguments) between vipassana teachers as to which way is the way to go.

Thought is definitely not the enemy. Your enemy is the lack of moment-by-moment clarity about rising and passing of thought. Thought is every bit as much part of the flow of nature as body sensations are. Your entire being is part of nature!

A time comes in meditation when you realize that the nature of thought is in fact just effortless vibration. At that point there's no need whatsoever to stop the thought process in order to meditate. You might say that you have cleaned away all the ignorance surrounding the thinking process.

Each individual, in my experience, has a major theme that blocks enlightenment. When you are able to "crack" that theme you break through; that is when you get your first real taste of freedom. With some people the theme is rage and anger. With other people it's fear. Those two are common. With you, based on what you've just said, it seems to be the ignorance surrounding the thinking process. So that's something you can explore and work with!

C. T. T.: The phrase "ignorance around the thought process" doesn't quite resonate with me. It's not that I have anything against my thoughts; I like my thoughts, I'm a good thinker. My thoughts are almost always interesting, fascinating. When I want to think about something I do it well. It's just that I've set an intention in a meditation session, or in practicing self-remembering in life, that I don't want to be off in thoughts then. Thought is not bad in itself, but my goal in meditation is to be in touch with body sensations.

Discussing this is tricky: It gets into a superego need to control on the one hand, but on the other hand I'm trying not to get swept away by thoughts in meditation because I know thoughts are major control mechanisms, building my reality, and they are running out of control. I believe that by learning to be in touch with the nonverbal aspects of my self, like body sensations in meditation, or being here and now to my sensory perceptions in self-remembering, I'm learning to live at a more effective and more rewarding level of existence. But what infuriates me is that I don't know that thoughts are starting. I'll be there, clearly *present*, I'm observing the flow of sensations. Then all of a sudden I find I've been off on automated thinking and imaging for a minute. I didn't know it started and I didn't know that I was lost in thought for a long time. That's the infuriating part.

S. Y.: Right. That's what I meant by ignorance. There's an unconsciousness, like a cloud, that surrounds the thinking process for you when it comes on. Thinking can sneak in through that cloud. But that cloud of unconsciousness can be cut through. If I were to work specifically with a student on the aspect of compulsive thinking I would probably take one of two strategies.

One strategy would be that I would have the student observe the *body sensations associated with the thinking.* First I'd determine the kind of thinking the student is doing. Is she worrying about things? Or thinking more as a sort of entertainment? I have no doubt that you, Charley, think to entertain yourself. In that case I would talk with the student and query her as she was meditating. Each time that I sensed that the student was getting involved in an entertaining thought pattern, I would bring her back to trying to detect the *pleasant* sensation in her body associated with entertaining thoughts.

Then I would have the student focus until she reached the level of what I call "detection." The student now has the ability to detect a distinctive somatic pattern of pleasure associated with interesting thoughts, entertaining thoughts, insightful thoughts. Then, once the student has localized that sensation, has found that flavor and the locations where that sensation is likely to come, I would ask the student if she could experience that sensation with some detachment. Just let it go. Just experience it without needing to cause it to continue.

The emphasis is on experiencing it as a physical sensation. Forget about what caused it, just experience it as a sort of mild pleasure like somebody stroking you, perhaps. It feels good, but could you let go of it? Could you develop an attitude of just watching it come and go, with acceptance?

Then, as the student would sit, I would ask her not to pay attention to the thinking, but to wait for that particular flavor of sensation to come up in the predictable locations. Then the student should immediately let go of that pleasure.

The *need* to be entertained would vanish at that point. I don't think anybody is addicted to thoughts; I think we are addicted to pleasant sensations. But the sensations are subliminal, and the addiction to subliminal sensations is behind most of the major addictions people have. The purpose of working with the body sensations is to sensitize the body to the point where you can begin to specifically detect what were formerly subliminal pleasures. You detect them in terms of "flavor qualities," intensity levels, rates of change and locations.

Once you are sensitized to the likely flavors and sensations, then you sit there and you're just watching, like somebody waiting in ambush. Watching those parts of the body where it's likely to come. And as soon as that pleasure sensation comes, you observe it and let it go, observe it and let it go, observe it and let it go. The thought process will stop cold.

Tension and Energy

C. T. T.: In my meditation observation I noted that I was able to turn tension into energy to fuel my meditation. Can you comment on this?

S. Y.: I think that is a valid perception. We lock immense amounts of energy in tension. But "tension" takes place at many levels. There's the gross physical tension that we're all aware of. But underlying that there's subtler tension, and underlying that there's even subtler tension. This is because the whole mind-body process is part of nature. Anything that comes up in the mind-body process will have the structure of things in nature. As science is just starting to discover with fractal geometry and the like, the important thing that shapes nature is the phenomenon of scale. You can take any natural object and look at it at finer and finer scales and there's always structure there.

Tension is like that. There is not just a single thing called tension. There's gross tension, and under that there's subtler tension, and under that there's even subtler tension. To use the vocabulary of fractal geometry, tension is a "scaling phenomenon." This is because tension is a process in nature. You haven't really relaxed until you've gotten down to the subtlest levels of tension.

It is in the subtle levels of tension that huge amounts of psychological energy are used up. It is analogous to friction in a mechanical device. The friction uses energy, but it accomplishes nothing. It's wasted energy. Most people have really no concept of how much energy is bound up in microscopic internal friction. So when some of that internal friction starts to break up, either by top-to-bottom relaxing, or bottom-to-top relaxing, then a lot of energy is freed up.

C. T. T.: You've been doing this kind of meditation for years now. Do you feel you've become much more energetic?

S. Y.: Yes, definitely. I am not in what we would call super-good health, partly because I don't have a thyroid gland, and also because of the fact that at one time I abused substances such as marijuana. Meditation eventually helped me and got me completely out of the use of those substances. But the substances had a deleterious effect on my body, which I think will always be with me on the physical level.

In spite of the fact that my body is not as healthy as it would have been if I'd taken care of it, I feel the meditation is an immense source of energy for me. If a person were careful with their health and were to meditate as much as I do, I believe that person would be feeling really good. For example, I probably average about five hours of sleep a night. That is quite a bit more than I think I would need if I was in really good shape, if I hadn't had these toxins in me. People who have meditated about the same length of time that I've meditated seem to be able to get by on three or four hours of sleep a night without too much difficulty.

Gentleness and Force

C. T. T.: Gentleness in attention seems common in meditation instructions, and in my meditation I find that being forcible in my intentions usually produces unnecessary tension. But if I'm sleepy or my mind is drifting very easily, I find that if I put more force in trying to focus I seem to get more results. Not always, but sometimes. I also remember reading stuff about how if you're really doing Zen meditation, for instance, you'll be sweating like a pig even if it is the middle of winter! There seems to be a real conflict here. Is it right to be gentle or should I be really concentrating?

S. Y.: The important thing is to avoid the conflict by realizing that there are no absolutes in meditation. One just feels one's way.

Everyone wants to know: "Am I doing it *right?*" Most people have to learn to meditate the way a baby learns to walk. It falls to the right, it falls to the left, and gradually it gets its equilibrium. So you just have to get a "feel" for what's right. Something could be said for either the gentle or forceful approach.

A similar question was once put to the Buddha. His response was that the meditation should be done the way that a person tunes a stringed instrument. You don't want to put too much tension on the strings, neither do you want the strings to be too slack. There is a middle degree that gives you the right tone. So one possible answer to the question is that you want to find that combination of bearing down versus gently focusing that works for you.

Another strategy in one of the Tibetan traditions is to consciously alternate the two. You do a period of really intense bearing down— ten minutes, half an hour, whatever—and then you do a comparable period of laying back and gently watching, and then bear down, then gently watch, and so on.

If you're feeling sleepy you should bear down. We call feelings like sleepiness *sinking*. Sinking is broader than just sleepiness, it is any sort of dimming of awareness. If you find that you're sinking, then bear down. If you find that you're getting real tense, then you can do gentle focusing. Which you do depends on the situation. It is what we might call an allopathic approach: You do the opposite of what the problem is.

Finding God

C. T. T.: I'd like to pick up a thread we were talking about before, when I asked you about aches and pains and what to do about these aches and pains. You said I was really asking two questions. One was what to do about aches and pains, and the other was what does sitting there and feeling your butt aching have to do with realizing God? Can you answer the second question now?

S. Y.: There are many valid descriptions of the meditative process, and there are many valid techniques to come to Realization. Further, there are many valid descriptions of what Realization is. Nowadays even Buddhist teachers sometimes speak of realizing God. I just happened to use that word God here, but we could just as accurately use words like "the Ground of Being," or the "natural state."

There was a really interesting philosopher, Spinoza, with whom I identify strongly. He shocked all of Europe by one little phrase in Latin, *"Deus sive natura,"* which means something like, "God or nature, pick whichever word you like."

People were shocked and outraged, and they attacked him for it. The interesting thing is that in ancient Chinese there's a single word, *tian*, which means both God and nature. Those concepts are not necessarily separate in the Chinese way of thinking. Anyway, I just happened to use that word God; meditation teachers just use whatever word pops into their head sometimes.

So what does feeling your butt ache have to do with realizing "God" or the "true nature of things"?

When we learn to feel sensations within the body with an attitude of equanimity, we are unlearning the habit of locking around sensation. This locking is the earliest habit we acquire, at the most primitive level. Our first tendency is to lock the flow of experience around raw body sensations. Then as the baby matures and begins to think, that habit carries over into locking around the thinking process and it spills over into the vision process, the hearing process, and so on. Pretty soon all six of the so-called "sense doors" have a habit of moment-by-moment microscopic freezing. That prevents us from experiencing these sense doors as part of the flow of nature.

So if you start with something very primitive, like any sensation whatsoever—pleasant, unpleasant, or neutral—and begin to observe it in what I refer to as a *skillful* way, you are beginning to unlearn the habit of blocking the flow of consciousness, unlearning it at the most primitive level, where that habit first started at the level of body sensation. As you continue to go through the unlearning process pretty soon you find that you are able to think without freezing the thinking process, the eye begins to function without freezing, and the flow of consciousness begins to take on the qualities of ripples spreading on a lake. The operation of the senses takes on an effortless, spontaneous, "just happening" quality. This unblocked flow is also the nature of the creative spirit that gives rise to the appearance of the world. So there is a direct link between just sitting there, watching your butt ache, and realizing God.

The Desire for More

C. T. T.: During concentrative meditation on my breathing I noted that I wanted much more from my meditative experience than the feeling of relaxed contentment. Would you comment?

S. Y.: Watch that desire for the deep spiritual experience with equanimity. Watch it come and go.

Watch your desire for enlightenment, your desire for God, in a meditative way. This can be very productive. One quick way to get to direct experience of God is to watch your desire for that experience come and go, until you realize the insubstantiality, the impermanence of that desire. Then the blockages to realization go away and the state that you want starts to shine through of its own.

In other words you can't reach out and get enlightenment. You can, however, eliminate the blockages to enlightenment, and then it will shine through of its own. Paradoxically a major blockage to enlightenment is the desire for enlightenment. So if you watch the desire for enlightenment, or the desire for something more in meditation come and go, then that's one way to come to the enlightenment experience.

Another way to put that is that *all you have to do to be completely happy is to break through each moment of unhappiness.* During meditation if you feel, "I want something more in this moment," then work through that feeling. If you can then you've worked through one tangible block to happiness. And then another feeling of wanting something, something different, something other, will come up, you transcend it, and so on.

C. T. T.: I understand that, but I have a strong reaction that I think you would get from many Westerners: You are talking about *wimpy* happiness, the happiness of somebody who gives up! What about the happiness that comes from competing and winning, from putting out your all and getting somewhere, from adventuring and triumphing?

A criticism that could be made of the whole Buddhist approach is that it is only an internal tranquilizer. You just give up wanting anything, so you're relatively happy by comparison. I know I'm putting this in extreme form, but what would you say to this hypothesis of wimpy happiness?

S. Y.: I'd say I am glad you brought it up, because it gives me another two hours to talk! Now we're getting down into some really nitty-gritty issues.

The crucial thing is to understand that there is a distinction between *conditional* happiness and *unconditional* happiness. The point is that they belong to different "dimensions."

Mathematicians sometimes refer to dimensions as "degrees of freedom." I think that gives you the answer. If you have a space that's two-dimensional you have two degrees of freedom, two directions in which you can move freely. Movement in one direction will not interfere with your movement in another direction.

I believe that human happiness is a two-dimensional space, but most people are only aware of one of those two dimensions. The dimension that we're all aware of is called "conditional happiness." I won, so I'm happy; I got money, so I'm happy; I'm successful, so I'm happy; I'm healthy, so I'm happy; I understand, so I'm happy. People say good things about me, so I'm happy.

All those are examples of moving in the positive direction along an axis of conditional happiness. I'm happy while I'm healthy—what happens when I'm not healthy? I'm happy when I'm successful—what happens when I'm not successful? When I'm not successful I'm moving in the negative direction along the axis of conditional happiness.

We devote our time and energy all day, every day, to moving as far as we can in the direction of conditional happiness.

There seems to be absolutely nothing in the meditative path that negates the importance or the significance of moving in the positive direction along the axis of conditional happiness. Meditation only claims that there exists a second dimension, independent of conditional happiness. Movements in that second dimension do not interfere with your ability to move in the first dimension, and vice versa. The second dimension of happiness might be called "unconditional happiness."

Our basic human problem is that we put *all* of our investment in the first dimension. Most people don't even intellectually consider the possibility of a second dimension; and even if they do consider it very few ever take the steps to turn 90 degrees and actually walk, even a toe's length, into that second dimension.

Want to put 80 percent, 90 percent of your time and energy into conditional happiness? Okay. But don't put 100 percent of your time and energy there. Reserve 5 percent, 10 percent, 20 percent at least for starters. Explore the second dimension, because positive movement in that first dimension depends on conditions and you cannot know or control conditions completely. In other words the degree to which you can consistently move up along the positive axis in that first dimension is very limited. The degree to which you move along the positive axis in the second dimension is also limited, but only by one's willingness to make consistent effort. Your movement is a direct function of your own efforts. In that sense it's completely within your control.

C. T. T.: Is there a negative axis on the second dimension? Could you work toward unconditional unhappiness?

S. Y.: Yes, there is a negative. You can go either way. A person who is creating a lot of bad karma is moving negatively, making it harder and harder to become enlightened. People actually move in this second dimension, but usually they do not move under their own conscious volition. They move willy-nilly.

You have these two axes, which create four quadrants. We might call the first axis "worldly success," and the second axis "spiritual success," for lack of a better word. Thus you can have the quadrant where you can be a worldly success and a spiritual failure. You can have the quadrant of being a worldly success and a spiritual success; you can be a worldly failure and a spiritual success; and you can be a failure in both realms. I know individuals in all four situations.

The specific form of vipassana that has had the strongest influence on me doesn't come from a lineage of monks, but of householders. The person who had the most immediate influence on the way I teach meditation (although I'm not his disciple officially in any way) is a man named S. N. Goenka, a very well known teacher. This man is also an exemplary successful entrepreneur in the business world and has raised a large family.

The man that taught Mr. Goenka was U Ba Khin, the first Accountant General of independent Burma. U Ba Khin was so successful as an administrator that when he reached mandatory retirement age they passed a special act in the Burmese parliament saying that although everyone must retire at a certain age, U Ba Khin should continue to work. They could not do without him!

In many Asian countries something like the Accountant General's office is the most lucrative opportunity for corruption that a bureaucrat can find. When U Ba Khin took over that job it was the most corrupt and inefficient part of the government. He cleaned it all up. Now you can imagine that you can't be a wimp and get in there and start cutting people's illicit activities. You've got to be pretty solid in what you're doing and ready to take some very serious flak and threats.

That is an example of "mysticism" and worldly success going together in the East. Let's look at the West. Two of the greatest Western mystics were St. John of the Cross and St. Teresa of Avila. They lived in the sixteenth century in Spain. They weren't just great mystics. They reformed one of the oldest orders in the Catholic church, the Carmelites, which had become very political and very corrupt. To reform an order in those days was roughly equivalent to leading a revolution. In fact St. John ended up being kidnapped by his political enemies, incarcerated, and abused. These are people who had attained unconditional happiness, yet continued to work to improve the conditions around them.

Psychedelics and the Spiritual Path

J. T.: Do you see any use for psychedelics or any other type of drugs on the spiritual path? Or, conversely, do you find that the effects that they have actually hold you back from where you want to go?

S. Y.: Answering this question is a good way for me to lose friends! But I do have some ideas on the subject. I abused mind-altering substances for over a decade, so I do speak from some experience. In point of fact I probably never would have gotten involved in meditation if I hadn't smoked marijuana. It got me interested in the possibilities of other states of consciousness.

I used to do a lot of meditation while I was stoned on marijuana and other substances. What I found was that, yes, I could learn things. But the price was that I developed a compulsion around the use of the substances. Any compulsiveness is antithetical to the ultimate goals of spiritual practice. That truth is particularly emphasized in the Buddhist tradition, but is also acknowledged in other traditions.

So, although I got insights and motivation and energy to practice, I developed, on the other hand, something that was, by definition, contrary to the goal of the practice. Thus there is a danger that, if one uses a substance to enhance one's spiritual practice, one will develop a neediness, a dependence, a compulsiveness about it.

Even subtle compulsions represent really major blocks to the deeper spiritual experiences. So that's an aspect that really has to be considered, because it is so easy to fool yourself. I fooled myself for years and years, thinking, well, the energy and the insights that I'm getting from this justify the fact that I'm hooked on it. It wasn't really true; that was the delusion.

J. T.: Would you say that the types of insights and experiences that you had on drugs were in any way the same as or similar to what you have as a result of meditating without drugs?

S. Y.: Anything that a drug would help you get you can get without it.

J. T.: Are you saying that the experiences and insights were the same quality, but they were just gotten in different ways?

S. Y.: Yes, but that should be clarified. When I would meditate using substances the meditation would get real interesting, I'd have a lot of energy to do it. I could look at very fine, microscopic levels of consciousness, pick up on stuff that was harder to pick up on when I wasn't stoned. By and large most drugs tend to magnify consciousness;

at least most of the ones that I would likely use—marijuana or psychedelics.

But anything that I saw when I was stoned I could see at other times, only maybe I'd have to wait six months or a few years for my awareness to be that way in an unstoned state. And maybe I'd have to work harder to raise the motivation to practice, because there wasn't that immediate sort of interest that the drugs generate. So drugs would give a boost to the practice. But there was an unacknowledged drivenness around their use and the name of the game in meditation is to reduce drivenness.

Attachment and Addiction

J. T.: You would have a compulsion to meditate?

S. Y.: If a compulsion around meditation develops, then it has to be addressed. More frequently we find that people develop needs with respect to the conditions they require to meditate, rather than around meditation itself. If a person needs to be in the presence of the guru in order to get into the meditative state, then the guru is in some way like a drug. Some people need to go off to the country in order to meditate, some people need a certain diet and feel that their body must be in a certain condition in order to meditate.

J. T.: Is there any reality to the idea that being in the presence of the guru can help in some way, that there is a kind of spiritual transmission?

S. Y.: If you have a *dependency* on the guru, that's a drug. That does *not* mean that having your body in a healthy condition, or being in the presence of the guru, or going off to the countryside is not a valid way to help your meditation. It can often help.

If you could use a drug and *really* not fool yourself, then that's the same as using the guru or using the country retreat, or having a healthy body. It is a condition that may help meditation. But if you develop a compulsiveness or a need around that condition then you are going against the direction of meditation. It's pulling in two directions at the same time.

There is another huge difference between making use of the presence of a teacher to help your practice and making use of a drug to help your practice: The drug can have a deleterious effect on the body. In addition to considering really whether you're hooked or not, you have to ask, "Am I willing to poison my body?"

It's very tricky: You might not think you're hooked, but you might have a very subtle craving or addiction or need. *Subtle is significant;* it can really get in the way. So there's the aspect of the cravings or compulsions that develop around drug use, and there is the aspect that by and large it is not good for the body to have these substances, especially with any kind of regularity.

Substances are used in some traditional cultures to enhance and explore consciousness. But in my experience (which is limited to the Native American Church, wherein peyote is used sacramentally) *discipline* is important. I used to hear people say, "Oh, that's just an excuse for those Indians to get high. They make a whole religion about it." But my rejoinder to that remark is that anybody who believes that should participate in a Native American Church ceremony.

The ceremony is usually done in a tepee: It involves sitting in that tepee without moving from your spot, without even getting up and going to the bathroom if you can, from the evening until late into the next morning, without sleeping and with a very prescribed and disciplined ritual. There is not a single minute for subjective "tripping out." Your eyes have to be open, you have to be present in the room. You have to be totally there with everything that's going on. There's a prescribed sequence in the ritual and everybody has to do their part. Peyote meetings are all done for a specific purpose.

There are no individual trips. You are just totally there with the purpose of that ceremony, hour after hour after hour, putting up with not moving and not sleeping all night. It's the very antithesis of "indulgence" in a drug.

The participants are eating peyote; people are vomiting, getting up and confessing their weaknesses, and crying, and praying, and going through catharsis. It's an incredible experience. Anybody who thinks that it is an indulgence or has anything to do with "getting high" should go to one of those meetings. The direct experience will change their minds real quick.

I don't know that every traditional culture that uses substances is that rigorous in terms of how the substance is to be used, but they may well be.

C. T. T.: Is there any traditional use of psychoactive substances in Buddhism?

S. Y.: When I first got involved in drug use, because of my scholarly proclivities, I researched the subject of substance use throughout world cultures. Since I was a specialist in Buddhism I naturally went into the ancient texts in several languages, trying to see if there was any evidence for this. In the Buddhist tradition, as far as I can see, there is none. I find no evidence of substance use ever in the Buddhist tradition—unless you count the fact that a lot of Zen masters like to drink; but a lot of Japanese men like to drink too. It's hardly that big a thing.

In Hinduism it is different. To this day there are dope-smoking yogis all over India. Some of them are phonies, some of them are schizophrenics. Occasionally you encounter somebody who has legitimate spiritual attainments and uses the substance in a sacramental, disciplined way.

Absorption

C. T. T.: Let's discuss the idea of becoming totally absorbed in the object of meditation. As I usually read instructions for concentrative meditation, the point seems to be to become totally absorbed in the object of concentration, breathing in this case. Every other sensation, thought, feeling, and so on, than the concentration object should cease to exist for the meditator with this degree of total absorption. But in my experience, moments when I start to become totally absorbed in my breathing, with everything else fading away, have always turned out to be moments when I either fell asleep or became enchanted by some thought train! When I am totally absorbed a dullness of mind occurs, and there is nothing or no one left to notice that I'm about to lose the concentration I do have. I have not satisfactorily dealt with this conflict. Sometimes during concentrative meditation I think I should just keep trying to be totally focused and hope that someday a novel state of total absorption in my breathing that isn't falling asleep or being enchanted by a thought will occur. At other times it seems perfectly clear to me that you cannot literally be totally absorbed in the object of concentration. Perhaps you can be 99 percent absorbed, but 1 percent has to be devoted to detecting the approach of a seductive thought or the sensations announcing that sleep is coming, and then initiating action to preserve the 99 percent concentration on the breath.

Here's an analogy: I may need to drive around town looking for something, and so I am trying to see what I see very clearly. But if I let 100 percent of my attention get absorbed in the looking around, I'm probably going to have an accident. I've got to keep a small percentage involved with the driving of the car.

Can you reconcile this with the traditional instructions for total absorption?

S. Y.: The mind will naturally become totally absorbed in whatever is in front of it, as long as it's not being pulled away by what is irrelevant. So, rather than look at it in terms of trying to get rid of what is irrelevant, I like to look at it as learning how not to be *pulled away* by what is irrelevant. In other words one is training the mind not to be pushed and pulled by craving and aversion.

As the mind becomes more purified, through the process of observing, these states of concentration will happen naturally because they are the natural state of the mind. It will naturally become concentrated. So what they're talking about in the traditional texts refers to the stage where you've purified consciousness sufficiently so that there doesn't have to be any sense of self or a guiding program to direct the concentration. One way to look at it is that the state of being totally absorbed will automatically happen to you.

Until that takes place, however, one does need a certain sort of guiding program. But the percent of your awareness or psychic energy necessary to guide the process gets less and less as you get more and more skilled. When you first drive a car it takes 100 percent of your awareness to drive, and you couldn't possibly talk to somebody at the same time. But once you master driving that car it takes very little of your awareness and you can talk at the same time.

The important thing is to realize that the concentration they are talking about, *complete* absorption, will happen automatically to anybody at any time as they work off enough of the cravings and aversions that would tend to pull them off.

C. T. T.: I see your basic point, that this just happens better at a more advanced stage, which certainly I'm not at. But I still have two problems with it. The first is that yes, I can get totally absorbed in my breathing, forget all about the fact that I was trying to do it, that I exist, and so forth; but after a moment a process of daydreaming or fantasy or falling asleep occurs. I may have been absorbed for an instant, but then it's just popped me through back into ordinary daydreaming.

The second problem is that the analogy I used has a misleading component built into it; indeed, as you learn to drive very well you can begin to drive unconsciously, but a common understanding of that process is that you have split off a part of your mind to handle things automatically. Now are you saying that a part of the mind can become an unconscious fragment, guide the absorption process, but be out of consciousness?

S. Y.: The answer to your last question is, "I think so." I feel that there are certain habits that have been imbued in me by years and years of practice. Those habits carry me, even when my ego center couldn't meditate too well.

For example, I have a bad habit: I tend to go to bed late and watch TV, even though I have to get up very early every morning to be at the Center and meditate. Typically, I meditate two hours each morning, from 5 A.M. to 7 A.M. I am completely spaced out at five in the morning! I get on the cushion and I can't meditate. But something starts meditating, even though my ego center is not organized quite enough to remember how to meditate. I can just feel eighteen years of meditation behind me directing a process, and meditation starts happening.

Let me also respond to your first question. In your particular case what happens is that you get absorbed and then you space out. That's an example of what we call a sinking state. It is quite true that there's a fine line between absorption and sinking. I would just recommend something practical with respect to that: Meditate with your eyes wide open. When you get absorbed the fact that the eyes are open will prevent you from going into a dreamy state at that time. But it is possible to be absorbed with the eyes open, or partially open.

C. T. T.: My experience is that switching to eyes-open meditation is helpful if it's great sleepiness that's tending to carry me away. But in terms of being carried away by ideas, it doesn't seem to matter much at all whether my eyes are open or closed.

Let me push this a little further. Buddhism classically distinguishes concentrative meditation and insight meditation. A traditional instruction for vipassana is to be aware of *everything* that happens. But in my experience to date they are not really two *qualitatively* distinct types. It's simply a matter of the width of what you choose to focus on. Even open-minded vipassana (insight meditation) is concentrative in the sense that some things are given more importance than others—for example, focusing on body sensations versus other events. If you take the ideal of attaining total consciousness of *everything* and anything in vipassana, doesn't this seem to conflict, at an intellectual level, with the idea that you train some automated part of your mind (in either vipassana or concentrative meditation) to run the show? Shouldn't you be aware of that controlling part of the mind rather than let it run on automatic?

S. Y.: The difficulty is in verbalizing: Our grammatical categories put constraints on us that make it difficult to describe what the process is like. The grammar makes us think there has to be a controller or watcher. But there's not a piece of the mind that does the work and is somehow separate and distinct from other pieces. There is a quality to the mind, or a habit, to be aware and equanimous. That habit is like a watch: You wind it up and it runs. You wind that habit up by years of practice within you and then it runs. So anything that comes up, at any level, becomes subject to awareness and equanimity. It's a *global characteristic* of the mind to have that habit of awareness and equanimity.

C. T. T.: I know semantic problems are a real danger here. Let me comment on that from my experience with self-remembering practice. Over the years my experience has been that I cannot remember myself out of habit. There's always a certain small but volitional effort required to be present. Now habit will make some difference. If instead of just talking "awake" or "asleep" in Gurdjieff's terms, self-conscious or lost in automated mental activity, we talk of *degrees* of wakefulness and asleepness, then habit that builds up from volitionally doing a lot of self-remembering can often keep me from falling very asleep, even though I'm not remembering to make that slight effort that actually triggers the waking-up process at a given time. I often experience "being asleep" as drowning in a sea of fantasies and sensations and external forces. So there can be a habit that keeps me pretty close to the surface instead of getting way, way down.

S. Y.: One has to have that volitional effort going until it just becomes second nature. The way that the habit is developed and becomes second nature is by making that volitional effort day after day, year after year; trying to create that "controller program" that constantly reminds you to be aware, equanimous. At first it is done by force of will. But somewhere along the line that program is not necessary any more; its properties start to infiltrate all of consciousness. That is when meditation starts to *happen* to you. That's what we might call the merit of years of work.

Expansion and Contraction

C. T. T.: I think your description, as far as I understand it, requires an emphasis on one further element: mindfulness of the process of going in and out. I'm comparing that to self-remembering, which also comes from a recognition of the fact that we're mechanically pulled in or out, but by processes we're not particularly conscious of, so in effect there is nobody really home; it's just a mechanical driving of processes.

The technique of self-remembering involves a deliberate going in and out *simultaneously*. For example, as I sit here watching you I give deliberate attention to being more precisely aware than usual of what I see. I don't just park my eyes on you and let my mind go on automatic. I pay deliberate visual attention, I deliberately hear the sounds in the room more. But simultaneously I take a part of my attention to be aware of my body and the sensations that are occurring in my body. That deliberate splitting and intensification of each side is what produces the mindfulness in the self-remembering. Could you elaborate your description in the light of what I've said?

S. Y.: You could be mindful of various things. When you start your practice you are usually mindful of the content of phenomena. That's a place to start. As time goes on the mindfulness becomes very much simplified. The content of phenomena is very complex, but the *contour* of phenomena is always made up of a little bit of expansion and a little bit of contraction. That's how the cosmic sculptor works, push out a little here, pull in a little here. Eventually all you have to be mindful of is the qualities of in and out. Those qualities form the content.

It's hard to verbalize how that process works. Imagine that you have a piece of sculpture, look at it. That's content. But there was a process that produced that content. A sculptor had to push in a little here, pull a little there, and that form was produced. If you would imagine that you had a sculptor who was working always with wet clay and constantly making new forms, there would always be a process of pushing in and pulling out, and there would be all these forms appearing. The sequence of experiences that we call life is actually this clay being pushed and pulled. I look at you and the cosmic sculptor pushes and pulls in a certain way, vibrates and moves in a certain way, and we get the appearance of Charley.

Now take away the idea that there's clay there, take away the idea that there are sculpting hands there, and just keep the idea that there's a process of expansion and contraction. Then you'll get some idea of the Buddhist experience of impermanence as the creative matrix of all appearances.

Within the expansion there are many little expansions and contractions, and within the contraction many little expansions and contractions. *In the folds of that vibrating the self and the world arise each instant. . . .*

Self-Remembering, Meditation, and the No-Self

C. T. T.: Gurdjieff developed the self-remembering technique for use in everyday life, when you're up and active. For instance, when I teach people to do a version of this I might tell them, "Leave 5 percent to 10 percent of your attention scanning your body in some specialized fashion, but most of the rest of it should be in hearing and especially vision. Don't put more than 5 percent or 10 percent of your attention in your body, because if you are crossing the street it is not smart to get overinvolved in the wonderful sensations in your body."

But in formal meditation you're not crossing the street, you're sitting inside where there are no things likely to bump you. So you can shift in the direction of far more attention on this internal process and explore some aspects of the fundamental nature of mind. I suppose there must be some advanced level of vipassana meditation where you can walk across the street and still be aware of the transitory nature of existence, but still get out of the way of the truck. Can you comment on that?

S. Y.: When we first come into this life we form an ego in order to cope with the world, but we also develop the habit of *solidifying* that ego. And that solidifying habit congests the flow of nature, leading to suffering.

The process of going from an infant to being an adult is the process of forming a healthy sense of self. Some adults decide to start the process all over again, at a meta-level, from being an adult to being a super-adult. In order to do that one has to learn the process of *unsolidifying* the sense of self.

An unsolidified self, which could be called the *no-self*, begins to be born within a person. That no-self has to gradually learn how to deal with more and more complex aspects of life, just as the solidified self did.

At the beginning the no-self may not be able to do anything except sit there, or maybe chant. That's a pretty easy one, chanting. That's why we have a lot of chanting in traditional spiritual practices. I don't use it at my center, but most centers do. It's an easy thing for the no-self to do. Then the no-self learns how to do more complex things, like maybe sweep the yard. Eventually it learns how to talk, how to drive a car, how to carry on contract negotiations, and anything else that needs to be done. But, just as for the self, it takes a while for that no-self to learn how to do complex things. Eventually most of ego's activities get taken over by the no-self activity.

Suggested Reading

Carrington, P. 1977. *Freedom in Meditation.* Garden City, N.Y.: Anchor.
Emmons, M. L. 1978. *The Inner Source: A Guide to Meditative Therapy.* San Luis Obispo, Calif.: Impact Pubs.

Goldstein, J. 1987. *The Experience of Insight: A Simple and Direct Guide to Buddhist Meditation*. Boston: Shambhala.

Goldstein, J., and J. Kornfield. 1987. *Seeking the Heart of Wisdom: The Path of Insight Meditation*. Boston: Shambhala.

Goleman, D. 1988. *The Meditative Mind: The Varieties of Meditative Experience*. Los Angeles: Jeremy P. Tarcher.

Gyatso, T. (The Dalai Lama). 1984. *Kindness, Clarity, and Insight*. Ithaca, N.Y.: Snow Lion Publications (P.O. Box 6483).

Hanh, Thich Nhat. 1987. *Being Peace*. Berkeley, Calif.: Parallax Press.

Hayward, J. 1984. *Perceiving Ordinary Magic: Science and Intuitive Wisdom*. Boulder, Colo.: Shambhala.

Hirai, T. 1978. *Zen and the Mind*. Tokyo: Japan Publications.

Johansson, R. E. A. 1969. *The Psychology of Nirvana*. London: Allen & Unwin.

Kadloubovsky, E., and E. M. Palmer, trans. 1978. *The Art of Prayer, an Orthodox Anthology*. London: Faber and Faber Limited.

Mullin, G. 1985. *Selected Works of the Dalai Lama III: Essence of Refined Gold*. Ithaca, N.Y.: Snow Lion Publications (P.O. Box 6483).

Murphy, M., and S. Donovan. 1988. *The Physical and Psychological Effects of Meditation: A Review of Contemporary Meditation Research with a Comprehensive Bibliography 1931–1988*. Big Sur, Calif.: Esalen Institute.

Naranjo, C., and R. E. Ornstein. 1971. *On the Psychology of Meditation*. New York: Viking.

Owens, C. M. 1979. *Zen and the Lady: Memoirs—Personal and Transpersonal—in a World in Transition*. New York: Baraka Books.

Shaffi, M. 1985. *Freedom from the Self: Sufism, Meditation and Psychotherapy*. New York: Human Sciences Press.

Shapiro, D., and R. Walsh, eds. 1984. *Meditation: Classic and Contemporary Perspectives*. New York: Aldine.

Shapiro, D. H. 1978. *Precision Nirvana*. Englewood Cliffs, N.J.: Prentice-Hall.

Shapiro, D. 1980. *Meditation: Self-Regulation Strategy and Altered State of Consciousness*. New York: Aldine.

Smith, H. 1982. *Beyond the Post-Modern Mind*. New York: Crossroad.

Solo-Loris, A. 1986. *Tranquility and Insight: An Introduction to the Oldest Form of Buddhist Meditation*. Boston: Shambhala.

Tart, Charles T. 1972. A psychologist's experience with transcendental meditation. *Journal of Transpersonal Psychology* 3:135–40.

Tulku, T., ed. 1975. *Reflections of Mind: Western Psychology Meets Tibetan Buddhism*. Emeryville, Calif.: Dharma Publishing.

———. 1978. *Openness Mind*. Berkeley, Calif.: Dharma Publishing.

Walker, S., ed. 1987. *Speaking of Silence: Christians and Buddhists on the Contemplative Way*. New York: Paulist Press.

West, M. A., ed. 1987. *The Psychology of Meditation*. Oxford: Clarendon Press.

Willis, J. D. 1972. *The Diamond Light of the Eastern Dawn*. New York: Touchstone Books, Simon and Schuster.

Part 6

DEATH

CHAPTER 27

Peace or Destruction?

Roger Walsh, a leading transpersonal psychologist, has written what I consider to be one of the most important books of our time: *Staying Alive: The Psychology of Human Survival.*[1] I want to share some of it as an inducement to getting you to read and think about it

It is easy to think of the problems in our world as "out there." Yet Walsh notes that

for the first time in millions of years of evolution all the major threats to our survival are human-caused. Problems such as nuclear weapons, pollution, and ecological imbalance stem directly from our own behavior and can therefore be traced to psychological origins. This means that the current threats to human survival and well being are actually symptoms, symptoms of our individual and shared mind set. The state of the world is therefore a creation and expression of our minds, and it is to our minds that we look for solution.

We can have no rational doubts about the horror of the current world situation. Succinctly, yet thoroughly, Walsh reminds us of the population bomb (6 billion more people expected within fifteen years); poverty (half the world's population lives in countries with less than $500 per year per capita income); malnutrition (15 to 20 million people—the population of California—die of malnutrition-related deaths each year); energy shortages; environmental pollution; loss of farmland to desert; and the possibility of nuclear war. Now we must add AIDS to the list. Yet this is not just a doom-and-gloom book: It is a call for individual and collective action in a way that can make a difference.

We have created a world situation that appears to demand unprecedented psychological and social maturation for our survival. Until now we have been able to cover or compensate for our psychological shortcomings. We have been able to consume without fear of depletion, discard wastes without fear of pollution, bear children without fear of overpopulation, and fight without fear of extinction. We have been able to act out our psychological immaturities rather than having to understand and outgrow them, to indulge our addictions rather than resolve them, and to revolve through the same neurotic patterns rather than evolve out of them. But if all the world is a stage, it is now no longer a big enough one for us to continue playing out our psychological immaturities. It is time for us to grow up, and we ourselves have created the situation that may force us to do so.

With the threat of nuclear annihilation hanging over the world, we all agree that establishing foundations for permanent peace is our most important task. The psychological and spiritual aspects of that task are more important than the more obvious political and economic aspects; for without firm psychological and spiritual foundations our so-called "practical" tasks, the political and economic actions, will not be effective.

This was shockingly illustrated for me recently. I heard a great spiritual leader, the Dalai Lama, talk about promoting world peace. I was very moved by his lecture, for he spoke from his heart as well as his mind. He stressed the many ways that external conflicts between people and nations stem from internal conflicts within ourselves, rather than arising only from external sources. We have to work on the external reasons for conflict; but if we want lasting external peace we must work for it from a solid, inner foundation of personal peace.

There were several other speakers at this meeting. Immediately following His Holiness's talk, a woman spoke about peace from a feminist perspective. She analyzed the way women have been mistreated in our own and other cultures, the ways in which war is a masculine activity that especially hurts women, and the need for women to use their power to stop war. Her analysis of the way sexism supports war opened new understandings to me. Intellectually I agreed with every point she made. They were clear, incisive, and very practical.

Emotionally, however, it was a different story. "Illogically" I found myself growing increasingly angry at her and everything she represented. My wife felt the same way, as did every other person in the audience with whom we later spoke. I was disturbed at feeling angry, as I knew it was both irrational and contrary to my own positive feelings toward feminism.

Through self-examination I realized that while the *conceptual* content of what she said was fine, indeed noble, the *emotional* tone of her talk was angry and aggressive and aroused automatic emotional defensiveness and opposition. I don't really know what was going on inside her, but she seemed to illustrate, unfortunately, His Holiness's main point.

If you don't have peace within yourself, your attempts to create peace in the outer world can backfire and may create even more hostility than if you hadn't done anything. I have noted a similar point in discussing Aikido in chapter 15.

Roger Walsh also spoke at this meeting, summarizing some of the points in his book. His practical suggestions for discovering and dealing with the psychological causes of our planetary problems were a fresh breeze in a realm of despair. There is hope.

Walsh calls for us to examine our beliefs, especially the ones that have become automatic habits of thought. We need to personally recognize, for example, that,"Beliefs operate as powerful, yet usually unrecognized, self-fulfilling prophecies." What, then, if we have a belief that nothing will really help? "Our ideologies are belief systems." What changes in our perspectives and possibilities can occur if we see that the "isms" we die for are beliefs, not ultimate truths?

Walsh encourages us to recognize that, "It is possible for us to choose skillful beliefs." We can choose consciously what we will give the energy of belief to and pick beliefs that promote mutual harmony rather than conflict. Not naively, but using intelligence and wisdom. Walsh quotes an anonymous verse that circulated widely in the meditation community a few years ago:

> The thought manifests as the word,
> The word manifests as the deed,
> The deed develops into habit,
> And the habit hardens into character.
> So watch the thought and its ways with care,
> And let it spring from love
> Born out of concern for all beings.

This is a sophisticated, readable, practical book with hope for our times. I cannot recommend it too highly. I reiterate the main point: If we do not establish peace in our hearts, our efforts to establish peace in the world are bound to fail.

Suggested Reading

Goldstein, J., and J. Kornfield. 1987. *Seeking the Heart of Wisdom: The Path of Insight Meditation*. Boston: Shambhala.

Gyatso, T. (The Dalai Lama). 1984. *Kindness, Clarity, and Insight*. Ithaca, N.Y.: Snow Lion Publications (P.O. Box 6483).

Hanh, Thich Nhat. 1987. *Being Peace*. Berkeley, Calif.: Parallax Press.

Sole-Leris, A. 1986. *Tranquility and Insight: An Introduction to the Oldest Form of Buddhist Meditation*. Boston: Shambhala.
Walsh, R. 1984. *Staying Alive: The Psychology of Human Survival*. Boulder, Colo.: New Science Library.

CHAPTER 28

A Dream of the Other Side

There has been a lot of death in my life lately. Like most of us I don't think about death much, and when I do I intellectualize it. In this chapter I am going to share some personal information and my feelings about death.

Our culture has developed a mythos of the "objective scientist," myths about the disinterested observer and investigator, above-normal human feelings and motives, relentlessly pursuing truth at all costs. We know it's not really true, but we all conspire in upholding this mythos. Scientists almost always communicate the results of their investigations in a cool, apparently objective language that fits our expectations of a detached, purely intellectual mind, and nonscientists support this style.

I have deliberately broken with this mythos in this chapter, even though I will be quite cool and intellectual for the most part in the following chapter on the possibility of survival of death in some form. Death, and the possibility of some kind of survival, is too important to be treated only intellectually, useful as that kind of treatment is. When I function as a scientist I try to be as objective as possible and to make it clear when I am functioning in the wider context of a human being who has other motives in addition to seeking truth. Please keep this human side of knowledge in mind as you read this chapter and the next. They are best read with your heart as well as your head.

It is usually unpleasant to be reminded of our mortality, but—on instructions from the dream world—I want to share with you an unusual dream event on just that subject. First, some background; I shall write for now from the perspective of June 1987, when these events started:

The Events of June 1987

A few months ago my mother discovered she has a thoracic aortic aneurysm, a swelling of an artery just outside her heart, that might burst at any time. The surgery that might correct it is very risky, so she decided to just live with it. It keeps death close to the surface of our minds.

Shortly before that discovery my close friend Anne (I'll use pseudonyms throughout this chapter) told me that her friend William had just died, quite young, of AIDS. Anne and I had talked about William's suffering and impending death for several months. AIDS is keeping all of us, even if we believe we are in a low-risk group, more aware of death. My wife, Judy, is a nurse in an infant intensive care unit. She frequently worries, like all the other nurses on her unit, about the possibility of contracting it from exposure to contaminated blood at work.

Anne and her husband, Bob, had also been talking with us a great deal the last couple of month's about Bob's father, who had been taken ill with cancer quite suddenly and was going downhill fast. He struggled for a while, but decided the pain wasn't worth it and that he wanted to leave. Last Friday night he died.

One of our oldest friends, Edna, entered the hospital early last week for a hysterectomy to stop constant bleeding. It's a relatively safe operation, but there's always some risk of death in any operation. Edna didn't want any visitors while she was in the hospital, so we planned to visit her Sunday morning, after she'd been home for a couple of days and was feeling better. Since Bob's father died that Friday night we decided that after seeing Edna Sunday morning we would visit Anne and Bob in Mountainview that afternoon and try to be helpful to them.

One more reminder of death: When we went to see Edna we found out that her husband, Harry, also one of our oldest friends, had been in the hospital the week before. Harry doesn't like people to worry about his problems, so he usually doesn't let us know about his frequent hospitalizations until they are over. He has been diabetic for a long time and has been losing circulation and sensation in his feet. An infected toe had to be amputated several years ago; a second toe had become infected and was amputated this time. Harry has developed other cardiovascular problems in the meantime so the operation was risky.

Harry's Dream

Harry had a dream four nights before we came down to visit him and Edna. Harry seldom dreams, and then only in disconnected fragments in black and white. Dreams have not been of much interest to Harry, and he has never bothered to take notes on them. But he felt compelled to take notes on this one and tell me about it instantly when we arrived, not only because it was vivid in color and unusual, but because it ended with an admonition from a dream character to tell me about the dream! I think Harry's dream is valuable to all of us. Here it is.

In this dream, instead of being my present age and health, I found myself young, virile, and in perfect health. I had a full head of hair, my hearing was acute instead of needing a hearing aid, and I had all my toes, none were amputated.

I was dressed in a yellow top, brown pants, and hiking boots, hiking along. I had to duck under a low tree, and on the other side was a cream-colored pickup truck, a 1978 Chevy. There was a guy of about fifty at the truck, wearing bib overalls, a trucker's green cap, white shirt, and boots.

He said he needed a copy of a book, the H to Z volume of the *Book of Knowledge* by Zalatos. He asked where I was from, and I told him Menlo Park. He said, "That's a long way from the Valley, how long have you been walking?"

"I don't know, a long time, I guess."

"My name is John. Come in the house and have some iced tea."

I followed John in. He didn't ask my name, nor did anyone else in the house ask. There was an older man and woman there that everybody called "Mom" and "Pop." They seemed to know me, but they didn't seem familiar to me.

They acted like simple country folk, but there was a strength and intelligence of superior nature in them. I was not ill at ease; on the contrary we spoke for quite a while with a comfortable, easy feeling. I felt at home.

I indicated I would like to see more of the Valley. They said their daughter Terry owned a Cessna 225. They took me to where she worked. I walked with them across the road and there was the white and red eight-passenger Cessna. They pointed to a small office building about a hundred yards away. I walked in the glass double door in the front.

There were no signs on the building. It was very plain, one story. To the left was a counter, behind the counter at the desk was an average, brown-haired 5'5" pleasant girl. She wasn't particularly beautiful, but I had to charm her away from her fiancé and marry her; I don't know why, not for sexual reasons.

When she saw me she spoke charmingly and completely ignored Jim, her fiancé. He finally went away in disgust.

We went to the Cessna and flew around the Valley for about one-and-a-half hours. It was beautiful. Completely rural, no factory buildings or towns, just farms.

When we landed she asked me to supper—not dinner, the word I would use, but supper. I agreed and we went down the road to the farm house and ate and ate. Vegetarian! It was the best food I ever ate! We complimented "Mom," and she just smiled. I don't know what we talked about, but it was late when I left, saying "I'll be back tomorrow to marry Terry." Everyone agreed, and I left.

It was only an instant when it was morning and I was back. We were married by John. There was no sexual feeling whatsoever in this entire dream, oddly.

Terry and I returned to the farm after driving the cream Chevy truck over very bumpy rural roads, seeing ordinary rural scenes. We arrived back at the farm about 9 P.M. and Terry said she would wait in the truck for me.

John, his brother "Pop," and "Mom" (his wife) were glad to see me. I said that Terry and I were going to Menlo Park. They seemed momentarily sad, but said it was probably best. John said "Don't forget my book at Kepler's," and he gave me twenty dollars for it. We all embraced and I went back to the truck.

Terry seemed distraught and ill. I told her she would love Menlo Park. She wanly smiled. She said that if something ever happened to her I had to "see Charley."

The dream ended.

I found this dream very moving, as it seemed to be a clear indication that some deeper part of Harry's mind (or something beyond his personal mind) was preparing him for death. I have no idea what the time frame might be: Harry could die next year or in twenty years, but the preparation was clear. That the dream clearly admonished him to tell me about it—Terry was clearly going fast—put me in an especially responsible position.

At the same time I was hesitant to say anything: It's not a normal part of polite conversation to tell someone that you think he's preparing to die. Might I upset him? But Harry was a good friend and a brave man who has lived with the possibility of death for a long time, so only honesty would be right. I also remembered that Harry had had a near-death experience when he was young that we had discussed occasionally, and so he did not have some of the usual fears of death. I told him my impression, and he agreed with me that it seemed appropriate. Here are the main points that we agreed on.

1. The unusual clarity, color, specificity, coherence, and long duration of the dream, plus the compulsion to write it down, meant it was an important message.
2. Harry's being in perfect health, young and virile, symbolizes transcending the limits of physical life in an afterlife. The prominent lack of sexual feeling in the dream acts like a statement that the dream is not about ordinary life.
3. He had had to journey a long way on his own—when people in the San Francisco Bay Area speak of the "Valley" we usually mean the Central Valley of California, which would be a one- or two-day hike from most places. Then he had to cross a barrier— ducking under the low-lying branches of the tree—to reach the beautiful country on the other side, symbolic of crossing to the other side.
4. The fact that he was completely accepted and felt so much at ease on the other side is typical of near-death experiences. Even though our ordinary mind may be surprised and not understand everything, the other side accepts and understands.
5. The rural setting of the dream was a puzzle and great attention-getter for Harry. He describes himself as a city boy, and his ancestors for hundreds of years have all been city dwellers. He and Edna spent several days with Judy and me in the country about twenty-five years ago, and that was the only time he's spent any time in a really rural setting. He's not a hiker and has never owned a pair of hiking boots.
6. The *Book of Knowledge* by "Zalatos" is most puzzling. Harry is sure of the name, but has never heard of Zalatos. It wasn't Zoroaster or Zarathustra, but Zalatos. Are the inhabitants of the Valley seeking more knowledge that can only be obtained from the living?

After we left and drove on to see Anne and Bob I felt that this dream, while clearly for Harry, was also intended for wider circulation, so I told it to Anne and Bob, who found it highly relevant for their grieving over Bob's father's death.

And now you have the dream . . .

What Happened Next

Death has stayed very close to me.

• In late June 1987 my mother's aneurysm suddenly started bleeding. We decided she should have the surgery anyway, risky as it was. She never regained consciousness and died on July 3.

- In the fall my godson Joshua was killed in an automobile accident in Colorado.
- On January 21, 1988, Harry died: a sudden, massive heart attack while he was brushing his teeth, a few frantic hours at the hospital as they tried to save him, but to no avail.

Death was a mercy, I think, because Harry was rapidly going downhill into invalidism and constant suffering. As a diabetic he had always had medical problems come and go, but he had a courageous spirit and a love for life that allowed him to cope very well and lead a satisfying life for many years. I have always taken him as an inspiration for others with chronic illnesses. Now his kidneys had failed badly and he was on dialysis, his liver wasn't functioning properly, another toe had been amputated because of an incurable infection, his hearing was worse, he could hardly read (and he loved to read), he needed an operation for cataracts, and on and on. He was taking dozens of different medications, suffering side-effects as his doctors tried to find medications that would slow his decline. The likely future was of a long, slow, undignified death, with all of his and his family's attention focused on coping with these many illnesses. For a man who was interested in so many things in life, who didn't like to impose on people, this coming constriction and suffering would have been terrible.

I like to believe he is hiking in that fertile valley now, with a perfect, youthful body. I like to think that Harry, a musician who had been partly deaf for many years, is hearing the most beautiful music. I will miss him.

We went to see Harry just a couple of weeks before he died, when he was on a temporary upswing and had enough energy to be himself for a couple of hours. He spontaneously told me that he loved me, and I told him the same. That was an incredible interaction for two guys who grew up in New Jersey. A capstone for a long, long friendship.

Harry never did go to Kepler's to look for the H-to-Z volume of the Zalatos *Book of Knowledge*. I wasn't sure I wanted him to, as that might mean the end of his time here, and I think he had the same ambivalence. Perhaps I shall go and look for it as a completion of his dream.

January 21, 1988

I had a long conversation with Edna earlier in the evening that Harry died. Among other things I told her that I had put a book in the mail for Harry about death and survival.[1] I particularly recommended the chapter by the noted Tibetan teacher Sogyal Rinpoche on Tibetan Buddhist ideas about what happens at and after death, and ways to help the recently deceased use the after-death experiences happily and to continue their personal evolution.

I expected that Harry might experience a variety of altered states in connections with his medical problems, so I also told her to remind Harry that he was still working for me: I expected reports on any interesting experiences he had! I had talked with Harry about many kinds of psychic and other experiences over the years, and this was a prominent area of our mutual interests. This was not only an interest Harry and I shared, but I thought that reminding him of our mutual interests would strengthen him in his difficulties.

Edna told Harry about our phone conversation, and he laughed happily about it. It was only about an hour later that he suddenly had his massive heart attack and died.

A Journey

In my meditation period this afternoon, which I devoted to Harry and Edna and their children, I suddenly thought about going to Harry in a "shamanic journey" sort of way. I was just sitting quietly, observing my experience (practicing vipassana meditation), when the idea came to me. I did not listen to any drumming, as I always have in years past when I tried this sort of "shamanic journey." Instead I pictured myself as entering my special tunnel to the "underworld" and finding one of my "helpers." He was right there. He took me on his back and we flew up into the sky.

There was Harry, looking great, flying around in the clouds, happy as a kid with a new toy. He didn't use words, but the feeling tone he communicated to me was, "This is wonderful! I can't wait to see more of it!" We embraced and said a quick goodbye, and Harry sailed up into the beckoning sky . . . I returned to sitting in my living room, meditating. My intellectual, scientific mind wanted to question the experience, attack its reality; but I have slowly learned to inhibit this when it is manifestly inappropriate.

Zalatos

Zalatos: a difficult character to track down. I found no author named Zalatos in *Books in Print*. There are three *Book of Knowledge* books listed: one by Maimonides, one by Al Ghazali, both well-known sages; the third is by Faris, someone whose name rings no bell and has no resemblance to Zalatos. I eventually tracked down a reference to a fourth *Book of Knowledge* by Strongcharges, which is a mixture of information on astrology and good husbandry. I also had a reference librarian look for anyone named Zalatos. No authors by that name, current or past. The best the librarian could come up with was "Simon called Zelotes," also known as St. Simon, one of Christ's disciples:

And it came to pass in those days that he went out into a mountain to pray, and continued all night in prayer to God. And when it was day he called unto him his disciples: and of them he choose twelve, whom also he named apostles; Simon (whom he also named Peter) and Andrew his brother, James and John, and Philip and Bartholomew, Matthew and Thomas, James the son of Alphaeus, and *Simon* called Zelotes [my emphasis]. (Luke 6:12–15)

Harry was a former church choir director and vocalist. He may well have heard the name of Simon Zelotes during sermons and readings, even if he had consciously forgotten it. I think this is probably the right Zalatos, and the symbolism of salvation is very strong. And perhaps the H to Z volume symbolizes from Harry to the end.

The Possibility of Survival

Our story goes on. Perhaps Harry's does too.

We are usually in a hurry to understand things, and I am no exception. Harry's dream made a lot of sense as soon as I heard it, and much more sense once we had discussed it.

The big exception was Terry. Who was this woman who played such a prominent role in Harry's dream? What did she represent?

The dream Terry was described as an "average, brown-haired 5'5" pleasant girl. She wasn't particularly beautiful . . ." She seems to have been rather well off, since she owned an eight-passenger Cessna airplane. She spoke charmingly to Harry and completely ignored her fiancé Jim. She flew Harry over the beautiful, completely rural valley for more than an hour. She asked him to a meal of the best food he ever ate. She married him. Then she became distraught and ill and told Harry that if something ever happened to her he had to "see Charley."

Harry was clearly puzzled by her in the dream. He had to charm her away from her dream fiancé Jim, but he didn't know why. It wasn't for the sexual reasons we normally associate charming someone with. Harry and Terry were married by John, but Harry remarked again in his account that there were no sexual feelings whatsoever on this occasion where one would usually expect some. I recall in my conversations about the dream with Harry that we could arrive at no clear meaning for Terry, a plain girl who had no associations for Harry.

Whether we're in a hurry for meaning or not, sometimes it takes time for things to reveal themselves more fully. News received from Harry's wife Edna has made Terry's presence much more interesting.

More than twenty-five years ago, when Harry and Edna lived back on the east coast, Harry's first teaching job was under the supervision of a teacher named Jimmy. Jimmy was a plain, down-to-earth man and became a good friend of Harry and Edna.

Jimmy was married to Terry.

Terry became a good friend of Harry and Edna, although they didn't know her as well as Jimmy.

Terry was also a plain, average looking woman, and she was wealthy from inherited money. She was charming and always smiling. Although she could afford whatever clothes she wanted, she often wore plaid shirts and jeans at a time when few American women dressed in this informal, "country" way.

Terry and Jimmy did a lot of things Harry and Edna would have liked to do in terms of "living the good life," such as frequent trips into New York City for dinner, nights out at the opera, and vacations to Europe and various islands.

The little town Harry and Edna lived in then was surrounded by rural, farming country in the Delaware Valley area of New Jersey and Pennsylvania.

Harry and Edna never saw Terry and Jimmy after they moved to California, but they corresponded about once a year, usually around Christmas time. This was not unique, as Harry and Edna regularly sent over a hundred Christmas cards and notes to various people. So there was some kind of relationship kept up, but a rather distant one.

Harry died in mid-January, a quick death. They had not received a Christmas card from Terry and Jimmy, but weren't, in Edna's recollection, consciously aware of this at the time of Harry's death. Edna doesn't recall realizing this until she checked a log book they had kept on cards sent a couple of months after Harry's death.

Then Edna received a letter from Jimmy. Terry had died a sudden unexpected death. She had a heart attack while shopping the previous year.

So there was a plain looking, wealthy real-life Terry who had once been a good friend of real-life Harry, who had preceded him into death, leaving behind real-life Jimmy. Dream Harry won dream Terry away from dream Jimmy.

Perhaps Harry had unconsciously known they had not received a card from Terry and Jimmy and this was at least partly responsible for dream Terry? Perhaps in some more real sense the deceased Terry was involved in delivering a message for Harry? Or perhaps . . .? As a psychologist there is so much more I would like to know about the psychological forces and meanings here that I will probably never know.

Thought provoking, to say the least. Whatever the ultimate realities, thank you Terry for telling Harry to tell me about this, and thank you Harry for sharing a dream of value to us all.

Suggested Reading

de Saint-Denys, H. 1982. In M. Schatzman, ed. *Dreams and How to Guide Them.* London: Duckworth.

Delaney, G. M. V. 1988. *Living Your Dreams: Using Sleep to Solve Problems and Enrich Your Life.* San Francisco: Harper & Row.

Faraday, A. 1972. *Dream Power.* New York: Coward, McCann & Geoghegan.

——. 1976. *The Dream Game.* New York: Harper & Row.

Garfield, P. 1974. *Creative Dreaming.* New York: Ballantine.

——. 1979. *Pathway to Ecstasy: The Way of the Dream Mandala.* New York: Holt, Rinehart & Winston.

Gendlin, E. T. 1986. *Let Your Body Interpret Your Dreams.* Wilmette, Ill.: Chiron Publications.

Kelzer, K. 1987. *The Sun and the Shadow: My Experiment with Lucid Dreaming.* Virginia Beach, Va.: ARE Press.

LaBerge, S. 1985. *Lucid Dreaming.* Los Angeles: Tarcher.

Mavromatis, A. 1987. *Hypnagogia: The Unique State of Consciousness between Wakefulness and Sleep.* London: Routledge & Kegan Paul.

Mindell, A. 1985. *River's Way: A Process Science of the Dream Body.* London: Routledge & Kegan Paul.

Tart, Charles T. 1969. Toward the experimental control of dreaming: A review of the literature. In C. Tart, ed. *Altered States of Consciousness: A Book of Readings.* New York: John Wiley & Sons. 133–44.

Taylor, J. 1983. *Dream Work: Techniques for Discovering the Creative Power in Dreams.* New York: Paulist Press.

Tholey, P. 1983. Techniques for inducing and manipulating lucid dreams. *Perceptual and Motor Skills* 57:79–90.

Ullman, M., and S. Krippner. 1970. *Dream Studies and Telepathy.* New York: Parapsychology Foundation.

——, and N. Zimmerman. 1979. *Working with Dreams.* Los Angeles: Tarcher.

Wolman, B., M. Ullman, and W. Webb. 1979. *Handbook of Dreams: Research, Theories and Applications.* New York: Van Nostrand Reinhold.

CHAPTER 29

Altered States and the Survival of Death

The essence of the ideas I want to share is expressed in the following two sentences:

After some initial shock and confusion resulting from the process of dying, I will not be too surprised if I regain consciousness. On the other hand I will be quite surprised if "I" regain consciousness.

To put it more precisely: I will not be too surprised if I regain some kind of consciousness after death, but that consciousness may be of a quite different sort than the ordinary state of consciousness to which I am accustomed. And I doubt that "I," in the sense of my ordinary self, will be the self that regains some sort of consciousness.

Will "I" Survive Death?

When we think about survival of death in terms of our ordinary, taken-for-granted "I" we inadvertently confuse the issue. It is no wonder that we do not have a clear answer about the possibility of survival.

What we call "I" is not a fixed identity: It actually changes from minute to minute. Some forms of "I" occur often. So it is useful, especially if we are interested in personal growth, to speak of our many "I"s or subselves.[1] As a personal example, I am a "writer" as I write this, specializing, as it were, in verbal expression. I will leave for an Aikido class in a few minutes, where I will switch to an "Aikidoist" subself that uses very little verbal expression, that, indeed, tries to "think" in kinesthetic images and feelings of energy, rather than words. When I come home from that class I will change to a subself of "husband" with much more emotional responsiveness, and so on.

Many of these ordinary "I"s often do not long "survive," in the sense of maintaining their presence and integrity, many of the small changes of ordinary life—such as those induced by strong emotions, hunger, sexual desire, fatigue, alcohol, and multitudes of other mind-altering drugs. If ordinary "I"s cannot survive these minor shocks, how could ordinary "I"s survive the vastly greater shock of death?

The question "Will I survive death?" cannot really be satisfactorily answered except as a subset of the larger question, "Who and what am I?"

The Nature of Ordinary Consciousness

Let us briefly look at the nature of ordinary consciousness (and the ordinary "I"s associated with it), and at the nature of altered states of consciousness.

The following represent processes or subsystems of the overall system of consciousness, as they are recognized by contemporary psychology. Let me briefly describe each process.[2]

1. *Exteroception* refers to the receptors we have for sensing the world external to our body, our ordinary senses. You read right now with an exterocepter, your eyes.

2. *Interoception* is the class of processes that give us information about the internal state of our bodies. Examples of interoception include noticing a cramped muscle, or sensing your balance or posture.

3. *Input processing* refers to the fact (amply documented by modern psychology) that our perception is not just given by the nature of the sensations reaching our exterocepters and interoceptors; it is a *construction*, a complex process whereby the input from our receptors is shaped, modified, added to, and subtracted from, until it becomes a percept of something familiar. The beliefs and prejudices of our culture result in many somewhat arbitrary habits of perception. These complex processes have all become fully automated in the course of enculturation, so we normally aren't aware of the steps in the process; it seems as if we just naturally see, hear, feel, and so on.

4. *Memory* refers to the many ways in which information about previous experiences, thoughts, and feelings is stored. Input processing relies heavily on memory for direction in its construction process.

5. *Awareness* is really beyond definition in words, as words are only a small subset of the total functioning of mind. It loosely refers to our ultimate ability to know that something exists or is happening. In ordinary consciousness awareness is usually almost totally wrapped up in words, internal talking to ourselves (which is what we usually mean by thought); but it is far more basic than words. (To jump ahead of my discussion for a moment, if something survives death it is going to be more closely connected with the nature of basic awareness than with ordinary consciousness.) Most of the other processes feed into awareness.

6. *Sense of identity* refers to a special quality of information that is added to certain contents of awareness. It is a feeling as well a cognitive quality that "This is me!"; an "I!" quality that gives whatever it is added to special priority for awareness and energy. The perception that "John Smith has a spider crawling toward his leg" doesn't have the feeling quality of the perception, "I have a spider crawling toward *my* leg!" Input from your body, by way of the interoceptors, is normally an important part of your sense of identity.

7. *Emotions* are the various ordinary (and not so ordinary) emotions that we experience, such as excitement, fear, anger, love, contentment, and so on.

8. *Space/time sense* is part of the process of constructing our perceptions of our self and our world. It provides a space and time reference. Experiences usually don't just happen, they happen *now, at this place*.

9. *Evaluation* refers to the various processes of evaluating information: Given what I am perceiving and what I already know, what does it mean, what should I do? Evaluation includes relatively formal, conventionally logical reasoning processes and *a*logical as well as *il*logical processes. The emotional processes are evaluation processes too, but have been separated out because of their special quality.

10. *Subconscious* processes are the normally invisible intelligent processes we invoke to explain organized experiences and behavior that don't make sense in terms of what a person consciously experiences. When someone claims he is quite calm, for instance, yet shows classical signs of fear, we suspect unconscious mental processes at work. I include positive processes here as well as the conventionally negative, Freudian ideas of the unconscious.

11. *Motor output* refers to processes for controlling our muscles and our bodies (hormonal, for example) that take the results of evaluations and decisions and allow us to act on them.

Now this is a far too static view of what is really an interlocking, mutually supportive collection of dynamic processes. Ordinarily the overall outcome of this dynamically acting and interacting system is *me*, my state of consciousness. To the extent that some of these processes are primarily functions of the physical body and nervous system rather than inherent qualities of the mind (motor output, for example), they will not survive death and so we can anticipate that the quality of what might be perceived as "I" after death must be quite different.

Stabilization of a State of Consciousness

An especially important quality of the system of functioning that makes up our state of consciousness is that it is *stabilized:* It generally maintains its overall pattern, its integrity, in spite of constant changes in our external world and our body. A sudden noise can occur, I can have a mild stomachache, and I still remain *me*.

The system generally compensates for changes so that it isn't pushed out of its range of optimal functioning. If you went into a state of mystical ecstasy whenever there was a flash of light you might enjoy it for a short while (by ordinary temporal standards), but you might not stay alive for very long. The sunlight glancing off the grill of the truck bearing down on you should not send you into ecstasy; it should be interpreted by ordinary-state standards as a warning that you should get out of the street!

A lot of the stabilization of ordinary consciousness comes about through the work load that all these processes impose on awareness. Because doing this work is almost completely automated, we ordinarily don't feel like we're working hard to maintain our ordinary state; we just seem to be in it. When a lot of that load is removed, as is typically done in inducing altered states of consciousness ("relax, don't evaluate, just float along," and so on), the nature of conscious experience can change drastically. To the extent that much of this loading stabilization of ordinary consciousness—our ordinary "I"—depends on bodily and nervous system processes, this loading will be removed at death, favoring the appearance of altered states.

Another major source of the stabilization of a state of consciousness (ordinary or altered) occurs through *feedback:* Information about results is sent back to processes intended to bring about those results. I want to push a heavy box across the room, but not hit the furniture. I don't just throw all my muscle power into a shove—I shove gradually, I perceive how well the box is moving. Is it too slow, can I shove a little harder? Is it too fast, getting too close to furniture, will I lose control and run into something?

Thus two major feedback loops are essential in stabilizing our ordinary consciousness. One, feedback via the external world, refers to the fact that we use our exteroceptors to monitor the results of our actions, as with the example of shoving the box. The second, feedback via the body, refers to the fact that sensations in our body also tell us about the results of our actions. If I feel a pain starting in my lower back as I begin shoving the box, I had better heed that feedback and work out a different way of moving the box if I don't want to injure myself.

To summarize, ordinary consciousness is a somewhat arbitrary construction. In the course of growing up we have built up huge numbers of habits: habits of perceiving, of thinking, of feeling, of acting. The automated functioning of these habits in our ordinary environment constitutes a system, the pattern we call our ordinary consciousness. Ordinary consciousness is stabilized, so it holds itself together in spite of varying circumstances. We forget the work we put into constructing this consciousness as children, and we don't realize the cultural relativity and arbitrariness of much of it; thus we take it for granted as "ordinary" or "normal" consciousness.

We usually think of survival in terms of the survival of personality. But personality, the set of characteristic behaviors and statements that distinguish us from others, manifests through our state of consciousness. For the purposes of this discussion, then, "personality" and our usual "state of consciousness" are largely synonymous.

Altered States

Every one of the psychological processes sketched above can undergo drastic changes. To mention just a few: You can see an ordinary face as that of an angel or devil. I don't mean that you *interpret* it that way; I mean the actual perception. You can feel you heart as a glowing mass of radiant energy instead of only a barely perceptible pulsation in your chest. Your memories can seem like those of someone else; or you may "remember" things that intellectually you know could not be known to you, yet they are "obviously" your memories. Totally new systems of thought can come into play for evaluating reality. What is most dear to you may change drastically. Space and time can function in whole new ways, as in experiencing eternity. Your muscles may seem to work in quite new ways.

Usually many of these sorts of changes occur simultaneously, and when they do we talk about experiencing an "altered state of consciousness." The change is too radical to see it as a variation of your ordinary state. It is qualitatively as well as quantitatively different.

Example of an Altered State of Consciousness:

Consider the following example of an altered state:

At one point the world disappeared. I was no longer in my body. I didn't have a body. . . . Then I reached a point at which I felt ready to die. It wasn't a question of choice, it was just a wave that carried me higher and higher, at the same time that I was having what in my normal state I would call a horror of death. It became obvious to me that it was not at all what I had anticipated death to be, except it was death, that something was dying. I reached a point at which I gave it all away. I just yielded, and then I entered a space in which there aren't any words. The words that have been used have been used a thousand times—starting with Buddha. I mean at-one-with-the-universe, recognize your Godhead—all these words I later used to explore what I had experienced. The feeling was that I was "home". . . It was a bliss state of a kind I never experienced before.[3]

This kind of altered-state experience is particularly relevant to the question of survival, and we shall return to it later.

The Dream State

Let's look at the most commonly occurring altered state: nighttime dreaming. We learned in chapter 1 that we all spend about 20 percent of our sleep time in a specific brain-wave state called stage 1 sleep, which is associated with the mental activity of dreaming. This is true whether we remember our dreams or not. We will look at the major processes or subsystems of consciousness in the same order as before and—to start thinking about some of the possible changes that an after-death state of consciousness might involve—we will see how nighttime dreaming might be like the after-death state.

In order to dream we must go to and remain asleep: We must induce an altered state of consciousness. Usually this means reducing exteroception and interoception to very low levels. We turn out the lights and close our eyes, eliminating visual input; we relax our bodies and don't move, eliminating interoceptive kinesthetic input. If we survive death in some form we will certainly not have the physical ex-teroceptors and interoceptors we had during life; so, as in dreaming, this customary input would be drastically reduced.

Further, we now know that there is a very active inhibition of what little input does reach our receptors. If you deliberately stimulate a sleeper (but not intensely enough to wake him) and then awaken him and get a dream report, you will find that most stimuli do not recognizably make it through into the dream world. The few that do are usually distorted so they fit in with the ongoing dream. Calling the dreamer's name, for example, could become another dream character asking him about the state of his health. If an after-death state is like a dream state might similar distortions of our questions to the deceased occur?

Memory functions in a quite different way in dream consciousness. In our waking state we usually know when we are drawing information from storage—a nonverbal "this is a memory" quality is attached to it. This quality disappears in dreams. The conventional view of dreams is that all the objects in the dream world are constructed from memory images, yet dreaming is experienced as *perceiving*, not as *remembering*.

Similarly our sense of identity, our emotions, and our evaluation processes can operate quite differently, as if the dream were of someone else with different emotional reactions and styles of thinking. What is sensible by dream standards may be outrageous by waking-state standards or vice versa. The space/time sense is totally changed: Instead of accurately putting your experiences in their "real" context of you lying in bed at night, you may be at a palm-lined oasis in the next century. If such alteration of the processing styles of emotion, evaluation, sense of identity, and space/time sense occurs routinely in dreams while alive, why couldn't these and other alterations occur after death? Suppose the after-death state is more like a dream state than an ordinary conscious state? Would someone who knew your personality in its ordinary state recognize your personality in something closer to its dream state?

Let us look at another common characteristic of dreams: Dreams usually seem to just *happen* to us. They don't often feel like our active creations. Who is creating this world and these actions? Where does the scenery come from, how do the various actors know when to come on stage? Will the after-death state be similarly passive? Will we care about trying to prove our survival to loved ones or researchers left behind?

We give our subconscious the credit for the intelligent and active creation of dreams. This is not a terribly good explanation, of course, but it is the best we have at this time . . . and a good reminder of how little we understand about our minds. If such a potent source of experience as dreams is controlled by mental processes we hardly understand at all, it reminds us of how careful we must be in extrapolating the characteristics of waking consciousness to the possible after-death state.

Finally note that the motor-output processes are also inhibited in the dreaming state of consciousness, just as input processing is. This reflects the fact that you perform all sorts of physical actions with what you take to be your physical body in your dreams, yet an outside observer sees that you lie still. Modern research has now shown that neural signals for movement are indeed sent to our muscles during dreaming, just as when we are awake. If you dream of lifting your arm, for example, all the necessary signals are sent to make your arm move that way. But an active paralysis of our muscles occurs during nighttime dreaming. Inhibitory signals are sent down the spinal cord to the muscles themselves so they will not respond. A good thing, too: It would be very dangerous to be physically moving about while our consciousness was in dreamland.[4]

No External Feedback in the Dream State

A state of consciousness is a dynamically interacting and *stabilized* system. Ordinary waking consciousness is especially stabilized by two major routes: feedback via the external world and the exteroceptors; and via the internal world, the body, through the interoceptors. In dreaming these major stabilization routes are lost.

In your dream you raise your arm and move a gigantic boulder that weighs tons. There is no actual input from the interoceptors in your physical arm to contradict the *idea* of your doing this. There is no actual perception through your physical eyes that there is no boulder there to contradict the *idea* of moving a gigantic boulder. What little "feedback" there is comes from your body image rather than your actual physical body. The *idea* thus has far more power to affect your construction of "reality"—the experience you realize—in the dream state because there is almost no input from a fixed, lawful, external reality that your internal idea must be consistent with. Might there be a similar lack of "reality checking" in an after-death state?[5]

In looking at dreams I have taken a conventional position: The dream is just a set of mental processes, based on physical brain and physical nervous system functioning, and nothing more. That is, a dream is all imaginary, unreal. Isn't it?

Altered-States Knowledge of Survival

A dream usually seems perfectly real at the time it is occurring (I exempt lucid dreams, in which you know that you are dreaming while dreaming, from this discussion). For me, for instance, dream reality is just as "real" as ordinary reality, if not sometimes more real. So where do we get the idea that it is imaginary? Let us look at the nature of experience.

Three Worlds of Experience

I can basically say that most of my experience readily falls into three general categories, which I shall call worlds. (We could just as well call them states of consciousness, but I want to stress their apparent "externality.")

1. *World 1* takes up most of my experienced life. It is a very rigid set of experiences; that is, its reality seems to be governed by some inflexible laws. Most situations in it cannot be altered directly by my desires or will. I have to do things according to laws that seem external to me. If I want to move a heavy boulder, for example, I have to get long levers or a block and tackle and exert my muscles strongly.

   World 1 is rigid, then, but it is also very reliable. The boulder will not move by itself or do anything unexpected unless quite specific events happen—someone else decides to move it using a block and tackle, or an earthquake shakes it loose. For normal conversational purposes I, like the apparently independently existing entities I meet in it, call this World 1 reality of experience my "waking consciousness" or the "real world."

2. *World 2* takes up the least amount of experienced time by the yardstick of my direct experience, but the second largest amount of time by some of the regular experiences of my World 1 reality. My usual direct experience of World 2 is of nothing happening at all; but a feeling of some unknown amount of time having passed occurs right at the end of World 2 experience. By World 1 standards, *insofar as they are appropriate to apply outside their own*

experiential realm, World 2 occupies almost a third of my life. When I am in the midst of World 1 experience I call my World 2 experience "dreamless sleep." When I am in the midst of World 2 experience I generally do not call it anything at all.

3. *World 3* is like World 1 reality in many ways. I see, taste, touch, and smell, I feel pleasure and pain, I reflect on things and reach conclusions, I plan and carry out actions. World 3 experience occupies only a small amount of my total experience by World 1 standards; but in its own terms it is sometimes brief, sometimes quite long. The apparently external laws and regularities that operate in World 1 experience make their appearance here, but generally are much more loosely applied. Sometimes I can move that boulder just by thinking about it, other times it may move by itself for no apparent reason. Sometimes I find principles or laws that only work for World 3 experience. I can fly by an act of will in World 3, for example. It is a special mental act that must be done correctly. This act of will has no effect in World 1.

When I am in the midst of World 1 I generally call my World 3 experiences "dreams." In the midst of World 3 my experiences are usually just as real as anything else I experience in any World.

Now this is the really curious thing: In World 1 I—along with practically all of the other ostensibly independently existing beings I experience as part of World 1—have convinced myself that only World 1 experience is real and worthwhile, and that World 3 experience, dreaming, is useless, unreal, and totally delusory. Why? Because it is not consistent in the way that World 1 experience is, and because it does not accurately mirror the regularities and events of World 1. I, a being who knows nothing directly but my own experience, have convinced myself that part of my direct knowledge and experience—which I know just as directly when I experience it as any other kind of direct experience—isn't real.

This dismissal of dream experience as unreal and delusory is, of course, culturally relative. Some cultures still accept dream reality as real and important, even if it isn't an accurate mirror of ordinary reality. Indeed it is only a historically recent development in our own culture to reject dreams so thoroughly. The rejection of the reality of dreams goes hand in hand with a mainstream rejection of the reality of altered states in general.

State-Specific Knowledge

We have been skirting around one of the most important qualities of knowledge, namely that it is *state-specific*. What you can know depends on the state of consciousness you are in.

Here's a simple analogy: You are using a net to troll through the ocean for fish. Your net has a one-inch mesh, so it will not pick up anything that is smaller than an inch. Thus you are excluding an enormous amount of life. If you understand this property of your net— your "data collection system"—there is no problem. If you are too enamored of your wonderful net, you are likely to think that ocean life is all bigger than one inch. You cannot study small life with your net.

Altered states of consciousness research has shown us that some kinds of human knowledge are state-specific. If you aren't in a certain state of consciousness certain things cannot be known.

Some knowledge is only partially state-specific in that it can be known in two or more states of consciousness. If I ask you the street address of your home, for example, you will probably give me a correct answer in your ordinary state, in a dream state (assuming I am some dream character asking the question), in a sexually aroused state, in a depressed state, and in a state of alcohol or marijuana intoxication. But there are things you can know in an altered state of consciousness that you cannot really remember in your ordinary state, much less tell others about in any adequate way.

If we want to know all that a human can know we must study some things in the appropriate altered state of consciousness. If we do not enter that state and work appropriately with it, we will never really know the answers. One of the tragedies of our time is that we have forgotten about the state-specificity of knowledge in regard to many vital spiritual questions. Thus we approach them only from an ordinary-states perspective and get answers that are distorted and pale reflections of reality. We have traded direct knowledge of the Unity of Life for abstract verbal statements and theories about unity, for example. It doesn't satisfy, and it doesn't work very well.

The Denial of Experience

What does this have to do with survival? Just this: *The direct experience of existing and experiencing in some form that seems partially or fully independent of the physical body is relatively common in various altered states of consciousness. This kind of experience constitutes the most direct knowledge*

of survival an individual may have. There is nothing inherently wrong
with indirect forms of evidence, of course; but this wholesale rejection
of direct altered-state-of-consciousness experience forces the survival
issue to be solely one of abstraction and deduction instead of direct
experience. This also amounts to throwing away some of the most relevant evidence about survival and may make it impossible to ever get
a *personally* satisfactory answer.

Contemporary research in humanistic and transpersonal psychology has shown that the wholesale rejection of dream and other altered-
states-of-consciousness experience has strong and largely pathological
consequences for our happiness and our full development as human
beings. Unfortunately many of our personal and cultural roots support
this rejection. Foremost among them is the dominance of materialism
as a philosophy of life.

The Materialist Position

The materialistic view of human beings, so widespread today, says
that our discussion about consciousness is nothing more than a discussion about biocomputer circuits. Consciousness is like an actively
running program in the biocomputer—that is, in us; and altered states
are simply different programs. The various aspects of consciousness
discussed above are merely subprograms of the larger program, which
is *nothing but* the totality of my biological, material self. The programs
and subprograms may produce all sorts of outputs and experiences.
Many of them are very useful to our pleasure and biological survival,
but many of them are quite arbitrary or even nonsensical.

I have programmed one of my laboratory's computers, for example,
to print out the statement, "I have just achieved ecstatic transelectrical
fusion with the great Chip in the Sky, experiencing all binary Knowledge and the depths of mystical electro-ecstasy!" We know that the
logical content of this statement is nonsense, of course. Computer chips
don't have "experiences" and do nothing but what the physical nature
of the computer allows them to do.

According to the materialistic reduction of consciousness to a set of
programs running in the human biocomputer, the program is totally
dependent on the hardware, the "bioware,"—the physical existence
and state of the material components the biocomputer is built from. If
the state of my computer's hardware is greatly changed, as by turning
off the power or physically destroying a component, the program dies.
When the hardware of human consciousness—the brain and body—
dies, consciousness dies with it. No belief or even mystical experiences

of being more than the body mean a thing in this view: When the brain and body die, you die. Period.

The materialistic equation is

$$mind = brain$$

and this is considered to be the complete story.

The Dominance of Materialism

Why has the materialistic view become so dominant?

One reason is purely functional: Materialism works exceptionally well for a very wide range of situations in life. It has, for example, made us materially richer than ever before, has given us enormous power over the physical world, and has alleviated pain and cured illnesses that were historically fatal.

On a purely intellectual level materialism appears to give us an intellectually consistent and straightforward understanding of the universe. This consistency is very intellectually satisfying.

Materialism also appears to give us protection against many "things" and "powers" that people were afraid of in the past. When belief in capricious, supernatural forces and malicious demons was widespread it was a matter of great practical concern to try to protect yourself, and it often seemed as if you had failed. Fear of the nonmaterial unknown was very real. But if you gave total acceptance to a belief system that said there were no supernatural forces or beings to begin with, then there was nothing to fear. All sorts of problems simply ceased to exist.

As a psychologist I suspect that materialism is not actually very solid as a belief system for many or most of the people who think they totally accept it; on a deeper level they have considerable unresolved fears of and hopes about the supernatural. Their passionate advocacy of materialistic philosophy may be a psychological defense, of the sort termed reaction formation, to try to avoid conscious awareness of conflict. I have written about this elsewhere with respect to the unacknowledged fear of psychic abilities and in a more general way.[6]

A completely materialistic philosophy, by invalidating vital aspects of human nature, creates a dismal outlook on life, an outlook that is usually not explicitly acknowledged precisely because it is so bleak. When hope, love, and joy, when intellect and the materialist philosophy itself are reduced to their "ultimate reality" of nothing but electrochemical impulses in a biocomputer that originated by chance in a dead universe, what is left?[7]

The Inadequacy of Materialism

If materialistic science and philosophy simply claimed to be a specialized branch of knowledge, useful in its own area but not especially relevant to things outside its area, it would lose most of the power it claims by virtue of being all-embracing. Plumbers, for example, have very useful knowledge about a very material subject; but I do not know of anyone whose spiritual outlook on life was deeply disturbed because plumbers are so good at the material things they do.

The practical and intellectual results of modern science are so powerful that we (including almost all scientists) are overly impressed with the materialistic philosophy intermixed with it. We can consciously reject materialism because of the loss of vital spirit it leads to, but it is hard to effectively reject the cultural conditioning and emotional involvement that we as Westerners almost invariably have in the scientistic outlook. Thus it is important for us to be able to rationally deal with the intellectual claim of comprehensiveness of materialism. We can't just take the position, "I don't like the way materialism feels, so even if I have to ignore my intellect I'm going to reject it."

The good news is that you don't have to be ignorant or unscientific in order to reasonably argue that the scientistic position is far from complete. It is not an all-powerful set of reasons for rejecting the possible reality of the spiritual. Please note that I'm not arguing the opposite and encouraging you to believe everything that is labeled "spiritual." There is a lot of nonsense under that label that should be sorted out and rejected. But not everything.

How Scientific Parapsychology Undermines Materialism

The good news is based on the findings of scientific parapsychology, a collection of thousands of naturalistic observations and at least seven hundred laboratory experiments in the last six decades. I believe these conclusively demonstrate that some aspects of the human mind simply cannot be reduced to materialistic explanations. Thus the equation "mind = brain" is woefully incomplete and should not be used to rule out spiritual realities or the possibility of survival on an a priori basis.

Parapsychological research has firmly demonstrated the existence of four major psychic abilities: telepathy, clairvoyance, precognition, and psychokinesis.[8]

1. *Telepathy* is the transmission of information from mind to mind, after we have ruled out ordinary physical means like talking to

one another or sign language, and ruled out inference from physically known data. The laboratory studies that firmly established telepathy were mostly card-guessing studies. A sender, isolated in his or her own room, looked at one card after another from a thoroughly shuffled pack of cards, trying to send his or her thoughts. A receiver isolated in another room wrote down his impressions of the cards. Perfect scores are extremely rare, but enough studies showed more hits than could be reasonably expected by chance to establish telepathy.

2. *Clairvoyance* is the direct extrasensory perception of information about the physical world without the intervention of another mind that already knows the information by ordinary sensory means. The classical card-test studies involved a percipient giving impressions of the order of a deck of randomized cards when no living human knew what the order of that deck was. Many studies showed enough hits to establish clairvoyance. The information transmission rate is about the same as in telepathy studies.[9] Both telepathy and clairvoyance seem unaffected by physical factors like spatial distance or physical shielding.

3. *Precognition* is the prediction of the future when the future is determined in a random way, such that inference from present knowledge would not be helpful. The classic experimental design is to ask a percipient to predict the order of a target deck of cards, but the cards will be randomly shuffled at some date in the future. Precognition of this sort has been successful at intervals of up to a year. Curiously the average information-transfer rate is much lower than in present-time telepathy or clairvoyance studies.[10]

Collectively telepathy, clairvoyance, and precognition are known as extrasensory perception (ESP), as they all involve information gathering.

4. *Psychokinesis* (PK) is the fourth well-established psychic phenomenon. It is popularly called mind over matter. The classic tests involved wishing which way machine-thrown dice would turn up; the target object is now usually an electronic random number generator. The frequency of PK appearance is about the same as precognition.[11]

The importance of these *psi phenomena* (as the four are now collectively referred to) is that they are manifestations of *mind* that have resisted all attempts to reduce them to known physical forces, or

straightforward extensions of known physical forces. I exempt some of
the speculations on the frontiers of quantum physics to explain psi as
"straightforward" extensions of physics because (1) they are controversial ideas in physics per se; (2) they involve such a radically different
view of what is "physical" that they should not be lumped in with the
old materialistic physics; and (3) quite important from a scientific view,
have not shown any notable degree of success in understanding and
controlling psi phenomena.

The psi phenomena are examples where we must say:

$$\text{mind} \neq \text{brain}$$

Although some aspects of mind and consciousness are partially or
wholly based in brain and nervous system functioning, psi phenomena
are not. They clearly demonstrate the need to investigate mind on its
own terms. These psi phenomena do not "prove" survival per se, but
insofar as mind has aspects that do not seem limited by space or time,
such aspects of mind are the sort we might expect to survive bodily
death.

Scientific Research on Survival

Modern parapsychological research has focused on the four aspects
of psi mentioned above. Originally, however, parapsychology was
called "psychical research" and focused specifically on the question of
survival of death.

Modern Spiritualism was born near the end of the last century when
mysterious rappings in the home of the Fox sisters were interpreted as
PK-like effects of departed spirits who were trying to communicate
with the living. In a short time Spiritualism became a worldwide religion. Its basic message was very appealing, and scientific in style.
Spiritualism accepted the fact that much that was called religion, based
on authority, was indeed just superstition. Scientists were right when
they said that experience, data, facts were more important than belief
or dogma. "Don't *believe* in survival," said the Spiritualists, "test the
idea of survival against the facts!"

Spiritualist mediums claimed to be mediums of communication,
channels between the living and the deceased for exchanging messages. For example, if you wanted to know if your Aunt Matilda had
survived death, you would not automatically believe or disbelieve the
idea. You would sit down with a medium at a seance and ask to speak
to Aunt Matilda. When the spirit who claimed to be Aunt Matilda was

contacted and speaking through the medium, you would ask her questions about herself until you were convinced that it was indeed Aunt Matilda speaking.

Many, many people carried out this kind of experiment. Some were not convinced of survival. The early psychical researchers noted that many of the so-called spirits gave only the vaguest details of their earthly lives, or were just plain wrong in what they said. Some seance communications from the ostensible spirits were of a very high quality, however, and convinced sitters of the reality of survival. Here is an example of the kind of high-quality sitting that has been reported:

After the war I went to a Scottish medium to see if she could pick up something about a friend, a German diplomat whom I feared had been killed either by the Nazis or the Russians. I simply didn't know what had happened to him. The medium very soon got onto him. She gave his Christian name, talked about things we had done together in Washington, and described correctly my opinion of his character. She said he was dead and that his death was a tragic he didn't want to talk about it. She gave a number of striking details about him and the evidence of personality was very strong . . .[12]

I believe any of us would be strongly impressed by this kind of evidence for the survival of death, and such accounts have convinced a few scholars and scientists of the reality of survival.

Complexities of Survival Research

Survival research is now a very small part of parapsychology (itself a minuscule field).[13] Compared to the central role it once had, survival research has been almost abandoned for half a century. The reason is quite interesting.

When psychical researchers first began investigating mediums the idea that living people had extraordinary psychic abilities was not generally accepted. If information from an ostensible surviving spirit was in accord with what the investigator knew about the deceased, he was inclined to accept it as evidence of survival: Who but he and the deceased knew it? As researchers gradually established that ordinary people sometimes showed telepathy, clairvoyance, PK, and precognition, however, the picture became more complicated. The validating information *might* have come from the deceased, but it might also come from the medium's unconscious telepathic reading of the investigator's (or from a friend of the deceased's) mind, or from a clairvoyant pickup of information from surviving documents and records. And if *precog*nition existed, how about the possibility of *retro*cognition, where the medium's unconscious psychic abilities went back in time to get information about the deceased when he was still alive?

Added to these psychic complications were the facts arriving from the study of hypnosis and of abnormal mental states like those involved in multiple personality, which showed that the subconscious part of a person's mind could do marvelous imitations of people. Further add in the fact that subconscious processes could distort a person's mental functioning to alter experience so it supported deeply held beliefs, and the grounds were established for a powerful alternative explanation of the best data for survival.

1. *Data:* Sometimes ostensible spirits, communicating through mediums, give very specific and characteristic information that was known to the deceased but could not have been known to the medium through normal, sensory means.
2. *Survival Theory:* This means that the deceased has indeed survived and is sometimes able to communicate with the living.
3. *Unconscious Impersonation Theory:* Because the medium believes in survival, and has a need to have experiences that reinforce her belief system, an unconscious part of her mind *imitates* deceased people. Because of occasional use of ESP abilities by this part of the subconscious mind to come up with information about the deceased that could not be normally known to the medium, these imitation personalities are very convincing. Because of the dissociation between the subconscious mind, the medium consciously feels like she is indeed simply a channel for personalities outside herself.

The Undead Deceased

To illustrate the complexities of survival research let us reread the high-quality case we looked at earlier:

After the war I went to a Scottish medium to see if she could pick up something about a friend, a German diplomat whom I feared had been killed either by the Nazis or the Russians. I simply didn't know what had happened to him. The medium very soon got onto him. She gave his Christian name, talked about things we had done together in Washington, and described correctly my opinion of his character. She said he was dead and that his death was so tragic he didn't want to talk about it. She gave a number of striking details about him and the evidence of personality was very strong. . . .

I did not present the whole report on the case before, so let me continue it:

If I had never heard any more, I would have thought it very impressive.

But after the sitting, I set about trying to find out something about him. Finally the Swiss Foreign Office found him for me. He was not dead. He had escaped from Germany and had married an English girl. He wrote to me that he had never been so happy in his life. So there I think the medium was reading my expectations. She was quite wrong about the actual facts, but quite right according to what I had expected.[14]

Most of the few scientists working in parapsychology abandoned survival research and focused on the psi abilities of the living because cases like this made it look just too difficult to decide between the survival hypothesis and the unconscious impersonation theory. The abandonment is probably premature, and a few investigators are still actively working to devise better tests of survival that could distinguish these two explanations. Ian Stevenson, for example, a psychiatrist at the University of Virginia, has proposed that subconscious ESP on the medium's part might account for factual knowledge shown by an ostensible surviving spirit, but would not account for complex skills if they were shown. For an ostensible spirit to *responsively* speak a foreign language you were sure was unknown to the medium, for example, rather than just mention isolated words or phrases from that language, would be very convincing. Unfortunately we do not have really good cases of that type—yet. Perhaps we will. The investigations of Ian Stevenson, one of the world's leading investigators of survival, are of great interest here.[15]

Models of Survival

As I stated at the beginning of this chapter, however, what little survival research has been done has implicitly been about the survival of ordinary consciousness, ordinary "I." We have seen how ordinary consciousness and ordinary "I"s are just one manifestation of whatever our more basic nature is. Let us now look at possibilities of survival that include some of the realities of altered states of consciousness.

Ordinary Consciousness-Equivalent Body Model

The *ordinary consciousness-equivalent* body model assumes that existence after death would be rather like permanent exile to a foreign land, but with consciousness and "external" reality much like they were before death. Given how much the structure of the body and brain shape the pattern of consciousness, we would expect some sort of nonphysical structure or process that mimicked most of the physical body's effects on consciousness in this sort of survival if consciousness was to be like it was when the physical body was still present.

Stable Altered-State-of-Consciousness Model

The *stable altered-state-of-consciousness* model would assume that there is a primary, "ordinary" (for the after-death state) state of consciousness after death, with stable and comprehensible (at least from within) qualities. It would be an altered state of consciousness compared to pre-death embodied ordinary consciousness. We would have to learn the qualities of this after-death state in order to fully comprehend and communicate with the deceased.

Multiple, Stable Altered-State-of-Consciousness Model

The *multiple, stable altered-state-of-consciousness* model assumes that the surviving person may exist in several altered states of consciousness from time to time. Communications from the same deceased person, but originating from different states, might seem contradictory or disjointed. The confusion could be lessened if (1) the surviving individual discriminated such states and indicated which state he was in and its characteristics; or (2) if we (in either our ordinary or some altered state of consciousness) could make such discriminations. Then by learning the characteristics of each state we would synthesize a coherent whole from the various communications.

To gather evidence in favor of the possibility of survival, we have to make an assumption in this and the previous model: that at least some of the altered states of consciousness the deceased can communicate from bear a clear enough resemblance to the living personality and state of consciousness so we can see the connection. It may be that people survive death in an altered state of consciousness that is so drastically different from their former state and personality that we can see no connection at all, but we can never gather evidence for survival from such a reality. Or, as suggested by some research and spiritual traditions, relations to the ordinary state may persist for a while after death but gradually fade, making it possible to gather evidence for survival for recently deceased persons but not for long-deceased ones. I personally incline toward a model of continual evolution of consciousness and would hope that I would not remain too fixed for too long after death.

Unstable, Transiting-States-of-Consciousness Survival

I have theorized elsewhere that the most comprehensive explanation for some of the altered states of consciousness phenomena we see (especially those induced by powerful psychedelic drugs in untrained individuals) is to recognize that we are not dealing with a single, stabilized altered state of consciousness but with continuous, unstable transitions from momentary configuration to momentary configuration.[16] The colloquial term "tripping" illustrates the flavor of the *unstable, transiting-states-of-consciousness* model. A person's condition is characterized (whether induced in life by a powerful destabilizing force like a drug or by the nature of the after-death state) by a lack of stability, a rapid shifting from one momentary configuration of conscious functioning to another. Such a condition would be rather like delirium. Both the person experiencing it and outsiders would perceive moments of sense and lucidity, perhaps moments of even greater lucidity than normal; but overall it is confused rambling.

The Body as a Stabilizer of Consciousness

Given the importance of the body and brain as stabilizing mechanisms for both ordinary and altered states of consciousness, as we discussed at the beginning of this chapter, the lack of a body and brain in an after-death state might well mean that it would be characterized by great instability. If we would investigate what happens to mental functioning in life when body awareness is greatly reduced or temporarily eliminated we might have a better understanding of what an after-death state might be like.

Our earlier discussion of dreaming (see Part 1) is quite relevant to this idea, for in dreaming we have almost no awareness of our actual physical bodies, only our mentally constructed dream bodies. Sensory deprivation studies also shed some light on this question. Ketamine intoxication might also be an excellent analog for studying the qualities of mind when no body is perceived in life. Ketamine, used as an analgesic in surgery, has also been used in much lower doses (about one-tenth the surgical dose) as a psychedelic drug. One of its major effects is to make the physical body effectively disappear from consciousness. The example of an altered state of consciousness at the beginning of this chapter was one that was induced by ketamine.

Interoceptive input from our physical bodies is not the only major source of stabilization of consciousness in physical life, of course. It may be possible for stable states of consciousness to develop in an after-death state based on other kinds of stabilization processes.

Communications Models

Another way of looking at the survival question involves a focus on the quality of the communications from the ostensible deceased spirits. Let's look at three of them.

The Noisy Telephone Line Model

Almost all survival research carried out to date has implicitly been based on what we might characterize as the *noisy telephone line* model. This assumes the ordinary consciousness-equivalent body model of survival: The deceased's mind and personality still function pretty much like normal, and includes a desire to communicate with surviving loved ones and convince them that they have survived death. The obvious inconsistencies, irrelevancies, and errors in mediumistic communications then call for a further step in modeling to explain the usually poor quality of communication.

Suppose you receive a long-distance telephone call, the essence of which is that the caller claims to be your long-missing sister. She says she was kidnapped but will be released if you leave a very large sum of money (essentially all of your savings) in a certain place. Otherwise they will torture and kill her. Naturally you want to save your sister, even if it means a great sacrifice.

Unfortunately the quality of the connection is very bad. There is hissing, crackling, and periods of silence. The voice quality is so badly distorted that you can't be sure it's really your sister's voice. Sometimes there is cross-talk, and other phone conversations are picked up. You are not always sure when something was said by your sister and when it was a fragment of a conversation by other people.

You want to be certain this is your missing sister before you part with your life's savings, so you ask questions about events that only you and your sister are likely to know the answer to. Sometimes you get answers that seem to make sense; but other times your sister claims she can't hear and understand you properly, or her answer is distorted or too general to be satisfying. Sometimes she claims she can't answer for reasons that aren't really satisfactory, such as "they" won't let her answer that one. All in all this would be a very unsatisfactory state of affairs.

The analogy is a good parallel to the quality of most mediumistic communications with the ostensibly surviving deceased. The problem is assumed by most Spiritualists and most investigators to be in the "telephone line," in the psychology of mediumistic communication: Your kidnaped sister is still pretty much who she was. There is an implicit faith that if we could just get better telephone connections the question of whether this was really your sister would receive an unequivocal answer.

The Delirious Phone Conversation Model

I believe the noisy telephone line analogy is useful. If people do survive, there may indeed be massive problems with the medium as communications channel, or problems with whatever kind of psi the medium uses to communicate with the deceased. Some information may not be transmitted at all or may be distorted in transmission (as in trying to get external stimuli into nighttime dreaming), and noise (generalizations, guesses, unconscious impersonation) may be added by the medium's unconscious mind. Hypothesizing all of the inconsistency and error of communication from the deceased as a communications problem is probably inadequate, however.

Suppose the reality of survival for many individuals is closer to the unstable, transiting-states-of-consciousness model, which we will here call the *delirious phone conversation* model. Yes, the deceased has survived, but the state of her consciousness is constantly changing, as in delirium. Imagine a telephone call from your kidnaped sister on our noisy telephone line while she is alive, but she is drugged or delirious. Indeed *she may never return to what used to be "normal" consciousness for her.* What kind of conversation will you have now? Will the occasional moments of "lucidity" (momentary configurations of states of consciousness that are like her ordinary state, so that ordinary sorts of information can be exchanged) produce sufficient evidence of your kidnapped sister's identity to counter the confusions, errors, and changed points of view that may dominate the communication?

The Altered-States Phone Conversation Model

In the *altered-states phone conversation* model your kidnaped sister is permanently in an altered state of consciousness, changed forever by the experiences she has gone through, but her altered state is stable. While we still have the problem of the noisy communication channel to deal with, we at least have a stable source of communications. Your sister may not be who she used to be, but she is an identifiable person, and that person has a definite relation to who your sister used to be.

Now we need to understand the nature of the state of consciousness she is in. Then we can ask her questions that will make sufficient sense in her altered state of consciousness to elicit relevant and intelligent responses. Similarly, if the after-death state involves a stable consciousness, even if it is altered by ordinary living-state criteria, we need to learn how to speak the "language" of that altered state of consciousness if we want to really learn whether someone has survived death.

Inappropriateness of Tests

If a person who survives is in a quite different state of consciousness than he or she was before death, the kinds of tests we use to establish identity might be quite inappropriate. They might give false-negative results (that is, they might say this is not the person when they should say it is), or give inconsistent and confusing results.

I am reminded of some experiences I had that illustrate this problem. When I was a graduate student I served as a subject in some studies of psychedelic drugs. One of the questions of interest was what such drugs did to color perception. Subjects uniformly reported that color was experienced as much brighter and more alive, and that they could obviously see more subtle distinctions among colors than they ordinarily could. I certainly had had that experience. Was this a purely subjective impression, or did psychedelics like psilocybin actually enhance the ability to discriminate different shades of color?

To test this a color discrimination test was used. I don't recall its technical name, but I called it the "bottlecap test" because it consisted of more than a hundred identical-size bottlecaps. The top of each bottlecap was a different color, and altogether they ranged through the whole color spectrum. They were shuffled in random order, and my job was to arrange them in a line from blue through red, with each adjacent color being the smallest change from the previous color. The shades of color were close enough that people taking this test in ordinary consciousness generally made a fair number of mistakes.

I took this test while near the peak of a psilocybin experience one day. This was scientific research so I had made a strong commitment before taking the drug to do my best, as I firmly believed it was important to test this question. As I began the test, however, my perspective in that altered state of consciousness was quite different. The test was so shallow; it could not begin to tap the profundity of what I was experiencing! Yet I understood that my earlier self, a distant thing but one I knew I would come back to some day, had made a commitment to do this test as accurately as possible. So I worked away at it.

The results of the test were very odd. My overall color discrimination accuracy was about the same as it ordinarily was. If you looked at individual parts of the test, however, there were long runs of perfect scores (implying better than ordinary color discrimination) mixed in with much larger errors than I ordinarily made (indicating worsened color discrimination). Had the psilocybin made me better or worse at perceiving color? The question could not really be answered on the basis of the test results. The question, as framed and worked on by ordinary consciousness methods, did not have a clear answer.

Fortunately we had a second perspective, an altered-state-of-consciousness perspective, because of my "inside" observations on what had happened during the test. I had been doing my best by ordinary-consciousness standards; but by the altered-state-of-consciousness standards of the psilocybin-induced state I was also quite impatient. If the bottlecap that I needed was nearby I saw it quickly and put it in the right place. When I couldn't find it right away, however, my rapidly changing mind—without my full recognition—picked almost any nearby bottlecap and hallucinated the right shade of color onto it. In this way I actually perceived just the shade I needed and could put the bottlecap in place, finish the silly test, and get on to more interesting experiences! In my altered state of consciousness this was an intelligent thing to do, given the inherent values of the altered state. Thus at times my color discrimination was superb; but when I became impatient the machinery of my mind put more value on finishing than on being consistent with another set of standards—ordinary-consciousness standards—that was foreign to my current state of consciousness. The result was massive mistakes by ordinary consciousness standards.

In this example we have the advantage that I returned to my ordinary state of consciousness with some memory of the altered state of consciousness and could report on why my functioning looked strange by ordinary-state standards. Insofar as someone who survives death may be in one or more altered states of consciousness, though, they may make similar "mistakes" by ordinary consciousness standards, and they may not be able to return to an ordinary state to explain their mistake.

How many of our tests for survival look meaningless, shallow, or silly to a person in some altered state of consciousness in an after-death state? How many of the "mistakes" made by ostensible surviving people in trying to prove their survival seem like intelligent actions from their altered-state-of-consciousness point of view? If someone had called me long distance while I was in the psilocybin-induced state and asked me to prove that I was me, beyond any shadow of a reasonable doubt, I would have found their request very odd, given my state of mind, and the "sensible" (to me in that state) answers I would have given might have seemed very strange to them. An obvious research project for survival research, then, is to investigate how people's sense of identity changes and how they communicate in a variety of altered states of consciousness while they are still living. Data from near-death experiences will be of great value here.

More Appropriate Tests for Survival

We can summarize the implications for improving the quality of survival research now around the question of "Who might survive death?"

The ordinary personality, ordinary "I," does not seem a likely candidate for more than temporary survival. It has little enough unity, being made of many subpersonalities, each of which often fails to "survive" the shocks of ordinary life for very long. The shock of dying might destroy many of these aspects of ordinary "I" either temporarily or permanently. In addition our ordinary-consciousness personality is heavily dependent on a number of body-based processes for its stabilization, processes like exteroceptive and interoceptive input. Without these processes consciousness can change drastically, as in ordinary dreaming. Unless something very analogous to an external world and a body is provided in the after-death state much of ordinary "I" would seem unlikely to survive.

If we want to ask "Does John Smith survive death?" we had better get to know the full range of possible manifestations of "John Smith" before he dies. Aside from knowing factual and personality details about the ordinary "John Smith," what is the drunken "John Smith" like? How about the "John Smith" when he has lost his body temporarily through sensory deprivation or ketamine administration? Or the "John Smith" in a disoriented state in unfamiliar surroundings? Or the "John Smith" after a profound meditative experience? Or the "John Smith" in a state of sexual arousal, or when carried away with anger, or in a state of depression? Or the "entity" that may appear in some altered states of consciousness that tells us the "John Smith" is a small and not very important manifestation of something much greater?

When we can identify all of these "John Smiths," we will be in a much better position to ascertain if any of them survive.

Suggested Reading

There is a large body of literature on investigations of the possibility of survival of death. The following small list of suggested readings will get you started on some interesting aspects of it.

Fielding, E. 1963. *Sittings with Eusapia Palladino and Other Studies.* New Hyde Park, N.Y.: University Books.

Gallup, G., and W. Proctor. 1982. *Adventures in Immortality.* New York: Mc-Graw-Hill.

Grof, S., and C. Grof. 1980. *Beyond Death: The Gates of Consciousness.* New York: Thames & Hudson.

_____, and J. Halifax. 1977. *The Human Encounter with Death.* New York: Dutton.

Gurney, E., F. W. H. Myers, and F. Podmore. [1886] 1962. *Phantasms of the Living.* New Hyde Park, N.Y.: University Books.

Kastenbaum, R., ed. 1979. *Between Life and Death.* New York: Springer.

Meyers, F. W. H. 1954. *Human Personality and Its Survival of Bodily Death.* New York: Longmans, Green & Co.

Moody, R. 1975. *Life After Life: The Investigation of a Phenomenon—Survival of Bodily Death.* Atlanta: Mockingbird Books.

_____. 1977. *Reflections on Life after Life.* Atlanta: Mockingbird Books.

Ring, K. 1980. *Life at Death: A Scientific Investigation of the Near-Death Experience.* New York: Coward, McCann & Geoghegan.

_____. 1984. *Heading Toward Omega: In Search of the Meaning of the Near-Death Experience.* New York: William Morrow & Co.

Roll, W. 1985. Will personality and consciousness survive the death of the body? An examination of parapsychological findings suggestive of survival. Ph.D. dissertation, University of Utrecht. 178–79.

Sabom, M. 1982. *Recollections of Death.* New York: Harper & Row.

Sidgwick, E. M. 1962. *Phantasms of the Living.* New Hyde Park, N.Y.: University Books.

Spong, J. S. 1987. *Consciousness and Survival: An Interdisciplinary Inquiry into the Possibility of Life Beyond Biological Death.* Sausalito, Calif.: Institute of Noetic Sciences.

Stevenson, I. 1974. Xenoglossy: A review and report of a case. *Proceedings of the American Society for Psychical Research 31.*

_____. 1987. *Children Who Remember Previous Lives: A Question of Reincarnation.* Charlottesville, Va.: University of Virginia Press.

Tart, Charles T. 1980. The possible nature of post-mortem states: A discussion, Part II. *Journal of the American Society for Psychical Research 74:418–24.*

_____. 1987. On the scientific study of other worlds. In D. Weiner and R.

Nelson, eds. *Research in Parapsychology 1986*. Metuchen, N.J.: Scarecrow Press.

White, S. E. 1977. *The Betty Book: Excursions into the World of Other Consciousness Made by Betty between 1919 and 1936*. New York: Dutton.

Epilogue

A book, by its nature, is a largely intellectual approach to communication, a cool medium. Yet some of the matters touched on here are more of the heart than of the head. For my final word (and gift) I want to share this Sufi teaching story.

THE TALE OF THE SANDS

A stream, from its source in far-off mountains, passing through every kind and description of countryside, at last reached the sands of the desert. Just as it had crossed every other barrier, the stream tried to cross this one, but it found that as fast as it ran into the sand, its water disappeared.

It was convinced, however, that its destiny was to cross this desert, and yet there was no way. Now a hidden voice, coming from the desert itself, whispered: "The wind crosses the desert, and so can the stream."

The stream objected that it was dashing itself against the sand and only getting absorbed: that the wind could fly and this was why it could cross a desert.

"By hurtling in your own accustomed way you cannot get across. You will either disappear or become a marsh. You must allow the wind to carry you over, to your destination."

But how could this happen? "By allowing yourself to be absorbed in the wind."

This idea was not acceptable to the stream. After all, it had never been absorbed before. It did not want to lose its individuality. And, once having lost it, how was one to know that it could ever be regained?

"The wind," said the sand, "performs this function. It takes up water, carries it over the desert, and then lets it fall again. Falling as rain, the water again becomes a river."

"How can I know this is true?"

"It is so, and if you do not believe it, you cannot become more than a quagmire, and even that could take many, many years; and it certainly is not the same as a stream."

"But can I not remain the same stream that I am today?"

"You cannot in either case remain so," the whisper said. "Your essential part is carried away and forms a stream again. You are called what you are even today because you do not know which part of you is the essential one."

When he heard this, certain echoes began to arise in the thoughts of the stream. Dimly, he remembered a state in which he—or some part of him, was it?—had been held in the arms of a wind. He also remembered—or did he?—that this was the real thing, not necessarily the obvious thing to do.

And the stream raised his vapor into the welcoming arms of the wind, which gently and easily bore it upward and along, letting it fall softly as soon as they reached the roof of a mountain many, many miles away. And because he had had his doubts, the stream was able to remember and record more strongly in his mind the details of the experience. He reflected, "Yes, now I have learned my true identity."

The stream was learning. But the sands whispered, "We know, because we see it happen day after day; and because we, the sands, extend from the riverside all the way to the mountain."

And that is why it is said that the way in which the Stream of Life is to continue on its journey is written in the Sands.[1]

Acknowledgments

All chapters in this book except chapters 10, 26, 28, 29, and the Prologue and Epilogue were originally printed in *The Open Mind* and are published in occasionally modified form here by permission of Psychological Processes, Inc.

Chapter 3, "The Sun and the Shadow," appeared in modified form in *Noetic Sciences Review* (Fall 1987). Vol. 1, No. 4, 15–18.

Chapter 4, "Beginning Dream Yoga," was published in modified form under the title "An Intriguing Results Connected with Beginning Dream Yoga" in R. Russo, ed., *Dreams Are Wiser Than Men* (Berkeley, CA: North Atlantic Books, 1987).

Chapter 9, "Firewalk," was published in modified form but under the same title in *Parapsychology Review* (1987). Vol. 18, No. 3, 1–5.

Chapter 13, "Identification," appeared in modified form as chapters 11 and 12 in Charles T. Tart, *Waking Up: Overcoming the Obstacles to Human Potential* (Boston: New Science Library, 1986), and is published here by permission of New Science Library.

Chapter 14, "The Game of Games," was first published in *Forum for Correspondence and Contact* (1985). Vol. 15, No. 2, 72–77.

Chapter 15, "Aikido and the Concept of Ki," was published in modified form under the title "Aikido: Harmony, Self-defense and Subtle Energies" in *New Realities* (1987), Vol. 7, No. 4, 45–49, and also in modified form under the title "Aikido and the Concept of Ki" in *Psychological Perspectives* (1987). Vol. 18, No. 2, 332–348.

Chapter 16, "Living in Illusion," was published in modified form in Charles T. Tart, *Waking Up: Overcoming the Obstacles to Human Potential* (Boston: New Science Library, 1986), and is published here by permission of New Science Library.

Parts of Chapter 19, "Prayer," were published in modified form in

Charles T. Tart, *Waking Up: Overcoming the Obstacles to Human Potential* (Boston: New Science Library, 1986), and is published here by permission of New Science Library.

Parts of Chapter 20, "Altered States of Consciousness and the Search for Enlightenment," were published in modified form as chapter 1 in Charles T. Tart, *Waking Up: Overcoming the Obstacles to Human Potential* (Boston: New Science Library, 1986), and is published here by permission of New Science Library.

Chapter 23, "Cultivating Compassion," was published in modified form as chapter 23, "Compassion," in Charles T. Tart, *Waking Up: Overcoming the Obstacles to Human Potential* (Boston: New Science Library, 1986), and is published here by permission of New Science Library.

Chapter 24, "Stray Thoughts on Meditation," by Shinzen Young, was originally published in R. Robinson and W. Johnson, eds., *The Buddhist Religion*, 3d ed. (Belmont, CA: Wadsworth, 1982), and is reproduced here by permission of Shinzen Young.

Selections from Chapter 26, "Meditation and Psychology: A Dialogue," were published in the *Noetic Sciences Review* (Autumn 1988). No. 8, 14–21.

Chapter 29, "Altered States and the Survival of Death," was originally published in J. Spong, ed., *Consciousness and Survival: An Interdisciplinary Inquiry into the Possibility of Life Beyond Biological Death* (Sausalito, CA: Institute of Noetic Sciences, 1987). A selection from the chapter appeared in the Institute's December 1985 "Special Report for Members." A small portion of this same chapter was published under the title, "Consciousness, Altered States, and Worlds of Experience" in *Journal of Transpersonal Psychology* (1986) and is reproduced by permission. Vol. 18, 159–170.

Notes

Introduction

1. See P. D. Ouspensky, *In Search of the Miraculous* (New York: Harcourt Brace, 1949).
2. A few of the original *Open Mind* articles that appear in this book were modified and integrated into my recent book *Waking Up: Overcoming the Obstacles to Human Potential* (Boston: New Science Library, 1986), which is a focused presentation of the idea of living in a state of illusion and techniques for awakening from such a state. If you have already read *Waking Up* you will not find that much overlap with this book; the few overlapping chapters have been considerably expanded here.
3. S. Troffer and C. T. Tart, "Experimenter bias in hypnotist performance," *Science 145* (1964): 1330–31.
4. C. T. Tart, "Initial integrations of some psychedelic understandings into everyday life," in L. Grinspoon and J. Bakalar, eds., *Psychedelic Reflections* (New York: Human Sciences Press, 1983), 223–33.

Prologue: The King's Son

1. Idries Shah, *Tales of the Dervishes* (London: Jonathan Cape, 1967), 217–18.

1. Lucid Dreams: Entering the Inner World

1. The *Proceedings* are unknown to most people, so few people had heard of the phenomenon until I reprinted van Eeden's description in 1969. See Charles T. Tart, ed., *Altered States of Consciousness* (New York: Wiley, 1969), 145–58. This book is temporarily out of print; it will appear in a revised third edition published by Harper & Row in 1990.
2. I find Tholey's work particularly fascinating as it ties in with my own work on consciousness, particularly attempts to create a state of "lucid waking" in my experimental Awareness Enhancement Training work, as discussed in Charles T. Tart, *Waking Up: Overcoming the Obstacles to Human Potential* (Boston: New Science Library, 1986).

3. For more information on this subject see Charles T. Tart, *States of Consciousness* (New York: Dutton, 1975; El Cerrito, CA: Psychological Processes, 1983).

4. Carlos Castaneda, *Tales of Power* (New York: Simon & Schuster, 1974), pages 18–20, 51, 67, 233, 235, 244, 245. My students and I hope to publish a comprehensive guide/index to all of Castaneda's ideas on inducing and using lucid dreaming, as well as all of the teachings attributed to Don Juan, sometime in 1990.

5. The complete reference on this subject is J. Schultz and W. Luthe, *Autogenic Training: A Psychophysiologic Approach in Psychotherapy* (New York: Grune & Stratton, 1959). You will have to filter out the authors' medical bias that only a physician can teach you to relax. There is also a comprehensive chapter on autogenic training in Tart, *Altered States of Consciousness.*

6. I have been reading *Life Extension* by D. Pearson and S. Shaw (New York: Warner, 1983). On page 195 they report a curious finding: For about half the people who try it, a 1000-microgram dose of vitamin B-12, taken *immediately* before bedtime, may greatly increase the intensity of colors in dreams. Taking it even thirty minutes before sleep may negate the effect. I think this would probably increase dream recall also: It did for me when I tried it. Tolerance develops rapidly, so you can only do this once in a while. I don't know if there are any medical problems that can result from taking B-12, so be cautious and consult your physician if you have already existing medical problems.

7. Detailed descriptions of the hypnagogic state can be found in chapters 5 and 7 of Tart, *States of Consciousness,* as well as in chapters 4 and 5 of Tart, *Altered States.*

8. This is a problem for narcoleptics, who suffer from "falling sickness," an undesired eruption of stage 1 dreaming sleep during ordinary waking activities.

9. Some readers will recognize that Tholey's Dual Body Technique for inducing lucid dreaming sounds exactly like some occult techniques for "astral projection." Tholey recognizes this but strongly points out in his article that the idea of an "astral body" is unscientific and he is not espousing it. I believe that occasionally there is some definite reality to it, however. See my "Out-of-the-body experiences" in E. Mitchell and J. White, eds., *Psychic Exploration: A Challenge for Science* (New York: Putnam, 1974); or chapter 9 in Charles T. Tart, *Psi: Scientific Studies of the Psychic Realm* (New York: Dutton, 1977); or Robert S. Monroe, *Journeys Out of the Body* (New York: Doubleday, 1971); and chapter 2 of this book. For now we will simply accept the Dual Body Technique as a way of inducing lucid dreaming.

10. This kind of waking wishing or autosuggestion has been used for years to influence the content of ordinary, nonlucid dreams. The interested reader can refer to a comprehensive review of such techniques in Charles T. Tart, "From spontaneous event to lucidity: A review of attempts to consciously control nocturnal dreaming," in B. Wolman, ed., *Handbook of Dreams* (New York: Van Nostrand Reinhold, 1979), 226–68. This is a comprehensive review of the technical literature on this subject through 1978, with extensive references.

11. See my article on the high dream in Tart, *Altered States of Consciousness.*

12. K. Stewart, "Dream theory in Malaya," in Tart, *Altered States,* 161–70. It is important to balance Stewart's persuasive writings by reading William Domhoff, *The Mystique of Dreams* (Berkeley: University of California Press, 1985).

13. Tholey treats lucid dream figures as imaginary, but he does report that some dream figures behave as if they possessed their own perceptual perspectives, cognitive abilities (thought and memory), and even their own motivation." See P. Tholey, "Consciousness and abilities of dream characters observed during lucid dreaming" in *Perceptual and Motor Skills 68* (1989): 567–78. I strongly recommend Michael Harner, *The Way of the Shaman* (San Francisco: Harper & Row, 1980) if you are curious about shamanism.

2. Beyond the Dream: Lucid Dreams and Out-of-the-Body Experiences

1. Stephen LaBerge, *Lucid Dreaming: The Power of Being Awake and Aware in Your Dreams.* (Los Angeles: Tarcher, 1985); Robert S. Monroe, *Far Journeys* (New York: Doubleday,

1985); and Robert S. Monroe, *Journeys Out of the Body* (New York: Doubleday, 1971). I suggest that before reading *Far Journeys* you first read Monroe's classic *Journeys Out of the Body*. *Far Journeys* will be difficult for many readers (including me) because most of the journeys in this second are not "local." Monroe and his students experience other worlds and communicate with beings in them, and there is no way we can evaluate their reality by ordinary criteria. Of course we might be interested enough to try to learn how to go there ourselves—but that is another story.

2. LaBerge, *Lucid Dreaming*, 1–2.

3. Keith Hearne, "Lucid Dreams: An Electrophysiological and Psychological Study" (Ph.D. thesis, University of Liverpool, 1978).

4. LaBerge, *Lucid Dreaming*, 243.

5. Ibid., 229–30. The dream by LaBerge quoted in chapter 21 is also quite relevant here.

6. Monroe, *Far Journeys*, 3.

7. Monroe, *Journeys Out of the Body*, 27–28.

8. This search is now embodied in the ongoing research and training seminars of the Monroe Institute of Applied Sciences. For information about the work of the Institute you may write them at Box 175, Faber, VA 22938.

3. The Sun and the Shadow

1. All excerpts in this chapter are from Kenneth Kelzer, *The Sun and the Shadow: My Experiment with Lucid Dreaming* (Virginia Beach, VA: A.R.E. Press, 1987).

4. Beginning Dream Yoga

1. K. Stewart, "Dream theory in Malaya," in Charles T. Tart, ed., *Altered States of Consciousness* (Garden City, NY: Doubleday, 1971), 161–70. William Domhoff recently carried out what we might call psychological detective work on Stewart's ideas about the Senoi, and he makes a convincing case that the Senoi never practiced the dream work Stewart imagined they did. Nevertheless the principles of Stewart's ideas were sound and have greatly benefited us in triggering off new approaches to dreams. See William Domhoff, *The Mystique of Dreams* (Berkeley: University of California Press, 1985).

2. For more information about the priming exercise and self-remembering see Charles T. Tart, *Waking Up: Overcoming the Obstacles to Human Potential* (Boston: New Science Library, 1986).

3. Charles T. Tart, "A possible 'psychic' dream, with some speculations on the nature of such dreams," *Journal of the Society for Psychical Research* 42 (1963): 283–89; and Charles T. Tart and J. Fadiman, "The case of the yellow wheatfield: A dream-state explanation of a broadcast telepathic dream," *Psychoanalytic Review* 61 (1974–75): 607–18.

4. Tarthang Tulku, *Openness Mind* (Berkeley, CA: Dharma Publishing, 1978).

5. Time: The Mystery Nobody Notices

1. The details of how I went about this, and the results I found, are fully presented in Charles T. Tart, "Information acquisition rates in ESP experiments: Precognition does not work as well as present-time ESP," *Journal of the American Society for Psychical Research* 77 (1984), 293–310.

2. See Charles T. Tart, *Psi: Scientific Studies of the Psychic Realm* (New York: Dutton, 1977).

6. Subtle Energies, Healing Energies

1. D. Krieger, *The Therapeutic Touch: How to Use Your Hands to Help or Heal* (Englewood Cliffs, NJ: Prentice-Hall, 1979).
2. I suspect most of us could actually do this kind of healing, but cultural blinders and prejudices keep us from even thinking of trying it. That's another story, however. Meanwhile Krieger's book is good reading.
3. The information concerning Grad's experiments presented in this chapter is from Bernard Grad, "Some biological effects of the 'laying on of hands': A review of experiments with animals and plants," *Journal of the American Society for Psychical Research 59* (1965): 95–127; and Bernard Grad, "The 'laying on of hands': Implications for psychotherapy, gentling, and the placebo effect," *Journal of the American Society for Psychical Research 61* (1967): 286–305.
4. Douglass Dean, "Infrared measurements of healer-treated water," in W. Roll, J. Beloff, and R. White, eds., *Research in Parapsychology 1982* (Metuchen, NJ: Scarecrow Press, 1983), 100–101.

7. Subtle Energies: Life as the PK Target

1. William Braud, "Conformance behavior involving living systems," in W. G. Roll, ed., *Research in Parapsychology 1978* (Metuchen, NJ: Scarecrow Press, 1979), 111–15.
2. William Braud, G. Davis, and R. Wood, "Experiments with Matthew Manning," *Journal of the Society for Psychical Research 50* (1979): 199–223.
3. William Braud, "Conformance behavior involving living systems." in W. G. Roll, ed., *Research in Parapsychology 1978* (Metuchen, NJ: Scarecrow Press, 1979), 111–15.
4. Braud, "Matthew Manning."
5. Braud, "Conformance Behavior."
6. Braud, "Matthew Manning." For further information, see William Braud, "Allobiofeedback: Immediate feedback for a psychokinetic influence upon another person's physiology," in Roll, *Research in Parapsychology*, 123–34; and William Braud and M. Schlitz, "Psychokinetic influence on electrodermal activity," *Journal of Parapsychology 47* (1983): 95–119.

8. ALB: The Misuse of ESP?

1. Boggle is a registered trademark of Parker Brothers, Inc.
2. As a psychologist with a lot of experience in investigating parapsychological phenomena I should be more specific about the word "unlikely," but trying to precisely calculate the probability that ALB will come up is very complex. If you are a mathematician you can get a copy of the game and try it. More on this later.
3. See Charles T. Tart, *Waking Up: Overcoming the Obstacles to Human Potential* (Boston: New Science Library, 1986).

9. Firewalk

1. H. Darbishire, ed., *Poems in Two Volumes of 1807* (Oxford: Clarendon Press, 1952), 321–32.
2. See H. Price, *Fifty Years of Psychical Research* (London: Longmans, Green & Co., 1939), chap. 14, for the full account of this fascinating experiment.
3. If you are interested in the few relatively scientific studies of firewalking, the fol-

lowing should be of interest: J. Blake, "Attribution of power and the transformation of fear: An empirical study of firewalking," *Psi Research 4*, No. 2 (1985): 62–88; M. Jamal, "The sacred fire," *Psi Research 4*, No. 2 (1985): 110–12; R. Heinze, " 'Walking on flowers' in Singapore," *Psi Research 4*, No. 2 (1985): 46–51; D. Stillings, "Observations on firewalking," *Psi Research 4*, No. 2 (1985): 51–59; and L. Vilenskaya, "Firewalking and beyond," *Psi Research 4*, No. 2 (1985): 89–110.

10. How to Use a Psychic Reading

1. "Channeling" is the popular word today; early in the century people who channeled or claimed to channel were called "Spiritualist mediums." The entities they claimed to manifest were mostly the spirits of the deceased. See chapter 29 for a detailed discussion of this aspect of channeling.
2. See Charles T. Tart, "An emergent-interactionist understanding of human consciousness," in B. Shapin and L. Coly, eds., *Brain/Mind and Parapsychology* (New York: Parapsychology Foundation, 1979), 177–200, for a detailed technical exposition of this idea.
3. I would like to recommend two excellent books on channeling. John Klimo has written a stimulating and encyclopedic work entitled *Channeling: Investigations on Receiving Information from Paranormal Sources* (Los Angeles: Tarcher, 1987). Arthur Hastings's *With Tongues of Men and Angels* is a sophisticated psychological treatment that is in preparation as of this writing.
4. I talk about the dismal track record with some hesitation. It certainly is a good general description of most formal channeling of ostensibly scientific and technical ideas. On the other hand where do successful inventors get their ideas? Some have admitted, usually late in life, to being "inspired"; but inventors have a difficult enough time getting new ideas accepted without mentioning that they may be "channeling" them.
5. Anonymous, *A Course in Miracles* (Tiburon, CA: Foundation for Inner Peace, 1975).
6. Lamar Keene, *The Psychic Mafia* (New York: Dell, 1976).
7. Charles T. Tart, "A survey on negative uses, government interest and funding of psi," *Psi News 1*, No. 2 (1978): 3.
8. I don't want to play social superiority games, but I do want people to distinguish between scientific parapsychologists—those who have scientific training and apply scientific method in their investigations of the paranormal—from too many people who call themselves parapsychologists but who don't have adequate and relevant scientific training or who don't use scientific method in their work. Those of us who have worked hard to get more acceptance of parapsychology in the general scientific community know what a loss it is when legitimate scientific work in this area gets lumped in with unscientific work that is advertised as if it were scientific work. This allows fervent opponents of the field to use the poor work to generally discredit the area. Practically it seems impossible to rescue the term parapsychologist from such loose usage, so I now stress that my own profession is psychologist, and psi phenomena are one of several areas of interest to me.
9. G. Gallup, Jr., *Adventures in Immortality* (New York: McGraw-Hill, 1982).
10. Louis Tannen, Inc., *Catalog of Magic*. You can find the cost of a current catalog by writing Tannen's at 1540 Broadway, New York, NY 10036.
11. An excellent psychic I know, Helen Palmer, by contrast, usually looks away or keeps her eyes closed during a reading. She usually doesn't want to be distracted from her psychic process by sensory feedback.
12. Detailed information on testing methods in the study of psychic phenomena can be found in B. Wolman, L. Dale, G. Schmeidler, and M. Ullman, eds., *Handbook of Parapsychology* (New York: Van Nostrand/Reinhold, 1977). An updating of these methods and extensive reviews of current findings can be found in H. Edge, R.

Morris, J. Palmer, and J. Rush, *Foundations of Parapsychology: Exploring the Boundaries of Human Capability* (Boston: Routledge & Kegan Paul, 1986).

13. Ibid.

14. Methods and excellent results of remote-viewing studies are described in Russell Targ and Harold Puthoff, *Mind-Reach: Scientists Look at Psychic Ability* (New York: Delacorte, 1977); Russell Targ and Keith Harary, *The Mind Race: Understanding and Using Psychic Abilities* (New York: Villard, 1984); and Charles T. Tart, Harold E. Puthoff, and Russell Targ, eds., *Mind at Large: Institute of Electrical and Electronic Engineers Symposia on the Nature of Extrasensory Perception* (New York: Praeger, 1979).

Basic material on ganzfeld studies my be found in Charles Honorton, "Psi and Internal Attention States," in B. Wolman et al., *Handbook of Parapsychology* (New York: Van Nostrand Reinhold, 1977), 435–72.

15. Actual practice calls for finer distinctions, such as ranking all the readings for degree of correspondence with you (first place, second place, and so on); or rating individual statements in each reading ("Not me at all"; "A little like me"; "Somewhat like me"; "A lot like me"; "Completely accurate description of me"). The technical references given elaborate on this.

16. Charles T. Tart and Jeffrey Smith, "Two token object studies with the 'psychic' Peter Hurkos," *Journal of the American Society for Psychical Research 62* (1968): 143–57.

17. I have been helped a great deal in my thinking in this area by participating in several invited conferences organized by Helen Palmer and sponsored by the Esalen Institute. At these unique conferences mature psychics and a few of us from the psychological world shared methodologies for obtaining information psychically, ethical concerns about the proper use of psychic abilities, and how the relationship between a psychic and a client could and should be used to be growthful with each other. My memory has blurred a little over time, so I may forget someone, but I particularly want to express thanks to Helen Palmer, Anne and Jim Armstrong, Angeles Arrien, Frances Cheyna, Marlene Cresci-Cohen, Laura Day, Hella Hammid, Keith Harary, Arthur Hastings, Robert Johnston, Rowena Pattee, Stephen Schwartz, Greg Schelkun, Joan Steffy, and Frances Vaughan. Edited papers from these conferences will, I hope, eventually be published by Helen Palmer.

18. Idries Shah, *Thinkers of the East* (London: Jonathan Cape, 1971), 111.

19. Charles T. Tart, *Waking Up: Overcoming the Obstacles to Human Potential* (Boston: New Science Library, 1986).

11. Who's Afraid of Psychic Powers? Me?

1. There actually is a drug called harmaline, one of whose common names is telepathine, that is used by South American shamans. It is a powerful psychedelic. They believe it facilitates access to the spirit world and psychic abilities.

2. See, for example, J. Eisenbud, "Psi and the nature of things," *International Journal of Parapsychology 5*, No. 3 (1963): 245–69; J. Eisenbud, *Paranormal Foreknowledge: Problems and Perplexities* (New York: Human Sciences Press, 1982); and J. C. Pierce, *Exploring the Crack in the Cosmic Egg* (New York: Julian Press), 1974. Other investigations of mine are reported in Charles T. Tart, "Acknowledging and Dealing with the Fear of Psi," *Journal of the American Society for Psychical Research 78* (1984): 133–43; Charles T. Tart, "Attitudes toward strongly functioning psi: A preliminary survey," *Journal of the American Society for Psychical Research 80* (1986): 163–73.

3. Charles T. Tart, "The controversy about psi: Two psychological theories," *Journal of Parapsychology 46* (1983): 313–20.

4. The Institute of Transpersonal Psychology, formerly called the California Institute of Transpersonal Psychology, is one of the few institutions in the world that provides graduate-level training in transpersonal psychology. If you are interested in this kind

of education, write for a list of schools to the Association for Transpersonal Psychology, P.O. Box 3049, Stanford, CA 94305.

5. See Idries Shah, *The Dermis Probe* (London: Jonathan Cape, 1970), 64–66, for the original story.

6. I have been given some fascinating material by practicing psychics on their fears of psi and have written about this in Charles T. Tart, "Psychics' fears of psychic powers," *Journal of the American Society for Psychical Research 80* (1986): 279–92. The obvious functioning of psychic abilities in their lives ups the ante, and their reactions are quite fascinating. I also recommend a landmark article by Arthur Hastings, "A counseling approach to parapsychological experience," in *Journal of Transpersonal Psychology 15*, No. 2 (1983): 143–68.

12. Real Effort

1. P. D. Ouspensky, *In Search of the Miraculous* (New York: Harcourt Brace, 1949), 363. Other introductions to Gurdjieff's ideas may be found in Kathleen Riordan Speeth, *The Gurdjieff Work* (Berkeley, CA: AND/OR Press, 1976); and in Charles T. Tart, *Waking Up: Overcoming the Obstacles to Human Potential* (Boston: New Science Library, 1986).

13. Identification

1. Charles T. Tart, *Waking Up: Overcoming the Obstacles to Human Potential* (Boston: New Science Library, 1986).

2. Charles T. Tart, *States of Consciousness* (New York: Dutton, 1975; El Cerrito, CA: Psychological Processes, 1983), 130.

3. Stimulating ideas on identification, and what might be hidden under our surface identifications, are given in Kathleen Riordan, "Gurdjieff," in Charles T. Tart, ed., *Transpersonal Psychologies* (El Cerrito, CA: Psychological Processes, 1983), 281–328; and in P. D. Ouspensky, *In Search of the Miraculous* (New York: Harcourt Brace, 1949).

14. The Game of Games

1. Robert Bathurst, 1985 Esalen catalog (seminar catalog).

15. Aikido and the Concept of Ki

1. K. Uyeshiba, *Aikido* (Tokyo: Hozansha, 1969), 5.

2. Note that I have written about Aikido at its best. As an art practiced by human beings, however, it is subject to change. Some students were attracted to Uyeshiba because he was the toughest martial artist in Japan; they paid little attention to all his talk about love and harmony. Others found that part central. If you seriously consider learning Aikido and can find one or more *dojos* (training centers) near your home, watch a few classes and try to sense the spirit of the teacher and the students before you commit yourself.

3. Robert Morris, personal communicaton, 1978.

16. Living in Illusion

1. N. Dixon, *Subliminal Perception* (New York: McGraw-Hill, 1971).

17. Self-observation

1. These psychological defense mechanisms and self-awareness practices are discussed at length in Charles T. Tart, *Waking Up: Overcoming the Obstacles to Human Potential* (Boston: New Science Library, 1986).
2. Anonymous, *A Course in Miracles* (Tiburon, CA: Foundation for Inner Peace, 1975).

18. Selecting a Spiritual Path

1. Charles T. Tart, *Waking Up: Overcoming the Obstacles to Human Potential* (Boston: New Science Library, 1986).
2. For more details of Ichazo's claim see Charles T. Tart, ed., *Transpersonal Psychologies* (El Cerrito, CA: Psychological Processes, 1983), 329–51.
3. I have given more specific advice on choosing a path in *Waking Up: Overcoming the Obstacles to Human Potential*.
4. The network of individuals and organizations in the Spiritual Emergence Network numbers more than ten thousand at present. By writing or phoning SEN you can receive information and referral for yourself or others. There is also an educational program, including articles, bibliographies, tapes, lectures, workshops, and conferences on aspects of spiritual opening and crisis. SEN's membership is open to anyone who is interested in the goals of spiritual awakening and what might be called spiritual midwifery.

    SEN needs support, volunteer networkers, and others to spread the word that they exist and are available to help out when needed. For more information on the Spiritual Emergence Network, write to SEN/CITP, 250 Oak Grove Avenue, Menlo Park, CA 94025.

19. Prayer

1. The texts for this class are my *Transpersonal Psychologies* and my *Waking Up*.
2. Charles Tart, *Waking Up: Overcoming the Obstacles to Human Potential* (Boston: New Science Library, 1986).
3. As this book was in press I discovered an interesting scientific study on the efficacy of petitionary prayer, Randolph Byrd's "Therapeutic Effects of Intercessory prayer in a Coronary Care Unit Population," *Southern Medical Journal* (July 1988): 826–29.

    Using a double-blind design (an essential element in this sort of study) 192 patients who had entered the Coronary Care Unit at San Francisco General Hospital were individually prayed for by a group of devout Christians, the intercessors. The intercessors had no direct contact with the patients, but were told only the patients' first names, diagnoses, and general medical condition. A matched group of 201 patients were used as controls in that the intercessors were not specifically asked to pray for them. The control patients required significantly more ventilatory assistance, antibiotics, and diuretics than those who were prayed for, and had a generally worse hospital experience. Whether such effects should be attributed to God or the more general effects of psychic healing mediated by prayer is an interesting question.

4. Charles Tart, "States of consciousness and state-specific sciences," *Science 176* (1972): 1203–10.

5. P. D. Ouspensky, *In Search of the Miraculous* (New York: Harcourt, Brace & World, 1949), 300–302.

20. Altered States of Consciousness and the Search for Enlightenment

1. In October 1984 I attended a unique conference on modern psychology and Buddhism, centered around a series of talks by His Holiness the Dalai Lama. As my contribution I tried to clarify for Westerners what is meant by the idea of "enlightenment," and to sketch how altered states of consciousness are essential to full enlightenment. This chapter is based on my remarks at the conference. Although Buddhist knowledge is clearly of enormous value in trying to understand altered states of consciousness, I am not very knowledgeable about it; so my remarks about altered states and enlightenment primarily arise from my Western scientific and personal knowledge. I hope that the East-West dialogues begun at this conference and at other places will lead to great advances in Buddhist knowledge, in Western scientific knowledge, and in general human knowledge, regardless of whether we label it "Buddhist" or "Western."

2. For precise scientific use I proposed in *States of Consciousness* that we reserve the term "state" for *major* alterations in the way the mind functions. See Charles T. Tart, *States of Consciousness* (New York: Dutton, 1975; El Cerrito, CA: Psychological Processes, 1983), chapter 1.

3. Ibid., 58.

4. Charles Tart, *Waking Up: Overcoming the Obstacles to Human Potential* (Boston: New Science Library, 1986).

5. This distinction between consciousness and awareness is further elaborated in Tart, *States of Consciousness*.

6. Ibid., 1983.

7. I believe that the great gift of the so-called "psychedelic revolution" was the fact that millions of people had at least a momentary glimpse of alternative modes of perceiving, thinking, feeling, acting, and being that they might never have had in the normal course of conditioned life. Some of these people forgot that vision and went back to their ordinary ways. Some turned the vision into fantasy and sank deeper into deluded consciousness. Some used the vision to begin transformative work on themselves.

8. P. D. Ouspensky, *In Search of the Miraculous* (New York: Harcourt, Brace & World, 1949).

9. H. Reed. "Dream incubation: A reconstruction of a ritual in contemporary form," *Journal of Humanistic Psychology 16*, No. 4: 53–70.

10. See Tart, *Waking Up*.

11. Specific tantric sexual practices are used in the East for moving toward enlightenment, but I do not feel qualified to discuss them.

12. Charles T. Tart, *On Being Stoned: A Psychological Study of Marijuana Intoxication* (Palo Alto, CA: Science & Behavior Books, 1971).

13. Unfortunately I do not have detailed knowledge of exactly what the problems associated with drug use are, from the Eastern point of view.

14. Self-remembering is similar to vipassana meditation in this way, and Tibetan Buddhist tradition has a variety of practices involving heightened awareness in everyday life.

15. Details on the rationale for self-remembering and methods of practiced are detailed in Tart, *Waking Up*.

21. Going Home

1. Anonymous, *A Course in Miracles*, Vol. 3, *Workbook for Students* (Tiburon, CA: Foundation for Inner Peace, 1975), 331.
2. Stephen LaBerge, *Lucid Dreaming: The Power of Being Awake and Aware in Your Dreams* (Los Angeles: Tarcher, 1985), 244–46.
3. Robert Monroe, *Journeys Out of the Body* (New York: Doubleday, 1971), 123–25.
4. Charles T. Tart, *States of Consciousness* (New York: Dutton, 1975; El Cerrito, CA: Psychological Processes, 1983), chapters 15 and 16.
5. Robert Monroe, *Far Journeys* (New York: Doubleday, 1985), 236–37.

22. What We Believe In

1. This cost is discussed in detail in Charles T. Tart, *Waking Up: Overcoming the Obstacles to Human Potential* (Boston: New Science Library, 1986).

23. Cultivating Compassion

1. Sogyal Rinpoche's teaching schedule in the United States can be obtained from the Rigpa Fellowship, Box 7866, Berkeley, CA 94707 ("Rinpoche" is an honorific title).
2. I discuss the nature of the Sense of Identity subsystem and its production of the "I!" quality at length in Charles T. Tart, *States of Consciousness* (New York: Dutton, 1975; El Cerrito, CA: Psychological Processes, 1983).
3. T. Gyatso (The Dalai Lama), *Kindness, Clarity, and Insight* (Ithaca, NY: Snow Lion Publications [P.O. Box 6483], 1984).
4. For more specific guidance with this exercise I have prepared a cassette tape, *The Musical Body*, with appropriate music and directions. It is available from the Institute of Noetic Sciences, 475 Gate Five Road, Suite 300, Sausalito, California 94965. Ask for their general catalog of books and tapes.

24. Stray Thoughts on Meditation

1. A version of this chapter was originally published in R. Robinson and W. Johnson, *The Buddhist Religion*, 3d ed. (Belmont, CA: Wadsworth, 1982), 226–35. It is reproduced here by permission. If you are in the Los Angeles area you may wish to attend meditation classes or retreats led by Shinzen Young. You can contact him at his Community Meditation Center, 1041 South Elden Avenue, Los Angeles 90006 (213) 384–7817.
2. The corresponding Pali terms are *samatha* and *vipassana*; in Tibetan *zhi gnas* (peaceful abiding) and *lhag thong* (penetrating vision); and in Chinese simply *chih* (stopping) and *kuan* (seeing).
3. This is analogous to what Thomas Kuhn in *The Structure of Scientific Revolutions* (Chicago: University of Chicago Press, 1962) calls a paradigm shift. As with the "Copernican revolution," that which was thought to be the center is no longer seen as such, and suddenly everything makes a lot more sense.
4. Patanjali defined a suitable meditation posture *(asana)* as "stable and comfortable."
5. See Janice Dean Willis, *The Diamond Light of the Eastern Dawn* (New York: Simon and Schuster, 1972). The Ch'an/Zen school of East Asia has a series of "ox taming pictures." But the Chinese ox pictures portray the entire course of Buddhist training beginning with confusion and passing through the stages of study and meditation,

initial breakthrough experience, the deepening and integrating of that experience, and culminating in "entering the marketplace offering gifts to all." The Tibetan elephant pictures merely depict stages of settling the mind.

6. See Charles T. Tart. ed., *Altered States of Consciousness* (Garden City, NY: Doubleday, 1972), 501–18; and Tomio Hirai, *Zen and the Mind* (Tokyo: Japan Publications, 1978).

7. This is a Chinese expression. The Japanese speak of "stealing moments" during the day.

8. Meaning not "to remember" but to "collect back" or gather in the mind. From Latin *re-con-ligere*, "back together tying." Compare Sanskrit *sam-a-dhi*, "together-back-putting."

9. For general treatment of Roman Catholic mysticism see Auguste Poulain, edited by J. V. Bainvel, *The Graces of Interior Prayer* (Windsor, VT: Celtic Cross Books, 1978). For the Eastern Orthodox tradition see Vladimir Lossky, *The Mystical Theology of the Eastern Church* (Crestwood, NY: St. Vladimir's Seminary Press, 1976); and E. Kadloubovsky and E. M. Palmer, trans., and Timothy Ware, ed., *The Art of Prayer, An Orthodox Anthology* (London: Faber and Faber Limited, 1978).

10. We see here the immense importance of context when dealing with spiritual vocabulary. In languages with long, rich histories, such as Sanskrit, Tibetan, and Chinese, the same word in different traditions may mean something entirely different or something slightly but significantly different. Even within the same tradition teachers may use terms in different senses. In fact, in the realm of spiritual discourse, the same teacher may use the same term in different senses on different occasions. Developing a sensitivity to such usage is an important aspect of intellectual maturity for students of religious experience.

11. When Freudians spoke of the "Nirvana Drive," meaning the drive to not exist, they were taking Nirvana in its commonly misunderstood sense of self-extinction. As a technical term in Buddhism Nirvana means freedom from any sense of being driven. Buddhism explicitly states that the drive to not exist *(abha vatrsna)* is as much a hindrance to Nirvana as the drive to exist is. Taken in that Buddhist sense the term "Nirvana Drive" is an oxymoron, a self-contradictory expression, like saying "wise fool."

12. For such a case see Flora Courtois, *An Experience of Enlightenment* (Wheaton, IL: Theosophical Publishing House 1986).

13. See Teresa de Avila, *The Interior Castle*, translated by E. Allison Peers (Image Books, 1961), chapter 7. For another classical Christian source that clearly distinguishes "trance mysticism" and "insight mysticism," see *The Cloud of Unknowing*, ed. by B. M. Horl. (London: Underhill, 1912) particularly chapter LXXI, which describes the fact "that some may feel the perfection of this work only in a time of ecstasy while others may feel it whenever they wish, in the common state of man's soul."

14. The notion that Theravadans as "Hinayanists" are only interested in individual liberation and not in helping others is quickly dispelled by examining the lives of highly attained representatives of that tradition. It is just that the "Mahayanist" tradition of East Asia and Tibet has a highly developed systematic philosophy and symbolism placing compassion on a par with wisdom and elucidating the inextricable interrelationship between the two. In Mahayana one is oriented from the very beginning to seek liberation for the sake of oneself and others. Such an orientation is technically called *bodhicitta* in Sanskrit. A person who meditates with this orientation is a *bodhisattva*.

15. In attempting to fully experience any event it is of utmost importance that the event's beginning and ending points be clearly noted. A line segment that includes its first and last point is mathematically very different from one that does not.

16. John Brodie, former quarterback of the San Francisco 49ers, recalled such experiences in an interview published in *Intellectual Digest* (January 1973): 19–20:

At times, and with increasing frequency now, I experience a kind of clarity that I've never seen adequately described in a football story. Sometimes, for example, time seems to slow way down, in an uncanny way, as if everyone were moving in slow motion. It seems as if I have all the time in the world to watch the receivers run their patterns, and yet I know the defensive line is coming at me just as fast as ever. I know perfectly well how hard and fast those guys are coming and yet the whole thing seems like a movie or a dance in slow motion. It's beautiful.

25. Observations of a Meditation Practice

1. See Charles T. Tart, "A psychologist's experience with transcendental meditation" *Journal of Transpersonel Psychology*, No.3 (1972): 135–40.
2. See Charles T. Tart, *Waking Up: Overcoming the Obstacles to Human Potential* (Boston: New Science Library, 1986). Self-remembering is a form of mindfulness meditation. See chapter 26 for the relationship between self-remembering and meditation.

27. Peace or Destruction?

1. Roger Walsh, *Staying Alive: The Psychology of Human Survival* (Boulder, CO: New Science Library, 1984).

28. A Dream of the Other Side

1. J. Spong, ed., *Consciousness and Survival: An Interdisciplinary Inquiry into the Possibility of Life Beyond Biological Death* (Sausalito, CA: Institute of Noetic Sciences, 1987).

29. Altered States and the Survival of Death

1. See Charles T. Tart, *Waking Up: Overcoming the Obstacles to Human Potential* (Boston: New Science Library, 1986).
2. Each process deserves at least a chapter and preferably a book in and of itself, but space limitations call for brevity. The interested reader will find more information in Charles T. Tart, *States of Consciousness* (New York: Dutton, 1975; El Cerrito, CA: Psychological Processes, 1983).
3. P. Stafford, *Psychedelics Encyclopedia* (Los Angeles: Tarcher, 1983).
4. The major exception to this overall inhibition is our eyes, which do move to follow the dream-world imagery, just as if we were awake and actually looking at it. There is no practical danger in moving our eyes around while we sleep, so no inhibition is needed.
5. Indeed some mediumistic communications suggest that the experienced reality of the ostensible surviving entities is largely one where their ideas and beliefs do construct the world they experience. They do not have the sorts of restraints that we have in the physical world, and which we need in order to harmonize what we perceive about the world with our ideas about it. This would make for a highly variable state of consciousness and make personal identity much less stable.
6. Charles T. Tart, "The controversy about psi: Two psychological theories," *Journal of Parapsychology 46* (1983): 313–20; this book, chapter 11; "Acknowledging and dealing with the fear of psi," *Journal of the American Society for Psychical Research 78* (1984): 133–43; "Defense mechanisms: Obstacles to compassion," *The Open Mind 3*, No. 2 (1985): 1–9.

7. In workshops I have been able to guide people to useful insights by having them go through a procedure I call a "belief experiment." This is the Western Creed exercise explained in chapter 22. It would be worth your time to review the Western Creed at this point. The ideas expressed in the Western Creed are generally claimed to be accurate representations of the best scientific *fact*, not just a belief system. If they are indeed facts then we must accept them, whether we like them or not. I certainly don't like them, but I must divorce my liking or disliking of ideas from my scientific investigation of their truth value. Are they well-proven facts? Or mainly the current cultural fashion?

8. "Psychic" means that while we observe information transfer or physical effects on the physical world as a result of mental desire, there are no reasonably conceivable physical means whereby the information transfer or physical effects can have come about. There may be other psychic abilities—I think there are—but they have not been investigated and established to the degree that these four have, so I focus on them as the foundations of parapsychology.

9. Charles T. Tart, "Information transmission rates in forced-choice ESP experiments: Precognition does not work as well as present time ESP," *Journal of the American Society for Psychical Research* 77 (1984): 293–310.

10. Ibid.

11. Charles T. Tart, "Laboratory PK: Frequency of manifestation and resemblance to precognition," in *Research in Parapsychology 1982* (Metuchen, NJ: Scarecrow Press, 1983), 101–2.

12. Collected after World War II by Rosalind Heywood. Quoted in W. Roll, "Will Personality and Consciousness Survive the Death of the Body? An Examination of Parapsychological Findings Suggestive of Survival" (Doctoral dissertation, University of Utrecht, 1985), 178–79.

13. Charles T. Tart, "A survey of expert opinion on potentially negative uses of psi, United States government interest in psi, and the level of research funding of the field," in W. Roll, ed., *Research in Parapsychology 1978* (Metuchen, NJ: Scarecrow Press, 1979), 54–55.

14. Roll, "Personality and Consciousness," 178–79.

15. See I. Stevenson, *Twenty Cases Suggestive of Reincarnation* (Charlottesville, VA: University of Virginia Press, 1974); *Cases of the Reincarnation Type. Volume 1* (Charlottesville, VA: University of Virginia Press, 1975); *Cases of the Reincarnation Type. Volume 2. Ten Cases in Sri Lanka* (Charlottesville, VA: University of Virginia Press, 1977); *Cases of the Reincarnation Type. Volume 3. Twelve Cases in Lebanon and Turkey* (Charlottesville, VA: University of Virginia Press, 1980); *Cases of the Reincarnation Type, Volume 4. Twelve Cases in Thailand and Burma* (Charlottesville, VA: University of Virginia Press, 1983); *Children Who Remember Previous Lives. A Question of Reincarnation* (Charlottesville, VA: University of Virginia Press, 1987).

16. Tart, *States of Consciousness*.

Epilogue: The Tale of The Sands

1. Idries Shah, *Tales of the Dervishes* (London: Jonathan Cape, 1967), 23–24.

Index

Abhidharma, 250
Ability to focus, 196
Absorption, 271, 309, 310
Acceptance by others, xii
Access to multiple states of consciousness, 198
Acocella, J., 173, 223
A Course in Miracles, 86, 169, 208, 212, 367, 370, 371
Acquired nature, 198, 195, 205
Active imagination, 16
Adamson, S., 212
Addiction, 299, 308, 320
Addiction to thought, 271
Advantages of Identification, 123
Aggressiveness, 31
AIDS, 319, 324
Aikido, xii, 139, 285, 286, 321, 369, ch. 15
Alcohol, 192
Alcoholics Anonymous, 281
Alertness, 295
Al Ghazali, 329
Aliveness, 267, 299
Allo biofeedback, 61
Alpha blocking, 249
Altered states of consciousness, xii, xv, 05, 111, 121, 106, 107, 108, 190, 213, 333, 334, 336, 338, ch. 20, ch. 31
Ambiguous perceptions, 160
Anchor point, 40
Anger, 72, 111, 142, 143, 144, 146, 166, 170, 199, 226, 231, 253, 285, 297, 320, 335
Anthony, D., 181
Anumana, 248
Apostle's Creed, 217, 219
Approval, xii, 104
Archaeus Congress on Holistic Medicine, 78
Archaeus Foundation, 171, 245
Archetypal, 111
Archetypal material, 111
Archetype, 259
Arhat, 280
Armor, 232

Armstrong, A., 368
Armstrong, J., 368
Arrien, A., 368
ASCs. See Altered states of consciousness
Association for Transpersonal Psychology, 369
Assumptions, xiii, 131
Assumptions, testing, 131
Astral projection, 364
Atheist, 182
Atkinson, R., 173, 223
Attachment, 94, 199, 203
Attacks, 233; blending with, 144; leading the energy of, 145; nature of, 144; psychology of, 143; verbal, 144
Attention, 54, 55, 62, 75, 81, 108, 122, 124, 126, 188, 207, 233, 238, 247, 272, 276, 300
Attentional focus priorities, 197
Attention energy, 121
Attention training, 216
Attitudes, 131
Attitudes toward prayer, 183
Available states dimension of enlightenment, 196
Auras, 67
Authenticity, 182
Authoritarianism, 262
Authority, x, 221
Authority figures, 215
Auto-biofeedback, 63, 64
Autogenic training, 9, 364
Automatization, 126, 160, 216, 231, 298, 321, 336, 337
Automatons, xi
Autosuggestion, 8, 364
Aversions, 254, 261, 310
Awakeness, 299
Awakening, xx, 201
Awareness, 194, 196, 247, 254, 255, 261, 276, 286, 289, 294, 301, 335, 371; basic, 198; nature of, 335
Awareness Enhancement Training, 108, 281

Background intentions, 267, 273
Bainvel, J., 373
Bakalar, J., 363
Balance, 110, 262
Balanced development, 225
Barley seeds, 58
Basic humanity, 129
Basic nature, 195, 198, 205
Bathurst, R., 130, 369
Beauty, 204
Being, 188
Being present, 142, 143, 146
Belief, 81, 214, 221, 321, 334, ch. 22
Belief experiment, 97, 99, 101, 107, 219, 220
Belief systems, 76
Beloff, J., 52, 366
Best, E., 79
Bias, 92, 131, 282, 283, 284, 286, 287, 288
Big Bang, 218
Biofeedback, 63, 64
Biological target systems, 61
Birds, 36, 37
Birge, W., 92
Birthday, 121
Black magic, 65
Black thumb effect, 59
Blake, J., 83, 367
Blending, 146, 147
Blind judging, 93
Bliss, 258, 269, 289, 295, 302, 338
Blockages, 303
Blood, 63
Blood pressure, 63
Boddhicitta, 373
Bodhisattva, 259, 373
Bodily/instinctive intelligence, 227
Body, x, 123, 125, 127
Body image, 340
Body sensations associated with the thinking, 298
Boggle, 67, 68, 366, ch. 8
Bootzin, R., 173, 223
Boredom, 295, 296
Boundaries, 109
Bourne, L., 173, 223
Brain waves, 11
Brainwaves, 249
Brain wave state, 338
Braud, W., 61–66, 366
Breathing, 21, 248, 250, 265, 267–271, 272, 300, 302, 309, 310; slowing of in meditation, 249
Brodie, J., 373
Buddha, xiv, 259, 261, 280, 284, 301, 338; definition of, 256
Buddhism, 26, 169, 182, 190, 198, 201, 206, 214, 234, 246, 247, 371, 372, 373, ch. 26

Budo, 140
Buffers, 230
Burden of precognitive ability, 51
Busyness, 170
Byrd, R., 370

California Institute of Transpersonal Psychology, 368
Calmness, 288
Cancer, 57
Carrington, P., 263, 277, 314
Castaneda, C., 8, 40, 41, 364
Caste system, 168, 169
Cat, 37, 38
Catharsis, 308
Chakras, 35
Chance, xii, 220
Change, 125
Channeling, 67, 84, 367, ch. 10
Chanting, 248, 314
Ch'an-Zen, 258
Charlatans, 85, 86, 88, 90, 179
Chenya, F., 368
Chih (stopping), 372
Childhood, 204, 209
Child mind, 75
Children and beggars, 168
Christian mystical tradition, 182
Churches, 221
Circadian rhythms, 165
Clairvoyance, 84, 85
Clarity, 21, 30, 72, 254, 257, 285, 286, 297; of awareness is preferable to murkiness of, 285
Claxton, G., 164
Clock time, 45
Closed mindedness, ix, xiv, 94
Cloud of Unknowing, 255
Coe, M., 83
Coffee cup exercise, 122
Cold readings, 46, 89, 90
Collective unconscious, 111
Color in dreams, 6, 364
Coly, L., 367
Combined technique, 9
Common sense, xvii
Community Meditation Center, 246, 372
Compassion, xiii, xvi, 166, 198, 199, 224, 256, 259, 260, 375, ch. 24; definition of, 226; developing it toward yourself, 237, 238; development of, ch. 24; intelligence needed, 228; obstacles to, 229, 230, 231, 232
Competition, 141
Completeness, 29
Compulsion, 307; (s), 308
Compulsiveness, 281, 306
Computerized psychotherapy, 55

Concentration, 247, 249, 251, 259, 263, 265, 271, 276, 288, 289, ch. 26
Concentrative meditation, 267, 271, 272, 300, 302, 309, 311
Conditioning, 124, 126, 130, 131, 198, 199, 200
Conflict, 104, 106
Conflicting desires, 184
Confusion, 253, 261
Conscience, 261
Consciousness, 3, 156, 333; construction of, 334; nature of, 156, 194; pattern of, 192, 202
Consensus consciousness, 167, 199, 200, 201, 202, 205, 206
Consensus trance, 124, 193, 238
Consistency, 295
Constellation of consciousness, 203, 226
Construction of perception, 173
Contact with the dead, 25
Content control of dreams, 13, 14, 15
Contentment, 335
Context, 131
Continuity of memory, 6
Contraction, 313
Contradictory messages, 104
Control, 4, 15, 21, 31, 111, 122, 298; of lucid dreams by wishing, 14; of lucid dreams by looking, 15
Controlling fish, 61
Costs of identification, 125
Counterattack defenses, 106
Courage, 30
Courtois, F., 255, 373
Cravings, 310
Crazy, 214
Creation of life, 218
Creation of the world, 218, 220
Creative problem solving, 201, 202
Creative thinking, 95–99
Cresci-Cohen, M., 368
Crutchfield, R., 173, 223
Crystals, 67
Cultural bias, 50, 103, 108, 129, 179, 186, 195, 206, 214, 262, 284, 292, 309, 323, 334, 337, 342, ch. 14, ch. 22
Cultural conditioning, 109, 170
Culturally given categories, 22
Cultural roles, 55
Culture, transcendence of, ch. 14
Curiosity, x, 75, 76, 79, 81, 82

Dalai Lama. See Gyatso, T.
Dale, L., 367
Dangers of spiritual path, 31
Darbishire, H., 366
Davis, G., 66, 366
Dawn, 37, 38
Day, L., 368

Daydreaming, 310
Deadening process, xi
Dean, D., 59, 60, 366
Dean, E., 52
Death, xii, xiv, 21, 22, 23, 32, 51, 85, 219, 221, 222, 253, 323, 333, ch. 30, ch. 31
Deeper self, 109
Deep meaning, 84
Defense, xv, 230, 231, 232, 233; psychology of, 143
Defense mechanisms, 166
Defense of time, 172
Defenses, 227, 229, 231, 232, 233, 375
Defensiveness, 235, 267, 320
Delaney, G., 33, 332
Delusion, xii, xv, xvi, xvii, 85
Delusions of grandeur, 111
Demons, 259
Denial, 104
Depersonalization, 169
Depression, 59, 111, 166, 192, 202, 208, 226
Dervish, 111, 112
De Saint-Denys, H., 17, 33, 332
Desire, 188, 247, 253, 254, 261, 302, 303; to help others, 227
Detachment, 247, 249, 251, 261
Detectives, 87
Development, xi, 110, 302, 314
Developmental tasks, 95
Devil, 30, 110
Dharana, 251
Dharmakaya, 260
Dhyana, 249, 251
Dice, 61
Diet, 307
Diet of impressions, 165
Dimensions of enlightenment, 196
Disassociated intellectual thinking, 167
Discriminating dreaming from waking, 6, 7, 9
Discrimination, ix, x, xv, xvi, xvii, 85, 90, 91, 93, 198, 199
Distancing defense, 171
Distractions, fighting, 268
Dividing Camels, 96
Dixon, N., 164, 369
Dogen, 260, 261
Domhoff, W., 33, 364
Don Juan, 8, 40, 41, 364
Donovan, S., 263, 277, 315
Doubt, x, 85, 90
Dream, 163, 192, 202; analysis, 5; body, 340; dissolution, 15; figures, entering into, 13; incubation, 201; recall, 10, 35, 36; world dissolution, 15; yoga, xvii, 35, 39, ch. 4
Dreaming, 191, 192, 202, 338, 342; the $50 bet, 191

Dreams, xiii, xiv, xv, xvi, 3, 4, 191, 200, 201, 323, ch. 30; analysis of, 29, 200; characteristics of, 6; discriminating dreaming from waking, 6; incorporation in. 339; inhibition of physical movement in, 340; lucid. See Lucid dreaming; passivity in, 339; time flow in, 20; wish fulfillment, 21
Drugs and Buddhism, 309. See also psychedelics, 307
Drunkenness, 6
Dry vipassana, 289
Dual body technique, 12, 364
Dualism, 252
Dullness, 263
Dvesa, 253, 255, 256
Dying, process of, 333

Ecker, B., 181
Eclipses, 218
Ecstasy, 32, 255, 336
Edge, H., 367
Effective action, 31
Effective compassion, 227
Effort, 312
Ego, 314
Ego inflation, 31
Ego-point technique, 13
Ehrenwald, J., 60
Eisenbud, J., 52, 113, 368
Ekstrand, B., 173, 223
Elation, 192
Electrical field, 61
Electrical resistance of the skin, 63
Electric knife fish, 61
Electromagnetic radiation, 157
Electromyogram, 20
Eliade, M., 83
Eliot, T.S., 260
Emmons, M., 263, 277, 314
Emotion, x, 54, 103, 108, 111, 121, 122, 131, 156, 160, 167, 184, 186, 192, 199, 202, 203, 206, 210, 225, 226, 229, 230, 234, 258, 320, 335, 339
Emotional development, 238
Emotional intelligence, 226
Emotional states, 199, 202, 203
Empathy, 147, 226, 227, 232
Empire analogy for our bodies, 65
Emptiness, 209
Encounter groups, xiii
Enculturation, 103, 105, 126, 130, 160, 195, 198, 204, 231, 237
Endarkenment, 206
Enemies, 221
Energies, 245; subtle, ch. 6
Energy, 47, 53, 111, 119, 126, 139, 225, 238, 250, 258, 267, 275, 287, 299, 300, 304, 306, 335; physical, 139; psychological container for, 111; psychological nature of, 53
Enlightenment, 140, 186, 190, 219, 220, 222, 254, 255, 256, 258, 260, 262, 282, 290, 295, 297, 303, 371, ch. 20; as a continuum, 193; available states dimension, 197, 198; desire for it as blockage, 303; presumptuousness of verbal definition, 193; tool analogy, 195, 196
Entering the stream of nobles, 254
Entities, 85, 86
Equanimity, 295, 302, 303
Equanimous, 312
Esalen, 65, 131, 181, 368
ESP, 47, 50, 67, 85, 194; electronic devices for testing, 49; misuse of, ch. 8; 67, signal-to-noise ratio, 48, 49; upper limits of performance, 49
ESP and physics, 47
Essence, 82, 126, 185, 227, 229, 231, 238
Essential self, 109
Estabani, O., 56, 57, 58
Eternity, 338
Evaluating psychic readings, 92
Evaluation, 167, 335, 339
Evans-Wentz, W., 33
Even-handed awareness, 295
Evolution, 218, 222
Excitement, 335
Exile, 208
Expansion, 109, 313
Expectations, 75, 95, 273, 283
Exterocepters, 334
Exteroception, 334, 337, 338, 340
Extinction, 319
Extrasensory perception. See ESP
Eye movement during sleep, 374

Fadiman, J., 365
Failure, 261
Fairbanks, AK, 121
Faith, 261
Fake world, 4
Fall, 238
Falling asleep, 269, 302, 309, 310
False color photographs, 158
False personality, 32, 126, 184, 224, 225, 230, 233, 234, 238
Fanaticism, 117
Fantasies of grandeur, 95
Fantasy, 108, 142, 170, 171, 203, 269, 285, 310
Faraday, A., 33, 332
Faris, N., 329
Fear, 15, 19, 30, 77, 79, 80, 101, 145, 162, 198, 199, 221, 231, 251, 295, 297, 319, 335, 369, 374, ch. 11; dealing with, 101; of being afraid, 30; of openness, 107

Feedback, x, 296, 336, 337, 340; during
    psychic reading, 367
Feelings, xii, 72, 105, 123, 127, 130, 181,
    237, 296; hidden, 148
Feinstein, D., 223
Femininity, 31
Fetzer Foundation, 165
Fire, 157
Firewalking, xv, 75, 81, 366, 367, ch. 9;
    danger of, 82; lack of burning of flesh,
    77; lack of effect on clothing, 80; paste
    applied to feet, 77, 78, 81; people's lack
    of interest in, 76; teaching, 79, 80; tem-
    perature of fire, 78, 81; temperature of
    soles of feet, 78; theories of, 76, 77, 81
First axiom of meditative practice, 284
Fish, 62
Fishing for information, 89
Flame, 40
Flight simulator, 159, 160, 163
Flying, 5, 191, 209, 210, 329
Food of impressions, 108
Foreigners, 130
Forestiere, B., 117, 118, 119
Forestiere Underground Gardens, 119
Forgetting yourself, 10
Formlessness, 260
Formless Self Society, 280
Fountain, 19
Four-minute-mile, xi
Fourth axiom, 295
Framework, 97
Freedom, 286, 297
Free will, 221
Fresno, CA, 118, 119
Freud, S., 29
Friends, 221, 222
Frustration, 166
Fulfillment, 286
Full lotus position, 292

Gackenbach, J., 17, 33
Gallup, G., 367
Game of Games, ch. 14
Ganzfeld, 93
Gardening, 98
Garfield, P., 33, 332
Gendlin, E., 332
Gentleness, 300
Gerbils, 62, 63
Getting off the line, 144, 147
Getting stuck in a good place, 262
Gibson, E., 83
Goal orientation, 65
God, xiv, 30, 112, 122, 127, 140, 169, 183,
    184, 185, 188, 217, 218, 220, 238, 252,
    255, 301, 302, 303
Goddesses, 259
Gods, 259

Goenka, 305
Goethe-Universität, 11
Goldstein, J., 128, 164, 207, 212, 241, 263,
    277, 315, 321
Goleman, D., 263, 277, 315
Goodness, 31
Grad, B., 55, 56, 57, 58, 59, 60, 61, 366
Grandparent, 235
Grasping, 291
Green, C., 17, 33
Green, M., 223
Green thumb effect, 58
Grinspoon, L., 363
Grof, C., 181
Grof, S., 181
Group pressure, 82
Growing flowers analogy, 224
Growth, xiv, xv
Growth needs, 107
GSR, 249
Guardian of the Spring, 19, 21
Gurdjieff, G., xi, 117, 121, 124, 126, 127,
    163, 165, 167, 172, 179, 183, 184, 185,
    187, 188, 201, 203, 205, 224, 225, 230,
    238, 281, 289, 312, 313, 369
Guru, 261, 307
Gyatso, T. (the Dalai Lama), 212, 235, 241,
    263, 277, 315, 319, 320, 321, 371, 372
Gymnotus carapo, 61

Habits, 337; of feeling, 96; of perception,
    96; of thought, 22, 96
Hair shirts, 292
Hall, E., 131
Hallucination, 259; in hypnosis, 192
Halo effect, 92
Hammid, H., 368
Hanh, T., 212, 263, 277, 315, 321
Happiness, 84, 262, 287, 303; conditional
    and unconditional, 303, 304, 305;
    wimpy, 303
Harary, K., 99, 368
Harmaline, 368
Harmony, 141, 143, 144, 146, 148
Harner, M., 17, 33, 329, 364
Haruspicy, 45
Hastings, A., 36, 37, 38, 86, 108, 109, 113,
    181, 367, 368, 369
Hatha yoga, 248
Haule, J., 109, 110
Hayward, J., 263, 277, 315
Hazrat Ali, 96
Healer, 53
Healing, 85, 139, 366, ch. 6; measuring
    rate of, 56
Healing blood, 63
Hearne, K., 20, 27, 365
Heart, xxi
Heart rate, 63

Heat capacity, 76
Heaven, xi, 209
Heinze, R., 83, 367
Hell, xi, 209, 217, 253
Hemolysis, 63
Heptascopy, 45
Here-and-now, 204
Here-and-nowness, 249, 286
Heywood, R., 375
High dreams, 364
Higher nature, 30
Higher order in the universe, 222
Higheyeque, 85, 93
Hilgard, E., 173, 223
Hinduism, 309
Hirai, T., 263, 277, 315, 372
Hisamatsu, 280
Hitler, A., 111
Holistic healing, 67
Holistic view of universe, 97
Holy Ghost, 217
Home, 260, ch. 21
Honorton, C., 368
Horl, B., 373
Hostile figures in dreams, 15, 16
Householders, 305
Houston, J., 212
Hsiao Chih-Kuan, 263
Humanistic psychology, 107
Humility, 178
Humor, 67, 262
Hungry ghost charlatan, 90
Hurkos, P., 93, 368
Hydraulic models of the mind, 156
Hypnagogic, 269, 270, 302
Hypnagogic state, 10, 11, 364
Hypnosis, xii, 9, 77, 190, 192; age regres-
    sion, 193; amnesia, 193; analgesia, 193;
    anosmia, 193; control of movement, 192;
    telepathic, 67
Hypnotic induction procedure, 192

Iannuzzo, G., 83
Ichazo, O., 179
I Ching, 97, 98, 99
Idea, 340
Identification, 30, 72, 109, 136, 170, 184,
    185, 230, 231, 233, 234, 237, 247, 254,
    259, 260, 369, ch. 13; objects of, 122,
    124; static quality of, 125
Identities, dropping, 127
Identity, xiv, 108; nature of, 333, 336, 339;
    student, 124
Identity states, 184, 187; examples of, 333
Ignorance, 298
Illusion, x, xi, 96, 170, 171, 205, 208, 214,
    224, 230, 285, 286; of separation, 169,
    170; living in, ch. 16
Image, 125, 255

Image-body technique, 12
Image-ego-point technique, 13
Imagery, 11, 12, 270, 296
Images, 258, 296, 297
Image technique, 11
Imagination, 117, 150
Imagining yourself dreaming, 9
Immobility, 12
Impermanence, 253, 291, 303, 313
Implicit social contract, 102
India, 165, 252, 309, ch. 17
Induction of consensus trance, 126
Information, 334
Information transfer, 49
Inhibition, 339; during sleep, 374
Input processing, 334, 335, 339
Insanity, 110
Insight, 5, 125, 225, 231, 247, 254, 258,
    259, 260, 263, ch. 26
Insight meditation, 216, 311. See also
    Vipassana
Insights, 216, 245, 287, 306
Inspiration, 367
Instinct, 167, 178
Institute of Noetic Sciences, 240, 372, 374
Institute of Transpersonal Psychology,
    108, 181, 368
Integration, 109, 110
Intelligence, xv, 218, 227, 232, 233; body,
    148
Intention, 10, 62, 267
Intentionality, 31
Intention technique, 8
Internal tribal problems, 133
Interoception, 334, 338
Interoceptors, 334, 335, 340
Inter-tribal competition, 133
Intimations of Immortality, 75
Intuitions, 245
Invention, 367
Involve, 154
Invulnerability, 230
Irritation, 295, 296

Jamal, M., 83, 367
Jesus, 182, 183, 217
Jhanas, 249, 253
Jodrey, 111
Johansson, R., 263, 277, 315
Johnson, W., 121, 246, 372
Johnston, R., 368
Jones, Indiana, 36
Joshua, 328
Joy, x
Judging, blind, 92
Judgments, 220, 222
Jung, C., 171
Just sitting, 260

Kadloubovsky, E., 263, 277, 315, 373
Kalamazoo, 165
Kalibaliwali, 81
Kaplan, B., 180
Karma, 172, 255, 304
Keene, L., 87, 88, 367
Kelzer, K., 22, 28, 29, 30, 31, 32, 332, 365
Kensho, 254, 258
Kesner, J., 52
Ki, 141, 148, 149, 150; definition of, 148;
    flowing water analogy, 149
Kindness, 31, 225
Klesa, 254, 259
Klesas, 253
Klimo, J., 86, 367
Knots, 295
Knowledge, intellectual vs. deeper, 170
Koan, 258
Kornfield, J., 128, 164, 207, 212, 241, 263,
    277, 315, 321
Korzybski, A., 22
Kretch, D., 173, 223
Krieger, D., 60, 366
Krippner, S., 223, 332
Kuan (seeing), 372
Kuda Bux, 78
Kuhn, T., 372

Labeling Experience, 22, 25
LaBerge, S., 17, 18, 19, 20, 21, 22, 25, 27,
    33, 209, 212, 332, 364, 365, 366
Lama, the Dalai. See Gyatso, T.
Laying on of hands, 53, 55, 60, 366
Laziness, 263
Leading, 146
Learning from mistakes, 179
Level of activation, 64
Levels of self-defense, 141
Lhag thong, 372
Liberation, 90, 204, 256, 260, 261, 288
Light, xi, 75, 82, 157, 210, 259
Lilly, J., 179
Limitations, x, 129
Living in a world simulator, 160
Living in illusion, xv, 90
Livson, N., 173, 223
Loading stabilization, 336
Locking around sensation, 302
Logic, 186, 287, 335
Lossky, V., 373
Lost toy, ix
Lotus, 35, 39, 40
Lotus position, 247, 291
Love, xii, 31, 32, 103, 120, 140, 141, 143,
    182, 197, 211, 224, 225, 229, 230, 231,
    233, 235, 236, 238, 240, 256, 262, 321,
    335
Loyal followers, 90
LSD, xv, xvi

Lucid dreaming, xiv, 201, 202, 205, 210,
    341, 364, 365; and enlightenment, 202;
    dangers of, 8; distinguishing from
    OOBEs, 25, 26; distinguishing from
    other experience, 25; formula for
    inducing, 9
Lucidity, 35, 39, 40
Lucid waking, 202, 205, 206
Luthe, W., 9, 364

McClenon, J., 83
MacKenzie, A., 52
Madras Institute of Magnetobiology, 165
Magic, 25, 26, 30, 123, 185
Magic, black, 65; catalogs of, 88, 367
Magnetic fields, 59, 165
Mahayana, 261
Maimonides, 329
Making your living with your left foot,
    117
Makyo, 259
Malaya, 365
Mania, 202
Manipulation, 168
Manning, M., 62, 63, 66, 366
Manual labor, 250
Marijuana intoxication, 6, 204, 205, 300,
    306, 308, 309, 371
Mark (sucker), 88, 89
Masao Abe, 280
Masculinity, 31
Maslow, A., 107
Masters, R., 212
Materialism, xiv
Maturity, 227
Mavromatis, A., 332
Maya, 214
Meaning, 182, 220
Medical students, 56
Meditation, viii, xiv, xv, 35, 71, 78, 142,
    149, 178, 182, 188, 190, 192, 198, 199,
    205, 206, 233, 234, 235, 236, 329, 372;
    and drugs, 306; and psychic abilities,
    261; and psychotherapy, 254; and self-
    remembering, 289, 314; as a utilitarian
    process, 285; axioms of, 295; basic types
    of, 247; compulsions created around,
    307; difficulties with, ch. 27, 265; effects
    on everyday life, 251; efficiency, 292,
    293; goal of Buddhist, 247; guided, 296;
    importance of practice, 252; mindful-
    ness. See Vipassana, 272; misconcep-
    tions about and perversions, 261, 262;
    misleading people, 281; no absolutes in,
    301; personal experience of, 245, 265;
    physiological effects of, 249; positions
    for, 248; postures for, 266, 282, 288, 289,
    290, 292, 372; settling in process, 267;
    teachers, 280; teaching and support by

peers, 280; teaching by "non-expert," 280, 281; walking, 257
Meditative perspective, 71
Mediums, spiritualist, 367
Memories, 337
Memory, 9, 19, 125, 163, 187, 191, 198, 204, 208, 212, 254, 255, 334, 339
Memory continuity, 8, 11, 12
Mental illness, 86
Merton, T., 293
Metabolism, 249
Metzner, R., 213
Miccha samadhi, 261
Mice, 56, 57
Mid-life crisis, 126
Mind, 156, 225; chemical models of, 156; computer models of, 156, 157, 158, 159, 163; nature of, 85
Mind-body relationships, xiii
Mindell, A., 332
Mindful, 294, 297
Mindfulness, xv, 71, 142, 224, 225, 231, 233, 234, 267, 270, 276, 289, 295, 296, 312, 313
Miraculous changes in dreams, 14
Misr, xiv, xx
Mitchell, E., 17, 33, 52, 364
Moha, 253, 254, 256, 258
Monasticism, 250
Monroe, R., 17, 23, 24, 25, 26, 27, 33, 209, 210, 212, 213, 364, 365, 372
Monroe Institute of Applied Sciences, 365
Moralities, 220, 222
Morality, 31, 251, 261
Morning liking exercise, 240
Morris, C., 173
Morris, R., 52, 60, 368, 369
Mother, 103, 104, 105
Motivation, 206, 249, 252, 306
Motives, 108
Motor Output, 336, 340
Mountain path, 21
Mouse, 37
Mullin, G., 263, 277, 315
Multiple personality, 184
Murkiness, 286
Murphy, M., 263, 277, 315
Music, 239, 252; celestial, 210, 211
Musical body; exercise, 239, 240; tape, 372
Mystical experience, xv, xvi, 140, ch. 21

Naranjo, C., 264, 277, 315
Narcolepsy, 364
Native American Church, 308
Nature, 302
Nature of consciousness, 29
Naval Postgraduate School, 130
NDE (near death experience), 85
Near death experience. See NDE

Nembutsu, 248
Neoplatonists, 252
Neurosis, 167, 214
New Age, 67
Niceness, 31
Nicoll, M., 189
Niem-Phat, 248
Nien-Fo, 248
Nightmare, 30
Nirmanakaya, 260
Nirvana, 210, 253, 256, 260, 262, 373; definition of, 253
Nirvana drive, 373
Noninterference, 286
Nonreturner, 280
Normalcy, xi, xii, 103, 117, 124, 167, 214, 216
Norris, Jo Ann, xi
No-self, 255, 314
Nuclear weapons, 319

OBE, 85, 209, 210, 259, 365, ch. 2, ch. 18; definition of, 23
Objectivity, xv, 283
Objects of identification, 123
Observation, 247
Observing your breathing, 234
Obstacles to compassion, 229
Once Returner, 280
One body technique, 12
Oneness, 254, 256
One-pointedness, 247, 248, 251, 253, 254
Open Mind, The, xi
Open mindedness, x, xv, xvi, xvii, 67, 93, 96, 204, 283
Openness, xiii, 107, 112, 166, 233, 234, 250
Oratio quies, 251
Orgasm, 203
Ornstein, R., 264, 277, 315
Ouspensky, P., 120, 127, 189, 207, 363, 369, 370, 371
Out-of-the-body experiences. See OBE
Overachievement, 97
Overexcitement, 266
Overpopulation, 319
Owens, C., 264, 277, 315
Ox taming pictures, 372

Pain, x, 77, 81, 123, 166, 193, 221, 230, 233, 253, 275, 291, 292, 293, 294, 301, 342; experiencing skillfully or unskillfully, 293
Palmer, E., 263, 277, 315
Palmer, H., 367, 368
Palmer, J., 368
Panic, 6, 192
Paradigm shifts, 372
Paralysis, 20, 340

Parapsychology, xii; size of the field, 87
Parents, 235
Passivity, 3
Patanjali, 251, 252, 372
Pathological, 236
Pathologies, 214
Patience, 31
Pattee, R., 368
Pauling, L., 319
Peace, xx, 129, 141, 210, 302, ch. 14, ch. 29; psychological foundations for, 320, 321
Peak experience, 32, 254
Pearson, D., 364
Perception, 108, 112, 129, 157, 158, 160, 167, 186, 197, 199, 203, 204, 206, 214, 230, 256, 257, 258, 286, 298, 334, 337; stages of, 162; tachistoscopic, 162; threshold of, 162
Perceptual defense, 162, 163, 164
Perfection, 95, 261
Perls, F., 29, 296
Personal growth, 28, 84, 88, 94–99, ch. 3
Personality, xiii, 337, 339
Personal power, 123
Pervasiveness of identification, 122
Petitionary prayer, 183, 185, 188
Petty charlatans, 88
Peyote, 308
Phenomena, contour of, 313
Physical correlates of ESP, 50
Pierce, J., 113, 368
Pinching yourself to test if you are dreaming, 6
Pirit, 248
PK, 59, 61, 76, 85, 139, 375, ch. 7; classic experiments in, 61; definition of, 61; size of effect, 61, 62, 64
Pleasure, x, xii, 253, 274, 275, 299, 342
Pollution, 319
Pontius Pilate, 217
Population bomb, 319
Position, 283
Possession, 259
Possessions, 125
Potentials, 103
Poulain, A., 373
Power, x, 102, 103, 122, 166, 230, 259
Prakrti, 252
Pratt, J., 92
Prayer, xv; ch. 19, 182; as consistent desire, 184; conscious, 187, 188; effectiveness of, 370; efficacy of petitionary prayer, 183, 184, 185; of quiet, 251; of the heart, 248; non-discursive, 251; research on, 183
Precognition, 45, 84, 85, 365, ch. 5; classical laboratory test, 46; definition of, 46
Predestination, 50

Pre-lucid dreams, 32
Premonitions, 45
Presleep control of dreaming, 14
Price, H., 83, 366
Priestley, J., 52
Primal conflict repression theory, 103, 104
Primal denial, 105
Priming exercise, 36
Prince Dhat, xix, xx
Principles, 256
Principles of Aikido, 144
Professor identity, 124
Projections on the teacher, 281, 282
Prophecies, 45
Proxy, 91
Pseudo-divination, 46
Psi, 49, 85; dangers of, ch. 11, 107, 110; definition of, 49, 85; labeling it evil, 107
Psychedelic drugs, xiii, xv, 204, 205; experience, xvi; revolution, 371
Psychedelics, 306, 308
Psychiatric disorders, xiv
Psychic, xvi, 62
Psychic abilities, 38, 86, 145; development of, 108, 113; energies, 67; experience, frequency of, 88; functioning, definition of, 375; healing, xv; openings, xiv; phenomena, xiv; reading, 88
Psychics, 87, ch. 10; personalities of, 88, 110; reliability of, 88
Psychokinesis. See PK
Psychological disorders, xiv
Psychological growth, xiv, 21, 22, 131, 180, 185, 188, 200, 205
Psychologizing as a defense, 171
Psychotherapy, 94, 203, 205, 231, 233, 234, 254
Punching exercise, 142
Purpose, 220, 222
Purusa, 252
Puthoff, H., 52, 99, 368

Raga, 253, 255, 256
Rage, 192, 197, 198, 202, 297
Raiders of the Lost Ark, 36
Rainbow, 22
Raja yoga, 251, 252
Randomization, 46
Rapid eye movement, 19, 20
Rationality, 221
Rationalization, 124, 172, 287
Real effort, ch. 12
Realism about capacities, 199
Reality, 18, 24, 26, 112, 125, 150, 163, 203, 214, 217, 219, 220, 221, 238, 285, 340, 341, 342; construction of, 25; contact, 8; losing contact with, 146
Realization, 301, 303
Recapitulation, 187, 188

Recollection, 251
Reducing the sense of "I!", 233
Reed, H., 371
Reflection technique, 7, 8
Reframing, 97
Reincarnation, 172, 375
Reinforcement, 217, 281
Reinforcements, of normal behavior, 216, 217
Rejection, 229, 232, 237, 253
Relationships, 250, 251
Relaxation, 39, 247, 248, 249, 266, 294, 295
Relaxing, 269, 294
Religion, 84
Remembering love, 234
Remote viewing, 92, 93
Repressing our psychic abilities, 104
Repression, 105, 106, 255
Research, xv
Researcher is part of experiment, xv
Resistance, 95, 102, 237, 238, 240
Rigidity, xiii
Rigpa Fellowship, 372
Rilke, R., 31
Rim Institute, x
Rinzai, 254, 262
Rinzai-shu, 258
Riordan, K., 120, 127, 369 (same as Speeth, K.)
Risk taking, x
Ritual, 111
Robinson, R., 110, 111, 246, 372
Rohan, R., 181
Role playing, 136
Roles, 123, 126, 127
Rolfing, xiii
Roll, W., 52, 66, 366, 375
Roman Catholic mysticism, 373
Roosevelt, F., 30
Root causes of suffering, 228
Rush, J., 368

Sadness, 111
Safety of the familiar, 171
Sages, 259
Saint John of the Cross, 305
Saint Paul, 30
Saints, 166
Saint Teresa de Avila, 252, 255, 305, 373
Sakyamuni, the historical Buddha, 256
Salamat, xx
Saline solution, 58
Samadhi, 210, 247, 249, 251, 252, 257, 260, 288
Samatha, 247–256, 258, 261, 368
Sambhogakaya, 260
Samsara, 214
Sankhya theorists, 252
Santa Fe, 245

Sanzen, 280
Sarmouni Brotherhood, 112
Satisfaction, 276
Satkayadrsti, 255
Satori, 254
Schatzman, M., 33
Schlitz, M., 66, 366
Schmeidler, G., 367
Schultz, J., 9, 364
Schwartz, S., 368
Schwarz, B., 83
Science, myths about, 323; method, 287
Scientific humanism, 84
Scientism, 183, 219, 220; definition of, 183
Scientistic creation myth, 217
Secondary denial, 106
Second axiom of meditative practice, 286
Secret names, 123
Secrets, 106
Security needs, 107
Seductive thoughts, 269
Selecting a spiritual path, ch. 18
Self, 10, 32, 82, 169, 255, 313, 314, 335; acceptance, 146, 236, 238; appraisal, 94; boundaries of, 108; concept of, 255; defense, ch. 15; definition of, 108, 109; extinction, 373; hypnosis, 9; image, 10, 102; knowledge, 105, 106, 178, 188, 226, 227; nature of, 254, 255, 270; observation, 108, 169, 224, 225, 238, 265, 370; pity, 117; remembering, 36, 40, 124, 205, 206, 224, 225, 233, 238, 265, 281, 289, 298, 312, 313, 365, 371, 374; transcendence, 21; understanding, 225
SEN. See Spiritual Emergence Network
Senoi, 35, 365
Sensations, 123
Sense of identity, 121, 335, 339
Sensory awareness, 205
Sensory detail, 3
Separateness, 108, 258
Separation, 169, 186
Seriousness, 188
Settling, 267, 268, 288, 294
Sex, 110
Sexism, 320
Sexual, encounters, 5; maturity, 162
Sexuality, 21
Shadow, 30
Shaffi, M., 264, 277, 315
Shah, I., 100, 111, 113, 179, 363, 368, 369, 375
Shaman, 16, 45
Shamanism, 259, 329, 364, 368
Shamanistic techniques, 16
Shapin, B., 367
Shapiro, D., 264, 277, 315
Sharq, xix
Shaw, S., 364

Shelkun, G., 368
Shinto, 140
Shortcomings, 94
Shuffling, 46
Siddhi, 38
Signaling from the dream world, 20
Sila, 261
Simon called Zelotes, 330
Simulation, 159, 214, 216, 218, 334, 337, 340
Simulation of reality, 214
Sin, 221
Sinking, 301, 311
Skepticism, 78
Skillful means, 230
Skin conductivity, 249
Sleep, 300; induction of, 10
Sleepiness, 271, 300, 301, 311
Smith J., 93, 368
SOC. See State of consciousness
Social approval, 109
Socialization, 82, 103
Social masking theory of psi inhibition, 102, 103
Society for Psychical Research, 78
Sogyal, Rinpoche, xiv, 225, 234, 235, 236, 329, 372
Sole-Leris, A., 164, 213, 264, 277, 315, 322
Solidified self, 314
Soto Zen, 260
Sounds, 297; felt in body, 274
Soviet-American relations, 130
Space/time sense, 335, 339
Specialness, 31
Specific heat, 76
Spectrum of consciousness, 32
Speeth, K., 120. See also Riordan
Spinoza, B., 302
Spirit, xv
Spirit helpers, 16
Spiritual, "Consumer Reports," 170, 100, Emergence Network, xiv, 180, 370, ch. 25; evolution, 32; growth, xiv, 94–99, 131, 180, 185, 189, 200, 203, 205, ch. 3, ch. 25; guides and teachers, 5, 97, 179, ch. 18
Spiritual beings, 222
Spirituality as a defense mechanism, 172
Spong, J., 374
Spontaneity, 17, 229
Sports, 252
Stability, 254, 290
Stabilization, 336, 340
Stabilization of a state of consciousness, 336
Stabilized, 336
Stafford, P., 338, 374
Stage, 20
Stage 1 sleep, 19, 338

Stage 2 sleep, 11
State of consciousness, 306, 336; altered, 192; changing, 198; concept of, 5; nature of, 191, 192; recognizing uses and limit, 197
State-specific, knowledge, 193, 198, 199, 212, 343; sciences, 186
Statistical significance, 71, 93
Steffy, J., 368
Stevenson, I., 375
Stewart, K., 33, 35, 364, 365
Sticks and stones, 123
Stillings, D., 83, 171, 367
Stilling the mind, 247
Stimulus driven, 233
Stopping, 262, 263
Stratton, G., 161
Stroking, 56
Strongcharges, 330
Stupidity, 262
Subconscious mind, 335, 340. See also Unconscious
Subjectivity, 45
Subsystems of consciousness, 121
Subtle energies, ch. 7
Suffering, xi, 111, 166, 199, 203, 206, 215, 227, 228, 230, 233, 238, 253, 286, 291; giving up your own, 238; useless, xi, 199
Sufism, xxi, 96, 111, 179, 182, 360
Suggestion, xii, 56, 60
Sukkha-Vipassana, 289
Superego, xii, 94, 188, 198, 298
Supermother, 103, 104
Suppression, 108
Surrender, 30
Survival of death, xii, 85, 130, 158, 186, 217, 218, 221, 222, 231, 374, 375, ch. 28, ch. 29
Sweat, 57
Sweating, 57, 61, 249

Tageson, C., 223, 241
Tale of the Sands, 360
Tannen, L., 88, 367
Tantra, 246, 259, 262
Tantric sexual practices, 204, 371
Targ, R., 52, 99, 368
Tart, C., 17, 33, 34, 52, 99, 113, 120, 127, 138, 164, 173, 181, 189, 207, 241, 264, 277, 315, 332, 363–372, 374, 375
Tart, J., 37, 119, 132, 180, 268, 279, 324, 327
Tarthang, Tulku, 39, 40, 264, 277, 315, 365
Taylor, J., 332
Teachers, 222; biases of, 284
Teaching stories, xix
Techniques for inducing lucid dreaming, ch. 5

Technobabble, 86
Technology, 86
Telepathic dreams, flags in, 38
Telepathic reception over 100 yard range, 102
Telepathine, 102, 107, 368
Telepathy, 38, 84, 85
Tension, 266, 267, 276, 294, 295, 296, 299, 300, 301; subtle, 300
Terrors of childhood, 104
Testing ideas, xvii; limits, x; theories, 287
Testing of psychic information sources, 91, 92, 93
Theorizing, 287
Theravada, 246, 248, 256, 262
Thinking, 296, 299, 335
Third axiom of meditative practice, 286
This is me!, 109
Tholey, P., 5–17, 34, 332, 363, 364
Thought, 105, 123, 203, 206, 255, 270, 273, 296, 297, 298, 299, 338; is definitely not the enemy, 297; as self-entertainment, 298; body sensations associated with, 298; observing, 40, 296
Threatening figures in dreams, 15
Three-brained beings, 148, 167
Thyroid, 57
Tian, 302
Tibetan, 259, 301, 329
Tibetan Buddhism, 22, 206, 225
Time, 45, 47, 338, ch. 5; barrier, 50
Tokyo University, 249
Tolerance, 31, 237, 238
Tong Len, 236
Touch, therapeutic, 366; value of, 54
Trance states, xii, 247, 249, 250–252, 255; value of, 247
Transcendence, 109, 137
Transcending tribalism, 131
Transference, 282
Transpersonal Creed, 221, 222
Transpersonal psychology, xiii, 156, 182, 203
Tribalism, 129, ch. 14
Tribal referees, 135
Troffer, S., 363
Trust, 31
Truth, x

U Ba Khin, 305
Ueshiba, M., 140, 369
Ullman, M., 332, 367
Unbalanced functioning, 167
Unbendable arm, 149
Unconscious 85, 335
Unconscious processes, 162, 254
Unity, 166
Unity of life, 222
Usefulness of identification, 124

Uyeshiba. See Ueshiba

Vajrayana, 246, 248
Value deficiency diseases, 84
Values, 126, 201, 214, 219–222, 251, 252
Van Eeden, F., 4, 5, 34, 363
Vaughan, F., 181, 368
Vibration, 272, 297
Victim signals, 142, 143
Vilenskaya, L., 83, 367
Vipassana, 142, 206, 248, 254–258, 260–262, 272–275, 280, 283, 288, 290, 297, 305, 311, 313, 329, 371
Vipasyana. See Vipassana
Virtue, 221
Vision, 118; inverted, 161
Visions, 45
Visualization, 8, 35, 39, 40, 64, 65, 150, 259, 260
Vitality, 57, 58, 204
Vitamin B-12, 364
Volition, 19
Vulnerability, 170, 231, 232, 233; of openness, 229

Waking in the morning, 75
Waking trance, xiii
Walker, J., 83
Walker, S., 264, 278, 315
Walking dead, xi
Walking meditation, 256
Walsh, R., 264, 277, 315, 319, 321, 322, 374
Ware, T., 373
Watcher, 312
Water, infra-red spectrum of, 59
Webb, W., 332
West, M., 164, 264, 278, 315
Western Creed, 214, 220, 375, ch. 22
White, J., 17, 33, 52, 364
White, R., 52, 366
Wholeness, 29, 31
Wilber, K., 181
Wildebeest, 29
Will, 9, 10, 31, 65, 188, 191, 202
Willing, 31
Willis, J., 264, 278, 315, 372
Wisdom, 254, 256, 258, 259, 263
Wishing, 14
Withdrawal, 252, 261
Within-state enlightenment, 202
Witness awareness, 294
Wolman, B., 332, 364, 368
Wonder, x, xii, 75
Wood, R., 66, 366
Words, inadequacy of, 193
Wordsworth, 75, 82, 83
Work, 185, 187, 188
Workaholics, 117

Working with a channel/psychic for
    growth, 94
World 1, 341, 342
World 1 invalidation of World 3, 342
World 2, 341
World 3, 342
Worldly success, 305
World simulation, 163, 164, 217, 218; ex-
    ample, 215; living in, 160, 161; model,
    162
Worlds of experience, 18
Worm in the mud, 262

Wounds, 56
Wu-Men, 251

Yoga, 182, 249, 252
Yombul, 248
Young, S., xiv, 245, 246, 274, 277, 372

Zarathustra, 327
Zelotes, 330
Zen, 149, 178, 246, 248, 249, 258, 259, 262,
    280, 290, 300, 309
Zhi gnas, 372
Zoroaster, 327